The Great Naval Game

D0886396

This book is about the theatre of power and identity that unfolded in and between Britain and Germany in the decades before the First World War. It explores what contemporaries described as the cult of the navy: the many ways in which the navy and the sea were celebrated in the fleet reviews, naval visits and ship launches that were watched by hundreds of thousands of spectators. At once royal rituals and national entertainments, these were events at which tradition, power and claims to the sea were played out between the nations. This was a public stage on which the domestic and the foreign intersected and where the modern mass market of media and consumerism collided with politics and international relations. Conflict and identity were literally acted out between the two countries. By focusing on this dynamic arena, Jan Rüger offers a fascinating new history of the Anglo-German antagonism.

JAN RÜGER teaches history at Birkbeck College, University of London. In 2002–3, he was a visiting fellow at the Yale Center for International and Area Studies, Yale University. His research on the cultural history of the navy and the sea has been awarded the Prize of the German Historical Institute London and the Julian Corbett Prize of the Institute of Historical Research, University of London.

Studies in the Social and Cultural History of Modern Warfare

General Editor

Jay Winter, *Yale University*

Advisory Editors

Omer Bartov, *Brown University*
Carol Gluck, *Columbia University*
David M. Kennedy, *Stanford University*
Paul Kennedy, *Yale University*
Antoine Prost, *Université de Paris-Sorbonne*
Emmanuel Sivan, *Hebrew University of Jerusalem*
Robert Wohl, *University of California, Los Angeles*

In recent years the field of modern history has been enriched by the exploration of two parallel histories. These are the social and cultural history of armed conflict, and the impact of military events on social and cultural history.

Studies in the Social and Cultural History of Modern Warfare presents the fruits of this growing area of research, reflecting both the colonization of military history by cultural historians and the reciprocal interest of military historians in social and cultural history, to the benefit of both. The series offers the latest scholarship in European and non-European events from the 1850s to the present day.

For a list of titles in the series, please see end of book.

The Great Naval Game

Britain and Germany in the Age of Empire

Jan Rüger

CAMBRIDGE
UNIVERSITY PRESS

CAMBRIDGE UNIVERSITY PRESS
Cambridge, New York, Melbourne, Madrid, Cape Town, Singapore,
São Paulo

Cambridge University Press
The Edinburgh Building, Cambridge CB2 8RU, UK

Published in the United States of America by Cambridge University Press,
New York

www.cambridge.org
Information on this title: www.cambridge.org/9780521875769

© Jan Rüger 2007

First published 2007
First paperback edition 2009

Printed in the United Kingdom at the University Press, Cambridge

A catalogue record for this publication is available from the British Library

ISBN 978-0-521-87576-9 hardback

In memory of
Nils Henning Rüger
27 January 1977–3 February 1979

Contents

List of illustrations

Acknowledgements

It is a great pleasure to thank the many people and institutions who have made this book possible. My largest scholarly debt is to Richard Evans, who was a wonderful supervisor during my Ph.D. at Cambridge and who has been a constant source of generosity and guidance since then. When I first suggested this topic to him some eight years ago, he commented that he saw 'more mileage' in it than in the other, more whimsical ideas that I had about islands and the North Sea. I hope the book shows that he was right.

I owe a particular debt of gratitude to Christian Meier and Gerhard Neumann, who were immensely inspiring teachers when I began to study history at Munich University in the early 1990s. Although I eventually abandoned their respective fields, ancient history and German literature, I hope that they would agree that some of their ideas have informed this study, if in a way that is not easily acknowledged in footnotes.

For his support and kindness at crucial times I am extremely grateful to Jay Winter. I was fortunate to be involved in the *Capital Cities at War* project, steered by him and Jean-Louis Robert. To work in this cheerfully international group of historians writing a comparative study of London, Paris and Berlin during the First World War taught me not only about the importance of language in history, but also that co-operation is possible in historical research, all too often deemed to be a necessarily solitary activity.

I am indebted, too, to David Cannadine and Chris Clark, for their questions and suggestions during the early stages of the manuscript, and to Eckart Hellmuth, Max Jones, Paul Kennedy, Michael Salewski and Hagen Schulze, for their advice over the years. Thanks are also due to Mark Bassin, Thomas Biskup, Michael Epkenhans, Dominik Geppert, Robert Gerwarth, Stefan Goebel, Ángel Gurría Quintana, Martin Kohlrausch, Angela Poulter, Nigel Rigby, Nicholas Rodger, Audrée-Isabelle Tardif, Heather Tilley, Carlos Alfaro Zaforteza and Katja Zelljadt.

I would like to thank especially the friends and colleagues at Birkbeck who make the School of History, Classics and Archaeology such an inspiring and exciting place. For their ideas and help I am very grateful to John Arnold, Joanna Bourke, Sean Brady, Christy Constantakopoulou, Emma Dench, Catharine Edwards, David Feldman, Matthew Innes, Lucy Riall, Hilary Sapire, Chandak Sengoopta, Naoko Shimazu, Julian Swann, Frank Trentmann, Filippo de Vivo and Nik Wachsmann. John Arnold read the entire manuscript and made many invaluable suggestions. My warm thanks, also, to Cambridge University Press's anonymous reader, whose comments were immensely helpful. At the Press, the combined patience and professionalism of Michael Watson, Rosina Di Marzo, Helen Waterhouse and Clive Unger-Hamilton saw the book through the publishing process.

I am glad to be able to thank the staff at the libraries and archives I visited in Germany, Britain, Australia and the United States. I am particularly grateful to Peter Gabrielsson (Staatsarchiv Hamburg), Herwig Müther (Historisches Archiv Krupp, Essen), Thomas Weis (Bibliothek für Zeitgeschichte, Württembergische Landesbibliothek, Stuttgart), Alexander Fiebig (Staatsbibliothek Berlin), Jörg Hillmann (Marineschule Mürwik), Marion Schreiber (Staatsarchiv Bremen), Hans-Henning Freitag (Stadtarchiv Kiel), Liz Rees (Tyne & Wear Archives Service, Newcastle), Matthew Sheldon (Royal Naval Museum, Portsmouth), Larry McKinna (British Pathé News Library, London), Neil Young (Imperial War Museum, London) and Kevin Hoey (National Archives of Australia). I am also grateful to Vickers Shipbuilding and Engineering Ltd, Barrow-in-Furness, who allowed me to study their dockyard records at Cumbria Record Office despite the fact that I seemed to have 'the wrong passport'.

I would like to acknowledge the kind permission of Her Majesty Queen Elizabeth II to make use of material that I consulted at the Royal Archives in Windsor. Pamela Clark, the Registrar of the Archives, read parts of the manuscript and prevented me from making a number of errors. Christopher Lloyd, formerly the Surveyor of the Queen's Pictures, was kind enough to show me the paintings of fleet reviews that survive in the Royal Collection. My warm thanks to both.

Visual sources played a key part from early on in the research for *The Great Naval Game* and I am very glad to have a larger than usual number of illustrations in the book. The reproduction of these images would have been impossible without the generous help of Nigel Rigby and Sara Grove (National Maritime Museum, Greenwich), Alan King (Portsmouth Central Library), Herwig Müther (Historisches Archiv Krupp, Essen) and Gudrun Müller (Wissenschaftliches Institut für Schiffahrts- und Marinegeschichte Peter Tamm, Hamburg). Jon Wilson and Christina Panagi were instrumental in putting the images together at Birkbeck, while the Isobel Thornley Bequest Fund very kindly helped with the costs. The publishers and myself have made considerable effort to trace and contact the copyright holders of the illustrations. In a very few cases this has not been successful and, if notified, we will endeavour to correct these omissions at the earliest opportunity.

The research for this book was funded by a number of British and German institutions: the Arts and Humanities Research Council, the German Historical Institute London, the Faculty of History at Cambridge, the Sir John Plumb Charitable Trust and Emmanuel College, Cambridge, to all of whom I am grateful. I was fortunate to have the *Studienstiftung des deutschen Volkes* accompany my studies for ten years and I remain indebted to this unique institution and the many individuals who work for it. In 2002/3, a Fox International Fellowship allowed me to carry out research as a visiting fellow at the Yale Centre for International and Area Studies. I am grateful to Mr and Mrs Fox for their generosity and hospitality, and to Larisa Satara for all her help during the year at Yale.

My largest debt of gratitude is to my wife, Jayne, who has contributed more to the making of this book than any other individual: she was the most critical and loyal reader I had. I am deeply grateful to her. I am also glad to be able to thank my parents and my sister finally for all their support and forbearance over the years. I owe them more than I could convey here. With them in my thoughts, I dedicate this book to the memory of my brother.

J.M.R.
London,
September 2006

The publication of this book in paperback has given me the opportunity to correct some typographical and factual errors. I am very grateful to readers and reviewers for pointing them out.

J.M.R.
London,
December 2008

Abbreviations

AA	Auswärtiges Amt
ADM	Admiralty
BA	Bundesarchiv
BA-FA	Bundesarchiv-Filmarchiv, Berlin
BA-MA	Bundesarchiv-Militärarchiv, Freiburg
BD	*British Documents on the Origins of the War*
BfZ	Bibliothek für Zeitgeschichte, Württembergische Landesbibliothek, Stuttgart
BPH	Brandenburg-Preußisches Hausarchiv
CLRO	Corporation of London Record Office, London Metropolitan Archives
CRO	Cumbria Record Office, Barrow-in-Furness
CUL	Cambridge University Library
DDF	*Documents Diplomatiques Français 1871–1914*
FAH	Familienarchiv Hügel, Krupp, Essen
FO	Foreign Office
GBRC	Glasgow Business Records Centre
GCA	Glasgow City Archives
GP	*Die Große Politik der Europäischen Kabinette 1871–1914*
GStA PK	Geheimes Staatsarchiv Preußischer Kulturbesitz, Berlin
HA	Historisches Archiv
Hansard	Hansard Parliamentary Debates
HO	Home Office
IWM	Imperial War Museum, London
LA	Landesarchiv
MVBl	*Marineverordnungsblatt*
NAA	National Archives Australia
NID	Naval Intelligence Department
NFTVA	National Film and Television Archive, British Film Institute, London
NL	Nachlass
NMM	National Maritime Museum, Greenwich

PA-AA	Politisches Archiv, Auswärtiges Amt, Berlin
PFDP	Pescott Frost Collection of Dockyard Photographs, Portsmouth Central Library
PGO	Portsmouth General Order
PP	Politische Polizei
PRO	Public Record Office (now: The National Archives), Kew
RA	Royal Archives, Windsor
RMA	Reichsmarineamt
RNM	Royal Naval Museum, Portsmouth
StA	Staatsarchiv
StadtA	Stadtarchiv
Sten. Ber.	*Stenographische Berichte über die Verhandlungen des Reichstages*
TWAS	Tyne and Wear Archive Services, Newcastle

Introduction

This book is about the theatre of power and identity that unfolded in and between Britain and Germany in the imperial age. It explores what contemporaries described as the 'cult of the navy': the many ways in which the navy and the sea were celebrated in the decades before the First World War. At the heart of this obsession were a host of rituals that put the navy and the nation on the public stage. Of these, fleet reviews and launches of warships were the most prominent. At once royal rituals and national entertainments, these were spectacles of power and pride, with hundreds of thousands regularly turning out to watch. They became a potent public theatre where tradition, power and claims to the sea were demonstrated to both domestic and foreign audiences. What role did this maritime stage play in the rise of the Anglo-German antagonism? What was its significance for nation-building and ideas of empire? And how might it change our understanding of the relationship between politics and culture, between public ritual and power?

In addressing such questions, this book understands the navy not only as a political and military instrument, but also as a powerful cultural symbol. Unravelling the spectacle created around this symbol opens a window to aspects of the history of Britain, Germany and the age of empire that have to date remained unexplored. This was a public theatre in which the domestic and the foreign intersected, where the modern mass market of media and consumerism collided with politics and international relations, and where identity and conflict were acted out between the nations. By focusing on this dynamic arena, *The Great Naval Game* explores the Anglo-German antagonism from a new perspective. Traditionally, historians have understood the growing rivalry between the two countries in diplomatic, strategic and economic terms. In the grand narratives that explained the 'rise and fall of the great powers' culture seemed a lesser category, a sub-field of the high politics of diplomacy and strategy.[1] True, a number of scholars have since explored important cultural aspects of the two countries' relations, such as exchange and transfer, as well as mutual stereotypes and images of 'the other'.[2] Yet, too often this enquiry has been left disconnected from the world of power and politics, as if to confirm the view of culture as a separate phenomenon and a source of subordinate influence, a view that has been prominent amongst political historians. This book has a different premise as its starting point. It aims to discover the cultural in politics and the political in culture. The two were inseparable in the celebration of the navy and the sea: ritual and theatre merged with power and politics. Focusing on this spectacle allows us to see the intensely political implications of public entertainment and forces us to understand international relations no longer as divorced from the cultural context in which they took place.

An examination of this public stage has to overcome, however imperfectly, the artificial boundaries between academic disciplines and specialisms. Indeed, it is the increasing separation into scholarly sub-disciplines that best explains why historians have had surprisingly little to say about the naval theatre. There has been a strong interest in public celebrations and royal rituals, especially so since the concept of 'invented traditions' rose to prominence. Eric Hobsbawm and David Cannadine have been particularly influential in explaining the growing pomp and circumstance of the late nineteenth century as a reaction to the rise of democracy and modern mass society: the less monarchs and governments could rely on traditional forms of legitimacy, the more they invented public rituals to

---

[1] Paul M. Kennedy, *The Rise of the Anglo-German Antagonism 1860–1914* (London, 1980); Paul M. Kennedy, *The Rise and Fall of the Great Powers: Economic Change and Military Conflict 1500 to 2000* (New York, 1987); Robert K. Massie, *Dreadnought: Britain, Germany and the Coming of the Great War* (London, 1991); Gregor Schöllgen, *Imperialismus und Gleichgewicht. Deutschland, England und die orientalische Frage 1871–1914*, third edition (Munich, 2000); David Stevenson, *Armaments and the Coming of War: Europe, 1904–1914* (Oxford, 1996); Klaus Hildebrand, 'Zwischen Allianz und Antagonismus. Das Problem bilateraler Normalität in den britisch-deutschen Beziehungen des 19. Jahrhunderts (1870–1914)', in *Weltpolitik. Europagedanke. Regionalismus. Festschrift Gollwitzer* (Münster, 1982), pp. 305–31.

[2] Rudolf Muhs, Johannes Paulmann and Wilibald Steinmetz (eds.), *Aneignung und Abwehr. Interkultureller Transfer zwischen Deutschland und Großbritannien im 19. Jahrhundert* (Bodenheim, 1998); Lothar Reinermann, *Der Kaiser in England. Wilhelm II. und sein Bild in der britischen Öffentlichkeit* (Paderborn, 2001); Michael Epkenhans, 'Aspekte des deutschen Englandbildes 1800–1914: Vorbild und Rivale', *Westfälische Forschungen* 44 (1994), pp. 329–42; Günther Blaicher, *Das Deutschlandbild in der englischen Literatur* (Darmstadt, 1992); Bernd-Jürgen Wendt (ed.), *Das britische Deutschlandbild im Wandel des 19. und 20. Jahrhunderts* (Bochum, 1984); Peter E. Firchow, *The Death of the German Cousin: Variations on a Literary Stereotype, 1890–1920* (Lewisburg, PA, and London, 1986).

display their continuing relevance and power.[3] In the twenty years since the emergence of this thesis, historians have explored national festivals and commemorations extensively.[4] Curiously, however, neither in Britain nor in Germany has this interest extended to the navy, one of the most powerful icons in this period, combining royal, national and imperial symbolism.

Nor has the intensive debate about national identity directed any attention to the navy as a cultural symbol. In Britain this debate has focused on the role of religion, conflict and state formation for the making and unmaking of 'the nation', with Linda Colley as one of the most influential recent protagonists.[5] The cult of the navy in fact offers a powerful stage for the issues examined in this debate, a stage on which notions of Britishness collided with English, Scottish, Welsh and Irish identities. The Royal Navy became one of the most important metaphors of Britishness in the nineteenth century, just as the German fleet was employed as a floating symbol of unity and national identification on the other side of the North Sea. Both played essential roles for the shaping of 'the nation', for ideas of empire, 'overseas' and difference. In exploring

---

[3] Eric Hobsbawm, 'Mass-Producing Traditions: Europe, 1870–1914', and David Cannadine, 'The Context, Performance and Meaning of Ritual: The British Monarchy and the "Invention of Tradition"', c. 1820–1977', both in Eric Hobsbawm and Terence Ranger (eds.), *The Invention of Tradition* (Cambridge, 1983), pp. 101–64, 263–307; David Cannadine, 'Introduction: Divine Rites of Kings', in David Cannadine and Simon Price (eds.), *Rituals of Royalty: Power and Ceremonial in Traditional Societies* (Cambridge, 1987), pp. 1–19.

[4] See Michael Maurer, 'Feste und Feiern als historischer Forschungsgegenstand', *Historische Zeitschrift* 253 (1991), pp. 101–30. The most important studies that have appeared since Maurer's survey are: Johannes Paulmann, *Pomp und Politik. Monarchenbegegnungen in Europa zwischen Ancien Régime und Erstem Weltkrieg* (Paderborn, 2000); Jakob Vogel, *Nationen im Gleichschritt. Der Kult der 'Nation in Waffen' in Deutschland und Frankreich, 1871–1914* (Göttingen, 1997); William M. Kuhn, *Democratic Royalism: The Transformation of the British Monarchy, 1861–1914* (London, 1996); Richard Williams, *The Contentious Crown: Public Discussion of the British Monarchy in the Reign of Queen Victoria* (Aldershot, 1997). See also Dieter Düding, Peter Friedemann and Paul Münch (eds.), *Öffentliche Festkultur. Politische Feste in Deutschland von der Aufklärung bis zum Ersten Weltkrieg* (Reinbek, 1988); Manfred Hettling and Paul Nolte (eds.), *Bürgerliche Feste. Symbolische Formen politischen Handelns im 19. Jahrhundert* (Göttingen, 1993); Karin Friedrich (ed.): *Festive Culture in Germany and Europe from the Sixteenth to the Twentieth Century* (Lewiston, 2000).

[5] Linda Colley, *Britons: Forging the Nation 1707–1837* (New Haven and London, 1992); Linda Colley, 'Britishness and Otherness: An Argument', *Journal of British Studies* 31 (1992), pp. 309–29. See also Raphael Samuel (ed.), *Patriotism: The Making and Unmaking of British National Identity*, 3 vols. (London, 1989); Raphael Samuel, *Island Stories: Unravelling Britain* (London, 1989); Robert Colls, *The Identity of England* (Oxford, 2002); Robert Colls and P. Dodd (eds.), *Englishness: Politics and Culture 1880–1920* (London, 1986); Keith Robbins, *Nineteenth-Century Britain: Integration and Diversity* (Oxford, 1988); Keith Robbins, 'National Identity and History', *History* 75 (1990), pp. 369–87.

the naval theatre, this book aims to contribute to our understanding of nationhood and its relationship with that 'remarkable transoceanic construct of substance and sentiment' called the empire.[6] Naval historians working on the late nineteenth and early twentieth centuries have shown sadly little interest in such issues. They have been interested in technology, administration and strategy, and they continue to be preoccupied with naval operations and sea battles.[7] What is sorely needed is a cultural history of the modern Royal Navy, an approach that inquires into the ways the navy and its past have been narrated and appropriated, an approach that investigates the cultural and political implications of the hero and tradition-worshipping that is so prevalent in accounts of the navy and the sea.[8] In *Losing Nelson* Barry Unsworth deconstructs such naval mythologizing by telling the (fictional) story of Charles Cleasby, a man unable to see himself separately from his hero Horatio Nelson. After years of re-enacting and reliving Nelson's battles and victories, Cleasby undergoes a painful metamorphosis. He begins to question his glorification of naval and national heroism and, in finally shedding his fixation, he comes to a better self-understanding.[9] Perhaps it is time that historians of the Royal Navy take a similar step. An inquiry into the symbolic role of the navy has important clues to offer for our understanding of sea power in the age of empire.[10] Strategy and battle tactics, diplomacy and politics alone do not explain why the Royal Navy mattered in the nineteenth and twentieth centuries. The 'great game for

---

[6] David Cannadine, *Ornamentalism: How the British Saw Their Empire* (London, 2001), p. 122. The vast literature on 'imperial cultures' has left the celebration of the navy almost entirely unexplored. See in particular John M. MacKenzie, *Propaganda and Empire: The Manipulation of British Public Opinion, 1880–1960* (Manchester, 1984); John M. MacKenzie (ed.), *Imperialism and Popular Culture* (Manchester, 1986); John M. MacKenzie (ed.), *Popular Imperialism and the Military 1850–1950* (Manchester, 1992); David Killingray and David Omissi (eds.), *Guardians of Empire: The Armed Forces of the Colonial Powers c. 1700–1964* (Manchester, 2000).

[7] For a survey that comes to a similar conclusion see Barry M. Gough, 'The Royal Navy and the British Empire', in Robin W. Winks (ed.), *The Oxford History of the British Empire*, vol. 5, *Historiography* (Oxford, 2000), pp. 327–41, here p. 339. The latest important studies of the Royal Navy in this period have been on administrative and technological reform: Jon Sumida, *In Defence of Naval Supremacy: Finance, Technology and British Naval Policy, 1889–1914* (Boston, MA, 1989); Jon Sumida, 'British Naval Administration and Policy in the Age of Fisher', *Journal of Modern History* 54 (1990), pp. 1–26; Nicholas A. Lambert, *Sir John Fisher's Naval Revolution* (Columbia, 1999).

[8] For a first step in that direction see John M. MacKenzie, 'Nelson Goes Global: The Nelson Myth in Britain and Beyond', in David Cannadine (ed.), *Admiral Lord Nelson: Context and Legacy* (Basingstoke, 2005), pp. 144–65.

[9] Barry Unsworth, *Losing Nelson* (London, 1999).

[10] For the twentieth century this point has been made by Ralph Harrington, '"The Mighty Hood": Navy, Empire, War at Sea and the British National Imagination, 1920–60', *Journal of Contemporary History* 38 (2003), pp. 171–85.

mastery in the North Sea'[11] was as much as a cultural phenomenon as it was a political one.

A cultural history of the German navy is similarly lacking. Here, historians have focused on the intentions behind the building of the fleet and its role in domestic politics. Was this an exercise in manipulating the masses, a palliative for the Wilhelmine electorate? Or was the building of the German navy a natural reaction to the rise of other powers in the age of imperialism and navalism? These questions, which were ultimately about how historians interpreted the relationship between foreign and domestic politics, have been impressively researched and hotly debated.[12] Yet, by focusing on such issues, historians have failed to investigate more closely the symbolic significance of the navy and the sea, described by Admiral von Tirpitz himself as a 'cultural space'.[13]

The Great Naval Game brings together these divergent historiographies. It is as much influenced by cultural, social and political history as it is by naval and maritime history. This is a book about the navy and the sea, about imperialism and Anglo-German rivalry, but also about ritual, identity and the imagination of 'the other'. Its title is intended to reflect this multi-faceted approach. The naval theatre was part of the imperial game, the struggle between great powers over spheres of influence and the domination of the sea. At the same time it was about entertainment, leisure and consumption. This was, as Henry Newbolt put it in his poem 'England', quite literally a 'game for man and boy'.[14] It could be played and enjoyed in numerous ways, ranging from the great fleet reviews themselves to a host of re-enactments in popular culture. The public collision of the intensely political and cultural dimensions of this game was precisely what made the naval theatre so relevant for Anglo-German relations.

The obsession with the fleet that flourished in Britain and Germany generated a vast amount of documents, ranging from central government

[11] Peter Clarke, *Hope and Glory: Britain 1900–1990* (Harmondsworth, 1996), p. 56.

[12] Jonathan Steinberg, *Yesterday's Deterrent: Tirpitz and the Birth of the German Battle Fleet* (London, 1965); Volker R. Berghahn, *Der Tirpitz-Plan. Genesis und Verfall einer innenpolitischen Krisenstrategie unter Wilhelm II.* (Düsseldorf, 1971); Paul Kennedy, 'Maritime Strategieprobleme der deutsch-englischen Flottenrivalität', in Herbert Schottelius and Wilhelm Deist (eds.), *Marine und Marinepolitik im kaiserlichen Deutschland 1871–1914* (Düsseldorf, 1972), pp. 178–210; Holger Herwig, *'Luxury' Fleet: The Imperial German Navy 1888–1918* (London, 1980); Michael Epkenhans, *Die wilhelminische Flottenrüstung 1908–1914. Weltmachtstreben, industrieller Fortschritt, soziale Integration* (Munich, 1991); Rolf Hobson, *Imperialism at Sea: Naval Strategic Thought, the Ideology of Sea Power and the Tirpitz Plan, 1875–1914* (Boston, 2002).

[13] Alfred von Tirpitz, *Erinnerungen* (Leipzig, 1919), p. 16.

[14] Henry Newbolt, 'England', in Henry Newbolt, *The Island Race* (London, 1898), p. 78.

records to the local files of the towns and dockyards where the navy was being celebrated; similarly from the highbrow press interpreting the naval theatre to the many layers of popular culture appropriating it. In order to reveal the often conflicting ways in which contemporaries participated in and made sense of this public spectacle, this book augments official and press sources with private diaries and journals. In addition, secret reports by undercover police and intelligence officers allow us to interpret the views of those who otherwise leave few traces in the archives. Through the help of such sources it becomes possible to contrast the role played by monarchs and ministers with that of the workers who built the ships, the lower ranks who kept them in order and the spectators who went to see them. Furthermore, it seems impossible to understand a spectacle so intrinsically visual without consulting a wide range of pictures, photographs and films. Taken by press correspondents and naval officers, commissioned by governments and film companies, these are essential sources that reflect the visual fascination of this public theatre.[15]

Two approaches are central for the way in which this book makes sense of such sources: the cultural and the comparative. Both require some explanation. Practitioners of cultural history have been remarkably successful in adopting the concerns and methods of other disciplines.[16] In focusing on the symbolic dimension of the navy, this book is clearly influenced by their endeavours. Yet, while taking important clues from scholars concerned with ritual and theatricality, it does not follow their tendency to neglect important political contexts and to view ritual as an end in itself. The kind of cultural history attempted here aspires to be neither naïve nor cynical: while interpreting the cult of the navy as a public theatre, with its own rules and rhetoric, the book is keenly aware

---

[15] One particular set of visual sources needs to be mentioned here: the Pescott Frost Collection of Portsmouth Dockyard Photographs (PFDP), held at Portsmouth Central Library. Mark Edwin Pescott Frost (1859–1953) was Secretary to the Admiral Superintendent at Portsmouth from 1899, a capacity in which he was responsible for naval ceremonies and celebrations. Between 1901 and the end of the First World War, he took numerous photographs of naval events and acquired additional material from local photographers, all collated as the PFDP, which presented an invaluable source for this book.

[16] Lynn Hunt (ed.), *The New Cultural History* (Berkeley, 1989); Peter Burke, *Varieties of Cultural History* (Cambridge, 1997); Peter Burke, *What is Cultural History?* (Cambridge, 2004). Particularly influential for this study have been Clifford Geertz, *Negara: The Theatre-State in Nineteenth-Century Bali* (Princeton, 1980); James MacAloon (ed.), *Rite, Drama, Festival, Spectacle: Rehearsals Toward a New Theory of Cultural Performance* (Philadelphia, 1984); Richard Schechner, *Performance Theory* (New York and London, 1988); Victor Turner, *The Ritual Process: Structure and Anti-Structure* (Harmondsworth, 1974) and Victor Turner, *The Anthropology of Performance* (New York, 1989).

of the politics involved, both domestically and internationally.[17] George Mosse and Hans-Ulrich Wehler, amongst others, have explained German national festivals and military spectacles as manoeuvres in the manipulation of the masses, foreshadowing the rise of the Nazis.[18] Historians of modern Britain have similarly interpreted public rituals as instruments of propaganda, producing imperialist sentiment and domestic consensus.[19] This book revisits such interpretations. It reassesses the direction and character of power in the 'age of the masses' and it asserts that, while certainly not an end in itself, naval and national pomp was more than simply a function of power.

The second key component in this interpretation is the comparative perspective. *The Great Naval Game* presents a parallel history of two countries. It compares their approaches to the navy and the sea and suggests conclusions about cultural and political differences. This comparison proceeds symmetrically; that is, it directs as much interest and attention to the one as to the other nation.[20] While not presupposing that the historical development of either Britain or Germany presents a model by which the other country's history should be judged, the book does contribute to the debate about 'German peculiarities'. Militarism, civil society and constitutional development are issues that must be studied comparatively if historians want to make assertions about whether or not

---

[17] The categorisation of approaches to public ritual as either naïve or cynical is taken from Peter Burke, *The Fabrication of Louis XIV* (New Haven and London, 1992), pp. 11 ff. See also Cannadine, 'Introduction: Divine Rites of Kings', pp. 1–19.

[18] George L. Mosse, 'Caesarism, Circuses and Monuments', *Journal of Contemporary History* 6 (1971), pp. 167–82; George L. Mosse, *The Nationalisation of the Masses: Political Symbolism and Mass Movements in Germany from the Napoleonic Wars Through the Third Reich* (New York, 1975), chs. 4, 5; Hans-Ulrich Wehler, *Das Deutsche Kaiserreich 1871–1918*, seventh edition (Göttingen, 1994), pp. 96–121, 171–8; Hans-Ulrich Wehler, *Deutsche Gesellschaftsgeschichte*, vol. 3, *Von der 'Deutschen Doppelrevolution' bis zum Beginn des Ersten Weltkrieges 1849–1914* (Munich, 1995), pp. 985–90, 1129–45.

[19] MacKenzie, *Propaganda and Empire*; James A. Mangan (ed.), *Making Imperial Mentalities: Socialisation and British Imperialism* (Manchester, 1990); Jonathan Schneer, *London 1900: The Imperial Metropolis* (New Haven and London, 1999), pp. 28–34; Scott Hughes Myerly, *British Military Spectacle: From the Napoleonic Wars Through the Crimea* (Cambridge, MA, 1996); Scott Hughes Myerly, '"The Eye Must Entrap the Mind": Army Spectacle and Paradigm in Nineteenth-Century Britain', *Journal of Social History* 26 (1992), pp. 105–31.

[20] Jürgen Kocka, 'Asymmetrical Historical Comparison: The Case of the German *Sonderweg*', *History and Theory* 38 (1999), pp. 40–50. See also Heinz-Gerhard Haupt and Jürgen Kocka, 'Comparative History: Methods, Aims, Problems', in Deborah Cohen and Maura O'Connor (eds.), *Comparison and History: Europe in Cross-National Perspective* (New York and London, 2004), pp. 23–39; Chris Lorenz 'Comparative Historiography: Problems and Perspectives', *History and Theory* 38 (1999), pp. 25–39; John Breuilly, 'Introduction: Making Comparisons in History', in John Breuilly, *Labour and Liberalism in 19th Century Europe: Essays in Comparative History* (Manchester, 1992), pp. 1–25.

Germany took a 'special path' in the modern age.[21] This book combines such a parallel history of Britain and Germany with a strong focus on the space between the nations. The rituals created around the navy and the sea in the two countries cannot be fully understood unless they are seen as closely interrelated phenomena that reacted to and influenced each other on many levels. Indeed, the naval theatre turned the sea, and the North Sea in particular, into a stage between the nations on which the key issues that defined the two countries were played out. In order to understand this Anglo-German phenomenon, we need to practise both comparative and transnational history. There need not be a contradiction between the two.[22]

By uncovering this Anglo-German stage, *The Great Naval Game* seeks to contribute to a new history of the sea as a cultural space.[23] Such an approach is particularly needed for Northern Europe. While the Mediterranean has been explored extensively since Fernand Braudel's pioneering work, first published in 1949, similar studies are lacking for the space between the British Isles and continental Europe.[24] Here, this book takes a first step. It attempts to convince its readers that a fruitful

---

[21] On the debate about Germany's 'path to modernity', see Richard J. Evans, 'Whatever Became of the *Sonderweg*', in Richard J. Evans, *Rereading German History: From Unification to Reunification 1800–1996* (London, 1997), pp. 12–22; David Blackbourn and Geoff Eley, *The Peculiarities of German History: Bourgeois Society and Politics in Nineteenth-Century Germany* (Oxford, 1984).

[22] German and French historians have been particularly prolific in debating the question of how to go beyond traditional comparative history, at times with the tendency of setting up a false dichotomy between comparison and transnational or 'transfer' history: Michel Espagne, 'Sur les limites du comparatisme en histoire culturelle', *Genèses* 17 (1994), pp. 112–21; Johannes Paulmann, 'Internationaler Vergleich und interkultureller Transfer. Zwei Forschungsansätze zur europäischen Geschichte des 18. bis 20. Jahrhunderts', *Historische Zeitschrift* 267 (1998), pp. 649–85; Michel Espagne, 'Au delà du comparatisme', in Michel Espagne, *Les transferts culturels franco-allemands* (Paris, 1999), pp. 35–49; Matthias Middell (ed.), *Kulturtransfer und Vergleich* (Leipzig, 2000); Michaël Werner and Bénédicte Zimmermann, 'Penser l'historie croisée. Entre empirie et réflexivité', *Annales* 58 (2003), pp. 7–36; Hartmut Kaelble and Jürgen Schriewer (ed.), *Vergleich und Transfer. Komparatistik in den Sozial-, Geschichts- und Kulturwissenschaften* (Frankfurt and New York, 2003); Jürgen Osterhammel, *Geschichtswissenschaft jenseits des Nationalstaats. Studien zu Beziehungsgeschichte und Zivilisationsvergleich* (Göttingen, 2001); Sebastian Conrad and Jürgen Osterhammel (eds.), *Das Kaiserreich transnational* (Göttingen, 2004).

[23] On recent initiatives in this field see Kären Wigen, 'Oceans of History', *American Historical Review* 111 (2006), pp. 717–21; Bernhard Klein and Gesa Mackenthun (eds.), *Sea Changes: Historicizing the Ocean* (New York, 2004); Daniel Finamore (ed.), *Maritime History as World History* (Gainsville, 2004).

[24] Fernand Braudel, *The Mediterranean and the Mediterranean World in the Age of Philip II*, translated by Siân Reynolds, 2 vols. (Berkeley, 1995); Peregrine Horden and Nicholas Purcell, *The Corrupting Sea: A Study of Mediterranean History* (Oxford, 2000); Peregrine Horden and Nicholas Purcell, 'The Mediterranean and "the New Thalassology"', *American Historical Review* 111 (2006), pp. 722–40.

starting point for a history of Britain and Germany, and indeed for modern Europe in general, may lie with a focus on the sea. Such an approach would combine the traditional emphasis on the centres of power, in this case London and Berlin, with a strong interest in the space where their influence met: how were Britain and Germany 'made' in the North Sea, how did the two countries project their power and identity in this maritime theatre?

The book is divided into five chapters, each of which follows a thematic approach, although they can be read chronologically. The first charts the rise of the public theatre celebrating the navy and the nation in the nineteenth century. It examines the transformation of key rituals and their emergence as professionally stage-managed and remarkably popular events before they met a sudden and unceremonious end in 1914. The chapter provides a close reading of the structure and choreography of launches of warships and fleet reviews, and investigates their historical background. It shows how, both in Britain and the *Kaiserreich*, these events became more frequent, more elaborate, more costly and more strongly regulated than at any time since the late eighteenth century.

One of the key factors influencing this rise was the unfolding of the political and cultural mass market towards the end of the nineteenth century. The second chapter therefore investigates how the naval theatre changed with the advent of the 'age of the masses' and explains the remarkable modernity of what was not least a spectacle of media, commerce and entertainment. The authorities in Britain and in Germany acknowledged that naval ceremonies had turned into a popular nationwide theatre and they saw the great potential of this stage for promoting the navy and 'educating the public'. However, while the governments and monarchs in both countries attempted to exploit this potential, the public itself became an important actor. Mass culture, popular papers and the cinema conveyed naval celebrations to millions of spectators, and in turn shaped the character of these events, often in a way that was beyond the control of the authorities. The entertainment provided by the naval theatre was thus never divorced from the fundamental political questions that characterized the 'age of the masses'.

For critics at the time and for many historians since, the naval theatre was a modern version of Rome's 'bread and circuses', designed to create loyalty and social cohesion amongst audiences. The third chapter reassesses this argument. Based on a wide range of first-hand accounts, it addresses three key questions. First, what was the role of the 'radical right' which historians have seen as so instrumental in the creation of naval enthusiasm? How, in particular, does it compare to the influence of other actors, who do not fall into the much-quoted, yet frustratingly imprecise, categories of 'above' and 'below'? Second, are claims about 'manipulation' or 'self-mobilization' borne out by the way in which people made sense of and participated in this public theatre? Third, how far does the concept of militarism, frequently employed by scholars of the 'manipulation' school, help us to understand the character of the naval theatre? In bringing these questions together, the chapter suggests a revision in our understanding of the 'mobilization of the masses' in the decades before 1914.

The symbolic quality of ships and the sea has intrigued observers as diverse as Admiral von Tirpitz and Michel Foucault. Chapter 4 follows their lead and asks why it was that the fleet was invested with so much meaning in the age of empire. Both in Britain and Germany the navy served as a prime symbol of national identity at a time when ideas of 'the nation' were contested both from within and without. While the army and its representation were rooted in regional traditions, the navy was a genuinely national institution that brought together key sources of identification such as monarchy, empire, geography and gender. Its public celebration aimed to reconcile local, regional and national contexts. The capability to symbolically merge different national signifiers into one potent display made this a unique arena for cultural nation-building.

Chapter 5 asks what the naval theatre meant for the Anglo-German antagonism. In the decades before the First World War, the North Sea became a stage on which international relations and naval rivalry intersected with popular culture and mass politics. In this inter-national theatre, the dreadnought fleets of Britain and Germany were floating platforms for the demonstration of sea power. Yet this was as much about concepts of nation, race and gender as it was about the command of the ocean. In the naval theatre, the Anglo-German antagonism was a dramatic game, in which important cultural issues were bound up with strategic and diplomatic developments. The significance of this game became particularly clear after 1909 when the staging and celebrating of the navy continued despite the fact that the Royal Navy had effectively won the naval race.

The epilogue, finally, goes beyond the timeframe that is usually associated with 'the age of empire'.[25] The imperial age did not end abruptly with the First World War, nor did the rivalry between Britain

---

[25] For two prominent examples see Heinrich Friedjung, *Das Zeitalter des Imperialismus 1884–1914*, 3 vols (Berlin, 1919–22) and Eric Hobsbawm, *The Age of Empire 1875–1914* (London, 1987).

and Germany. The naval stage was revived in the 1920s and 1930s, reaching a new climax before the Second World War. The re-emergence of this theatre sheds light on important continuities and discontinuities in German and British history. The book concludes by considering the remarkable longevity of the naval theatre in the twentieth century and its slow, but seemingly inevitable decline in recent years.

1   The rise of the naval theatre

On 17 July 1909 Britannia came to town. The Thames was 'thronged
with expectant people' when the bascules of Tower Bridge opened at 1pm
to let the procession of warships enter.[1] Small cruisers and destroyers had
already moored at Greenwich and Woolwich. More destroyers anchored
opposite the Tower of London and at London Bridge. A line of black
torpedo boats went further up the river, a detachment mooring off
Somerset House, a further four of them at Westminster Bridge. Then
the most modern and intriguing vessels of the fleet followed, the submarines. Two of them moored at Temple Pier, watched by the crowds
with 'awe' and 'quiet fascination', another four at Westminster, close to
the Houses of Parliament.[2] At the same time the fleet's big battleships,
including the latest Dreadnoughts, anchored down the river at Southend
in two long lines, flanked by torpedo boats. They were reportedly greeted
by 'a pressing, eager mob of sightseers'.[3] By 3pm a grand total of 150
warships, almost the entire Home Fleet, had assembled in the Thames,
stretching from the very heart of the capital eastwards towards the sea, a
floating chain of forty miles.

The fleet's visit was officially at the invitation of the Lord Mayor, who
was to receive naval officers and sailors at the Guildhall for the first time in
the history of the Corporation.[4] Yet there was little doubt that the
spectacle was more than a meeting between the navy and the figurehead
of the City. The visit had been consciously designed as mass entertainment. The arrival and departure of the fleet both took place on a
Saturday, when most Londoners would have time to go to the river.
The navy remained in the Thames for an entire week, to allow for a
long programme of attractions. There were mock-fights, illuminations,

---

[1] *Daily Mail*, 19 July 1909.
[2] *Daily News*, 19 July 1909; *Daily Mail*, 19 July 1909; *Daily Express*, 19 July 1909.
[3] *Daily News*, 19 July 1909.
[4] For the official announcement of the event see Hansard, Fifth Series, House of Commons,
vol. 7, cl. 23 (28 June 1909). The preparation for the visit is documented in PRO, ADM
1/8048.

fireworks and searchlight displays. Naval marches and parades passed through the streets of London, the most spectacular on 21 July, when 1,200 men and 40 officers marched from the Embankment to the Guildhall, dragging an artillery of 12-pounder field guns behind them. All ships, excluding the submarines, were open to visitors. The navy even had special programmes for children wanting to visit one of the dread-noughts. 'Sensation followed sensation' was how one spectator described the show.[5]

It is doubtful that 'London thought and talked of nothing but the Navy' for the whole week, as the *Naval and Military Record* claimed.[6] Yet, the sheer numbers of spectators were remarkable. According to newspaper reports, close to four million people went to see the ships between 17 and 24 July. More than a million Londoners watched the arrival of the fleet on the first day, and tens of thousands went on board the ships for guided tours.[7] Along the Embankment and at Westminster the crowds were so large that the police had to force them into queues that were kept moving. At Southend, the main pier leading to the *Dreadnought* had to be repeatedly closed due to overcrowding. In the morning of 18 July, an estimated 20,000 people rushed onto the pier. There were broken ribs, people were fainting and 'nasty rushes and collisions' occurred between the police and the crowds.[8]

Just as dazzling as the numbers of visitors were the rich layers of commercial and voluntary initiative formed around the fleet visit. Shipping and tourist businesses had a field day, with an armada of excursion boats and pleasure steamers surrounding the navy. Thomas Cook and Son offered luxury cruises, promising Londoners a close view of 'The Great Naval pageant on the Thames' for £1. 1s. There were countless stalls along the river, offering souvenirs, postcards and programmes. Here and in the high streets naval outfits and flags were on sale. News-vendors were busy selling special issues, amongst them the 'wonderful naval double number' of the *Illustrated London News*, covering 'every naval event of importance, every new device of offence or defence; every phase of naval life'. Advertisements for chocolates employed the theme of 'naval manoeuvres', showing a sailor talking to an officer while slipping the officer's wife a bar of chocolate behind his back. There were Dreadnought biscuits and Dreadnought toys. A sign outside a tailoring business declared: 'Dreadnought and Wear British Clothing'. There were

[5] *Daily News*, 21 July 1909.   [6] *Naval and Military Record*, 29 July 1909.
[7] *Times*, 26 July 1909; *Naval and Military Record*, 29 July 1909; *Daily Mail*, 19 July 1909.
[8] *Daily News*, 19 July 1909.

even 'Dreadnought trams', fashioned as battleships, complete with imitation guns levelled at intending passengers.[9]

The spectacle's significance clearly went beyond London: it was situated at the intersection between local, national and imperial contexts. For *Punch*, Britannia herself had come to town in the guise of the navy. In a full-page illustration the magazine showed Britannia triumphantly entering London, presenting the trident, with the White Ensign fluttering proudly behind her. While flanked by modern warships, her toga and helmet alluded to Ancient imperial greatness. This was not really about the Corporation of London, the illustration made clear, but about nation and empire, coming together in a dazzling display that had a parallel only in the splendour of Ancient Rome.[10] Most of the popular press agreed. A 'gigantic array of battleship and cruiser, of torpedo-boat and submarine that lies like a gleaming sword across the threshold of the imperial city' was how the *Daily Mail* described the display in the Thames.[11] The *London Illustrated News* had few doubts about the feelings of 'the Briton' watching this spectacle. Pride and the excitement of power dominated amongst the emotions best captured, the magazine believed, by Rudyard Kipling in *A Fleet in Being*:

And the whole thing was my very own (that is to say yours); mine to me by right of birth. Mine were the speed and power of the hulls, not here only but the world over; the hearts and brains and lives of the trained men; such strength and such power as we and the World dare hardly guess at. And holding this power in the hollow of my hand; able at the word to exploit the earth to my own advantage; to gather me treasure and honour, as men reckon honour, I (and a few million friends of mine) forbore because we were white men. Any other breed with this engine at their disposal would have used it savagely long ago.[12]

In this dense prose, nation and empire, race and masculinity, weaponry and power merged with the lure of and mastery over the sea. Those marvelling at this machinery of might, the quote suggested, had experienced the sensation of being part of a larger entity, defined by race ('white men'), nation ('Britons') and gender ('as men reckon honour'). In this

[9] For these and other examples see *The Navy League Guide to the Thames Review, 17th to 24th July 1909: Many Illustrations and Diagrams and Plans of the Fleet*, edited by Benedict W. Ginsburg (London, 1909). See also *Times*, 16 July 1909; *Daily News*, 21 July 1909.

[10] *Punch*, 14 July 1909: 'Britannia comes to town'.

[11] *Daily Mail*, 19 July 1909. Similarly: *Daily Express*, 19 July 1909.

[12] *Illustrated London News*, 17 July 1909. The quotation was taken from Rudyard Kipling, *A Fleet in Being: Notes of Two Trips with the Channel Squadron* (London, 1898), first published in the *Morning Post* between 5 and 11 Nov 1898. For a similar language used in the depiction of the 1909 fleet display see Bart Kennedy, 'The Grey Guards', in the *Daily Express*, 19 July 1909.

spectacle 'me and a few million friends of mine' appeared as one, united by the power to operate (and restrain) the 'engine of strength' that was the navy.[13]

How can this powerful fascination with the fleet and the sea be explained? Clearly, a number of dynamics came together in this arena that celebrated navy, nation and monarchy with unprecedented pomp and popularity. These included the intersection of government initiative with voluntary and commercial agendas; the rapid rise of mass media, leisure and entertainment; the attractiveness of the naval stage for the projection of local, regional, national and imperial loyalties; its increasingly central role for royal ritual; the curious combination of modern and traditional themes through the navy as an instrument that acted at once as the pioneer of technological advance and as an arbiter of the nation's past; the unique symbolic value that the fleet had as a result of all these aspects; finally its obvious role in imperial rivalry and the Anglo-German antagonism. Consecutive chapters will examine these factors in detail. This chapter begins by tracing the rise of the public rituals celebrating the navy during the nineteenth century. It provides a close reading of the choreography and structure of these displays and examines their remarkable transformation into professionally stage-managed national rites that took place with unparalleled frequency. In doing so, this chapter suggests that events such as the fleet's visit to the Thames in July 1909 are best understood as a powerful public theatre played out for both national and international audiences.

Discipline and ceremonial

The nineteenth-century celebration of the navy had its origins in an arena famously identified by Michel Foucault as paradigmatic for the power structures at work in modern societies. In *Discipline and Punish* Foucault analysed how power was enshrined as a quasi-anonymous force in modern institutions such as prisons, hospitals and schools.[14] For Foucault, military parades and inspections offered particularly clear examples of the mechanisms established in the seventeenth and eighteenth centuries to create 'docile bodies'. One of the illustrations in *Discipline and Punish* shows a medal commemorating Louis XIV's first

---

[13] *Illustrated London News*, 17 July 1909.
[14] Michel Foucault, *Discipline and Punish: The Birth of the Prison*, translated by Alan Sheridan (London, 1977), for the following particularly pp. 135–69.

military review in 1668.[15] It was at such rituals that the body entered 'a machinery of power that explores it, breaks it down and rearranges it'.[16] Military inspections exemplified how individual soldiers were formed into part of a 'multi-segmentary machine', their bodies disciplined through one 'collective and obligatory rhythm' of marching, exercising and parading.[17] It makes sense to read the original function of fleet reviews in a similar way. In his famous book on naval customs, first published in 1848, Admiral Rudolf Brommy described the procedures that the Royal Navy and most other navies had established in the age of sail. When taking up his command, an admiral would inspect his fleet assembled outside harbour. After the fleet's ceremonial showing of respect to its commanding officer, ships would 'clear for action', with officers and sailors taking up their battle stations. The admiral would board each vessel where, accompanied by the ship's commander and surgeon, he would inspect the state of *matériel* and *personnel*. Afterwards he would have the muster-book read out, signalling the completeness of the ship's crew and its readiness to put to sea.[18]

It was on this procedure that royal fleet reviews were originally modelled. The monarch as the titular head of the navy took the place of the inspecting officer. When George III held a review of the fleet in 1773 and again in 1781, these were still inspections in the original sense of the word. Accompanied by the naval lords, the King went on board the flagship and inspected the crew and the ship personally.[19] However, as they developed between the late eighteenth century and the First World War, royal reviews brought important changes that emphasized less the disciplining of bodies and more the theatrical display of monarchical and national power. At none of the reviews in the second half of the nineteenth century did the monarch board warships for inspection.[20] Instead, an elaborate procession was established in which the Queen or King sailed through the lines of warships and received the acclamation of the navy, a

---

[15] Ibid., plate 1.   [16] Ibid., p. 138.   [17] Ibid., pp. 151–2, 164.
[18] Rudolf Brommy, *Die Marine. Eine gemeinfassliche Darstellung des gesammten Seewesens*, third edition (Vienna, 1878), pp. 378–401. See also Hans-Peter Stein, *Symbole und Zeremoniell in deutschen Streitkräften vom 18. bis zum 20. Jahrhundert* (Herford, 1984), pp. 229–44 and Peter Kemp (ed.), *Oxford Companion to Ships and the Sea* (Oxford, 1976), pp. 569–70.
[19] *The Diaries of Colonel The Honourable Robert Fulke Greville, Equerry to His Majesty the King George III*, edited by Frank McKno Bladon (London, 1930), pp. 39–41; H. W. Wilson, 'Previous Naval Reviews', in *The Navy League Guide to the Coronation Review* (London, 1902), p. 17; *Times*, 31 July 1909 ('Sea Pageants of the Past'); *Naval and Military Record*, 3 Aug 1910.
[20] This excluded the 'semi-private' inspections of 1910 and 1912.

1. The royal procession through the lines of warships during the fleet review at Spithead, 31 July 1909. The royal yachts *Victoria and Albert* and *Alexandra* are preceded by the Trinity Yacht *Irene* and followed by the Admiralty yacht *Enchantress* and the *Fire Queen*, the yacht of the Commander-in-Chief Portsmouth.

movement that consciously imitated the rituals by which earlier ages had celebrated the entry of heroes and saviours.[21]

It was the ritualized honouring of the monarch that dominated naval reviews now.[22] Victoria's fleet review of 1887, on which all subsequent Spithead ceremonies were to be based, provides the best example.[23] At 3pm on 23 July 1887, the *Victoria and Albert*, with the Queen on board, left its buoy at Osborne, Isle of Wight, and took course towards the fleet. The royal yacht was met outside the boundaries of the 'review ground' by the Trinity Yacht, the official vessel of the Trinity Brethren, responsible

---

[21] See the section 'Sailor King and *Flottenkaiser*' in Chapter 4 for a more detailed analysis of this point.

[22] For a similar transformation that German army parades underwent in the nineteenth century see Vogel, *Nationen im Gleichschritt*, pp. 27–32.

[23] PRO, ADM 179/54; PRO, ADM 179/55: Review Orders; PRO, LC 2/146: Admiralty report on the Naval Review at Spithead on Saturday, 26 June 1897.

for the buoys and lighthouses of the English coast.[24] Its ceremonial
function was that of a maritime harbinger, heralding the entry of the
monarch.[25] Preceded by the Trinity Yacht, the *Victoria and Albert* entered
the lines of the fleet, arranged in two columns of battleships and two
smaller lines of torpedo boats. Two other royal vessels followed in its
wake, the *Osborne* and the *Alberta*, accommodating more members of the
royal family and household. Then came the Admiralty Yacht, the
Enchantress, followed by vessels for the diplomatic corps, the House of
Lords, the Commons and colonial officials. When the royal yacht entered
the lines of warships, the fleet fired a royal salute. Officers and sailors were
paraded on deck and the crews cheered the Queen as her yacht passed
each warship. At the end of the procession, the *Victoria and Albert* anchored and the Queen received the commanding officers.[26]

This elaborate maritime procession showed that the function of fleet
reviews had changed fundamentally. This was clearly no longer an
'inspection' in the original sense of the word. The distance at which the
royal yacht passed the warships during the procession precluded any
meaningful appreciation of the state *matériel* and *personnel* were in. One
of the admirals on board a vessel following the royal yacht during the
coronation review of 1911 found that the guests had had 'great difficulty
in distinguishing the ships even with the help of the chart'.[27] Midshipman
John Southby noted at the same occasion that the distance of the royal
yacht to the warships was so great that the monarch could only be made
out with a telescope.[28] The royal message at the conclusion of reviews
('His Majesty is greatly pleased with the efficient condition of the Home
fleet') was hardly more than a rhetorical gesture which acknowledged that

[24] On the Trinity Yacht, which had originally acted as a pilot, see *Encyclopaedia Britannica*,
vol. 27 (Cambridge, 1911), p. 286 and Kemp (ed.), *Oxford Companion*, pp. 889.

[25] From 1911 onwards three torpedo boats preceded the royal yacht additionally. For
accounts of the effect of this see NMM, HTN/201: Journal of Admiral Sir Louis
Henry Hamilton, 31 July 1911; RNM, 1980/127: J. H. Edelsten, midshipman's journal,
24 June 1911.

[26] For Victoria, this seems to have been the least enjoyable part. She noted in her diary: 'I
received all the Admirals and Captains of the Fleet, which took a long time. We only got
home at 9. I was very tired' (RA Queen Victoria's Journals, 23 July 1887). Her successors,
in contrast, expanded this reception into fully-fledged dinners and parties. Compare the
description that the Prince of Wales sent to his wife from the royal yacht at the end of the
1902 review: 'As soon as we had anchored, all the Admirals and Captains came
onb[oard] and Papa made them a little speech and gave them each a Coronation
medal'. This was followed by a 'large party' with 'many old friends' (RA GV/CC, 3/31,
16 Aug 1902).

[27] PRO, ADM 116/1157: Admiral Tupper to Commander-in-Chief Portsmouth,
27 June 1911.

[28] RNM, 1986/422: John H. P. Southby, midshipman's journal, 23 June 1911.

the navy had put on a good show. Fleet reviews were no longer held to inspect the ships and muster the crews, but in order to allow for an elaborate theatrical display of monarchical and national power. Naval officers now described them as 'shows' or 'theatre'.[29]

This functional change was paralleled by a strong rise in the frequency and professionalism with which these public rituals were being staged in the last decades of the nineteenth century. In 1907, Percival A. Hislam, naval author and commentator, noted that of late, fleet reviews had become recurrent features on the public stage. It was 'a remarkable fact', he wrote, that the number of 'naval pageants at Spithead' had increased dramatically in the recent past. Hislam saw the beginning of this expansion in 1887 when Queen Victoria had held a grand fleet review as part of her Silver Jubilee.[30] This spectacle set important precedents for the naval theatre. It established the 'Jubilee Review' as a new royal ritual, celebrating the Queen's fifty years of reign with a fleet assembly in the Solent, which was repeated in 1897 with the 'Diamond Jubilee Review'. This was further expanded in 1902 with the invention of the 'Coronation Review'.

Most of the press followed the lead of the Admiralty in describing this ceremony as part of royal tradition and 'ancient prescription'.[31] Only very few observers pointed out that there was no such tradition. John Leyland, naval author and historian, wrote in June 1911: 'The custom of gracing a Sovereign's Coronation with the magnificence of a naval review appears to be of entirely modern origin'. He concluded rightly that 'no record exists of any Coronation Naval Review before that one of 1902'.[32] The new feature in royal and naval ceremonial was repeated with much pomp in 1909, 1911, 1937 and, for the last time, in 1953. Queen Victoria's 'Golden Jubilee Fleet Review' thus stood at the beginning of a string of ceremonies that advertised the link between monarchy and navy more strongly in public. Between 1887 and 1914, the stretch of water in the Eastern Solent between the Isle of Wight and Portsmouth was formalized as a ritual arena for the display of the monarch's 'ocean throne'.[33]

---

[29] NMM, HTN/202a: Admiral Sir Louis Henry Hamilton, private diary, 29 July 1914; IWM, 85/11/1: Edward W. H. Blake, midshipman's journal, 12 June 1909.

[30] Percival A. Hislam, 'Reviews of Other Days', *Daily Express*, 3 May 1907. See also Lord Brassey, 'The Navy', in Thomas Humphry Ward (ed.), *The Reign of Queen Victoria*, vol. 1 (London, 1887), pp. 234–80.

[31] *Naval and Military Record*, 21 Aug 1902. The invention of the 'coronation review' is documented in PRO, ADM 116/131 and ADM 179/56.

[32] John Leyland, 'The Navy and the Coronation', *Mariner's Mirror* 1 (1911), p. 165.

[33] John Huntley Skrine, *The Ocean Throne: Verse for the Celebration of the Fiftieth Year of the Reign of Victoria* (Uppingham, 1887).

Originally the point of muster before fleets put to sea, Spithead was turned into the prime ceremonial stage of the fleet, a busy amphitheatre of power and pride, in which nation, monarch and navy met.

Victoria's jubilee review set a precedent not only for royal ritual, but also for Admiralty planning and stagecraft. If the symbiotic celebration of monarchy and navy was to become a regular and professionally managed feature on the public stage, it required systematic recording and central supervision. Until 1887, no substantial archive had existed at the Admiralty where the regulations for public rituals could be consulted. Nor had the naval leadership been particularly keen on getting closely involved in the planning of naval ceremonies. The 1887 review marked a radical departure from this hesitance. All preparations made at Portsmouth were now supervised and documented centrally. The Secretary of the Admiralty wrote specifically to the Commander-in-Chief at Portsmouth:

As it is desirable that a complete record should be kept at the Admiralty of the various steps taken on this occasion, I am to request that a duplicate copy of whatever Port Orders you may issue may be transmitted to the Admiralty.[34]

After the review, the memoranda, telegrams, orders and charts documenting the preparations were bound in six heavy volumes. They showed the close central control and meticulous attention to detail that had begun to characterize the celebration of the navy.[35] It was in these 'ceremonial books', which served as the blueprint for subsequent occasions, that the Admiralty codified all important procedures, including the order of the royal procession through the lines of warships and the evolution of 'manning yards', applied for the first time in 1887 to non-rigged ships.[36]

Beyond setting these precedents, Victoria's Golden Jubilee review marked a watershed in the frequency with which such rituals were staged. Between 1773 and 1887, only eight royal reviews had been held. Between

---

[34] PRO, ADM 179/54: Secretary of the Admiralty to Commander-in-Chief, Portsmouth, 7 June 1887.

[35] The six volumes are contained in PRO, ADM 179/54 and ADM 1/6871. On Admiralty planning see also Jeffrey L. Lant, 'The Spithead Naval Review of 1887', *Mariner's Mirror* 62 (1976), pp. 67–79.

[36] PRO, ADM 179/54: Memo Willes, 29 June 1887; ibid.: Proposal for (a) dressing ships with flags (b) performing evolution of 'manning yards' in Turret and Barbette ships, 2 July 1887. On the evolution of 'manning ship' see also Stein, *Symbole und Zeremoniell*, p. 232, Walter Transfeldt, *Wort und Brauch in Heer und Flotte* (Stuttgart, 1986), p. 363; Brommy, *Marine*, pp. 380–1.

1887 and 1914, in less than a quarter of the same time span, eleven took place.[37] In addition, George V held a review of the merchant navy in 1913 and there were four major fleet displays that took place in the absence of the monarch. Taking these into account, Britain witnessed sixteen public fleet assemblies in twenty-eight years.[38] In 1909, an unprecedented three fleet displays took place in one year, marking the beginning of a six-year period in which a royal review of one sort or another took place every year.[39] Never before in British history had there been so many naval displays in such short a period. And not only did these public rituals take place more often than ever before, they also involved rapidly rising numbers of ships. There were 128 naval vessels assembled in 1887, 165 in 1897 and 173 in 1907. The 1911 Coronation Review counted 167 ships, to be topped in 1914 when 205 vessels were on display.[40] The rising number of warships, combined with their steady increase in size, meant that the assembled fleets had to be displayed in an increasing number of lines. There were four lines of warships in 1887, six in 1897, eight in 1902, ten in 1911 and eleven in 1914. This meant that royal reviews took markedly longer. At the Jubilee Review in 1887 the procession through the lines of the fleet had taken roughly an hour. In 1911, it took, as junior officer John Cardew of HMS *Defence* noted, 'nearly 2 hours for the [royal] yacht to go around', an unprecedented amount of time.[41]

The real subject of these rituals, then, was no longer the fleet, but the public. What had originally been inspections of *matériel* and *personnel* had turned into ostentatious displays of monarchical and national power. Their primary purpose was no longer the disciplining of crews, the creation of 'docile bodies', as Foucault put it, but the public acclamation of the monarch. This functional change went hand in hand with the remarkable stagecraft and professional planning that developed at the Admiralty and was mirrored in the rising frequency and expanding scale of these rituals.

---

[37] This number includes the royal reviews at Spithead as well as the royal 'inspections' at Cowes, Torbay and Weymouth.

[38] If one compares the 114 years between 1773 and 1887 with the 28 years between 1887 and 1914, this was an increase in frequency of 714 per cent.

[39] This included a royal review at Spithead, an assembly of the fleet for the Imperial Press Conference, also at Spithead, and the navy's visit to the Thames described at the beginning of this chapter.

[40] For these numbers see Hislam, 'Reviews of Other Days'; Wilson, 'Previous Naval Reviews'; *Naval and Military Record*, 21 Aug 1902 and 22 July 1914; *Times*, 22 July 1887, 25 June 1897 and 24 June 1911.

[41] RNM, 1982/1716: John Cardew, midshipman's journal, 1909–1915, 23 June 1911.

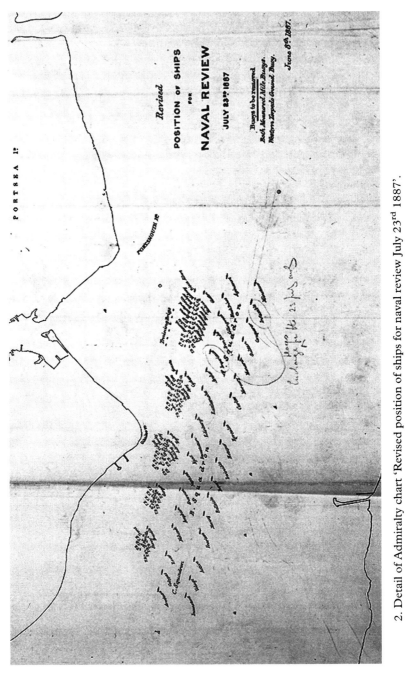

2. Detail of Admiralty chart 'Revised position of ships for naval review July 23rd 1887'.

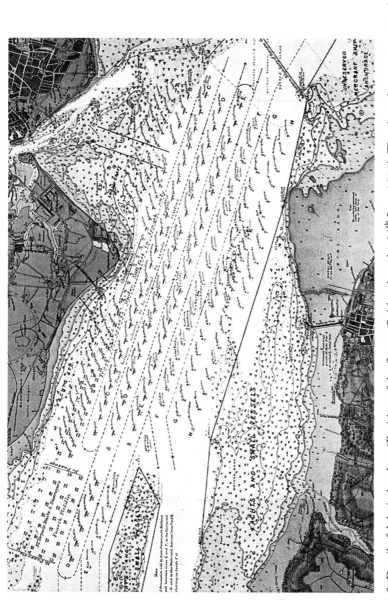

3. Detail of Admiralty chart 'Position of the fleet at Spithead on the 24th June 1911'. The chart documents not only the expansion in the size of fleet reviews (compare illustration 2), but also the rising professionalism of Admiralty planning. By 1902, the chart came in a standardized, multi-colour version, which was released to newspaper offices and the souvenir industry weeks in advance. It was reprinted in the press, official programmes and even on 'naval souvenir handkerchiefs'.

Maritime theatre

It is no exaggeration to describe the expanding celebration of the navy as the rise of a new form of public theatre. The accounts by observers were impregnated by the language of theatre. Spithead, the location for most naval reviews, was an 'amphitheatre', the preparations there were 'dress rehearsals'.[42] The pieces shown on this stage were 'spectacles' or 'pageants'.[43] Newspapers compared them directly to the latest shows in the West End. The *Daily Express* wrote about the fleet's visit to the Thames in 1909: 'It was like watching a cinematograph' and spoke of the 'animated pictures' displayed on the river.[44] The *Daily News* commented on the same event that it offered better viewing and more attractions than the shows 'at the old Adelphi'.[45] Correspondents reviewed naval displays as dramatic performances, describing the main actors, judging the *mise en scène* and discussing the best places for viewing.[46] They analysed the movements of the royal yacht and revelled in the details of the *Victoria and Albert* putting 'her head to the eastward' or describing 'a graceful semi-circle'.[47] Here is how the naval correspondent of *The Times* previewed the 'gridiron movement', an especially artful manoeuvre to be performed at the 1902 coronation review:

In this formation, and preserving the distance, the columns will approach the [royal] yacht; but before reaching her they will exchange the position of the columns by turning the ships simultaneously inwards and passing through the intervals, firing a Royal Salute while they are passing through. This is the gridiron movement; and, though it looks somewhat complicated in a diagram, it is as simple and pretty a movement as could well be devised [. . .]. The two divisions, having exchanged positions, will once more be twelve cables apart, and will now pass the yacht; and when the last ship is again well clear the division will turn inward sixteen points, the leaders counter-marching, as it were, to the right and left and the remainder of the ships following in succession.[48]

---

[42] *Times*, 1 June 1909; *Daily Chronicle*, 15 Aug 1902.
[43] See the coverage of the 1902 royal review in *Daily Telegraph*, 19 Aug 1902; *Daily Express*, 15 Aug 1902; *Daily Mail*, 18 Aug 1902; *Standard*, 19 Aug 1902; *Times*, 18 Aug 1902; *Sunday Times*, 17 Aug 1902; *Daily Chronicle*, 15 Aug 1902, with headlines such as 'The Spithead Spectacles', 'Excellent Maritime Spectacle', 'The Naval Spectacle', 'Sea Pageant', 'Fleet Pageant' and 'Naval Pageant'.
[44] *Daily Express*, 20 July 1909; *Daily Express*, 22 July 1909.
[45] *Daily News*, 21 July 1909.
[46] See for example *Times*, 14 Aug 1902; *Times*, 24 June 1911; *Daily Mail*, 2 Feb 1911; *Daily Express*, 2 Feb 1911.
[47] *Morning Post*, 24 June 1897; *Times*, 28 June 1897; *Times*, 12 and 14 June 1909; *Times*, 31 July 1909; *Times*, 9 July 1912.
[48] *Times*, 18 Aug 1902. In the event, the 'gridiron movement', which, according to the *Daily Telegraph*, 19 Aug 1902, had 'excited so much interest', had to be abandoned due to bad weather.

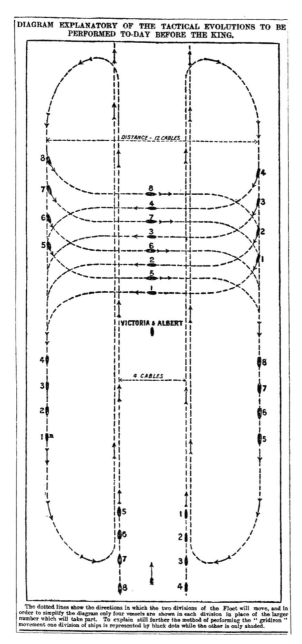

4. Maritime ballet. The gridiron movement, to be performed at the coronation review in 1902 (*Times*, 18 August 1902).

This was an elaborate maritime ballet, performed by warships. The Portsmouth Review Orders for exercises such as the gridiron read like carefully scripted naval choreographies.[49] John MacNeill, MP for South Donegal and Professor of Constitutional Law, called the programme for the 1909 fleet review the 'cross between a libretto and a funeral march'.[50] And while officials were at odds to stress that naval reviews and displays showed 'the Fleet in working guise', the officers on board agreed that this was empty rhetoric.[51] These were well-rehearsed forms of entertainment that had little practical value in terms of training and which scarcely gave an accurate picture of the fleet's condition. Lieutenant (later Admiral Sir) Louis Henry Hamilton, on board HMS *Cumberland* during the fleet assembly of July 1914, noted that officers often made fun of 'the whole show exercises'.[52] Watching a mock-attack carried out by torpedo boats and submarines, midshipman Edward Blake wrote on 12 June 1909: 'a fine spectacle, but practically, of course, absurd'.[53]

The rise of this naval theatre was reflected in official and popular terminology. In official Admiralty usage there were only *royal* reviews of the fleet, typically taking place at Spithead in the Solent. Assemblies of the fleet not attended by the monarch were 'mobilizations', 'displays' or 'visits'. Yet, with the ever-growing number and variety of demonstrative fleet assemblies, these distinctions were lost on most people outside the navy. As the Secretary of the Admiralty lamented in 1910, the wider public referred to naval displays indiscriminately as 'reviews'.[54] Most of the press called the fleet's visit to the Thames 'The Great Naval Review' or 'The Thames Review', despite the fact that the King neither visited nor inspected the assembled fleet.[55] When the Admiralty introduced a

---

[49] For an example see PRO, ADM 179/56, pp. 10–35.

[50] Hansard, Fifth Series, House of Commons, vol. 8, cl. 1356 (29 July 1909).

[51] 'The Fleet in working guise' was how T. J. Macnamara, Parliamentary Secretary to the Admiralty, described the 1912 inspection in Parliament. See Hansard, Fifth Series, House of Commons, vol. 40, cl. 299 (26 June 1912).

[52] NMM, HTN/202a: Admiral Sir Louis Henry Hamilton, private diary, 29 July 1914. See also his entry for 31 July 1911 (coronation review) in NMM, HTN/201.

[53] IWM, 85/11/1: Edward W. H. Blake, midshipman's journal, HMS *King Edward VII*, 12 June 1909. For similar examples see RNM, 1997: Diaries of James Colvill, 1910–1920, 24 June 1911; *The Navy and Defence: The Autobiography of Admiral of the Fleet Lord Chatfield* (London, 1942), pp. 79–80; Stephen King-Hall, *A North Sea Diary 1914–1918* (London, 1936), p. 26.

[54] PRO, ADM 1/8197: Memorandum by J. W. S. Anderson, 1 Nov 1910.

[55] Even the Navy League ignored Admiralty terminology and spoke indiscriminately of a 'review' whenever the fleet was assembled for public purposes. Cf. *The Navy League Guide to the Thames Review 17th to 24th July 1909* (London, 1909). See also *Daily News*, 20 July 1909; *Annual Register* (London, 1912), p. 174 and, for similar examples in the correspondence between various businesses and the Admiralty, PRO, ADM 1/8197 and 1/8317.

number of variations to the format of fleet assemblies ('parliamentary inspections', 'royal inspections' and 'imperial fleet assemblies') even *The Times*, otherwise eager to follow official terminology, referred to them simply as 'reviews'.[56] George V himself seems to have been uncertain what exactly the name and purpose of the naval assemblies were that he attended. In his telegram to the mobilized fleet in July 1914 he expressed his high appreciation of the 'splendid appearance' that the navy had made during the '*review* of the Fleet'.[57] The Admiralty was much obliged for the praise, but it could not help gently correcting the King. The Commander-in-Chief of the assembled fleet wired back to Buckingham Palace: 'The Home Fleets are honoured by Your Majesty's *inspection*'.[58]

For most of the press and the public (as well as the King in this example) 'review' had come to simply mean a spectacular assembly of ships, in most cases warships, with a strong demonstrative and public character. This change in meaning was yet another indicator of the functional transformation that fleet assemblies had undergone in the nineteenth century. Originally service rituals aimed at mustering and disciplining crews, they had turned into professionally stage-managed performances that ran according to codified procedures and were supervised at the central government level. By the end of the nineteenth century this theatre took place more frequently and on a larger scale than ever before. The Royal Navy was no longer just an instrument for battle; it had turned into a cultural tool, employed for theatrical displays played out in front of national and international audiences with unprecedented pomp.

A similar transformation took place, if in a much shorter span of time, in Imperial Germany. It was under Wilhelm II, who came to the throne in 1888, that the celebration of the navy was transformed into one of the key public arenas for the projection of monarchy, nationhood and Germany's mission abroad.[59] Fleet reviews, which until then had been of hardly any significance, were turned into annual rituals that marked the climax of the 'naval season'. In parallel to Germany's ambitious

---

[56] *Times*, 16 July 1907; *Times*, 26 July 1910; *Times*, 2, 3, 4 and 7 May 1912.
[57] PRO, ADM 116/1313: His Majesty the King to the Commander-in-Chief Home Fleets, 20 July 1914 (added emphasis).
[58] Ibid. (added emphasis).
[59] His grandfather, Wilhelm I, had held only one fleet review during his reign as emperor. See Georg Neudeck and Heinrich Schröder, *Das kleine Buch von der Marine. Ein Handbuch alles Wissenswerten über die deutsche Flotte nebst vergleichenden Darstellungen der Seestreitkräfte des Auslands* (Kiel and Leipzig, 1899), p. 16.

naval programme, they expanded continuously in scale and duration.[60] In establishing this maritime ritual, the Kaiser and the Imperial Navy were at pains to distance themselves from the Royal Navy. For many German observers there was too much theatricality and ostentation in the way in which the British celebrated their navy. The correspondent of the *Frankfurter Zeitung*, reporting from Spithead in 1909, wrote that British fleet reviews were pure 'naval theatre'.[61] In July 1914 the *Berliner Tageblatt* declared that the latest Spithead assembly had been all about outward appearances. The 'ostentatious showpiece' (*äußerliches Prunkschauspiel*) given by the Royal Navy had stood in sharp contrast to German fleet reviews which were part of 'real' manoeuvres and training.[62]

Wilhelm II himself, while clearly admiring the Royal Navy and its tradition, considered British public ritual as curiously 'backward'. In his memoirs he spoke of 'the superficialities and the pomp [...] which are common at such occasions in England'. The British attached 'more importance to an almost medieval display of splendour' than the Germans who emphasized exercise and training.[63] Reading about the elaborate preparations for Edward VII's coronation fleet review in 1902, the Kaiser could not help exclaiming: '*echt englisch!*'[64] Summing up what he saw as the essential difference between the two countries, he wrote that the Imperial Navy did 'not exist for ceremonial, but for war'.[65]

The Kaiser's fleet reviews were therefore designed to set the German navy apart from the British example. Rather than borrow from the Royal Navy's ceremonial tradition, the Kaiser and his admirals turned, characteristically, to the Prussian army as a role model. They transferred, quite literally, the army's well-developed repertoire of public parades onto the sea. Just as the army manoeuvres were preceded by a *Kaiserparade*, the

---

[60] In 1911, the fleet under review comprised for the first time more than a hundred vessels, forming a line fourteen kilometres long. A year later 118 vessels were on display. As Helmuth von Moltke, witnessing the spectacle on board the flagship, noted in his diary, it took the *Hohenzollern* 'almost an hour' to pass this armada: Helmuth von Moltke, *Erinnerungen, Briefe, Dokumente, 1877–1916*, edited by Eliza von Moltke (Stuttgart, 1922), p. 370 (16 Sep 1912). See also *Frankfurter Zeitung*, 17 Sept 1912, Zweites Morgenblatt and *Times*, 17 Sept 1912.

[61] *Frankfurter Zeitung*, 17 July 1909, Abendblatt.

[62] *Berliner Tageblatt*, 16 July 1914. Similarly *Berliner Lokal-Anzeiger*, 18 July 1914.

[63] Wilhelm II, *Ereignisse und Gestalten aus den Jahren 1878–1918* (Leipzig and Berlin, 1922), pp. 120–1. On Hohenzollern distaste for 'English ostentation' see also Lamar Cecil, *Wilhelm II: Prince and Emperor, 1859–1900* (Chapel Hill, 1989), p. 277. For a similar assessment see Constantin von Zedlitz, 'Lebende Geschichtsbilder', *Berliner Lokal-Anzeiger*, 21 July 1909, Abendausgabe, who saw British public life characterized by the 'worshiping of historical relics'.

[64] BA-MA, RM 2/164, Bl. 111: Marginalia to *Naval and Military Record*, 20 March 1902.

[65] BA-MA, RM3/9688, Bl. 54–5: Marginalia to *Daily Telegraph*, 8 May 1902.

naval exercises were now opened by a grand fleet review, the *Flottenparade*.[66] The procedures followed during this review were based on Prussian army parades, which had essentially two parts: the *Aufstellung*, which saw infantry and cavalry standing in line while the Kaiser rode past, and the *Vorbeimarsch*, which involved the troops, usually grouped in platoons, marching past the Kaiser and his entourage.[67]

The navy imitated these procedures in its fleet reviews, which took place in two different formats. The first, resembling the *Aufstellung*, displayed the fleet at anchor in a number of lines.[68] These were up to six kilometres long, with ships arranged in squadrons. 'Just like the detachments [*Staffeln*] of an army corps on parade', observed the *Frankfurter Zeitung* at the 1902 review.[69] On board his royal yacht, the naval equivalent of the Kaiser's *Paradepferd* (the show horse used at army parades), Wilhelm II would then sail through the lines of warships.[70] In contrast to British tradition, there were no vessels for royal guests, the Admiralty, Parliament and the diplomatic corps following the Kaiser; nor was there a maritime herald like the Trinity yacht that would have preceded the *Hohenzollern* at these occasions.[71] The second formation in which the Kaiser regularly reviewed his navy, the *Vorbeifahrt*, was modelled on the army's *Vorbeimarsch*.[72] This involved the royal yacht and the fleet passing each other 'under way': the fleet sailed in line at ten to twelve knots towards the *Hohenzollern*. First in the line passing the Kaiser at 300 metres' distance came the flotillas of torpedo boats. They

---

[66] As the official German Nautical Dictionary explained, *Parade* was a military term, referring to infantry and cavalry. See *Deutsches Seemännisches Wörterbuch. Im Auftrag des Staatssekretärs des Reichs-Marine-Amts heraus gegeben von A. Stenzel* (Berlin, 1904), p. 289; H. Frobenius (ed.), *Militär-Lexikon*, Ergänzungsheft 2 (Berlin, 1903), p. 53; G. von Alten (ed.), *Handbuch für Heer und Flotte*, vol. 5 (Berlin, 1913), p. 226. For a comprehensive analysis of army reviews see Vogel, *Nationen im Gleichschritt*, pp. 27–91. On the Kaiser's naval thinking as governed by military analogies see Berghahn, *Tirpitz-Plan*, pp. 28–9.

[67] Von Alten, *Handbuch für Heer und Flotte*, vol. 5, p. 226; Julius Castner (ed.), *Militär-Lexikon* (Leipzig, 1882), p. 279; *Meyers Konversationslexikon*, vol. 13 (Leipzig, 1897), p. 509. For a detailed description see Vogel, *Nationen im Gleichschritt*, pp. 53–4.

[68] Until 1904, this formation usually involved only two lines. With the rapid expansion of the German fleet, a third line of ships became standard, as seen at the 1907, 1909 and 1910 reviews. See BA-MA, RM 2/100, Bl. 345: Paradeskizze; BA-MA, RM 2/106, Bl. 284: Skizze B.

[69] *Frankfurter Zeitung*, 14 Sept 1901, Zweites Morgenblatt.

[70] On the *Paradepferd* see Vogel, *Nationen im Gleichschritt*, p. 53.

[71] For an analysis of the constitutional imagery that this involved, see Chapter 4.

[72] On the following see BA-MA, RM 2/106, Bl. 282: Programm für die Vorführung der Flotte; ibid., Bl. 284: Defilierplan für die Flottenparade am 5. September 1911; BA-MA, RM 2/107, Bl. 269: Programm für die Vorführungen der Flotte vor Sr. Majestät; ibid., Bl. 272: Paradeskizze für die Vorführungen der Flotte am 16. September 1912; and BA-MA, RM 3/10237, Bl. 283: Reihenfolge der Schiffe.

were followed by the battleships and cruisers, keeping 350 and 400 metres between each other. In the press and in internal correspondence the fleet was described as 'marching past' the Kaiser or as 'standing on parade', underlining how much these procedures were borrowed from the army.[73]

Both formats of the *Flottenparade* involved the fleet manning ship upon arrival of the Kaiser, firing a royal salute and the crews cheering while the royal yacht passed. These were, just as in Britain, the signs of the navy honouring its head. In contrast to the Spithead spectacles, however, the Kaiser disembarked from the royal yacht at the end of fleet reviews and boarded the flagship. Wilhelm II put strong emphasis on this demonstrative joining of the navy that concluded each fleet review. He insisted on going on board the flagship even in choppy seas. At occasions when the weather forbade disembarking at open sea he was prepared to leave the royal yacht at harbour and hold the review on board the flagship.[74] Having joined the navy in this way, the Kaiser would then watch the part of the manoeuvres specially prepared for him, occasions at which he regularly (and often to the irritation of his admirals) decided to command the fleet himself.[75]

And yet, despite all this public emphasis on functionality, German fleet reviews were just as theatrical and removed from any real training purpose as their British equivalents. When the Kaiser claimed that his navy's *Flottenparaden* were 'training for war' while British naval spectacle was 'mere ceremonial', this was largely based on self-deception. To begin with, the vocabulary used to describe the naval exercises that he observed, betrayed a strong element of theatricality. 'Performances' (*Vorführungen*) and 'battle images' (*Gefechtsbilder*) were the official titles.[76] These were

---

[73] *Frankfurter Zeitung*, 31 Aug 1909, Erstes Morgenblatt; *Deutsche Nachrichten*, 3 Sept 1911; *Frankfurter Zeitung*, 6 Sept 1911, Erstes Morgenblatt; *Berliner Neueste Nachrichten*, 11 Sept 1904. See also the articles by the *Norddeutsche Allgemeine Zeitung*, *Der Tag* and *Kölnische Vokszeitung*, in *Presse-Stimmen zur Flotten-Parade* (Berlin, 1911), pp. 5–18. Internal instructions for this type of review were called *Defilierplan*, again a military term (*defilieren*: to march past in file). Technically, of course, the Kaiser marched just as much past his ships as they past him, with the *Hohenzollern* usually going two knots faster than the approaching fleet. See BA-MA, RM 2/107, Bl. 269; BA-MA, RM 2/108, Bl. 53: Admiralstab to Marine-Kabinett, 16 Feb 1914; BA-MA, RM 2/106, Bl. 284: Defilierplan für die Flottenparade am 5. September 1911.

[74] For an example see *Frankfurter Zeitung*, 17 Sept 1912, Zweites Morgenblatt.

[75] On the 'difficulty and anxiety' that this caused see Count Robert Zedlitz-Trützschler, *Twelve Years at the Imperial German Court* (London, 1924), p. 87 and Wilhem Deist, 'Kaiser Wilhelm in the Context of His Military and Naval Entourage', in John C. G. Röhl and Nicolaus Sombart (eds.), *Kaiser Wilhelm II: New Interpretations* (Cambridge, 1982), pp. 169–92.

[76] BA-MA, RM 2/107, Bl. 222: Chef Admiralstab to Kaiserliches Kommando der Hochseeflotte, 31 Aug 1912; BA-MA, RM 2/100, Bl. 347: Gefechtsbild 21 am 7. September [1904]; BA-MA, RM 2/107, Bl. 269: Programm für die Vorführungen der Flotte vor Sr. Majestät in der Helgoländer Bucht am 16. September 1912.

well-rehearsed dramatic pieces, staged for the entertainment of His Majesty and the wider audience.[77] The officers present at these occasions were painfully aware of this. Commanding SMS *Rheinland* at the 1911 review, Albert Hopman criticized the fact that the drill for the parade and the show exercises had been 'more than excessive'.[78] In fact, so much time was taken up by rehearsing the show evolutions that the actual manoeuvres, to take place later in the absence of the Kaiser, had to be curtailed heavily.[79] Wilhelm Groener, observing the training of the fleet as a general staff officer in 1908, found the navy increasingly obsessed with ceremonial and mock battles. Groener noted that the exercises that he witnessed were 'not a preparation for war, but merely a means of making the fleet ready for being paraded'. Naval displays were occasions 'at which officers and men do not show their real abilities, but only what they have rehearsed for this very moment'. Groener called this the '*Besichtigungstürken*',[80] a word that had made it into the military dictionaries during this period. *Einen Türken stellen* or *etwas türken*, they noted, meant to 'pretend something for inspection' or to 'drill a show exercise'.[81] Just as in Britain, the theatrical display of monarchical and national power had come to dominate the original purpose of fleet reviews.

Going down the ways

A similar dynamic can be seen at work in the rise of the second main genre staged in the naval theatre: launches of warships. In Britain, three major changes expanded the scope and significance of these rituals between the late eighteenth and the late nineteenth century. The first concerned the gender of the patron at the centre of these ceremonies. Launching a warship had originally been a strictly male domain and was usually performed by dockyard officials. This changed at the beginning of the nineteenth century. In 1803, a female patron launched a warship for

---

[77] For a particularly striking example of this choreography see BA-MA, RM 2/106, Bl. 285: Anlage zum Flottentagesbefehl Nr. 87 vom 12. August 1911. Anordnungen für das Zeremoniell bei Besichtigung der Hochseeflotte durch Seine Majestät den Kaiser am 5. September 1911.

[78] Albert Hopman, *Das Logbuch eines deutschen Seeoffiziers* (Berlin, 1924), p. 373.

[79] Ibid., p. 374. Hopman became later head of the RMA's *Zentralabteilung*.

[80] Wilhelm Groener, *Lebenserinnerungen* (Göttingen, 1957), p. 124, watching the fleet's review drill on board SMS *Pommern* on 5 May 1908.

[81] Paul Horn, *Deutsche Soldatensprache* (Giessen, 1899), p. 76; Bernhard v. Poten (ed.), *Handwörterbuch der gesamten Militärwissenschaften*, vol. 9 (Bielefeld and Leipzig, 1880), p. 181; *Grimms Wörterbuch*, vol. 2, 1. Abteilung, 2. Teil (Leipzig, 1952), cl. 1853. See also Tirpitz, *Erinnerungen*, p. 43, commenting on the growing theatricality that he saw as characterizing the public rituals of the Imperial Navy.

5. Cutting the cord. The Duchess of Wellington at the launch of HMS
Iron Duke, Portsmouth, 12 October 1912.

the first time and this became the regular custom after 1811. As a result,
the ceremonial gained new momentum and generated greater public
attraction. The ladies chosen as launch patrons were usually aristocrats
or the wives of high naval officers; they stood at the centre of a range of
polite and social functions that had not previously been associated with
ship launches.[82]

---

[82] Margarette Lincoln, 'Naval Ship Launches as Public Spectacle 1773–1854', *Mariner's
Mirror* 83 (1997), p. 470; Silvia Rodgers, 'The Symbolism of Ship Launching in the
Royal Navy', D.phil. thesis, University of Oxford (1983), pp. 271–6; *Admiralty Manual of
Seamanship*, vol. 1, p. 401.

The ceremonial was, secondly, enlarged when Queen Victoria set a crucial precedent in the mid-nineteenth century. Monarchs since Henry VIII had occasionally watched launches of warships, but they had never played an active role in the ceremony. If present, 'the Royal personages were merely lookers-on at the ceremony', as Edward Fraser, a naval author with an enduring interest in the ceremonial of the service, noted.[83] In 1854, however, Victoria launched a ship of the Royal Navy herself, the first monarch in British history to do so. Watched by the Prince Consort, it took her three attempts to break the bottle against the stem of the *Royal Albert*, before wishing 'success' to the ship and releasing it.[84] The precedent drew royalty and aristocracy closer to the ceremony and made the spectacle more popular with the public.

A third important innovation came when the Admiralty introduced a religious service to be held at all launches of warships. While much of the romanticizing naval literature of the Edwardian period assumed that such a service was part of the 'age and custom' that distinguished the ceremony, this was an invention of the 1870s that came as part of the new attention paid to public ritual by the leadership of the navy. It was between the Admiralty, the Archbishop of Canterbury and the Queen that the form of the service was decided in the course of October 1874. The service was put into effect at the beginning of 1875. On 16 January the *Army and Navy Gazette* announced that 'the launches of Her Majesty's ships are to be no longer a mere secular ceremony'.[85] The order of service, which the Admiralty believed would 'commend itself to the feelings of the people of this country',[86] regulated precisely what readings and hymns the dockyard chaplain or local priest were to use. The religious ceremony, as it has been conducted at ship launches in Britain ever since, begins with a reading of Psalm 107, verses 23 to 31 and 43:

They that go down to the sea in ships: and occupy their business in great waters;
These men see the works of the Lord: and his wonders in the deep.

---

[83] *Times*, 10 March 1902. The papers of Edward Fraser, who collected a plethora of information on naval ceremonies between the 1890s and the 1930s, are held at the National Maritime Museum, Greenwich. Material for and a draft of his article on ship launches, cited above, can be found in NMM, FRS/49. See also his explanation of 'the launching ceremony of old-time England' in *Bellerophon* (London, 1909), pp. 6–7.
[84] *Times*, 15 May 1854.
[85] *Army and Navy Gazette*, 16 Jan 1875.
[86] Hansard, Third Series, vol. 222, cl. 393: George Ward Hunt, First Lord of the Admiralty, 16 Feb 1875. For the background see D. Bonner-Smith, 'Religious Ceremony at Launches', *Mariner's Mirror* 35 (1949), pp. 43–6, where the correspondence between the First Lord of the Admiralty, the Archbishop of Canterbury and Queen Victoria is given. See also NMM, FRS/57.

They are carried up to the heaven, and down again to the deep: their soul melteth away because of the trouble.

They reel to and fro, and stagger like a drunken man: and are at their wits' end.

So when they cry unto the Lord in their trouble: he delivereth them out of their distress.

For he maketh the storm to cease: so that the waves thereof are still.

Then are they glad, because they are at rest: and so he bringeth them unto the haven where they would be.

O that men would, therefore, praise the Lord for his goodness: and declare the wonders that he doeth for the children of men!

Whoso is wise will ponder these things: and they shall understand the loving-kindness of the Lord.[87]

The verses tell of storms, distress and trouble, of staggering men at their wits' end – a remarkable choice for a reading intended to instil confidence and pride in naval crews. The psalm contrasts the fragility of men and the 'perils of the deep' with the blessings of God. These themes of guardianship and hope also dominate the prayer that follows in the order of service ('O Thou that sittest above the water floods, and stillest the raging of the sea . . .). Only after this and the Lord's Prayer does the service mention war and duty, in a hymn by L. M. Sabine Pasley. It is for 'home and country' that the crew will sail in the new ship. If having to face 'war's dread engines', they will fight as 'men of might, brave hearts and true'. Led by the dockyard choir, the assembled officers and ratings sing:

> O Father, King of Earth and Sea,
> We dedicate this ship to Thee;
> In faith we send her on her way,
> In faith to Thee we humbly pray, –
> O hear from heaven our sailors' cry,
> And watch and guard her from on high.

> When duty calls to risks unknown,
> Where help must come from Thee alone,
> Protect her from the hidden rock,
> From War's dread engines' fatal shock;
> O hear from heaven our sailors' cry,
> And in peril be Thou nigh.

> May England's sons, her destined crew
> Be men of might, brave hearts and true;
> Yet theirs the better sort of fame
> To be of those that love Thy Name.

---

[87] *Service to Be Used At the Launching of Ships of His Majesty's Navy* (London, 1902).

O hear from heaven our sailors' cry,
In war and conflict be Thou nigh.

And when at length her course is run,
Her work for home and country done;
Of all the souls that in her sailed,
Let not one life in Thee have failed;
But hear from heaven our sailors' cry,
And grant eternal life on high.[88]

After this hymn, the chaplain blesses the ship and 'all those who sail in her'. The patron is then asked to release the ship by cutting the launching cord. With the joint singing and praying, the display of Church symbols and the blessing of ship and men, the service lends to the proceedings a moral authority and solemnity which naval ceremonial alone does not offer. By the mid 1870s, launches of warships had thus become substantial pageants that took twice as long as at the beginning of the century, involving a range of religious and ritualized acts as well as the increasingly active participation of the monarchy.

In the decades up to 1914, a range of further innovations and regulations added to the growing theatricality of these occasions. A number of Admiralty orders were issued to ensure, amongst other things, that larger numbers of officers and sailors attended and that ships and installations were routinely 'dressed' on launch days.[89] The social functions created around launches expanded too, so much so in fact that the Controller of the Navy demanded in 1911 that whenever royalty or other esteemed guests were to perform a launch, dockyards submit an estimate and gain official sanction before commencing preparations.[90] Just as with fleet reviews, this was part of the increasing professionalism that marked the Admiralty and its new interest in public displays from the 1880s onwards. Until then, the planning of naval celebrations had been left in the hands of local dockyard officials and there had been no systematic recording of launching ceremonies.[91] Now, there were uniform regulations that

---

[88] Ibid.

[89] This display, usually seen at royal reviews, was ordered for a launching ceremony for the first time in October 1912, when the *Iron Duke* was launched at Portsmouth. See *Evening News and Southern Daily Mail*, 12 Oct 1912. Another new custom was the invitation and ceremonious positioning of regiments that had an association with the new ship's name, see *Naval and Military Record*, 30 Oct 1912.

[90] See the digest in PRO, ADM 12/1493, 91/3. The correspondence on this subject, CN 9407/1911, is not enclosed in ADM 1. Further evidence for the rising costs of launches is given in PRO, ADM 1/7461B: Controller to Superintendent of Chatham Dockyard, 5 April 1900.

[91] See PRO, ADM 1/7363: Minutes by the Secretary and Chief Clerk, 21 July 1898, confirming that there had been no systematic records of launching ceremonies at the Admiralty prior to the 1890s.

governed the launching of warships, a public ritual that was staged with an ever-increasing frequency and with unprecedented central supervision.[92]

A range of other, related ceremonies accompanied the transformation of fleet reviews and ship launches into a well-choreographed form of public theatre in Britain. The laying of a new warship's keel plate was one of them. For most of the nineteenth century this was a small-scale and private event. The Admiral Superintendent of Chatham Dockyard wrote to Edward Fraser in 1899: 'In the Government Dockyards it is not the practice to hold any ceremony on the occasion of laying down a new ship'.[93] Only three years later the Admiralty changed its policy radically. In March 1902, it asked the King to perform this ritual publicly to mark the beginning of the building of HMS *King Edward VII*. *The Times* judged the occasion 'admirably stage managed'.[94] Observers were quick to establish that this was the 'first ceremonial laying of a keel-plate by a royal personage'.[95] From then until 1914, the new ritual expanded continuously. It became customary to have a band play 'Britannia Rules the Waves' while the keel plate was lowered and to ask a female patron to drive the first rivets into it.[96] In 1911, Fraser noted that almost all occasions at which a new warship was laid down were now celebrated with an extensive ceremony.[97] In 1913, after a huge crowd and a group of illustrious guests, amongst them Winston Churchill, had celebrated the laying down of the *Ramillies* at Dalmuir, the *Scotsman* commented: 'Until recently the laying of a new keel was a matter that passed without ceremony in the Clyde yards, but times are changed'.[98] Within just a few decades, a range of rituals had been newly invented and others dramatically expanded. They celebrated navy, nation and monarchy with unprecedented frequency and professionalism.[99]

---

[92] For the process of codification see the minutes by the Secretary and Chief Clerk of the Admiralty written after the launch of HMS *Ocean* (ibid).

[93] NMM, FRS/49: Swinton Holland, Admiral Superintendent of Chatham Dockyard, to Fraser, 11 Oct 1899.

[94] *Times*, 10 March 1902.   [95] *Illustrated London News*, 15 March 1902.

[96] *Naval and Military Record*, 25 Feb 1909. For the increasingly elaborate character of keel-laying ceremonies see TWAS, 696/23 and PFDP, vols. 4 to 6.

[97] NMM, FRS/49: Note, 3 Jan 1911.

[98] *Scotsman*, 13 Nov 1913. Similar examples in *Glasgow News*, 12 Nov 1913; *Glasgow Herald*, 13 Nov 1913; *Daily Record and Mail* (Glasgow), 13 Nov 1913.

[99] These findings stand in contrast to interpretations which argue that royal spectacle in the late Victorian and Edwardian era should be seen as within the tradition of the first half of the nineteenth century and not as cases of 'invented traditions'. See Walter Arnstein, 'Queen Victoria Opens Parliament: The Disinvention of Tradition', *Historical Research* 63 (1990), pp. 178–94; John Plunkett, *Victoria: First Media Monarch* (Oxford, 2003), p. 17 and Norman Davies, *The Isles* (London, 1999), p. 743, who sees 'no inventions' in the coronation ritual of 1902.

6. The laying of the first keel plate of HMS *Queen Elizabeth*, Portsmouth, 21 October 1912.

Launching the Imperial Navy

Launches of warships underwent a similar transformation in Imperial Germany. Traditionally, this had been a modest ceremony. The regulations issued by the naval chief of staff, Albrecht von Stosch, in 1876 specified that 'all costly elaborations [*aller kostspielige Aufwand*]' should be avoided at ship launches.[100] In the 1890s, however, the humble service ritual was transformed into a major imperial pageant. Wilhelm II occupied himself with every detail. Assisted by a naval leadership happy to see the fleet more prominently represented on the public stage, the Kaiser ordered that ship launches were to be turned into key national and royal rituals. His *Allerhöchster Kabinettsorder* of 27 September 1900 decreed that warships were to be launched in an entirely new way.[101] A range of innovations was introduced both at government and private yards. The

---

[100] *MVBl* 7 (1876), p. 15: Bestimmungen, betreffend das Arrangement und Ceremoniell bei dem Stapellauf eines S.M. Schiffe oder Fahrzeuge auf Kaiserlichen Werften, 31 Jan 1876. For the origins of this ritual in Germany see C. B. Hansen, 'Schiffstaufen', in Volker Plagemann (ed.), *Übersee. Seefahrt und Seemacht im deutschen Kaiserreich* (Munich, 1988), pp. 140–2.

[101] *MVBl* 31 (1900), pp. 397–8: Das Zeremoniell bei Stapelläufen. The preparation of the order is documented in BA-MA, RM 3/117.

custom of having the oldest local naval officer act as launch patron was superseded by the Kaiser's personal choice: 'It will be decided by Me who will perform the launch of one of My ships'.[102] This usually meant that Wilhelm II selected a name from a list of dignitaries suggested to him by Tirpitz or von Müller, the Chief of the Naval Cabinet.[103] Royals, members of the high nobility and military leaders were preferred choices. For smaller vessels, the Kaiser could be persuaded to appoint mayors or burgomasters as patrons.

Not only was the role of the launch patron enlarged, but also military representation. The honorary guard attending warship launches was to consist no longer of sixty men, but a whole company, complete with standard and military band, comprising up to 640 men, a commander and a number of additional officers. Taking account of this strong increase, the regulations no longer referred to an 'honorary guard' (Ehrenwache), but an 'honorary company' (Ehrenkompagnie).[104] As a ceremony within the ceremony the Kaiser reserved for himself the right to inspect this detachment on the way to the launch platform. Additionally, the new regulations ordered all naval and military commands in the vicinity to send detachments. Even officers on leave had to attend.[105] From 1901, all ceremonial routes that the Kaiser was to take were to be lined by troops on both sides. This required 400 to 500 additional soldiers filing into dockyards already crowded by guards, detachments from ships and garrisons as well as the assembled officer corps.[106] In August 1902, Wilhelm II decreed that all officers present at launches had to wear their decorations.[107] And in March 1904, he ordered that the honorary guard had to present arms and the band play the Ehrenmarsch not only for royalty, but also for the Burgomasters of

---

[102] MVBl 31 (1900), p. 397.
[103] The process of choosing the launch patron is best illustrated in GStA PK, I Rep 89, Nr. 32225, Bl. 12: Chef Marinekabinett to Chef Geheimes Civil-Kabinett, 4 June 1908, discussing who should launch the Rheinland. See also BA-MA, RM 3/118, Bl. 128 where the choice of patron for the Helgoland is documented.
[104] MVBl 31 (1900), p. 398. For the preparation of honorary guards see BA-MA, RM 3/184, Bl. 22: RMA to Königlicher Hauptmann und Kompagniechef Hübner, 26 May 1913.
[105] MVBl 31 (1900), p. 398. See also BA-MA, RM 31/93, Bl. 185: Kaiserliche Werft Kiel to Kommando Kiel, 17 June 1901.
[106] BA-MA, RM 31/93, Bl. 179: Staatssekretär RMA to Kaiserliches Kommando Kiel, 18 June 1901. See also MVBl 32 (1901), p. 274: Nr. 15, 31 July 1901. BA-MA, RM 31/93 includes the details on the procedure for the lining up of troops (Spalierbildung) as it was practised at the Kiel yard, where 33 officers and 400 men were ordered for this purpose, rehearsing the task a day before the launch.
[107] MVBl 32 (1902), p. 249: Nr. 228, 4 Aug 1902.

Hamburg, Bremen and Lübeck, who attended a large number of ship launches.[108]

Perhaps the most remarkable element in this ever-expanding pageantry was the *Ablaufpavillon*. This platform, complete with canopy and draping, was set up close to the water to give the 'highest and all-highest personages' a prime spot from which to watch the ship enter the water.[109] Its effect was to create more ceremonial and make ship launches take considerably longer. The key figures involved in the ceremony (the ship's patron, royal guests, admirals and entourage) now had to visit two platforms, which were located at opposite ends of the festive arena created around the hull. On arrival, they first proceeded to the 'christening platform', the *Taufkanzel*. After the speech, the naming of the ship and the breaking of the bottle, they left this platform at the ship's stem and proceeded towards the 'viewing platform', the *Ablaufpavillon*, situated close to the ship's stern. The route led alongside the entire hull and was lined by soldiers, guards and spectators. Only after this procession and once the 'highest guests' had arranged themselves in the pavilion, the sign was given for the ship to be released.[110] In the stage management of this ritual, the *Ablaufpavillon* thus represented an equivalent to the 'retarding element' in classical drama. It allowed for an interlude between the naming of the ship and its launching, which created suspense and space for further ceremonial.[111]

---

[108] BA-MA, RM 31/1067, Bl. 123, Staatssekretär RMA to Kaiserliches Kommando Kiel, 4 March 1904; RM 3/129, Bl. 55: Memorandum, 27 July 1903, where the ceremonial rank of the mayors of Hanseatic cities is discussed for the first time; BA-MA, RM2/1618, Bl. 44: Müller to Tirpitz, 20 Jan 1909, where the ceremonial elevation of the Hanseatic mayors is explained retrospectively. See also *Flaggen-, Salut- und Besuchsordnung für die Kaiserliche Marine* (Berlin, 1904), pp. 55–6 and ibid., plate 5.

[109] The *Ablaufpavillon* was usually restricted to launches of capital warships and the presence of royalty. It was however also used at a number of launches performed not by royal but other dignitaries, such as Graf von Schlieffen in 1906. After increasing financial objections, this use was cut back at government yards in the course of 1908, while private yards kept using *Ablaufpavillons* or *Ablauftribünen* up to 1914.

[110] BA-MA, RM 31/93, Bl. 185: Kaiserliche Werft Kiel to Kommando Kiel, 17 June 1901; ibid., Bl. 191: Beitrag zum Stationstagesbefehl. The lengthened ceremonial route made necessary by the *Ablaufpavillon* can be seen in the drawings for launch arrangements in BA-MA, RM 3/153, Bl. 16; RM 3/130, Bl. 25; RM 3/133, Bl. 46; RM 3/134, Bl. 125; RM 3/135, Bl. 116; RM 3/142, Bl. 41; RM 3/152, Bl. 135; RM 3/159, Bl. 81; RM 3/170, Bl. 19; RM 3/171, Bl. 13; RM 3/188, Bl. 24. See also BA, R43/955: Situationsplan für den Stapellauf S.M. Linienschiff 'M'.

[111] The *Ablaufpavillon's* retarding effect is neatly captured in B. Henrici, *Deutsches Flottenbüchlein* (Hamm, 1907), pp. 34–5. In 1912, this effect was taken to a new extreme at the launch of the *Imperator* in Hamburg. The *Ablaufpavillon* was set up on the shore opposite the Vulcan yard, so that after the naming of the ship the Kaiser, his entourage as well as the Senators had to be shipped across the harbour in the Senate's *Staatsbarkasse* before the hull could be released: StA Hamburg, 132–1 I, 2282, Bl. 97a.

The transformation of ship launches into a new form of national and imperial theatre was further signalled by the introduction of the 'launch speech'. The Kaiser decided that the launch of a warship should be a profoundly 'solemn act'.[112] However, military ceremonial and the breaking of a bottle alone did not make for much *Feierlichkeit*. In Britain, such an aura was evoked by the religious service that had been introduced in 1875. The Kaiser, in contrast, was opposed to having any higher authority than his own represented at ship launches. He rejected any Church involvement and chastised Protestant critics who argued that the 'christening' of warships was blasphemy or superstition if it did not include a religious service.[113] It was the 'christening speech', the *Taufrede*, which was to create the solemnity that the Kaiser sought in ship launches. This speech was held before the breaking of the bottle and the releasing of the vessel. In it, the speaker revealed the name of the new ship that had been kept secret until then.[114] Directly addressing the vessel in the intimate second person singular (*'Du'*), he bestowed a mission on to the ship and charged its name with associations of honour, bravery and victory before it was 'solemnly sent out on to the water'.[115]

The administrative effort involved in the planning and editing of these speeches reflected how seriously the erstwhile modest ceremonies were being taken now. The content of each speech was controlled by Tirpitz's public relations office in Berlin, the *Nachrichtenbureau*. In advance of each launch it sent a collection of past speeches as guidance to the high guest invited to deliver the speech, reminding him of the requirement to

---

[112] Penzler (ed.), *Reden Kaiser Wilhelms II.*, vol. 2, p. 176: Speech by Wilhelm II at the launch of the *Kaiser Karl der Große*, 18 Oct 1899.

[113] During the 1903 General Synod a number of Protestant pastors had urged the Kaiser to change the launching ceremonial because of its blasphemous associations. At the very least, the expression *Schiffstaufe* and the ceremonial utterance 'I christen thee' should be dropped, they argued. W. Meyer, a pastor from Niedergebra, Saxony, sent petitions to the Imperial Navy Office and the Kaiser for over two years. In 1905, however, the Provincial Synod of Saxony decided that no religious offence was committed by calling the launching of a warship a 'christening'. See *Der Pfarrerverein. Organ der evangelischen Pfarrervereine*, 15 May 1903, p. 71; BA-MA, RM 2/1618, Bl. 99: Provinzial-Synode Sachsen, Antrag 33 der Petitionskommission, 13 Oct 1905 and BA-MA, RM 3/9958, Bl. 64: 'Der Kampf um die Schiffs-Taufe'. For the Kaiser's interventions see BA-MA, RM 2/1618, Bl. 27 and BA-MA, RM 3/9958, Bl. 80–1.

[114] Great efforts were made to keep the designated names of new ships secret until their launch. In the press, in official statements and in the Reichstag new vessels were referred to by a single letter or as the *Ersatz* of the predecessor ship. See in particular BA-MA, RM3/40: Namengebung von Schiffen, 1899–1914, ganz geheim. In Britain ship names were made public before the keel laying.

[115] For an analysis of the content of these speeches see Chapter 4.

mention the Kaiser and suggesting suitable themes in connection with the name of the ship and the place of the launch. The speaker then drew up a draft and sent it back to Berlin, where the *Nachrichtenbureau* scrutinized it and suggested alterations. This process was explained to the dignitaries, who had to submit their speeches, as 'making sure that no errors or contradictions arise in the press coverage', but it effectively amounted to censorship.[116] In three quarters of cases, the drafts were sent back with only minor corrections 'for better understanding'. However, in roughly a quarter of cases, Tirpitz's press officers changed the text substantially, at times cutting entire passages or rewriting them. In almost all of these cases the aim was to avoid provocation in Britain.[117]

The transformation of warship launches from the humble affairs they had resembled in the 1870s to major imperial pageants after the turn of the century caused a remarkable rise in expenditure, so dramatic in fact that the Imperial Audit Office felt it had to reprimand the naval leadership. In November 1908, it wrote to the Imperial Navy Office and the Treasury, lamenting the massive increase in the cost of launch celebrations. Citing particularly extravagant examples, the Audit Office asked the *Reichsmarineamt* to find ways of limiting expenditure.[118] The Treasury agreed. At a time when expenditure on new battleships had reached unprecedented heights and was straining the Imperial budget, its Minister of State argued, the cost associated with representation and ceremonial could not be allowed to rise any further.[119] The Imperial Audit Office did not fail to remind the government that originally, when von Stosch had first set up uniform regulations in 1876, launches of warships had been regarded as low-key affairs that were meant to create only a minimum of expense. Now, in 1908, wrote the Audit Office, 'costs

---

[116] BA-MA, RM 3/153, Bl. 21: RMA to General Freiherr von der Goltz, 25 March 1908.
[117] This process is recorded in detail for the years 1898 to 1914 in BA-MA, RM 3/9958–61. Compare Chapter 5 on the Anglo-German theatre.
[118] BA-MA, RM 3/118, Bl. 99–100: Reichsrechnungshof to Staatssekretär RMA, 17 Oct 1908. The audit office was especially appalled by the excessive expenditure on coaches and hotels as well as the custom of giving *two* luxurious dinners to mark launches. It also criticized the fact that there was no agreed limit to the rise in expenses, and that the cost of launches was charged to the general construction expenses of ships without a separate subhead.
[119] BA-MA, RM3/118, Bl. 97: Staatssekretär Reichsschatzamt to Staatssekretär RMA, 24 Nov 1908. The irony of economizing on the festivities rather than the hugely expensive vessels themselves was not lost on satirical magazines, see illustration 7.

30. Oktober 1908 — No 44 ULK

Reichssparsamkeit.

Tirpitz: Wir müffen fparen, hohe Taufpathin! Taufen Sie alfo gütigft diefes Zwanzigmillionenfchiff ftatt mit Sekt mit diefer Flafche Fürftenbergbräu!

7. 'Imperial Thriftiness'. Admiral von Tirpitz offers a bottle of beer to the launch patron, explaining: 'We have to save money, esteemed patron! So will you please christen this twenty-million ship with a bottle of *Fürstenbergbräu* instead of champagne!' (*Ulk*, 30 October 1908).

for such celebrations, which had formerly never been considerable' had reached 'very substantial heights'.[120]

Local authorities struggled to keep costs at bay too, especially in Hamburg and Bremen. Policing these events, decorating streets and town halls, hiring coaches and steamers was expensive enough, but it was the elaborate dinners and banquets given after launches which strained the Hanseatic purses most.[121] In 1909, the Bremen Senate topped all records with the expensive festivities created around the launching of HMS *Thüringen*. It put on a dinner for Prince Eitel Friedrich, the Duchess of Saxony-Altenburg and a host of 'high guests', costing a staggering 10,000 marks. Realising that such a sum was not to be found in the city's coffers, the Burgomaster rushed a budget amendment through the Senate and the *Bürgerschaft*, the lower chamber. He did so by evoking paragraphs 49 to 51 of the Bremen Constitution, extraordinary powers reserved for moments of crisis that allowed the Senate to speed up the legislative process if the 'welfare of the state' (*das Staatswohl*) was under threat.[122] To keep all this from public scrutiny, the Senate obliged the members of the *Bürgerschaft* to treat the amendment as top secret, and the official printer was instructed to destroy all references to the amendment.[123] These were remarkable financial and political manoeuvres, undertaken for the celebration of a warship. They demonstrated how far these rituals had come since the 1870s, when naval ceremonial had aimed to avoid 'all costly elaborations'.[124]

---

[120] BA-MA: RM 3/118, Bl. 99: Reichsrechnungshof to Staatssekretär Reichsschatzamt, 17 Oct 1908. Tirpitz eventually agreed to cap costs. Importantly, however, launches marked by the presence of 'highest or all-highest personages' (*Hohe oder Höchste Persönlichkeiten*) were exempted. Since it was the Kaiser's prerogative to decide who launched ships, this provided a convenient means for circumventing the agreed limit. See BA-MA, RM3/118, Bl. 117: Staatssekretär Reichsschatzamt to Staatsekretär RMA 21 Dec 1908; BA-MA, RM 3/118, Bl. 131: Kiel dockyard to RMA, 26 Aug 1909; StA Hamburg, 132–5/2, HG VII y 32, Bl. 6: Klügmann to Burchard, 13 June 1911.

[121] For details of the celebrations and dinners given at Hamburg and Bremen see StA Hamburg, 132–1I, 28, 33, 57 and 63; StA Bremen 3-B. 16, 1, 4, 7, 10 and 17. See also the detailed report on the splendour and decorum of local launch celebrations in HA Krupp, FAH 3 B 181: Jencke to Krupp, 2 April 1898.

[122] *Verfassung der freien Hansestadt Bremen* (Bremen, 1854), pp. 8–9.

[123] StA Bremen, 3-B. 16, Nr. 10, Bl. 20a: Senatssekretär an die Carl Schünemannsche Druckerei, 6 Nov 1909, streng geheim. Consequently, neither the *Verhandlungen zwischen dem Senate und der Bürgerschaft* (1909), vol. 2, p. 1197, nor the *Verhandlungen der Bürgerschaft* (1909), p. 697 refer to the amendment. Nor do the original *Bürgerschaft* minutes held at StA Bremen, 6,40-P.3, Nr. 56. The extraordinary measure is only recorded in a secret minute to be found in StA Bremen, 3-B. 16, Nr. 10, Bl. 20: Sonderprotokoll. Vertraulich. Mitteilung des Senats vom 5.11.1909. Stapellauf des Linienschiffes 'Ersatz Beowulf'.

[124] *MVBl* 7 (1876), p. 15.

Expensive pictures

In Britain, too, the expansion of the naval theatre was mirrored by rising costs. In 1887, the Admiralty footed a bill of £3,500 for the accommodation and entertainment of visitors and an additional, unspecified amount for illuminations and fireworks.[125] In 1897, the total sum which the Admiralty was responsible for was £23,324 10s. 3d. In 1902, this had risen to £28,701 9s. 6d., with an additional £6,200 spent on the illumination of the fleet, a sum which alarmed the navy's Accountant General.[126] In 1909, when the Admiralty staged three major fleet assemblies and costs threatened to spiral out of control, the government had to face parliamentary inquiries.[127] In 1911, the expenses for the royal fleet review rose to a record £31,800.[128] This sum included payment for the entertainment of guests, the hire of vessels, the catering on board steamers and extra pay for police officers. However, it excluded expenditure for the illumination of the fleet, which was carefully distributed across a labyrinth of accounts, presumably to spare officials from more embarrassing questions in the Commons.[129]

Between 1911 and 1914, a continuous battle took place between the Treasury and the Admiralty about the rising costs of this public theatre. In June 1912 the Secretary of the Treasury wrote an internal memorandum about what he saw as the excessive cost of naval celebrations. The forthcoming 'parliamentary inspection' of the fleet at Spithead seemed particularly wasteful. He complained that the Admiralty had asked for 'an enormous sum for this "picture"'. 'I can conceive of no reason at all', he

---

[125] PRO, ADM 1/6871: Treasury to Admiralty, 9 June 1887.

[126] PRO, ADM 116/133: Report on the meeting of the Coronation Review Committee, 10 Feb 1902; ADM 1/7602: Accountant General to Controller, 10 Dec 1902. Originally, the Admiralty had asked the Treasury for an overall sum of £25,000 (RA VIC/W56/16: Treasury Chambers to H.M. Private Secretary, 6 Feb 1902). A further rise in costs could only be averted by accepting offers from shipping companies for vessels free of charge, to be used for the accommodation of guests and foreign dignitaries: PRO, ADM 116/133: Report on the meeting of the Coronation Review Committee, 10 Feb 1902; ibid: Peninsular and Oriental Steam Navigation Co. to Admiralty, 18 Feb 1902.

[127] Hansard, Fifth Series, House of Commons, vol. 8, cl. 614 (statement by C. E. Hobhouse, Financial Secretary to the Treasury, 22 July 1909); ibid., cl. 1978 (statement by Reginald McKenna, First Lord of the Admiralty, 5 Aug 1909).

[128] PRO, ADM 116/1156.

[129] PRO, ADM 1/8230: Director of Stores to Controller, 17 May 1911; ibid.: Memorandum by Accountant General, 23 May 1911; ibid.: Statement showing the value of illuminating stores specially supplied to H.M. Ships in connection with the Coronation Naval Review, 1911; ibid.: Admiral Superintendent of Portsmouth Dockyard to Controller of the Navy, 19 Sept 1911; ibid.: Controller to Portsmouth Dockyard, 9 Nov 1911; ibid.: Portsmouth Dockyard to Controller, 2 April 1912; ibid.: Controller to Portsmouth Dockyard, 3 May 1912.

continued, 'why it should take place this year – which has neither a Coronation or Colonial Office Celebration: and talk about Members of Parliament "inspecting" the fleet is of course absurd.'[130] In a letter to the Admiralty, the Secretary of the Treasury objected strongly to the 'altogether excessive' use of funds.[131] Yet, faced with pressure in the Cabinet, the Chancellor of the Exchequer footed the bill for the unprecedented spectacle. Only in June 1914 did he succeed in reining in the Admiralty's expenditure for this public theatre. Sir John Bradbury, Permanent Secretary to the Treasury, argued the case in a scathing memorandum. Referring to the planned fleet review and an elaborate scheme for the entertainment of special guests, MPs and the press, he wrote:

The last picnic of this character was two years ago, the one before three years before that. It will no doubt soon become [...] annual. As will be seen from the papers herewith these entertainments have given rise in the past to parliamentary criticism and in 1912 the Treasury attempted without success to cut down the amount accounted for.[132]

It was as a result of the Treasury's steadfast refusal to sanction a rise in costs that the Admiralty decided to stage the 1914 fleet assembly in a more 'functional' format, as a 'test mobilization' inspected by the King, but without a formal royal procession and without a long guest list.[133]

Two aspects are worth noting about the spiralling costs that accompanied the rise of the naval theatre in Britain. First, none of the sums quoted above included the expenditure for the daily functioning of the fleet during public displays and visits. The money spent on victualling and coaling, and the remuneration of officers and men was added to the normal expenses of each vessel. It was, as McKenna conceded in the Commons, 'impossible to say' how much these costs were.[134] That they were significant is beyond doubt. A summary of the quantities issued by Portsmouth Victualling Yard illustrates this. At the 1902 Coronation Review, 138 tons of meat and vegetables were issued. This rose to 273 tons in 1907, to 337 tons in 1909 and to 635 tons in 1911. During the 1911 review, the Commander-in-Chief of Portsmouth dockyard wrote that 135 tons of meat and vegetables had to be supplied on a single day,

---

[130] PRO, T 1/11642: Minutes, 15 June 1912.

[131] PRO, ADM 1/8317: Secretary of the Treasury to Secretary of the Admiralty, 17 June 1912; ibid., Secretary of the Admiralty to Secretary of the Treasury, 20 June 1912.

[132] PRO, T 1/11642: Minute by Sir John Bradbury, 26 June 1914. See also ibid., Bradbury to Secretary of the Admiralty, 3 July 1914.

[133] For the fleet assembly of July 1914, see the epilogue.

[134] Hansard, Fifth Series, House of Commons, vol. 7, cl. 1020 (6 July 1909).

'the largest issue for one day in the history of the yard'.[135] Second, the rise in expenditure for naval displays was not caused by inflation or other circumstances beyond the control of the Admiralty. Instead, it was a direct consequence of the arrangements getting bigger, with more guests invited for longer and to more spectacular displays. The fleet review in 1902 provides a case in point. An Admiralty memorandum, drawn up after the event, summarized the arrangements and compared them with previous reviews: 'Nothing on a similar scale has ever previously been attempted by the Admiralty'. The document noted that 'the arrangements of 1897 were much less extensive and many new details were introduced at the present occasion'. The preparations and additional costs of 1902, in contrast, had been taken 'with a view to giving the arrangements more of a national and representative character'.[136]

More than anything, it was the rising social and cultural function of the naval theatre that made it so expensive. The royal court, government, the diplomatic corps, thousands of special guests and large numbers of press correspondents had to be catered for. By the late nineteenth century, naval celebrations had become part of 'The Season'. The combination of royal ritual, naval spectacle, yachting events and polite entertainment established Cowes/Portsmouth, but also Kiel, as fixtures in the annual calendar of 'the best circles'.[137] Sir Bryan Godfrey-Faussett, George V's naval equerry, conveys a vivid impression of this in his journals. The time before and after naval events was taken up by tea parties, 'lunch en route', excursions, receptions and dinners.[138] At fleet reviews special trains brought the invited guests to Portsmouth, with compartments and seats assigned in accordance with status and precedence.[139] The Admiralty

---

[135] PRO, ADM 116/1156: Commander-in-Chief Portsmouth to Secretary of the Admiralty, 5 Aug 1911.

[136] PRO, ADM 116/132, Memorandum on the work of the Naval Review Committee, 1902.

[137] Leonore Davidoff, *The Best Circles: Society Etiquette and the Season* (London, 1986), ch. 4; Kai Detlev Sievers, 'Die "Kieler Woche" im wilhelminischen Deutschland. Ihre nationale und soziale Bedeutung', *Mitteilungen der Gesellschaft für Kieler Stadtgeschichte* 67 (1980), pp. 213–28; Jürgen Jensen, 'Die Kieler Woche, Deutschland und die Welt', in Jürgen Jensen and Peter Wulf (eds.), *Geschichte der Stadt Kiel* (Neumünster, 1991), pp. 457–75, here 457–62; Hedwig Sievert, 'Die Kieler Woche', in Plagemann, *Übersee*, pp. 49–52.

[138] Churchill Archives, Churchill College, Cambridge, Godfrey-Faussett Papers, BGGF, 1/60, 3 Aug 1909. See also the notes by Wiedenmann, *Marine-Attaché*, pp. 120–32 and the diary of Hamburg's Burgomaster Mönckeberg: StA Hamburg, 622–1 Mönckeberg 21A, Bl. 285.

[139] On precedence and seniority see the Lord Chamberlain's papers in PRO, LC 2/146. For a flavour of the arrangements: *Review of the Fleet by His Majesty The King: July 31, 1909* (London, 1909); *Official Visit of the Houses of Parliament to the Fleet at Spithead: Tuesday, 9th July, 1912* (London, 1912).

Gruß von der Kieler Woche!

Kaisersalut der Kriegsflotte. *am 24. Jun. 190Y.*

8. The naval theatre and 'The Season'. Postcard from Kiel Week, showing the Imperial Navy firing the imperial salute.

was inundated with requests for tickets for vessels in the royal procession through the lines of warships. So important seemed the social and political status of fleet reviews that the Lord Mayor of London tried to establish a right for himself to have his own vessel follow the royal yacht. He appeared in person at the Admiralty and 'begged that the ship which Donald Currie had now placed at his disposal might be allowed to be in the procession'.[140]

Punch mocked this 'naval season' in 1897, when the Queen's jubilee review at Spithead had brought about an exodus of London society. Its caricature showed a lady posing in front of a mirror, surrounded by boxes of shoes and dresses, deciding what to wear for the event. Carrying a case for opera glasses, she wore miniature Union Jacks on her shoulders and on her hat. 'We had a rare good time in London, and now I'm off for a "whiff of the briny" at the naval review', said the caption.[141] The naval theatre had become a prime arena in which privilege and precedence were

---

[140] PRO, ADM 1/7336B: Memorandum, Secretary of the Admiralty, 3 June 1897. The Lord Mayor was not granted the privilege, but the Admiralty was happy to give him a ticket for one of its own vessels. See also ADM 179/60, pp. 128–31, where the Lord Mayor's preparations for the 1911 review are recorded.

[141] *Punch*, 26 June 1897: 'A quick change'.

played out, both in front of invited guests and wider audiences. This was just as much the case in Germany as it was in Britain. 'I lead the princess, the prince leads [my wife] Emmy', noted Hamburg's Burgomaster Burchard with satisfaction in his diary after the dinner celebrating the launch of the *Friedrich der Große*. 'I had instructed Klügmann, the [Hanseatic] envoy [at Berlin], to demand this seating plan. Admiral von Tirpitz, apparently not very pleased about this arrangement at first, shows no sign of being disgruntled'.[142] To be assigned the right place, to note names and faces, and to be noted by them, seemed paramount. All this was amplified by the press, who regularly published seating plans and complete lists of 'invited guests'. German newspapers even began to discuss the wardrobe worn by upper-class ladies at ship launches.[143]

By the end of the nineteenth century the celebration of the navy had become a busy public stage on which culture and politics merged. Fleet reviews, launches of warships and a range of related rituals were now more elaborate and professionally stage-managed, and they took place more often and on a larger scale than at any time since the late eighteenth century. In Germany, dictionary entries for *Flottenparade* emphasized the new status of these rituals. Both the *Handwörterbuch der Militärwissenschaften*, a comprehensive dictionary of military sciences, and the venerable *Meyers Konversationslexikon* recognized that the erstwhile private meetings between the Kaiser and the navy had turned into an elaborate public theatre.[144] How much this cultural arena mattered for politicians was mirrored in the rising costs that they were prepared to fund. Indeed, the naval authorities themselves acknowledged that the celebration of the navy had turned into a key national and international theatre. One remarkable example for this can be seen in the Annual Statement of the First Lord of the Admiralty, distributed each year in Parliament with the navy estimates. In March 1910, this official report, traditionally restricted to financial and administrative information, listed for the first time the key naval celebrations of the previous year. It gave details about displays such as the Coronation Naval Review at Spithead and the Home Fleet's visit to the Thames. From 1912, the Statement

---

[142] StA Hamburg, 622-1 Burchard A1: Johann Heinrich Burchard, Betrachtungen und Erinnerungen, 1904–1909, Bl. 154. A similar sentiment can be found in Burgomaster Mönckeberg's description of the launch of *Kaiser Karl der Große* in StA Hamburg, 622-1 Mönckeberg 21a, Bl. 291.

[143] *Hamburger Nachrichten*, 23 May 1912, Abend-Ausgabe: 'Stapellauftoiletten'.

[144] *Militär-Lexikon. Handwörterbuch der Militärwissenschaften*, edited by H. Frobenius, *Ergänzungsheft 2* (Berlin, 1903), p. 53; *Meyers Konversations-Lexikon*, sixth edition, vol. 15 (Leipzig and Vienna, 1908), p. 415.

featured an entire separate section called 'Ceremonies and Visits'.[145] This acknowledged the navy's new public role: it was no longer only its function as an instrument of defence that mattered, but its cultural role as a symbol that celebrated monarchy, empire and the nation with unprecedented pomp and professionalism.

[145] 'First Lord's Statement Explanatory of Navy Estimates', *Naval Annual* (1910), p. 379; *Naval Annual* (1911), pp. 389–90; *Naval Annual* (1912), p. 373; *Naval Annual* (1913), pp. 426–7; *Naval Annual* (1914), pp. 405–6.

2 Culture, politics and the mass market

There can be little doubt that the celebration of the navy was an arena in which monarchs and governments were busy projecting their power. Both in Britain and Germany the royal yachts, those seafaring thrones, were at the centre of a range of maritime rituals that were aimed at impressing domestic and foreign audiences alike with the continuing relevance of monarchy.[1] Yet it would be wrong to explain the rise of the naval theatre merely as an exercise in the 'invention of tradition'.[2] By the end of the century, monarchs and governments had to contend with new actors and new audiences that lay outside their direct control, yet had a key influence on the character of public ritual. The dynamic relationship between these new forces and the traditional masters of ceremony is the focus of this chapter. It analyses how the coming of the 'age of the masses' transformed the naval theatre and how the authorities responded to these changes. It shows that, while they attempted to exploit the potential of the maritime stage for promoting the navy and the monarchy, the Admiralty and the *Reichsmarineamt* were forced to acknowledge that popular culture and the mass market shaped this arena just as much as they themselves. The way in which the naval theatre changed in the decades before 1914 thus reflected wider social and political transformations.

New audiences, new media

Four million people came to see the fleet during its visit to the Thames in July 1909. During the course of the week, the popular press published pictures of 'the crowd' with captions such as 'London awaits the fleet' or 'hungry crowds'. The masses shown in these pictures were not merely

---

[1] On the use of royal yachts as tools of monarchical representation, see Brigitte Marschall, *Reisen und Regieren. Die Nordlandfahrten Kaiser Wilhelms II.* (Hamburg, 1991); Paulmann, *Pomp und Politik*, pp. 177–8, 426; C. M. Gavin, *Royal Yachts* (London, 1932), pp. 283–93.
[2] Hobsbawm, 'Mass-Producing Traditions'; Cannadine, 'Context, Performance and Meaning of Ritual'.

passive audiences; rather, they represented a new force in the political culture of both countries. Increased primary education, widespread literacy, urbanization, new means of transport and communication, an increase in leisure time and the commercialization of this time through new forms of tourism, entertainment and consumerism: these were the factors driving the popularization of culture and public life.[3] As far as the naval theatre was concerned, two new forms of media were especially important: the popular press and the cinema. After the turn of the century, new tabloids like the *Daily Mail* and the *Daily Mirror* sold close to or more than a million copies each day.[4] In contrast to the traditional broadsheets, they relied on advertising rather than the selling price for revenue. The new mass-circulating newspapers that rose towards the end of the century in Germany followed a similar strategy, with Scherl's *Berliner Lokal-Anzeiger* and Ullstein's *Morgenpost* and *BZ am Mittag* as the flagships.[5] In both countries this flourishing popular press adopted important aspects of the 'new journalism' pioneered by American newspapers, which meant easy reading, entertainment, practical advice, sensation – and images.[6]

---

[3] Jose Harris, *Private Lives, Public Spirit: Britain 1870–1914* (London, 1994), pp. 17–23; Colin Matthew, 'Public Life and Politics', in *Short Oxford History of the British Isles: The Nineteenth Century* (Oxford, 2000), pp. 85–133; Werner K. Blessing, 'Fest und Vergnügen der "kleinen Leute"', in Richard van Dülmen and Norbert Schindler (eds.), *Volkskultur. Zur Wiederentdeckung des vergessenen Alltags (16.–20. Jahrhundert)* (Frankfurt, 1984), pp. 352–79; Lynn Abrams, *Workers' Culture in Imperial Germany: Leisure and Recreation in the Rhineland and Westphalia* (New York, 1992); Kaspar Maase, *Grenzenloses Vergnügen. Der Aufstieg der Massenkultur 1850–1970* (Frankfurt, 1997), pp. 16–114; Erika Rappaport, *Shopping For Pleasure: Women in the Making of London's West End* (Princeton, 2000); Frank Trentmann, 'Knowing Consumers – Histories, Identities, Practices: An Introduction', in Frank Trentmann (ed.), *The Making of the Consumer: Knowledge, Power and Identity in the Modern World* (Oxford and New York, 2006), pp. 1–27.

[4] Alan J. Lee, *The Origins of the Popular Press in England 1855–1914* (London, 1976); Joel H. Wiener (ed.), *Papers for the Millions: The New Journalism in Britain 1850 to 1914* (New York and London, 1988); Stephen Koss, *The Rise and Fall of the Political Press in Britain*, vol. 1 (London, 1984).

[5] Peter Fritzsche, *Reading Berlin 1900* (Cambridge, MA, 1996); Rudolf Stöber, 'Der Prototyp der deutschen Massenpresse. Der "Berliner Lokal-Anzeiger" und sein Blattmacher Hugo von Kupffer', *Publizistik* 39 (1994), pp. 314–30; Andreas Schulz, 'Der Aufstieg der "vierten Gewalt". Medien, Politik und Öffentlichkeit im Zeitalter der Massenkommunikation', *Historische Zeitschrift* 70 (2000), pp. 65–97; Ernst Bollinger, *Die goldenen Jahre der Massenpresse*, second edition (Freiburg, 2002); Thomas Nipperdey, *Deutsche Geschichte 1866–1918*, vol. 1 (Munich, 1994), pp. 797–811.

[6] James D. Startt, 'Good Journalism in the Era of the New Journalism: The British Press, 1902–1914', in Wiener, *Papers for the Millions*, pp. 275–98. See also Frank Esser, *Die Kräfte hinter den Schlagzeilen. Englischer und deutscher Journalismus im Vergleich* (Freiburg, 1998); Jörg Requate, *Journalismus als Beruf. Entstehung und Entwicklung des Journalistenberufs im 19. Jahrhundert. Deutschland im internationalen Vergleich* (Göttingen, 1995); James Retallack, 'From Pariah to Professional? The Journalist in German Society and Politics, from the late Enlightenment to the Rise of Hitler', *German Studies Review*

Even more important for the naval theatre was the cinema. Both Britain and Germany experienced a rapid expansion of this new medium.[7] From the turn of the century, cinemas became a common feature of cities and smaller towns, offering, as one observer put it in 1913, 'the most popular form of amusement of the day':

> Fifteen years ago there were no picture palaces [...]. The number of picture theatres throughout the world is now believed to be about 60,000, and the number increases by scores daily [...]. Six years ago the total number of employees in cinematograph theatres in Great Britain was about 500. They now exceed 125,000.[8]

By 1914, 568 cinemas were registered in central and suburban London, typically seating between 200 and 800 guests, although some had as many as 2,000 seats.[9] A similar increase was experienced in Germany. In 1905, Berlin had 20 registered cinemas. Seven years later, the number had risen tenfold. By the outbreak of war, nearly 350 cinemas existed in Berlin, with a total capacity of 120,000 seats.[10] Observers spoke of the 'high tide of the cinematographic movement'.[11] The remarkable rise of the cinema was by no means restricted to urban centres. Contemporary studies stressed that this was a nation-wide development, with provincial towns and even villages housing cinemas in Germany in the years before 1914.[12] The same applied to Britain, where large towns with more than 100,000 inhabitants had typically between 20 and 40 cinemas, smaller cities up to a dozen and even villages regularly had their own

16   (1993), pp. 175–223; Frank Bösch, 'Volkstribune und Intellektuelle: W. T. Stead, Harden und die Transformation des politischen Journalismus in Großbritannien und Deutschland im 19. und 20. Jahrhundert', in Clemens Zimmermann (ed.), *Politischer Journalismus, Öffentlichkeiten, Medien im 19. und 20. Jahrhundert* (Ostfildern, 2006), pp. 99–120.

[7]   Much of the recent scholarship on pre-First World War cinema in Britain and Germany is represented in two edited volumes: Andrew Higson (ed.), *Young and Innocent? The Cinema in Britain, 1896–1930* (Exeter, 2002); Thomas Elsaesser (ed.), *A Second Life: German Cinema's First Decades* (Amsterdam, 1996).

[8]   Valentia Steer, *The Romance of the Cinema: A Short Record of the Development of the Most Popular Form of Amusement of the Day* (London, 1913), p. 11–12.

[9]   *Kinematograph Yearbook 1915* (London, 1914), pp. 445–53.

[10]   Karl Brunner, *Der Kinematograph von heute – eine Volksgefahr* (Berlin, 1913), p. 8–9. These numbers are confirmed by the material presented by Gary D. Stark, 'Cinema, Society, and the State: Policing the Film Industry in Imperial Germany', in Stark and Bede Karl Lackner (eds.), *Essays on Culture and Society in Modern Germany* (Arlington, Texas, 1982), pp. 122–66, here p. 124.

[11]   Emelie Altenloh, *Zur Soziologie des Kinos* (Jena, 1914), p. 49.

[12]   Ibid., pp. 49, 55; Arthur Wolf, *Denkschrift betreffend die Kinematographentheater* (Berlin, 1913), p. 9; Stark, 'Cinema, Society, and the State', p. 122. This stands in contrast to Nipperdey, *Deutsche Geschichte*, vol. i, p. 796, who sees the pre-war cinema as 'limited to the big cities'.

picture house.[13] By the outbreak of the First World War, an average of one million people went to the cinema daily in Britain, and in Germany an average of one-and-a-half million.[14] Cinema had turned into the most popular form of entertainment.[15]

The new audiences addressed by the cinema and the popular press were not simply passively consuming, they were increasingly politically active. Since 1871 the German Reichstag was elected by universal male suffrage. In Britain, the 1884 Reform Act had extended the male franchise significantly, with the effect that the majority of adult men were now enfranchised. It had important implications for the political culture of both countries that this widening of the electorate coincided with the rise of mass media. Politicians and intellectuals may have disliked the sensationalist style of popular papers such as *BZ am Mittag* and the *Daily Mail*. Yet they had to acknowledge that these publications represented a new force in the political process. The popular press spoke to and claimed to speak for exactly those audiences that were newly enfranchised and were using their votes increasingly to project their entitlement and participation.[16]

[13] 'Directory of Picture Theatres in Great Britain', *Kinematograph Yearbook 1915*, pp. 445–507. In 1914 there were eleven registered cinemas on the Isle of Wight and even remote small towns in Cornwall had their own picture houses, underlining how much the new medium had expanded geographically.

[14] *Kinematograph Yearbook 1915*, pp. 55–6; *Times*, 4 March 1914 and Brunner, *Kinematograph*, pp. 8–9. The numbers are corroborated by Stark, 'Cinema, Society, and the State', p. 125 and by David Welch, 'Cinema and Society in Imperial Germany, 1905–1918', *German History* 8 (1990), pp. 28–45, p. 29. See also Jerzy Toeplitz, *Geschichte des Films*, vol. 1, *1895–1928* (Munich, 1975), p. 106 and Nicholas Hiley, ' "Nothing More Than a 'Craze' "': Cinema Building in Britain from 1909 to 1914', in Higson, *Young and Innocent*, pp. 111–27.

[15] On the cultural transformations provoked by film and the cinema see Leo Charney and Vanessa R. Schwartz (eds.), *Cinema and the Invention of Modern Life* (Berkeley, 1995); Thomas Elsaesser, *Filmgeschichte und frühes Kino. Archäologie eines Medienwandels* (Munich, 2002); Daniel Morat, 'Das Kino', in Habbo Knoch and Alexa Geisthövel (eds.), *Orte der Moderne* (Frankfurt, 2005), pp. 228–37 and Bernhard Rieger, *Technology and the Culture of Modernity in Britain and Germany, 1890–1945* (Cambridge, 2005), ch. 4.

[16] Margaret Anderson, *Practicing Democracy: Elections and Political Culture in Imperial Germany* (Princeton, 2000); Larry Eugene Jones and James Retallack (eds.), *Elections, Mass Politics, and Social Change in Modern Germany* (Washington, DC, 1992); James Retallack, *Notables of the Right: The Conservative Party and Political Mobilisation in Germany 1876–1918* (Boston, 1988); Axel Grießmer, *Massenverbände und Massenparteien im wilhelminischen Reich. Zum Wandel der Wahlkultur 1903–1912* (Düsseldorf, 2000). For an impressive regional study see Thomas Kühne, *Dreiklassenwahlrecht und Wahlkultur in Preußen 1867–1914. Landtagswahlen zwischen korporativer Tradition und politischem Massenmarkt* (Düsseldorf, 1994). On Britain: Brian Harrison, *The Transformation of British Politics* (Oxford, 1996), pp. 157–80; Jon Lawrence, *Speaking For the People: Party, Language and Popular Politics in England, 1867–1914* (Cambridge, 1998).

Playing to this new audience became an important feature of political culture. Historians of modern Germany have spoken of a 'new style' of politics that was commonplace from the 1890s onwards.[17] Extra-parliamentary agitation and direct appeals to the electorate became more important, outflanking the discreet and 'gentlemanly' style of politics, the *Honoratiorenpolitik* of the 1870s. Not all aspects of the 'new politics' of appealing to voters and 'mobilizing the masses' were inventions of the turn of the century. Nor are they necessarily best captured by the terms 'demagoguery' or 'populism', phrases used by contemporaries and historians alike with radically different associations.[18] However, it is clear that a novel situation developed from the 1890s onwards, not just in Germany, but also in Britain. A significantly extended electorate, the majority of whom were exercising their right to vote, met with new strategies of electoral mobilization and political campaigning. This political change coincided in both countries with important cultural transformations. The popular culture of media, entertainment and consumerism that rose from the 1890s onwards provided key instruments for new styles of political mobilization. It was not only that politics were no longer the monopoly of notables and patricians; politics could now be played with new instruments, reaching the reading, spectating and voting masses. Popular culture *was*, in this sense, political culture.

This was the fundamentally changed context in which public ritual was situated at the end of the nineteenth century. The coming together of new communication and consumption practices with significant extensions in the franchise and new strategies of mobilizing voters and consumers opened a dynamic public market in which politics and culture were increasingly inseparable. To describe this transformation as the advent of the 'political and cultural mass market' does not imply the overtly pessimistic reading that has been enshrined in the texts of the Frankfurt School.[19] The popular culture that rose in the decades before 1914 may

---

[17] David Blackbourn, 'The Politics of Demagogy in Imperial Germany', in Blackbourn, *Populists and Patricians: Essays in Modern German History* (London, 1987), pp. 217–45; David Blackbourn, *History of Germany, 1780–1918: The Long Nineteenth Century* (Oxford, 2002), ch. 9; Geoff Eley, *Reshaping the German Right: Radical Nationalism and Political Change after Bismarck*, with new introduction (Ann Arbor, 1991).

[18] As James Retallack, 'Demagogentum, Populismus, Volkstümlichkeit. Überlegungen zur "Popularitätshascherei" auf dem politischen Massenmarkt des Kaiserreichs', *Zeitschrift für Geschichtswissenschaft* 48 (2000), pp. 309–25 has argued convincingly.

[19] Max Horkheimer and Theodor W. Adorno, *Dialektik der Aufklärung* (Amsterdam, 1947); Jürgen Habermas, *Strukturwandel der Öffentlichkeit. Untersuchungen zu einer Kategorie der bürgerlichen Gesellschaft. Mit einem Vorwort zur Neuauflage* (Frankfurt, 1990), first published in 1961. For the idea of the *politischer Massenmarkt* see Hans Rosenberg, *Große Depression und Bismarckzeit* (Berlin, 1967), p. 18; Maase, *Grenzenloses Vergnügen*, pp. 25–9 and Kühne, *Dreiklassenwahlrecht*, pp. 17–38.

have contributed to the demise of 'critical-rational discourse', as Jürgen Habermas famously lamented, but it also signalled democratization and new forms of political participation. The new media of the Edwardian and Wilhelmine period expressed the political entitlement of 'the masses' as much as they entertained them.

The unfolding of this mass market in the late nineteenth century introduced a new tension into the naval theatre. Commercial actors such as the popular press, the cinema and the tourist industry began to have a direct influence on its shape and character. To begin with, there was the new presence of the media. The 1897 naval review was attended by 203 reporters, twice as many as in 1867.[20] The Secretary of the Admiralty wrote that the number of applications for press tickets were 'in excess of what was anticipated in so many ways'.[21] In 1911, a record number of 267 correspondents were accredited; 217 of them worked for British newspapers and agencies, 50 for foreign ones.[22] While the number of correspondents from the quality press stayed roughly the same between 1897 and 1914, the number of those from popular and pictorial newspapers rose dramatically. Of the thirty-three London daily and weekly newspapers accredited for the 1911 review, only eleven were traditional titles such as *The Times*, the *Pall Mall Gazette*, the *Westminster Gazette* and the *Daily Telegraph*. They were easily out-numbered by the reporters of the tabloids and illustrated magazines, amongst them the *Daily Graphic*, *Daily Mail*, *Daily Mirror*, *Daily News*, *Graphic*, *London Illustrated News*, *Illustrated Sporting and Dramatic News*, *News of the World*, *People*, *Sketch* and *Sphere*.[23] Even amongst foreign correspondents, those associated with the popular press began to dominate.[24] Overtaking the established press in their coverage of naval celebrations, the new tabloid papers and magazines had become a central actor in this public theatre.

The influence of the popular press went hand in hand with the expanding role of the leisure and entertainment industry. By the late nineteenth century the seaside had become one of the most popular

---

[20] PRO, ADM 1/7336B: Jubilee Review 1897, Applications for Tickets; ADM 1/6871: Memorandum by Lord Charles Beresford, 17 May 1887.

[21] PRO, ADM 1/7336B: Memorandum, Secretary of the Admiralty, 18 June 1897.

[22] PRO, ADM 116/1159: Coronation Naval Review, Saturday 24th June, 1911. The Parliamentary review of 1912, at which no royalty were present, still managed to attract 130 press correspondents to Portsmouth, see PRO, ADM 179/53: Memorandum, Admiral Superintendent, Portsmouth, 8 July 1912.

[23] PRO, ADM 116/1159: Coronation Naval Review 1911, Press. In addition, fifty provincial English papers had sent correspondents, as well as eight Irish, eight Scottish and four Welsh newspapers.

[24] PRO, ADM 1/8049: Cowes Review 1909, Press applications.

destinations for urban excursionists and short-term holidaymakers.[25] Given the strong connection between the sea, leisure and entertainment, it was perhaps predictable that the tourist industry should discover the naval theatre as a prime attraction. For the royal fleet review in 1902, the London and South-Western Railway Company had on a single day sixty-seven special trains running from Waterloo to Southampton. More than 100 ships were scheduled to depart from Southampton to ferry spectators to Spithead.[26] Dozens of them were chartered by Thomas Cook, Henry Lunn and the like, offering package tours ranging from inexpensive one-day tickets to luxury deals including dinner and accommodation.[27] So high was the demand that Henry Lunn had to resort to chartering liners from outside Britain, handing the German HAPAG a tidy profit. The combination of modern transport and a thriving tourist and leisure industry allowed more people to watch naval events then ever before. Reporting from Portsmouth in August 1902 during what it called the 'Spithead Spectacles', the *Daily Express* wrote:

The town is as gay as a Hindoo bazaar with bunting and devices, and you are haunted by a sense of holiday-making from the appearance of the crowds in the streets, go where you will [...]. On Saturday, all regular railway traffic will be suspended, and from a very early hour of the day an immense procession of excursion trains will pour such a concourse of spectators into the old town as it has probably never yet witnessed.[28]

The police authorities also observed that these events were drawing increasingly large crowds. In November 1900, officers in Bremen noted during the preparations for the launch of SMS *Medusa* that '[t]he rush of spectators at these occasions increases from year to year'.[29] At British

---

[25] Gary S. Cross, *The Playful Crowd: Pleasure Places in the Twentieth Century* (New York, 2005); James Walvin, *Beside the Seaside: A Social History of the Popular Seaside Holiday* (London, 1978); John K. Walton, *The English Seaside Resort: A Social History, 1750–1914* (Leicester, 1983), ch. 7; Alain Corbin, *The Lure of the Sea: The Discovery of the Seaside in the Western World 1750–1840* (London, 1995); Maase, *Grenzenloses Vergnügen*, pp. 81–3. See also Thomas Richards, *The Commodity Culture of Victorian England: Advertising and Spectacle, 1851–1914* (Stanford, 1990), p. 240 on the emergence of the 'sea-side girl' as an advertising icon.

[26] *Times*, 17 June 1902.

[27] See the Henry Lunn catalogue *Coronation Procession, the Naval Review, Summer Cruise and Tours* (London, 1902) and the Thomas Cook catalogue *Coronation of H. M. King George V: Programme of Facilities for Witnessing the Royal Naval Review at Spithead on June 24th and the Coronation Processions in London on June 22nd and 23rd 1911* (London, 1911). See also PRO, MT 9/732: Board of Trade, Marine Department, to Towey Steam Eng. Company, 25 June 1902 and Piers Brendon, *Thomas Cook* (London, 1991), p. 239.

[28] *Daily Express*, 15 Aug 1902.

[29] StA Bremen, VIII.F.31, Nr. 22, Bl. 1. For a similar statement in the British press see *Daily Record and Mail* (Glasgow), 1 May 1911.

fleet reviews the number of spectators rose so much that the Home Office had to mount a concerted effort to control the crowds. Writing to the police authorities along the south and south-east coasts in the weeks before the 1902 Spithead review, it emphasized the 'urgent importance of paying strict attention to this matter at the time of the forthcoming Naval Review'. It predicted that there would be unprecedented numbers of passenger ships and pointed out that 'great danger to the public is likely to arise from the overcrowding of these steamers unless the police make every effort to prevent it'.[30]

Remarkable as the rising numbers of spectators were in themselves, more decisive was the widened geographical background from which they came. According to Edward Fraser, ship launches in the late eighteenth and early nineteenth century drew visitors from an area of a dozen miles around the location.[31] In the decades before the First World War this radius had widened dramatically. Special trains and tourist steamers brought spectators from hundreds of miles away. During the 1897 review, correspondents remarked that people from all over the country were arriving. The *Morning Post* estimated that about 20,000 sightseers alone came 'principally from the Midlands'.[32] For the 1902 royal review in the Solent, special steamers came from as far as Orkney and the Shetlands.[33] At the 1911 German *Flottenparade* at Kiel, correspondents observed that tourists and spectators came from 'from deep inside the country'.[34] The effect was, as the *Kieler Neueste Nachrichten* observed, that there was an 'effervescent mix of dialects' in the crowds of spectators.[35] The naval theatre had become a spectacle that could be participated in without geographic or social limitations.

The naval game

The unfolding of the mass market of leisure, entertainment and consum- erism turned the celebration of the navy into a commodity that could be bought and, quite literally, played anywhere. A vast range of products

---

[30] PRO, MT 9/729: Home Office Circular, 26 May 1902, sent to twenty-four county and borough police forces, as well as to the Commissioner of the Metropolitan Police and the Commissioner of the City Police. See also ibid.: West Sussex Constabulary to Home Office, 18 June 1902.

[31] Fraser, *Bellerophon*, p. 2.

[32] *Morning Post*, 24 June 1897; *Barrow News*, 3 July 1897. At the launch of the *Ocean* in 1898, *The Times* explained that the 'enormous crowds of spectators' were the result of excursion trains running from all over Southern England (*Times*, 6 July 1898).

[33] PRO, ADM 116/132.   [34] *Tägliche Rundschau*, in *Presse-Stimmen*, p. 9.

[35] *Kieler Neueste Nachrichten*, 6 Sept 1911, Erstes Morgenblatt. Similarly *Berliner Lokal-Anzeiger*, 4 Sept 1911, Zweites und Drittes Blatt, Abendausgabe.

linked naval themes with consumers' desires. This included tobacco, rum, soap, soup, sweets, perfume, clothes and men's grooming products. Picture books, guides, charts, postcards and other memorabilia were sold not just at the sites of naval celebrations, but all over the country.[36] There was the much-cited sailor suit, the *Matrosenanzug*, worn by boys, and the equivalent for girls, the *Matrosenkleid*.[37] And there were popular songs, plays and musicals, written to celebrate ship launches and fleet reviews.[38]

Even more intriguing were the many products that allowed both adults and children to re-enact the naval theatre. Two genres, often combined, were particularly popular: toy ships and war games. German toy manu-facturers such as Bing and Märklin were quick to export model tinplate warships to Britain, each with a miniature white ensign and Union Jack. Often enough children in Britain thus played with model dreadnoughts that were in fact 'made in Germany'.[39] You could stage your own ship launch with such toys or play 'fleet review' (see illustration 9). And you could use them as part of the commercial war games that enacted naval battles. *Panzerflotte*, made by Heyde in Germany, for example, was sold in a box complete with replica warships, chart and instructions.[40] Other war games catered for the more advanced player who demanded an exact

---

[36] Collections of these are held at the NMM, the RNM and at Portsmouth Central Library (Naval & Lily Lambert McCarthy Collections). For Germany see especially the Wissenschaftliches Institut für Schiffahrts- und Marinegeschichte Peter Tamm, Hamburg. The popularity of the Admiralty chart detailing the position of warships during fleet reviews is documented in ADM 116/132: William Lyon, manufacturer of stationery, to Secretary to the Admiralty, 5 June 1902 and in PRO, ADM 1/8197: Hydrographer to Secretary Admiralty, 31 May 1911 and 1 June 1911. See also *Die Bildpostkarte in Deutschland* (Hamburg, 1965), ill. 10 and 14; also Tori Smith, ' "Almost Pathetic...But Also Very Glorious": the Consumer Spectacle of the Diamond Jubilee', *Histoire Sociale* 29 (1996); Richards, *Commodity Culture of Victorian England*, ch. 2.

[37] Robert Kuhn and Bernd Kreutz, *Der Matrosenanzug. Kulturgeschichte eines Kleidungsstückes* (Dortmund, 1989); Ingeborg Weber-Kellermann, *Der Kinder neue Kleider. 200 Jahre deutscher Kindermoden in ihrer sozialen Zeichensetzung* (Frankfurt, 1985), pp. 105–19; Dora Lühr, 'Matrosenanzug und Matrosenkleid. Entwicklungsgeschichte einer Kindermode von 1770 bis 1920', *Beiträge zur deutschen Volks- und Altertumskunde* 5 (1960/61), pp. 19–42; Walter Hävernick, *Der Matrosenanzug der Hamburger Jungen 1890–1939* (Hamburg, 1962). For a striking example see the portrait in Jörg Duppler, *Germania auf dem Meere. Bilder und Dokumente zur Deutschen Marinegeschichte 1848–1998* (Hamburg, 1998), p. 67.

[38] Theo Bonheur, author of numerous operettas, wrote *The Dreadnought: Descriptive Fantasia* (London, 1906) for the launch of HMS *Dreadnought*. See also Arthur Martyn, *Souvenir Song: The Naval Pageant* (London, 1909) and Mary Amabel Nassau Strachey, *The Sea-Power of England: A Play for a Village Audience* (London, 1913).

[39] For examples see Jacques Miller and Robert Forbes, *Toy Boats 1870–1955: A Pictorial History* (Cambridge, 1979), pp. 61–5 and Basil Harley, *Toy Boats* (Haverfordwest, 1987), pp. 13–7.

[40] Miller and Forbes, *Toy Boats*, p. 99. *Britannia: Naval War Game* (London, 1894) was a similar British example. See also Donald F. Featherstone, *Naval War Games: Fighting Sea Battles with Model Ships* (London, 1965).

9. 'Fleet Review, front seat 2*d*.'. From Rosa Petherick, *Toy Boats* (London, 1910).

tracing of sea battles past and future. One of these was invented by Fred T. Jane, who was not only a successful publisher of naval annuals, but also the secretary of a naval war games society.[41] The *Jane Naval War Game* proved popular enough to merit three different editions of rules between 1898 and 1912. Jane described it as a '*Kriegsspiel* simulating all the movements and evolutions of every individual type of modern warship, and the proportionate effect of every sort of gun and projectile'.[42]

In a league of its own, if the advertisements are to be trusted, was the most popular German naval game, the award-winning *Seestern*. It allowed the players to let mines explode, vary the cruising speed of vessels and take wind and weather into account. Manufactured by Schmidt in Hamelin, it featured twelve replica battleships, cruisers, torpedo boats

---

[41] The society met regularly at the George Hotel in Portsmouth, where Nelson had reportedly spent his last night on English soil. Here, Jane restaged past naval battles and refined his game, which was played by royal and naval dignitaries such as Prince Louis of Battenberg, Lieutenant R. Kawashima of the Imperial Japanese Navy and Grand Duke Alexander Mihailovitch of Russia. See Richard Brooks, *Fred T. Jane: An Eccentric Visionary* (Coulsdon, 1997), ch. 2 and Featherstone, *Naval War Games*, ch. 17.

[42] *Rules for the Jane Naval War Game* (London, 1898); *Hints on Playing the Jane Naval War Game* (London, 1903); *How to Play the "Naval War Game": With a Complete Set of the Latest Rules, Full Instructions, and Some Examples of "Wars" That Have Actually Been Played: Official Rules, 1912, Cancelling all Others* (London, 1912).

and merchant vessels, all made of metal. The game, which could be ordered by post for 5.50 marks, allowed you to stage your own naval battles at home, but it also claimed to improve the players' minds. As the advertisements proclaimed, '*Der Seestern* combines captivating entertainment for young and old with the enrichment of knowledge and the invigoration of the spirit [*Anregung des Geistes*].'[43] The naval theatre could now not only be experienced in the seaside towns where fleet reviews, mock fights and ship launches took place; it could be played at home with a large variety of games and toys that engaged the fascination for modern technology, weaponry and power as much as they played on the adventure of empire and the lure of the sea.

Another effect of this entertainment culture was that the naval theatre could be watched publicly in cities and towns far removed from the coast. Nowhere was this more strikingly the case than in the model shows that re-enacted the naval theatre in Britain and Germany. Initially, such shows were part of imperial and commercial exhibitions, notably in London in 1891 and in Berlin in 1896.[44] However, these re-enactments, called *Flottenschauspiele* or *Marineschauspiele* in Germany, were so popular that they became established as a new entertainment genre of their own. Their stage was a pool or artificial lake, surrounded by stands for the audience, which could reach thousands.[45] The demonstrations were performed by model warships, each large enough to allow a mechanic to lie inside to steer the vessel (see illustration 11).[46] A regular high point was 'His Majesty's review of the fleet'. This is how the *Deutsche Marineschauspiele* announced it:

It is one of the most beautiful spectacles when a fleet of powerful warships lies at anchor, dressed in full ornament, waiting for the arrival of His Majesty. A warship on its own is imposing – how much more impressive is a whole fleet. Here are the small boats, hustling between the battleships, conveying orders and despatches. Finally all the busy activity stops: the Imperial Yacht *Hohenzollern* is in sight. And as the yacht passes, each warship fires the Imperial salute, the crews are paraded and a thundering 'Hooray!' can be heard. To watch this spectacle makes the heart beat faster – especially when the imperial review takes place in beautiful sunshine.[47]

---

[43] 'Das neue Seekriegsspiel "Der Seestern" allein preisgekrönt Berlin 1907', *Die Flotte* 11 (1908), p. 31.

[44] Paul Lindenberg (ed.), *Pracht-Album photographischer Aufnahmen der Berliner Gewerbe-Ausstellung 1896 und der Sehenswürdigkeiten Berlins und des Treptower Parks* (Berlin, 1896), p. 171; Pieter van der Merwe, 'Views of the Royal Naval Exhibition, 1891', *Journal of Maritime Research*, Sept 2001 (http://www.jmr.nmm.ac.uk/server.php?show=conJmrArticle.29). See also *Times*, 5 May 1905 with a review of the naval entertainments given at the 1905 Naval Exhibition at Earl's Court.

[45] The *Flottenschauspiele* that opened in Berlin in 1904 could seat up to 4,000 visitors.

[46] BA-MA, RM 3/9834, Bl. 6: Programm der Deutschen Flottenschauspiele.

[47] BA-MA, RM 2/1873, Bl. 86: leaflet 'Flottenschau'.

Even a critical observer like Alfred Kerr, author of many scathing literary and theatre reviews, found them peculiarly attractive:

The *Marineschauspiele* are very captivating. Their entrance looks like a ship. Behind this large construction is a square, especially built pool. Its background looks like a coastline with a fort – naturally made of *papier mâché*, but very deceptive. Reproductions of German warships, three meters long, move on the water [...], steered by a man, hidden inside. And they shoot, electrically propelled, with truly lightning-like speed over the surface of the water. [...]
In this fashion, the biggest victories are won and at the end the wonderfully white *Hohenzollern* sweeps through the waves, salutes are shot, the air is full with the smoke of gunpowder. The illusion is truly great while you can sit at the side and have a beer. These victorious battles are fought five or six times a day, in intervals of two hours. To watch them costs only fifty *Pfennige*.[48]

The *Marineschauspiele* promised the audience music between the different acts of naval drama and two intervals in which drinks and snacks could be purchased.[49] As Kerr observed, compared to the real thing, the *Schauspiele* had the great advantage that you could have a beer while watching the miniature fleet gain command of the sea.[50]

Strikingly similar naval games were popular in the United Kingdom and its colonies. One of the dramatists claiming copyright for this genre came from Australia. Arthur Francis Russell, a dental surgeon in Melbourne, applied in 1913 for the registration of the copyright for what he called an 'entertainment in dumb show'. Its title was 'Naval Review and Battle', and it consisted of a number of historic sea battles re-enacted by model warships. This began, naturally, with a replication of Nelson's fleet defeating the French at Trafalgar and ended with 'boats so constructed that they represent exactly in outward appearance the most modern battleships, dreadnoughts, torpedo boats and submarines of the present day'. All of this took place against the backdrop of an idyllic coastal scene:

At the back of the sheet of water, which may be of any convenient measurement according to the size of the allotment of ground on which the show is placed, there is erected special scenery built and painted to represent a coastal city with forts and light-houses.

[48] Alfred Kerr, *Wo liegt Berlin? Briefe aus der Reichshauptstadt 1895–1900* (Berlin, 1998), p. 156. Kerr had visited the naval shows performed on the artificial lake at Berlin Treptow as part of the *Gewerbeaustellung* in May 1896.
[49] BA-MA, RM 3/9834, Bl. 6: Programm der Deutschen Flottenschauspiele.
[50] Kerr, *Wo liegt Berlin*, p. 156. For the related genre of the 'Marine-Schauspiel-Theater', given in variety shows, see Florian Dering, Margarete Gröner and Manfred Wegner, *Heute Hinrichtung. Jahrmarkts- und Varietéattraktionen der Schausteller-Dynastie Schichtl* (Munich, 1990), pp. 72–8.

10. Poster by C. Schön, advertising the *Flottenschauspiele* that opened on Kurfürstendamm, Berlin in 1904. Up to 4,000 spectators could watch a model-size battlefleet conquer the sea in a gigantic artificial pool, twice on weekdays, three times on Sundays.

At each side of the water are placed 'wings' of rockwork etc; and in front seating accommodation for the audience to witness the entertainment. Other representations in the way of scenic effects may be employed without departing from the spirit of my entertainment.[51]

Russell's model warships were powered by electricity, just as those in the German *Flottenschauspiele*. At ten to twenty feet length, they could carry a concealed mechanic 'who manoeuvres the model man of war, and fires at the proper time in the exact manner of a battleship in action'.[52] The naval drama, which the Australian authorities registered as literary copyright No. 2831, featured impressive special effects, including flames and explosions. Just as in the naval amphitheatres of Hamburg or Berlin, it ended with a review of the victorious model-size fleet.

---

[51] NAA, Canberra, A1336/2831.   [52] Ibid.

11. *Marineschauspiele* at the 1902 industrial exhibition, Düsseldorf. The photograph shows a model-size *Hohenzollern* receiving the imperial salute.

Such naval re-enactments drew on a long tradition. In Imperial Rome sea battles had been staged for public entertainment time and again. Caesar had started the custom of hosting *naumachiae*, fought by prisoners, as part of triumphal games in 46 BC. Consecutive emperors had the Colosseum flooded or artificial lakes dug for the re-enactment of sea battles.[53] Such naval theatre was reinvented during the Renaissance and it was still popular in August 1814, when the British Prince Regent presented a string of naval battles on the Serpentine in London to celebrate the end of the Napoleonic Wars.[54] In contrast to this older tradition, the naval re-enactments staged in Germany and Britain in the decades before the First World War were not given by emperors, kings or princes.[55] Nor were they one-off events. The *Flottenschauspiele* were commercial entertainment, repeated throughout the day. They provide a striking example of the way in which the naval theatre was transformed into a visual experience that could be reproduced and restaged.[56]

The singularly most important factor in this transformation was the cinema, the rise of which was described at the beginning of this chapter. The first public event ever to be filmed in Germany was the opening of the Kaiser-Wilhelm-Kanal in 1895.[57] Pictures showing launches of warships were marketed as early as 1897 when the pioneering German cinematographer Oskar Messter advertised a film of the launch of the *Wilhelm der Große*. Praising the 'outstandingly focused and clear

---

[53] For a detailed discussion see K. M. Coleman, 'Launching Into History: Aquatic Displays in the Early Empire', *Journal of Roman Studies* 83 (1993), pp. 48–74 and 'Naumachie' in *Paulys Realencyclopaedie der classischen Altertumswissenschaften*, vol. 32 (Stuttgart, 1935), cl. 1970–74.

[54] For a contemporary account, see Charles Lamb's letter to William Wordsworth from August 1814, in *The Letters of Charles Lamb*, edited by Russell Davis Gillman (London, 1907), pp. 239–40. On Elizabethan naval festivals see Roy Strong, *Art and Power: Renaissance Festivals 1450–1650* (Woodbridge, 1984), plates 50, 96, 99 and, for the context, N. A. M. Rodger, 'Queen Elizabeth and the Myth of Seapower in English Politics, 1568–1815', *Transactions of the Royal Historical Society*, 6th series, vol. 14, 2004, pp. 155–76.

[55] While not objecting to the *Flottenschauspiele*, neither the Kaiser nor the *Reichsmarineamt* had an active role in them. See BA-MA, RM3/9834, Bl. 11: RMA to Chairman, Deutsche Flottenschauspiele, 8 June 1904 and RM2/1873: Karl Leps, Flottenschauen Hamburg, to Marinekabinett, 17 May 1900.

[56] This was one of the main advertising points stressed by the promotional literature, see BA-MA, RM 2/1873, Bl. 79: leaflet 'Flottenschau'.

[57] Hauke Lange-Fuchs, *Der Kaiser, der Kanal und die Kinematographie* (Schleswig, 1995); Martin Loiperdinger, 'Wie der Film nach Deutschland kam', *KINTop* 1 (1992), pp. 114–8. A copy of the famous film by Birt Acres is kept at the NFTVA, title ref. 500866.

pictures', Messter offered the film to cinemas for seventy-five marks.[58] In Britain, the symbiosis between the new film technology and the expanding naval theatre was epitomized by Alfred J. West. West turned a small photographic atelier into a flourishing company of international reputation by specializing in filming naval and maritime subjects. His numerous series of naval films were marketed as *West's Our Navy* and leased to cinemas and theatres. In October 1899, *Our Navy* opened as a permanent show at the Polytechnic in Regent Street, London, where it remained for fourteen years.[59] The naval programmes at the Polytechnic changed frequently. An advertisement from October 1902 announced moving images of the coronation naval review as part of an 'entirely new programme'. Tickets were available for as little as one shilling.[60] When West published a catalogue of his films in 1912, it listed 371 naval films with a total length of roughly 38,000 feet.[61] By then, over two million people had visited the Polytechnic in London to see the fleet on the screen.[62]

The importance of the cinema for the transformation of the naval theatre is clear from the correspondence between the main film companies and the Admiralty. As these documents show, pictures of naval celebrations were in heavy demand, not only in Britain and its empire, but also on the European Continent. When applying for permission to film the 1911 naval review, the cinema company Gaumont wrote that:

in addition to representing as film producers several hundred theatres in this country, we are firmly established in every large continental city, and what is perhaps more important, in the colonies. We have four branches in Canada and five in Australia. There is a great demand for a thoroughly representative series of films.[63]

---

[58] *Special-Catalog No. 32 über Projektions- und Aufnahmeapparate für lebende Photographie, Films, Graphophons, Nebelbilder-Apparate etc. der Fabrik für optisch-mechanische Präcisions-Instrumente von Ed. Messter* (Berlin, 1898), reprinted in *KINtop Schriften*, vol. 3 (Basel and Frankfurt, 1995), p. 75. For a short introduction to the pioneering work by Messter see Thomas Elsaesser, 'Wilhelminisches Kino: Stil und Industrie', *KINtop* 1 (1993), pp. 18–19.

[59] *British Journal of Photography* 46 (1899), p. 642. On West's early years see John Barnes, *The Beginnings of the Cinema in England*, vol. 3 (Exeter, 1996), pp. 45–53; vol. 4 (Exeter, 1996), pp. 97–102; vol. 5 (Exeter, 1997), pp. 55–60.

[60] *Times*, 3 Oct 1902. See also *Times*, 8 and 13 Oct 1902.

[61] Alfred West, *Our Navy: A Synopsis of the Life-Work of Alfred West, FRGS, Depicting Scenes of Life in Our Navy and Our Army, Our Mercantile Marine: An Illustrated and Descriptive Catalogue* (London, 1912), pp. 1–49. Barnes, *Beginnings*, vol. 5, p. 267, quotes a 1911 leaflet in which West claimed that he had photographed 100,000 feet of film of naval and military subjects between 1898 and 1911. Some films of West's *Our Navy* series survive at Hampshire Record Office, Ref. AV56.

[62] West, *Our Navy*, p. i. See also *Bioscope*, 7 March 1912, p. 659.

[63] PRO, ADM 116/1157: Gaumont Co. to Secretary of the Admiralty, 5 April 1911.

Pathé Frères, the biggest cinematographic company of the pre-war era, claimed that 'more than 10 million people all over the world' would see its images of the review.[64] Two years later the number had risen to 'more than twenty million people in London, the British Isles, and the Empire'.[65] Requesting passes for two cameramen in the same year, the London branch of Eclair Film wrote that the pictures would be 'shown throughout the entire world and especially in England and the British Colonies, to about 38 million people'.[66]

Charles Urban, one of the most influential figures in the early British film industry, wrote in 1907 that naval topics ranked highly amongst the most popular subjects in cinematography, with pictures of 'naval demonstrations' and the 'launching of war vessels' in especially high demand.[67] When Alfred Döblin, German novelist and critic, commented on the rise of the cinema in 1909, he found that the most popular cinematographic topics were crime stories, sentimental pieces and warships.[68] In the years before 1914, fleet reviews and ship launches could be seen in urban cinemas on the same evening as the event itself.[69] An early historian of the new medium explained in 1913:

In the early days of the cinematograph a "topical event" was frequently not shown on the screen until two or three days after the pictures had been taken. To-day [sic] a subject can be shown at a West End theatre in less than two hours after the return of the operators with their negatives.[70]

[64] PRO, ADM 116/1157: Pathé Frères Cinema Ltd. to Secretary of the Admiralty, 3 June 1911.

[65] PRO, ADM 179/53: Eric E. Mayell of Pathé Frères Cinema Ltd. to Admiral Superintendent of Portsmouth Dockyard, 5 Feb 1913.

[66] PRO, ADM 1/8319: Eclair Film Co. to Secretary of the Admiralty, 15 May 1913. For further correspondence of this type see PRO, ADM 1/8268. Similar letters to German naval authorities can be found in BA-MA, RM 3/9871–4.

[67] Charles Urban, The Cinematograph in Science, Education and Matters of State (London, 1907), pp. 22–3. On Urban see Luke McKernan, 'Putting the World Before You: The Charles Urban Story', in Higson, Young and Innocent, pp. 65–77.

[68] Alfred Döblin, 'Das Theater der kleinen Leute', in Alfred Döblin, Kleine Schriften (Olten and Freiburg, 1985), p. 72, first published in Das Theater, Dec 1909. See also the naval scenes advertised as part of cinema gazettes such as Gaumont-Woche and Pathé Journal in BA-MA, RM 3/9874. The prominence of the navy in the early cinema is emphasized by Rachael Low and Roger Manvell, The History of the British Film, 1896–1906 (London, 1948), p. 61 and Rachael Low, The History of the British Film, 1906–1914 (London, 1948), pp. 146–7. See also Martin Loiperdinger, 'Kaiser Wilhelm II. Der erste deutsche Filmstar', in Thomas Koebner (ed.), Idole des deutschen Films (München, 1997), pp. 47–8.

[69] Times, 11 Sept 1908; Newcastle Daily Journal, 21 March 1912.

[70] Steer, Romance of the Cinema, p. 84. One can detect the beginnings of the 'society of the spectacle' here: the modernity of the image itself was just as, if not increasingly more, important than what it referred to. See Guy Debord, The Society of the Spectacle, translated by Donald Nicholson-Smith (New York, 1992), first published in 1967. That fleet

Footage of fleet reviews or ship launches remained on the programmes for weeks and months, in spectacular cases even for years. One of *Pathé's Animated Gazettes* of 1913 still featured pictures of the 1911 launch of the German battleship *Kaiser*. A film of the 1906 launch of the *Dreadnought* was still on the 1912 list of moving images shown at the London Polytechnic.[71] It was the cinema more than any other medium that turned the naval theatre into a spectacle that could be reproduced nation-wide. As Valentia Steer wrote about the 1911 coronation, what transformed the event for the public was that 'by paying sixpence at a picture theatre the same evening they could see the whole thing in comfort from a cushioned seat'.[72] For the first time, the navy's great displays could be experienced not only by travelling to the seaside or by reading about them. People could now watch this theatre in their home town. Tens of millions did so in the decade before the First World War.[73]

Secrecy and publicity

How did the authorities react to this dynamic unfolding of popular culture? What was their understanding of the role played by the media, entertainment and tourism? And what strategies did they develop to exploit the naval theatre?[74] There can be little doubt that Tirpitz and the *Reichsmarineamt* recognized the great publicity potential presented by the celebration of the navy. The visits to the fleet organized by Tirpitz for the members of the Reichstag bear witness to this, as does the advertising tour on which a squadron of torpedo boats was sent down the river Rhine in 1900.[75] While the *Nachrichtenbureau* discovered naval reviews

reviews and ship launches could be seen in urban cinemas on the same evening of the event was repeatedly stressed in the press, for example: *Times*, 11 Sept 1908; *Newcastle Daily Journal*, 21 March 1912.

[71] British Pathé News Library, London, ref. no. N.23; West, *Our Navy*, p. 35, film no. 246.
[72] Steer, *Romance of Cinema*, pp. 16–7. See also Altenloh, *Soziologie*, p. 36.
[73] On the popularity of the navy in cinema see also PRO, ADM 1/8265: Agnes E. Weston to Secretary of the Admiralty, 26 June 1912 and BA-MA, RM3/9871, pp. 97–9: Vorsitzender, Flottenverein für den Stadt- und Landkreis Kattowitz, to Deutsche Mutoskop und Biograph Gesellschaft, 8 March 1901.
[74] Studies on 'naval propaganda' offer little answer to such questions. While providing a wealth of material on press manipulation, the 'pens behind the fleet' and the naval leagues, they have curiously little to say about the public celebration of the navy: Wilhelm Deist, *Flottenpolitik und Flottenpropaganda. Das Nachrichtenbureau des Reichsmarineamtes 1897–1914* (Stuttgart, 1976); W. Mark Hamilton, *The Nation and the Navy. Methods and Organization of British Navalist Propaganda, 1889–1914* (New York and London, 1986); Juerg Meyer, *Die Propaganda der deutschen Flottenbewegung 1897–1900* (Bern, 1967).
[75] The Rhine tour is documented in BA-MA, RM 3/9814. See also Deist, *Flottenpolitik und Flottenpropaganda*, pp. 99, 211; Jörg-Uwe Fischer, 'Die Faszination des Technischen. Die parlamentarischen Studienreisen zur kaiserlichen Flotte vor 1914', *Zeitschrift für Geschichtswissenschaft* 40 (1992), pp. 1150–6.

comparably late and only in response to public and commercial interest, launches of warships had an intended public dimension from the outset of the naval programme. The 1900 orders regulating launching ceremonies stated explicitly: 'As far as circumstances permit, the public should be given access to the celebration'.[76]

However, while Tirpitz and the *Nachrichtenbureau* were acutely aware that the naval theatre provided an ideal stage for the 'mise en scène' of the fleet,[77] there were important reasons why they did not fully exploit this potential. The *Reichsmarineamt*'s mounting concern with espionage played a central role. Only few documents detailing its counter-intelligence activities have survived, mostly because the correspondence was '*streng geheim*' (strictly confidential) and usually kept out of the files.[78] It is clear, however, that Tirpitz was concerned about intelligence gathering at dockyards as early as 1900.[79] Launches were especially sensitive. These were occasions when dockyards were opened to the public and when visitors could inspect a new ship closely. With the unfolding of the Dreadnought era, counter-espionage measures played an increasingly important role in launching preparations. In 1908, Tirpitz complained to the Prussian Home Office, which had established a central office for counter-espionage, that the surveillance at Kiel was still 'insufficient'. He urged that 'more attention has to be paid to counter espionage'.[80] The Berlin head of Police reported in the same year: 'It is a fact that the facilities of the Imperial Navy are currently the object of foreign espionage, conducted with the help of large funds by foreign powers'.[81] As a consequence, it became standard practice to camouflage sensitive parts of a ship before it was launched.[82] Additionally, the number of secret policemen employed to keep an eye on suspicious persons was increased. Tirpitz ordered plain-clothes officers

[76] *MVBl* 31 (1900), p. 397.
[77] This is how Eulenburg described Tirpitz's propaganda efforts in a letter to the Kaiser in April 1898, cf. *Philipp Eulenburgs politische Korrespondenz*, edited by John C. G. Röhl, vol. 3, *Krisen, Krieg und Katastrophen, 1895–1921* (Boppard, 1983), p. 1888, doc. 1365.
[78] BA-MA, RM 3/188, Bl. 4: RMA to Direktor Carlson, Schichau-Werft, 19 Sept 1913.
[79] StA Bremen, XII.G.3.a, Bl. 9: Abschrift Schreiben des Staatssekretärs RMA, 7 Sept 1900, ganz geheim, zu Neubau von Schiffen und Geheimhaltung; Bl. 11: Memorandum of Bremen Police on the same subject, 19 Oct 1900.
[80] GStA PK, I. HA Rep. 77, Titel 872, Nr. 12, Bd. 1: Tirpitz to Minister des Innern, Berlin, 17 Oct 1908. For the co-operation between regional *Zentralstellen* and the Berlin office for counter-espionage see StA Hamburg, 132-1I, 3405.
[81] GStA PK, I. HA Rep. 77, Titel 872, Nr. 12, Bd. 1: Polizei-Präsident, C[entral]St[elle] Berlin, to Minister des Innern, Berlin, 4 Nov 1908.
[82] The RMA's *Geheimhaltungsvorschriften* are documented in StA Hamburg, Blohm & Voss, nos. 858 and 864. See also BA-MA, RM 3/9958, Bl. 199: Tirpitz to Werft Wilhelmshaven, 5 March 1908; RM 3/171, Bl. 12: RMA to Kaiserliche Werft Kiel, 23 Feb 1911; RM 3/188, Bl. 4: RMA to Direktor Carlson, Schichau-Werft, 19 Sept 1913.

from Berlin to be present at ship launches. This had become necessary, he wrote to the Kiel yard, since local police seemed no longer capable of containing espionage attempts.[83] At the same time, the question of access for the press was reassessed. Film and photography seemed particularly problematic. The Kaiser, alarmed by the reports about espionage, decreed in 1908 that no person carrying a camera was to be admitted to the launch of a warship.[84]

The increasingly obsessive concern with espionage presented the *Reichsmarineamt* with an acute conflict between secrecy and publicity. The head of the harbour police in Kiel wrote in 1913 that:

taking pictures of a warship that is being launched seems extremely worrying, especially as the ship's hull with all its complex installations is put on to film and through the cinematograph shown to the widest public. I assume that such films are being bought by foreign countries.[85]

Naturally, the naval authorities shared these concerns. However, they were also aware of the case against too much restriction. As *Oberwerftdirektor* Henkel of the Kiel naval dockyard argued, an altogether too restrictive handling of photography and cinematography was to be avoided, 'since the very welcome distribution of pictures of His Majesty's ships and of life in the navy should not be hindered'.[86] There was thus an acute dilemma. While the concerns about espionage called for secrecy, the aim of fostering naval enthusiasm called for publicity. This was the case not only in Germany, but also in Britain, where similar concerns about espionage and foreign intelligence existed.[87]

What made matters worse in Germany was the *Tirpitz-Plan* or, more precisely, the *Gefahrenzone*, the 'danger zone' that it envisaged. This was the period during which the German navy would not yet be powerful enough for a confrontation with a force such as the Royal Navy. However, the ambitious expansion of the German navy might provoke exactly such a confrontation. Thus, naval muscle-flexing and too much foreign attention was to be avoided during this period, lest it provoke, if not a

---

[83] BA-MA, RM 3/9958, Bl. 238: Tirpitz to Werftdirektor Kiel and Chef der Marinestation der Ostsee, 1 April 1908.

[84] BA-MA, RM 3/9899, Bl. 23: Marinekabinett to Kommando Kiel and RMA, 21 Feb 1908.

[85] BA-MA, RM 3/9899, Bl. 102: Polizeibehörde Abt. VIII, zur Vorlage Polizeipräsident, 14 May 1913.

[86] BA-MA, RM 3/9899, Bl. 103–4.

[87] Special counter-intelligence officers were employed for the launch of the *Dreadnought*, a measure that became standard procedure and contributed to the sharp rise in police surveillance between 1906 and 1914. See PRO, MEPO 2/929: Undersecretary of State, Home Office to Commissioner of Police of the Metropolis, 9 Feb 1906; MEPO 2/1441: Secretary Admiralty to Commissioner of the Police of the Metropolis, 14 Feb 1911; Police Portsmouth to Commissioner of the Police of the Metropolis, 20 March 1914.

'Copenhagen' for the German fleet, then at least a further acceleration of British naval building.[88] Launches and reviews, however, attracted precisely such attention, as Tirpitz was painfully aware. There are a number of letters in which he states that he wished less public fuss would be created around launches of battleships, since such events were given a great deal of press coverage in Britain.[89] Yet how could public rituals be exploited as the most effective form of domestic naval advertising, when at the same time such publicity was feared with regard to the foreign arena? The concerns about the *Gefahrenzone* and a potential confrontation with Britain exacerbated the dilemma between publicity and secrecy.[90]

It was in response to these contradictory demands that the *Reichsmarineamt* established its policy of denying access while feeding the press news material. This policy was followed at naval manoeuvres which were, just as in Britain, strictly off-limits for the press. From the late 1890s onwards, the *Nachrichtenbureau* commissioned retired officers or trusted naval writers to attend manoeuvres and write semi-official press reports.[91] In addition to these heavily edited *offiziöse Berichte*, the press office gave photographs taken by naval officers free to the press.[92] From the turn of the century the *Reichsmarineamt* adopted a similar policy with regard to photography at ship launches. While news correspondents were rarely denied access, only specially commissioned photographers were admitted to dockyards to take pictures of the ceremony. Often, only the yard's *Werksphotograph* was allowed to take pictures. However, these images still had to be submitted to the *Nachrichtenbureau* in Berlin. From there, after censoring, the pictures were offered to the press. Newspapers and magazines repeatedly asked for their own photographers to be admitted – and received the same standard answer: this was

---

[88] Jonathan Steinberg, 'The Copenhagen Complex', *Journal of Contemporary History* 1 (1988), pp. 23–46; Kennedy, 'Maritime Strategieprobleme', esp. p. 182.

[89] BA-MA, RM 3/118, Bl. 141: Tirpitz to Großadmiral von Koester, 19 Sept 1911; HA Krupp, FAH 4 C 55: RMA to Krupp, 26 May 1909. See also Tirpitz, *Erinnerungen*, pp. 98, 133.

[90] This dilemma also characterized the *Nachrichtenbureau*'s editing and censoring of the speeches given at launches, compare Chapter 1 and 5.

[91] For the dissemination of these articles the Nachrichtenbureau relied heavily on Wolffs Telegraphen Bureau (WTB). Compare BA-MA, RM 3/10236, Bl. 35–6: Denkschrift zum Immediatsvortrag betreffend Berichterstattung für die Presse über die Herbstmanöver, 2 May 1900; ibid., RM 3/10237: Notiz zum Immediatsvortrag betreffend diesjährige Manöverberichterstattung, 29 May 1903; ibid., RM 3/10238, Bl. 87–91 with an exemplary correspondence between RMA, the Wilhelmshaven Station and the WTB. For examples of how the *Manöver-Berichte* were edited see BA-MA, RM 3/10237, Bl. 89–107.

[92] BA-MA, RM 3/10237, Bl. 69–73 has a list of such photographs offered to the press. See also ibid., Bl. 83: Notiz zum Immediatsvortrag, 22 Oct 1903 and ibid., Bl. 305: Chef Marinekabinett to RMA, 15 July 1912.

impossible, but a set of pictures would be provided for them.[93] As a result, the pictures printed in the papers tended to be repetitive and unvaried. A sense of irritation about this effect is evident in the letters sent by press agencies and newspapers to Tirpitz's press office.[94] Private dockyards too complained that the policy of controlling and censoring was slow and counter-productive. The Germania yard wrote to the *Nachrichtenbureau* in 1904:

The arrangement to which we have adhered so far – namely taking pictures, developing and submitting them for inspection [to the *Nachrichtenbureau* in Berlin], and then receiving permission for distribution – takes up considerable time, so that the interest in photographs and their publication has already lessened. We allow ourselves therefore to ask most devotedly whether in future the submission of pictures taken by our photographer could be refrained from.[95]

However, the *Nachrichtenbureau* was not willing to ease the regulations and the policy criticized by the Germania yard remained unchanged.

The same policy applied to the filming of naval events. The Hanover cinematographer Buderus wrote in June 1901 that, until recently, local officials had always granted him access to naval events. This had included celebrations at which the Kaiser had been present. 'As of late however', he noted, 'the authorities have become very anxious and hesitant to grant such permission'.[96] In the decade before 1914, the *Reichsmarineamt* restricted the number of cinematographers who had access to ship launches to a very few either official (*amtliche*) cameramen or to individuals with special permission granted by the Kaiser.[97] Both at private and naval yards they were accompanied by an officer charged with their supervision.[98] Once developed, the films had to be sent to the *Nachrichtenbureau* for clearance. Only after approval from Berlin were the distributing companies allowed to market their pictures. Cinematographers were dismayed by these regulations, which meant that naval films tended to be of predictable content and reached the cinemas with considerable delay.

While Tirpitz's *Nachrichtenbureau* is usually seen as an effective propaganda machine, these findings point to the contrary. Confronted with the new influence of mass media and popular entertainment,

[93] For an example see BA-MA, RM 3/9874, Bl. 75–6: Photo-Union to RMA, 22 March; ibid.: RMA to Photo-Union, 18 April 1913.
[94] BA-MA, RM 3/9871, Bl. 168: Redaktion *Überall* to RMA, Dec 1902.
[95] BA-MA, RM 3/9899, Bl. 18: Germaniawerft Krupp to RMA, 11 Nov 1904.
[96] BA-MA, RM 3/9871, Bl. 113: C. Buderus to RMA, 17 June 1901.
[97] BA-MA, RM 3/9899, Bl. 68: Chef Marinekabinett to Staatssekretär RMA, 3 Feb 1912.
[98] BA-MA, RM 3/9899, Bl. 70: Staatssekretär RMA to Kaiserliche Werft Kiel-Gaarden, 13 Feb 1912.

Tirpitz and the Imperial Navy opted for a complicated process of control and manipulation. The belief that the press had to be led and fed, rather than left alone, proved to be a limiting factor in the promotion of the naval theatre. This was aggravated by the Imperial Navy's obsession with espionage and the *Gefahrenzone*. As a result, the *Nachrichtenbureau* worked against rather than with the dynamics of modern media. While the popular press and the film companies were keen to exploit the naval theatre, the combination of control, censorship and semi-official press feeding hindered rather than helped this.[99]

A silent navy?

The fact that Tirpitz's approach was an inefficient way of dealing with the modern media is all the more evident when compared to the strategy adopted in Britain. Surprisingly, the Admiralty's attitude towards the press and the public has attracted very little attention. Indeed, there seems to be a historiographical consensus that the Admiralty, and the British government in general, were incapable of something as disreputable as propaganda in this period. Mark Hamilton sees 'a strong core of highly motivated individuals and associations' at work in British naval agitation, but the Admiralty itself is left curiously unexamined in his study.[100] Christopher Bell goes even further. He claims that the navy first became involved in propaganda activities during the First World War, but reluctantly so and without giving up its tradition of a 'silent navy'. Only in the 1920s did the Admiralty begin to develop its own publicity policy and advertise the navy actively. The propaganda activities of the inter-war years, Bell claims, stood in sharp contrast to the pre-war era when the Admiralty had regarded any form of actively engaging with public opinion as 'sordid' or distasteful.[101] Such ideas of the pre-war British Admiralty as 'silent' with regards to press and propaganda are strongly influenced by Paul Kennedy's assessment in his seminal study of *The Rise of the Anglo-German Antagonism*. Kennedy compares official British and German attitudes to public opinion and concludes that, in contrast to the *Nachrichtenbureau*'s activities, 'such blatant press-influencing

---

[99] On the limits of official press manipulation in Wilhelmine Germany see also Gunda Stöber, *Pressepolitik als Notwendigkeit. Zum Verhältnis von Staat und Öffentlichkeit im Wilhelminischen Deutschland 1890–1914* (Stuttgart, 2000) and Martin Kohlrausch, *Der Monarch im Skandal. Die Logik der Massenmedien und die Transformation der wilhelminischen Monarchie* (Berlin, 2005), esp. pp. 69–72.

[100] Hamilton, *Nation and Navy*, p. 11.

[101] Christopher M. Bell, *The Royal Navy, Seapower and Strategy between the Wars* (Stanford, 2000), ch. 8.

did not exist' in Britain.[102] 'Government-press relations in Britain were usually managed in a "gentlemanly" fashion', Kennedy writes and points to occasional private contacts between politicians and journalists, typically at one of Pall Mall's gentlemen's clubs.[103]

Perhaps even more influential in perpetuating this image of the British Admiralty as 'above' public opinion and propaganda has been the Admiralty itself. Its official statements regularly suggested that there was no involvement of naval authorities with the press. In 1907, the Parliamentary Secretary to the Admiralty, Edmund Robertson, was pressed in Parliament

if he can state the nature of the obligation and the rule or rules, if any, which regulate the communication to the public or the Press by the Sea Lords and their subordinates of information regarding the Navy, or of the views of all or any of them upon naval matters.

Robertson's response was short: apart from the 'usual obligations of official secrecy' there were 'no regulations'.[104] The impression he gave was that it was beneath the Admiralty to concern itself with thoughts about the public and the press. This impression was encouraged at a number of similar occasions in the years to follow. Moreover, it was actively fostered at the outbreak of the First World War, when the British Government published diplomatic correspondence that highlighted German attempts at influencing domestic and foreign public opinion in the pre-war years.[105] And it was reinforced after the war when officials again invoked the Wilhelmine example as a negative contrast: while the Germans had engaged in propaganda, the British had refrained from such dirty tricks. The Royal Navy had remained a 'silent service'.[106]

This official and historiographical orthodoxy needs to be corrected. Contrary to the image of a 'silent service', the Admiralty followed a well-defined publicity policy and did not hesitate to influence the press directly through a number of measures. The Admiralty engaged in naval propaganda just as much as and ultimately more successfully than the *Reichsmarineamt*. Because there was no special department within the Admiralty that would have been solely concerned with public relations,

---

[102] Kennedy, *Rise of the Anglo-German Antagonism*, p. 365.   [103] Ibid., p. 366.
[104] Hansard, Fourth Series, House of Commons, vol. 179, cl. 946–7 (31 July 1907).
[105] *Despatches from His Majesty's Ambassador at Berlin Respecting an Official German Organisation for Influencing the Press of Other Countries: Presented to both Houses of Parliament, September 1914*, Cd.7595 (London, 1914).
[106] Davys Manning, 'The Silent Service', *Naval Review* 15 (1927), p. 614, qtd. in Bell, *Royal Navy, Seapower and Strategy*, p. 165.

there are not nearly as many well preserved sources as in the German case, and this is aggravated by the heavy weeding of archives that used to be Admiralty practice. However, if one traces the correspondence of the Secretary of the Admiralty, the papers of the Naval Intelligence Department and the despatches by naval attachés, a number of key documents emerge which reveal that lengthy discussions took place amongst the leadership of the Royal Navy about the public, its role in naval politics and the strategies available for influencing it. These sources make clear that, while its attitude towards the press and the public differed markedly from that followed by Tirpitz and his *Nachrichtenbureau*, the Admiralty was just as publicity-conscious as and ultimately more insightful than its German counterpart.

As early as 1887, during the preparations for the Queen's jubilee review, the strong interest shown by the press in naval pageants led the Admiralty to make these rituals more accessible to the media.[107] In 1897 it organized for the first time an official press boat for correspondents and photographers.[108] After the turn of the century, it began to develop a systematic approach to the media. In May 1902, a 'Memorandum on Press Representatives' was drawn up and subsequently printed for office use and included in the *Collection of Admiralty Office Memoranda*. It set out guidelines for how to deal with press representatives. The office staff in London were instructed not to enter into conversations with the press unless authorized:

Press representatives who may call at the Admiralty for information are to be politely conducted to one of the Waiting Rooms on the Ground Floor, and are not to be permitted to roam about the Office or enter any of the rooms. [...] No interviews are to be held with them. The name of the representative is to be taken to the Private Secretary of the Permanent Secretary, who will only give information under authority.[109]

The memorandum indicates that contacts between the Admiralty and the press were frequent and that they went beyond private conversations in gentlemen's clubs. It also suggests that the Admiralty actively reflected about how to manage its dealings with the press. The memorandum was a product of important discussions that took place at the Admiralty in 1902 about the role of the press and the public. Two developments furnish the

---

[107] PRO, ADM 1/6871: Memorandum by Lord Charles Beresford, 17 May 1887. On the admission of journalists to the jubilee celebrations in London see Plunkett, *Victoria: First Media Monarch*, p. 237.

[108] PRO, ADM 1/7336B: Memorandum, Secretary of the Admiralty, 18 June 1897.

[109] PRO, ADM 1/7597: Memorandum on Press Representatives, 6 May 1902. See also *Collection of Admiralty Office Memoranda* (London, 1907), p. 87.

background to these discussions. First, critical views on naval matters had increasingly appeared in the press, including information that was, in the eyes of the Admiralty, either plainly wrong or excessively misleading. As a result, the Admiralty considered whether such negative news should be countered and how the press and public opinion were best influenced. Second, the activity of Tirpitz's *Nachrichtenbureau* had become known. Closely observed by the Admiralty and the Foreign Office, it provided an example of how the press might be manipulated. It was against this example that the Lords of the Admiralty and a number of other influential officials defined the Admiralty's own publicity policy.

The memoranda and minutes documenting these discussions are crucial for an understanding of the Admiralty's attitude towards the press and the public. In April 1902, Captain A. W. Ewart, the British naval attaché at Berlin, wrote to the Admiralty explaining what he saw as a promising strategy by which to influence public opinion in favour of the navy. It was disturbing, he wrote, to repeatedly read articles 'finding fault wrongfully' with the Royal Navy.[110] Such criticism, aggravated by critical statements from public figures such as Lord Beresford, was 'doing a great deal of harm to our prestige'. It 'should therefore be corrected officially or semi-officially'.[111] As a model of how this might be done, Ewart pointed, in a second despatch, to Tirpitz's press office:

I neglected to emphasize my remarks by failing to inform you that a section actually exists in the German Admiralty for this purpose. This section is called the 'Nachrichten Bureau', and its duties are defined as follows: 'The News section has the task of correcting erroneous public opinion, and of contributing information for the enlightenment of the public on all important Naval questions'. The principal organ of the bureau is the 'Marine Rundschau', but I am under the impression that articles are sent to other periodicals, and Naval news in the press is generally controlled.[112]

Ewart's reports and his suggestion of an imitation of the *Nachrichtenbureau* triggered a discussion within the Admiralty about the attitude that it should take towards the press and the public. Reginald Custance, the Director of Naval Intelligence, wrote that the subject was 'so important' that he submitted the papers to the Senior Naval Lord, Vice-Admiral Lord W. T. Kerr, and the First Lord of the Admiralty, the Earl of Selborne. The Secretary of the Admiralty, Sir Evan MacGregor,

---

[110] PRO, ADM 1/7596: Ewart to Sturdee, 26 April 1902, A. Ewart's letter is marked 'A', his memorandum 'B'. Both were addressed to F. C. D. Sturdee, Assistant Director of Naval Intelligence, who submitted them to the Director of Naval Intelligence, Reginald Custance.

[111] PRO, ADM 1/7596: Ewart to Sturdee, 26 April 1902, B.

[112] PRO, ADM 1/7596: Ewart to Naval Intelligence Department, 1 May 1902.

and the Parliamentary Secretary to the Admiralty, Hugh Arnold-Forster, were also involved. It is clear from their discussions that the leadership of the Royal Navy was convinced that public opinion was crucially important for the navy. In contrast to the *Reichsmarineamt*, the Admiralty came to the conclusion that it was best not to force the press coverage of naval events into a process of control and censorship. Kerr and Selborne agreed that, if the Admiralty wanted to continue enjoying the publicity brought by a press massively interested in the navy, then the press should not be stifled. Indeed, the benefits of press attention could not be reaped without accepting occasional damage. This argument was developed further in a memorandum written by F. C. D. Sturdee, Assistant Director of Naval Intelligence, in response to Ewart's despatch. This was an internal and confidential document, restricted in its distribution to the leadership of the Royal Navy; it therefore could state its matter openly and clearly. Ewart wrote:

I believe it may be generally accepted that Public opinion has been largely responsible for all the great increases of our Fleet &c. This has led to many wild statements being made & has undoubtedly painted the British Fleet in its worst colours, which may influence public opinion abroad adversely to us, but not official opinion as they are probably better informed. [...]. I believe it would be very serious for the welfare of the Navy to stifle public opinion & if the official denial is given to every exaggeration a tendency to optimism will prevail which is even more dangerous for the welfare of the Navy. – It is proverbial that the Treasury are bound to try and check all increases of expenditure & that official life tends to dislike changes & criticism. Therefore criticism if fair is very beneficial. [...] For the above reasons I believe it would be a mistake to check criticism except when officials whether in the Navy or civil service make wild statements which are taken abroad as correct. These can best be neutralized by getting a question asked in the House (if it is sitting).[113]

From this and other documents it is evident how acutely aware the British Admiralty was of the public and its role in modern politics.[114] Leading officials saw public enthusiasm for the navy as crucial for the political climate required to achieve a successful bidding for naval increases and they actively reflected on how best to nurture this enthusiasm.

To this end, the Admiralty followed a policy that was both passive and active: passive in that it refrained from attempts at controlling and correcting the press, especially when negative news was published; active in that it staged spectacular public displays, at which it catered for and at

---

[113] PRO, ADM 1/7596: Memorandum by Sturdee, undated.

[114] PRO, ADM 1/7872: Director, Naval Intelligence Department, to First Sea Lord, 20 Jan 1906; ibid.: Director, Naval Intelligence Department, to Secretary of the Admiralty, 2 June 1906.

times openly courted the press. The Admiralty not only encouraged public interest in traditional royal and naval ceremonial, it also staged a range of novel displays exclusively for publicity reasons. The Thames visit of the Fleet in July 1909, described in Chapter 1, provides a key example. There was no naval, royal or other precedent for the occasion. More than anything, the visit was an exercise in entertaining and attracting urban mass audiences. Whether they approved or disapproved of the visit, the press were unanimous in seeing it as a spectacular case of naval advertising. While the *Labour Leader* criticized the 'tempting display' that it considered was designed to further the 'appetite for armaments', *The Times* lauded the great entertainment value of the naval show.[115] 'Even the man in the street who professes no knowledge of the problems that lie hidden in these walls of iron must be impressed', wrote the *Daily Mail*, certain that the spectacle 'cannot fail to quicken the pulse of patriotism'.[116] The *Naval and Military Record* went as far as to calculate the visit's effect on forthcoming elections: 'This will find due expression both privately, and on the platform, and not the least, in the ballot boxes.'[117]

There were numerous other occasions at which the fleet was, in the Admiralty's own words, paraded 'for show purposes'.[118] Only a month before the display in the Thames, the Admiralty had staged an unprecedented fleet assembly at Spithead, not for British royals or visiting dignitaries, but for the journalists and correspondents attending the Imperial Press Conference. As the *Naval and Military Record* observed: 'The assembly of a fleet at Spithead for the special benefit of the Empire's press is a new feature in our history'.[119] The same was true of the 1912 fleet review given for Members of Parliament.[120] The Admiralty's efforts in courting the press and Parliament at such occasions accounted for a substantial part of the rise in costs of this public theatre. In 1909, the Admiralty paid for all travel expenses of the members of both Houses of Parliament attending the fleet review. This included travel arrangements for the families of MPs, as well as free accommodation and catering on board a steamer that the Admiralty had chartered for this purpose. As C. E. Hobhouse, Financial Secretary to the Treasury, had to concede in the Commons, there was no precedent for such generosity.[121] The cost of 'parliamentary inspections' rose more than threefold between 1909 and

---

[115] *Labour Leader*, 11 June 1909; *Times*, 1 June 1909.   [116] *Daily Mail*, 19 July 1909.
[117] *Naval and Military Record*, 29 July 1909.
[118] PRO, ADM 1/8215: Memorandum, Naval Branch, April 1911.
[119] *Naval and Military Record*, 17 June 1909. See also *Times*, 1 June 1909.
[120] On the 1912 'parliamentary review' see PRO, ADM 179/53; on the Imperial Press Conference the section 'The floating empire' in Chapter 4.
[121] Hansard, Fifth Series, House of Commons, vol. 8, cl. 614 (22 July 1909).

1912. In explaining this rise to the Treasury, the Admiralty wrote that, in order to make the spectacle more attractive for MPs, it planned to show them not only the fleet anchored at Spithead during the day, but also how it put to sea in the evening.[122]

In facilitating the press coverage of such events, the Admiralty took the opposite approach from the German authorities. Rather than restrict access to a small number of trusted or semi-official representatives, the Admiralty went out of its way to accommodate as many correspondents, photographers and cinematographers as possible.[123] From 1897, the Admiralty provided special press boats at all fleet reviews, carrying hundreds of journalists, with extensive catering on board and officers in attendance to provide information.[124] It readily granted cinematographers, both British and international, access to naval celebrations.[125] And it was happy to accommodate, as far as possible, their special requests. At ship launches, for example, film companies were keen to have more than one camera covering the events, so that different angles could be shown at cinemas. As Charles Urban, the cinematographer, explained:

Two cameras at least are trained on the vessel to be launched, one covering a sweeping view of the vessel from the bow end, and the other from the stern; both cameras are located so that every movement [...] is covered as much as it possibly can.[126]

To facilitate such footage, the Admiralty offered cameramen different platforms and enclosures from where to film, and it installed special facilities on its press boat so that cameramen could take pictures from

---

[122] PRO, ADM 1/8317: Secretary of the Admiralty to Secretary of the Treasury, 20 June 1912.

[123] This applied to royal reviews, fleet visits and launches of warships. Naval manoeuvres and launches of submarines remained strictly private affairs. See PRO, ADM 198/3, p. 269 and ADM 198/4 pp. 339–41.

[124] PRO, ADM 1/7336B: Memorandum, Secretary of the Admiralty, 18 June 1897.

[125] For a general discussion see PRO, ADM 116/1157: Naval Review, Facilities for Photographing, 8 May 1911; and ADM 179/60: Secretary Admiralty to Commander-in-Chief Portsmouth, 11 May 1911.

[126] Urban, *Cinematograph*, p. 23. A similar arrangement is described in PRO, ADM 116/132: Hepworth & Co Cinematographers to Secretary of Admiralty, 18 March 1902. See also the letters sent by, amongst others, Pathé Animated Gazette, the Topical Budget and the Co-operative Cinematograph Company to the Admiralty, contained in PRO, ADM 1/8268. One of the most spectacular and still surviving films shot by Urban in this fashion, alternating between two angles, is of the launch of HMS *Dreadnought* in Feb 1906. See NFTVA, ref. no. 531432: 'King Edward VII launches HMS *Dreadnought* from Portsmouth Dockyard' (Charles Urban Trading Company, 1906). See also NFTVA, ref. no. 530107: 'The launch of the *Thunderer*' (Warwick Trading Company, 1911), shot in the same fashion.

aboard. At the 1909 Thames fleet display, it even allowed large numbers of photographers to take pictures on the upper decks of the latest dreadnoughts.[127] There were, however, restrictions to such access. The launching of submarines and the few 'private' inspections of the fleet that the King held were strictly off limits.[128] Also, photographers and cameramen were routinely supervised by police or naval officers.[129] Yet there was no censorship, no screening of journalists or limiting of their numbers. On the occasion of the launch of HMS *Orion, The Times* praised the Admiralty for its 'excellent arrangements for representatives of the Press and for photographers'.[130] When the press facilities were found wanting, the Admiralty bent over backwards to rectify the matter. At the 1909 Spithead review, the press boat had returned to harbour considerably later than advertised and the journalists on board had not been offered any dinner. The Admiralty responded to the mishap with a major exercise in damage limitation. A comprehensive report was ordered and assurances were given that the fullest possible amenities would be guaranteed at the next event. The First Lord of the Admiralty, Reginald McKenna, apologized to the press in Parliament, 'acknowledging in the fullest terms that a blunder has been made, and I am very sorry for it. I regret it exceedingly'.[131]

In order to ensure strong press coverage, the Admiralty even supplied journalists with background information in the run-up to important events. In the days before the launch of the *Dreadnought* in 1906, it sent a booklet with material to editors and journalists. In the accompanying letter, the Secretary of the Admiralty wrote:

As the First Lord is anxious that the Press should be able to know something of the main features of this new development in warship building, he is glad to put this statement in your hands, but he particularly wishes that in commenting on it, you should not quote it or any part of it verbatim. – The whole object is to prevent anything being published which has an official character.[132]

---

[127] PRO, ADM 116/1157: Orders as regards Photographers visiting H.M. Ships at Southend, July 1909.

[128] Even Alfred West was denied access to the 1912 inspection at Weymouth: PRO ADM 1/8268: Secretary of Admiralty to West, 4 May 1912 and 6 May 1912.

[129] For two examples see TWAS, PA/NC/1/5: Newcastle upon Tyne City Police, General Orders, 26 Oct 1905–23 Nov 1906, pp. 229–30 and PRO, ADM 116/132: Hepworth & Co Cinematographers to Secretary of Admiralty, 18 March 1902.

[130] *Times*, 20 Aug 1910.

[131] Hansard, Fifth Series, House of Commons, vol. 8, cl. 1935 (4 Aug 1909). See also the report in PRO, ADM 1/8049. See also PRO, ADM 1/8197: Hydrographer to Secretary of Admiralty, 31 May 1911 and 1 June 1911, showing that the official programme and chart for fleet reviews were released with meticulous timing to newspapers and agencies as well as the souvenir industry.

[132] PRO, ADM 1/7873: Press communication, private and confidential, 7 Feb 1906.

12. Press stand at the launch of HMS *Queen Elizabeth*, 16 October 1913.

The brochure sent to editors and journalists was one that the *Nachrichtenbureau* would have been proud of. It detailed on three pages why the *Dreadnought* was 'the first of a new type of ship', praising the new design and underlining that it had taken only four months for the hull to be built. The brochure went as far as providing headlines and sound-bites, such as 'The battleship is the embodiment of concentration of gun-power'. This was a sophisticated press release directly aimed at influencing public opinion. On the cover it noted in bold: 'This statement is not for official publication, but to serve as a guide to the press, and is not to be quoted *verbatim*'. The Secretary of the Admiralty explained this caution in the letter that accompanied the brochure:

The Board [of the Admiralty] are particularly anxious that no statement should appear in the Press or anywhere else concerning this vessel, which bears an official imprimatur, as it is plainly undesirable to put in the hands of foreign Governments any definite and official information concerning her.[133]

Whether the brochure included any confidential information was debatable. And in any case, such information would have appeared in *Brassey's Annual* before long. Rather, the Admiralty's request that the press prevent any 'official imprimatur' in its usage of the information was informed by domestic considerations, namely to avoid any public impression that the Admiralty was tinkering with the press.

All this suggests a considerable revision of our understanding of the Admiralty and the British government in the 'age of the masses'. It seems to make little sense to think of British officials in the decade before the First World War as conducting no other press relations than cultivating a few private contacts with journalists and editors. The Admiralty shed such reticence long before 1914 and not during the war or in the inter-war period.[134] The sources show a government that was acutely aware of the public and its role in modern politics. In order to ensure extra-parliamentary support, the Admiralty followed a simultaneously passive and active policy: passive in that it refrained from attempts to control or correct the press; active in that it staged a range of public displays, many of them solely for publicity reasons, at which it catered for and at times openly courted the press. In comparison to the *Nachrichtenbureau's* policy, the Admiralty's approach must be regarded as the more insightful

---

[133] Ibid.
[134] Nor was it a novelty when the Admiralty allowed cinematographers to film the navy during the war and after, as Bell, *Royal Navy, Seapower and Strategy*, pp. 168, 174 suggests. This practice had been in use as early as 1897. Alfred West's catalogue of 1912 listed 371 naval films, very few of which had been produced without the active co-operation of the navy. See West, *Our Navy*, pp. 1–49.

and effective response to the changes taking place in the public sphere during this period. While the Admiralty aligned itself with the dynamics of the modern mass media, Tirpitz's apparatus forced the press into a long-winded process of *offiziöse Pressepolitik*, interfering and controlling to such a degree that the coverage of the naval theatre was often hindered rather than encouraged.

The intrusion of the masses

While the Admiralty and the *Reichsmarineamt* employed different means of influencing public opinion, both approaches would qualify as propaganda: as an 'ensemble of strategies aimed at creating political meaning and at directing opinions and perceptions', or simply as the 'mobilization of consent'.[135] Contemporaries in both countries called it 'naval education'.[136] Yet official strategies were only one of numerous factors at work in the naval theatre. Most of these did not operate in the 'above-below' fashion suggested by the concept of propaganda.[137] And while the naval theatre was certainly intended as a stage for naval advertising by the authorities, it underwent fundamental changes that were clearly beyond their control. The 'age of the masses' brought not only a dramatic social and geographical widening of audiences, it also changed the shape of public ritual itself. At its heart was the dynamic relationship between new media and new audiences on the one hand, and the traditional masters of ceremony on the other.

The way in which German fleet reviews were opened to media and tourist participation provides a case in point. Originally, Wilhelm II had established the ritualized meetings between himself and the fleet as private ceremonies. Their preparations constituted some of the navy's most well guarded information. All correspondence referring to them was marked 'top secret'. This included the planned location for fleet

---

[135] Ute Daniel and Wolfram Siemann, 'Historische Dimensionen der Propaganda', in Daniel and Siemann (eds.), *Propaganda. Meinungskampf, Verführung und politische Sinnstiftung 1789–1989* (Stuttgart, 1994), p. 12; Jay Winter, 'Propaganda and the Mobilization of Consent', in *The Oxford Illustrated History of the First World War* (Oxford, 1998), pp. 216–26.

[136] 'Die Flotte als Erzieherin' was a recurrent phrase in Germany, coined by the semi-official naval writer von Gottberg (BA-MA, RM 3/10237, Bl. 303). This is how the *Naval and Military Record*, 17 June 1909, described the object of naval spectacles: 'To bring home the lesson of sea power to every individual man, woman, and child in that portion of the earth which lies beneath the shadow of the Union Jack, and to show them that their very existence depends on this force'.

[137] For a critique of traditional approaches to propaganda see Rainer Gries and Wolfgang Schmale (eds.), *Kultur der Propaganda* (Bochum, 2004).

reviews.[138] It was only under the pressure exerted by media and commercial interest that these 'private' ceremonies were opened to the public. This process began locally, in towns such as Wilhelmshaven, Kiel and Danzig, which had harbours close to the locations where the Imperial Navy's reviews usually took place. Discovering the commercial potential of these occasions, shipping companies began to offer excursions and day trips to see the fleet assembled in review formation. Once bigger players in the leisure industry like HAPAG and *Norddeutscher Lloyd* had caught on, the Kaiser's annual naval review turned into a professionally marketed tourist attraction. The shipping lines and the press became increasingly skilled at gaining information about the date and location of the annual fleet review. As a result, the Kaiser's yacht was greeted by an armada of tourist steamers, private vessels and boats chartered by the press. In 1907, the *Berliner Lokal-Anzeiger* noted that local boats were outnumbered by tourist vessels from distant ports bringing 'huge masses' to see the navy.[139] And two years later, the *Deutsche Tages-Zeitung* observed that the number of these pleasure steamers was so high that they seemed to 'encircle' the fleet.[140]

It was only in 1911 that Wilhelm II and the naval leadership openly acknowledged the extent to which their fleet reviews had changed due to the influence of commercial and media forces. For the first time, the *Reichsmarineamt* organized an official press boat. This was explicitly in response to the numerous enquiries by the press.[141] What was more, the Kaiser then decreed that not only the press boat, but also all tourist steamers should be allowed into the ritual centre of the spectacle. Setting a precedent, he permitted press and pleasure boats to follow the *Hohenzollern* in its procession through the lines of warships.[142] More than fifty commercial steamers followed the Kaiser's yacht past the fleet, taking an estimated 40,000 spectators to watch the review close up.[143] Newspapers noted approvingly that the Kaiser had formally opened a previously private royal and naval ritual to the public.[144]

[138] BA-MA, RM 2/104, Bl. 17: Chef des Admiralstabes to Chef des Marinekabinetts, 15 April 1909: Ganz Geheim. Von Hand zu Hand!; BA-MA, RM 2/106, Bl. 282: Kommando der Hochseeflotte, Ganz Geheim, Programm für die Vorführung der Flotte vor Sr. Majestät am 5. September 1911; BA-MA, RM 2/107, Bl. 15: Chef des Admiralstabes to Chef der Hochseeflotte, 11 Jan 1912, Ganz Geheim: Kaisermanöver.
[139] *Berliner Lokal-Anzeiger*, 3 Aug 1907, Zweite Ausgabe, Abendblatt.
[140] *Deutsche Tages-Zeitung*, 30 Aug 1909.
[141] BA-MA, RM 3/10237, Bl. 273: RMA to Flottenkommando, 23 Aug 1911; RM 3/10237, Bl. 52 and Bl. 272: Flottenkommando Kiel to RMA.
[142] BA-MA, RM 2/106, Bl. 188: Marinekabinett to Flottenkommando Kiel, 22 Aug 1911.
[143] *Kieler Zeitung*, 6 Sept 1911, Erstes Morgenblatt.
[144] *Leipziger Illustrierte Zeitung*, in *Presse-Stimmen*, p. 22. See also *Berliner Lokal-Anzeiger*, 4 Sept 1911, Zweites und Drittes Blatt, Abendausgabe.

The influence of public, commercial and media interest was even more clearly on display in 1912, when the naval authorities and the Kaiser decided to hold a strictly private fleet review. Wilhelm II specifically decreed that there should be no press or tourist boats during the fleet assembly off Heligoland scheduled for 16 September.[145] While the *Reichsmarineamt* was still busy explaining this to tourist boards and travel agencies, the shipping companies in Bremen, Hamburg and Wilhelmshaven were already advertising 'fleet review cruises' and 'day trips to see the navy'.[146] In late August, the naval authorities caved in, realizing that the fleet review could hardly be kept 'private'. The Chief of Naval Staff asked the Kaiser for permission to 'open' the ceremony.[147] Against his original intentions, Wilhelm II agreed to allow pleasure steamers to participate actively in the forthcoming review. Having been overtaken by commercial and media initiative, the navy's leadership then hastily drew up a plan of how to contain public participation in the review, so that it would not spill over into the manoeuvres.[148] Against the stated intentions of the Kaiser and the navy, the forces of commerce and media had turned this 'private' ceremony into a public spectacle. It is clear then that the way in which the Kaiser's annual fleet reviews were opened to the public, had little to do with Tirpitz's public relations office or other agents of manipulation 'from above'. Rather, it came about as the result of a process in which media and commercial interest outflanked the Admiralty.[149]

The same was true in Britain. Here, the naval theatre had been opened to the wider public much earlier. Yet a similar feeling of 'the masses' encroaching on royal and naval ceremonial existed at the turn of the century. Both the press and the naval authorities observed that fleet reviews were changing under the influence of mass entertainment and tourism. During the 1902 coronation fleet review, the tradition-conscious naval correspondent of *The Times* was dismayed at how 'little decency or respect' there was in the way in which the large number of excursion

[145] BA-MA, RM 3/10237, Bl. 305: Chef Marinekabinett to Chef Admiralstab, 15 July 1912. See also BA-MA, RM 2/107, Bl. 15: Chef des Admiralstabes to Chef der Hochseeflotte, 11 Jan 1912.
[146] BA-MA, RM 3/10238, Bl. 4–12.
[147] BA-MA, RM 2/107, Bl. 212: Chef Admiralstab to Chef Marinekabinett, ganz geheim, 29 Aug 1912.
[148] BA-MA, RM 2/107, Bl. 222: Chef Admiralstab to Kaiserliches Kommando der Hochseeflotte, ganz geheim, 31 Aug 1912.
[149] The *Reichsmarineamt* acknowledged this in the letters that it sent to shipping companies and tourist boards a week before the occasion. For an example see BA-MA, RM 3/10238, Bl. 30: RMA to Seebäderdienst der Hamburg-Amerika-Linie, 11 Sept 1912. On the wider debate about 'manipulation' and 'self-mobilization' see Chapter 3.

13. The intrusion of the masses. Spectators after the launch of HMS
Dreadnought, 10 February 1906.

steamers surrounded the royal yacht. He was not alone in lamenting
'all this intrusion'.[150] After the event, the Commander-in-Chief at
Portsmouth wrote to the Admiralty:

Complaints have been made to me by several of the [war]ships at Spithead, during
the late assembly of the Fleet, of the behaviour of the Excursion Steamers; that
they proceed at excessive speed through the lines, regardless of the traffic regulations, shave the ships dangerously close, to give their passengers a good view,
and swamp boats, damage ladders &c, by their wash, to say nothing of the danger
to smaller boats. These vessels carry on in this way with impunity, as they are well
aware of the impossibility of stopping them when loaded with passengers and
going 10 to 12 knots, and action at law is costly, difficult, producing doubtful
results, but that something should be done is certain. On the occasion of the
presence of a large Fleet at Spithead, they make use of the opportunity to make
money, by rushing the vessels round the Fleet as often as possible, regardless of
anything but getting back to take a fresh lot round, knowing that being crowded
with passengers and going a good speed everything afloat makes way for them.

[150] *Morning Leader*, 18 Aug 1902.

I have personally observed this want of consideration, having to suddenly alter course to avoid being run down by the [steamer] 'Duchess of Fife'.[151]

The Admiralty felt that the safety and sanctity of its most important public ritual was being threatened. It complained to steamship companies and tightened the regulations published in the *Notice to Mariners* before reviews.[152] Yet the transformation of fleet reviews under the influence of the leisure and tourist industry continued. The number of excursion steamers and their intrusive presence increased further in the years leading up to 1914.[153] Their role as active participants was formally acknowledged in 1911, when they were allocated their own berths to anchor within the review field. As *The Times* observed, the lines of commercial vessels next to the assembled fleet now constituted 'a not inconsiderable review in themselves'.[154] Whether the Admiralty liked it or not, the pleasure boats had turned from outside spectators into active participants in the ritual. The authorities' difficulties in maintaining the boundary between the highly structured ritual core of the celebrations and their outer circles of mass participation showed the direct, spatial impact of the 'age of the masses' on the naval theatre.

In Germany, the 'intrusion of the masses' was felt in particular with regard to cinematography. The *Reichsmarineamt* was adamant that no foreign cameramen ought to be admitted to ship launches. Yet international film distributors found ways of circumventing these restrictions. When denied access, they purchased pictures from local German firms and marketed them under their own label. Some even recruited German cameramen who had been commissioned by the authorities. Pathé, the French firm, for example, made a contract with the cinematographer Eugen Hamm. Hamm was on a good footing with the Kaiser, for whom he had taken a private film during a hunting trip. He was favoured by the court and given a *Sondererlaubnis* to film naval and imperial events. It was only when his competitors tipped the police off that the *Nachrichtenbureau* scrutinized his background. In May 1913, the Head of Police in Berlin informed Tirpitz:

that the Catholic photographer Ernst Eugen Hamm, born on 3 April 1869 at Baden, does not have his own studio. Rather, he works exclusively for the German

---

[151] PRO, ADM 1/7579: Hotham to Secretary of Admiralty, 3 July 1902. See also PRO, ADM 179/56: Commodore SMS *St. George* to Hotham, 1 July 1902.

[152] PRO, ADM 1/7579: Minute, Secretary of Admiralty, 21 Aug 1902; PRO, ADM 179/60, p. 39: *Notices for Mariners*; PRO, ADM 198/3, pp. 327–8: Excessive speed of passenger steamers.

[153] RNM, 1986/422: John H. P. Southby, midshipman's journal, 24 June 1911.

[154] *Times*, 26 June 1911.

representation of the well-known French film company Pathé frères to whom he always sends his films. The allegations that have been made against him are thus right and it would seem appropriate to exercise some restraint towards him.[155]

A range of other examples show how difficult the authorities found it to control the media at naval events. Carl Speck, a cinematographer from Kiel, established a particularly fine record of covert filming. Again and again he managed to find a way into dockyards or neighbouring buildings before ship launches. On 5 May 1913, in the hours before the launch of the *Großer Kurfürst*, the Hamburg police discovered him inside the Vulcan yard with his camera positioned close to the launching-ways. From there he escaped on to the roof of a nearby coffee hall, where he continued to film until police dragged him away.[156] What his example and that of Eugen Hamm illustrate is that there were significant limits to the authorities' power to control the ways in which mass media and the entertainment industry influenced the naval theatre. They struggled to rein in photographers and cameramen as well as tourist boats and commercial steamers. Whether they liked it or not, the Admiralty and the *Reichsmarineamt* were forced to acknowledge that the new forces of media, leisure and entertainment were directly influencing the shape of the naval theatre.

Theatricality and the crowd

The impact of the unfolding mass market on the naval theatre was particularly clearly expressed in the discourses and practices concerned with the role of 'the crowd' and 'the masses'. While these terms had mostly negative connotations in intellectual discourse,[157] the popular press styled itself as speaking for the vast audiences that took part in

---

[155] BA-MA, RM 3/9874, p. 107: Polizei-Präsident Berlin to Nachrichtenbureau RMA, geheim, 18 May 1913 (Abschrift). See also BA-MA, RM 3/9900, Bl. 50–1: Hamm to Nachrichtenbureau RMA, 20 May 1913; BA-MA, RM 3/9960, Bl. 130–1: Hamm to Nachrichtenbureau RMA, 17 Nov 1913 and ibid.: reply by Löhlein, Nachrichtenbureau. On Hamm see also BA-MA, RM 3/9874, Bl. 57.

[156] BA-MA, RM 3/9899, Bl. 99–100: Polizeibehörde Hamburg, Abteilung VIII (Hafenpolizei), Distrikt I Wache 10, betr. Photogr. Carl Speck, wegen verbotswidrigen Photographierens von Kriegsschiffen, 5 May 1913; ibid., Bl. 105: Polizeibehörde Hamburg, Abteilung IV (Politische Polizei), Bericht des Wachtmeisters Hinz, 27 May 1913.

[157] Gustave Le Bon, *The Crowd: A Study of the Popular Mind* (London, 1896), first published in French in 1895, is often cited as the main influence in interpreting the dangers arising from 'the crowd'. That his book expressed attitudes which were widely shared amongst intellectuals, has been shown by John Carey, *The Intellectuals and the Masses: Pride and Prejudice amongst the Literary Intelligentsia, 1880–1939* (New York, 1992). See also J. S. McClelland, *The Crowd and the Mob: From Plato to Canetti* (London, 1989).

public rituals. There were special sections analysing the mood of 'the masses'. From around the turn of the century, images of 'the crowd' appeared increasingly in films and on the front pages of the newspapers. Coverage of naval events recurrently included photographs of 'the eager masses', 'the crowd' or 'the ship and the spectators'. The language and imagery employed in the press showed a strong tendency to personify the crowd as a homogenous, single entity. The *Daily Express* wrote of 'the cry' that 'went up from thousands of throats' at the launch of HMS *Thunderer*.[158] The *Daily Mail* had 'one cry' arising from 'the crowd'.[159]

The emergence of 'the crowd' as a new actor was reflected in the strategies developed by the authorities. Both in Britain and Germany, a host of measures was introduced to shape 'the crowd' and impose boundaries on it. It became standard procedure to use separate gates and access streets for the mass audiences on the one hand and the specially invited guests on the other. The arrival of dignitaries was usually scheduled earlier than the opening of the gates for the general public, thereby avoiding any direct contact.[160] At most ship launches, authorities designated a space in which the crowd was to be contained. Apart from the police, deputations of *Vereine*, Boy Scouts and guards of soldiers were positioned with the aim of keeping the wider audience in its designated space. The ubiquitous *Spalierstehen*, the lining of streets by guards of honour, thus became an exercise both in ceremonial representation and in shaping and controlling the crowd.[161]

Yet mass audiences could no longer simply be 'regulated' or 'controlled'. They also had to be catered for. This began with safety. By 1910, it was standard procedure at launches to have teams of stretcher-bearers under the orders of a fleet surgeon on stand-by.[162] At the 1911

---

[158] *Daily Express*, 2 Feb 1911.
[159] *Daily Mail*, 2 Feb 1911. See also *Naval and Military Record*, 30 Oct 1912; *Daily Express*, 15 Aug 1902. For examples in the local press see *Portsmouth Evening News*, 10 Feb 1906; *Hampshire Telegraph*, 17 Feb 1906; *Jarrow Guardian*, 22 March 1912. For similar examples in Germany see *Danziger Neueste Nachrichten*, 27 May 1903, Erste Beilage; *Hamburger Hausfrau*, 2 June 1912; *Hamburger Correspondent*, 20 June 1914; *Hamburger Correspondent*, 16 Dec 1895, Hauptblatt.
[160] See the programmes and drawings of launching arrangements in BA-MA, RM 3/153, Bl. 16; RM 3/130, Bl. 25; RM 3/133, Bl. 46; RM 3/134, Bl. 125; RM 3/135, Bl. 116; RM 3/142, Bl. 41; RM 3/152, Bl. 135; RM 3/159, Bl. 81; RM 3/170, Bl. 19; RM 3/171, Bl. 13; RM 3/188, Bl. 24.
[161] The police strategies aimed at 'shaping the crowd' are particularly well documented in the case of Bremen. See StA Bremen, VIII.F.31, Nr. 22, Bl. 17: Staatssekretär RMA to Senatskommission, 2 April 1902; StA Bremen, VIII.F.31, Nr. 22, Anlage 8, Bl. 25; *Bremer Nachrichten*, 9 July 1903, Erstes Blatt; *Bremer Nachrichten*, 25 Jan 1909.
[162] PRO, ADM 179/33: PGO, 20 Aug 1910. Documented for the following years in ADM 179/72: PGO 1248/1911; ADM 179/73: PGO 1537/1912; ADM 179/74: PGO 204/1913.

Spithead naval review, 150 members of the St John's Ambulance Association were enlisted to ensure the well-being of spectators.[163] Yet catering for 'the crowd' was not limited to safety issues. Authorities were aware of the demand for good viewing and entertainment, a demand that was amplified by a press increasingly focusing on the facilities offered to spectators.[164] Badly prepared events could draw scathing reviews. When not enough food stalls had been licensed for the 1909 fleet visit to the Thames, the *Daily News* ran the front-page headline 'Hungry crowds'.[165] Concessions to 'the masses', in contrast, were lauded.[166] All this demonstrated that the mass audience had acquired an active role in the naval theatre. Indeed, dockyard officials and naval officers showed a strong awareness of 'the masses' and the need to entertain them. They acknowledged that 'pleasing the audience' had become a main aim of fleet reviews and ship launches. They reflected on the image that the fleet would create, how 'the show' would look from ashore, how the 'effect of the whole fleet', the 'display' and 'image' would be received by the spectators.[167] The presence of cameras, press boats and hosts of journalists was a constant reminder of the millions that would watch the spectacle. Playing both to this distant mass audience and to the crowds present had gained a new importance. Serving the demand for dramatic effects and spectacular novelties, 'impressing the audience', as Eduard Blohm, one of the directors of the Blohm & Voss dockyard, put it in his diary, had become a central function of naval celebrations.[168]

Taken together, these findings suggest that the rise of the naval theatre cannot be explained simply by reference to governments and monarchs. It was in the dynamic relationship between the traditional masters of ceremony and their attempts at the 'invention of tradition' on the one hand, and the new audiences and new media on the other hand, that this

---

[163] Portsmouth City Records Office, CCM 1/23, Council Records: Minutes of Watch Committee, 23 May 1911. On the problem of overcrowding see PRO, MT 9/729: HO Circular, 26 May 1902, sent to twenty-four county and borough police forces, as well as to the Commissioner of the Metropolitan Police and the Commissioner of the City Police. See also West Sussex Constabulary to Home Office, 18 June 1902.

[164] *Daily Chronicle*, 15 Aug 1902; *North-Western Daily Mail*, 22 Feb 1909; *Times*, 14 Aug 1902.

[165] *Daily News*, 20 July 1909. See also *Naval and Military Record*, 24 Aug 1910.

[166] *Daily Mail*, 29 April 1911; *Evening News and Southern Daily Mail*, 12 Oct 1912; *Illustrated [Newcastle] Chronicle*, 21 March 1912; *North-Western Daily Mail*, 22 Feb 1909; *Glasgow Leader*, 29 June 1906; *Naval and Military Record*, 29 Aug 1907.

[167] RNM, 1997: James Colvill, 24 June 1911; RNM, 1982/1716: John Cardew, 23 June 1911; RNM, 1986/422: J. H. P. Southby, 23 June 1911. See also IWM 85/11/1: Edward W. H. Blake, midshipman's journal, 12 June 1909; Hopman, *Logbuch*, p. 373.

[168] StA Hamburg, 622-1/2: Eduard Blohm, Werfterinnerungen 1877–1939, p. 257.

public theatre unfolded in the decades before 1914. Modern transport and tourism brought a dramatically widened radius of direct participation, turning naval ceremonies into mass events. Cinema, *Flottenschauspiele* and other forms of urban entertainment restaged the naval game in places that were distant from the coast. The naval theatre had become a commodity, readily available as a game that could be purchased and played all over the country. Yet the impact of mass culture and commercial initiatives went considerably beyond simply 'popularizing' the naval stage. Popular culture represented a new source of power and participation. The 'opening' of private aspects of ritual to the public, the intrusion of mass participation into the core of royal ceremonies, the changing spatial character of naval rituals, the increasingly prominent role that 'the crowd' played in stagecraft and choreography: these were important new features brought about not by the authorities, but by mass media and popular culture.

The transformation that the naval theatre underwent in this period was thus never divorced from fundamental political questions. The crowds shown prominently in images of naval celebrations were not merely passive audiences. Styled and appropriated in popular culture and the mass media, they represented a new force in politics. Rather than simply a cynical tool, 'invented' to appease or manipulate 'the masses', the naval theatre expressed their new influence. Both the Admiralty and the *Reichsmarineamt* acknowledged this in internal memoranda. They saw the huge potential of this maritime stage for promoting the navy and the monarchy in the age of mass politics. In their attempts to exploit this potential they took remarkably different paths. Tirpitz and the *Nachrichtenbureau* established a complicated mechanism of control, censorship and feeding of the press, which ultimately hindered rather than helped the initiatives taken by the media and the leisure industry to commercialize the naval theatre. The Admiralty's approach, in contrast, presented a more effective response to the changes taking place in the public sphere. Rather than attempting to control or channel the forces of the market, the Admiralty aligned itself with them and made the naval theatre as accessible as possible to the media.

While the authorities attempted to utilize the naval stage for their own interests, they had to acknowledge that the forces of mass culture had a strong grip on this arena. Nowhere was this more obvious than in February 1910, when the Royal Navy was rattled by a scandal that showed how transient public prestige could be. Disguised with brown face-powder and false beards, a party of six, amongst them Virginia Woolf, announced themselves to the Commander of the Home Fleet by

HOW THE OFFICERS OF H.M.S. DREADNOUGHT WERE HOAXED: PHOTOGRAPH OF THE "ABYSSINIAN PRINCES" WHO HAVE MADE ALL ENGLAND LAUGH.

14. 'All England is laughing at the practical joke played a few days ago on the officers of HMS *Dreadnought* by five men and a young woman who, with the aid of elaborate "make-ups", passed themselves off as Abyssinian princes, an interpreter and a representative of the Foreign Office, and were accorded royal honours and shown all over the mighty battleship by Admiral Sir William May and the Dreadnought officers' (*Daily Mirror*, 16 Feb 1910). The photograph was taken before the party, led by Horace Cole, went on their trip to visit the *Dreadnought*. On the very left, wearing a false beard, is Virginia Woolf as 'Prince Sanganya'.

telegram as 'Prince Makalen of Abbysinia [sic] and suite'.[169] They were promptly received with royal honours and shown around the

---

[169] PRO, ADM 1/8192: Telegram purporting to be from Sir Charles Hardinge, Foreign Office, but sent by Horace Cole to Commander-in-Chief Home Fleet, 7 Feb 1910.

Dreadnought, the flagship of Admiral Sir William May. As the internal Admiralty report put it, the *Dreadnought*'s officers 'never detected anything' about the party that 'consisted of four dark skinned persons in Oriental costumes and two Europeans'.[170] The press had a field day, while at the Admiralty 'the question of what should be done about that wretched hoax' was still 'a matter of perplexity', as its Secretary admitted in a private letter to Admiral May.[171] There were full-page reports and large photographs in the tabloids, mocking the navy and its public theatre.[172] The same newspapers that usually lauded the navy's public pageantry now ridiculed it. More than anything, the 'Dreadnought hoax' demonstrated that the balance of power between governments and monarchs on the one hand and new media and new audiences on the other was in flux. Clearly, the naval theatre was about entertainment and amusement, but this was never divorced from the fundamental political questions that characterized the 'age of the masses'.

---

[170] PRO, ADM 1/8192: Admiral Sir William May to Secretary of the Admiralty, 17 Feb 1910, confidential.

[171] PRO, ADM 1/8192: W. Graham Greene, Secretary of the Admiralty, to Admiral Sir William May, 16 Feb 1910, private. See Adrian Stephen, *The 'Dreadnought' Hoax* (London, 1936) for an account by one of the participants and Dudley de Chair, *The Sea Is Strong* (London, 1961), pp. 131–2 for the reaction amongst naval officers.

[172] For a flavour of the press coverage: *Daily Express*, 12 Feb 1910, front page: 'Amazing naval hoax: Sham Abyssinian Princes Visit the Dreadnought: Bogus Order'; *Globe*, 12 Feb 1910: 'Bogus "Princes" on the Dreadnought'. See also Peter Stansky, *On Or About December 1910: Early Bloomsbury and Its Intimate World* (Cambridge, MA, 1996), ch. 2.

3   Bread and circuses

In the eyes of critical observers, the naval theatre had an obvious historical parallel: the games of Ancient Rome. Indeed, to some it seemed as if the Kaiser and his navy were aiming to upstage the Roman emperors and their ostentatious festivals. The most compelling depiction of this parallel was Ludwig Quidde's famous pamphlet *Caligula: A Study in Imperial Insanity* of 1894, which sold close to a quarter of a million copies before 1914 and provoked one of the major scandals that came to characterize Wilhelm II's reign. Quidde wrote of the emperor's 'love of display and extravagance', the 'hunger for military triumphs' and 'manoeuvre-amusements', all of which he saw as characterized by an overarching sense of ostentation and the 'theatricality that is an ingredient in imperial insanity'.[1] While he wrote this about Caligula, it was clear that his subject was the Kaiser: too obvious were the allusions to Wilhelm II's 'love of the sea' and his 'fantastic idea' of conquering it.[2] The similarities between the megalomania of the ancient past and the Wilhelmine present became a standard argument used by critics of the naval theatre.[3] In contrast to Quidde, though, most of them saw in the Kaiser's celebrations more than simply 'imperial insanity'. They argued that this public theatre had a decidedly political function. Again, Imperial Rome provided a key historical parallel. 'Bread and circuses' was the catch-phrase, first used by the satirist Juvenal to describe the Roman games as part of a strategy by

---

[1] Ludwig Quidde, *Caligula. Eine Studie über römischen Cäsarenwahnsinn* (Leipzig, 1894), pp. 10–11. On the 'Caligula affair' see Kohlrausch, *Monarch im Skandal*, pp. 118–54; Karl Holl, Hans Kloft and Gerd Fesser (eds.), *Caligula – Wilhelm II. und der Cäsarenwahnsinn. Antikenrezeption und wilhelminische Politik am Beispiel des 'Caligula' von Ludwig Quidde* (Bremen, 2001); Ludwig Quidde, *Caligula: Schriften über Militarismus und Pazifismus*, edited and introduced by Hans-Ulrich Wehler (Frankfurt, 1977). For an English translation see *The Kaiser's Double, Being a Translation of the Celebrated Pamphlet by Prof. Ludwig Quidde Entitled 'Caligula: A Study in Imperial Insanity'* (London, 1914).

[2] Quidde, *Caligula*, pp. 11–12.

[3] For a particularly readable example see *Die Zukunft*, 15 June 1895, pp. 527–8. See also Graf Ernst Reventlow, *Kaiser Wilhelm II. und die Byzantiner*, second edition (Munich, 1906), esp. pp. 156–70.

which emperors won the favour of the masses – and kept them politically docile.[4] For many critics, the Wilhelmine and Edwardian naval theatre followed a similar strategy: to keep the masses enthralled by spectacular shows and to orchestrate them into willing subjects. Ship launches and fleet reviews were part of a theatre that was designed to distract attention from social problems and political deficits, lamented socialist newspapers both in Britain and Germany.[5] Indeed, the *Vorwärts*, the organ of the German Social Democratic Party, saw in the Kaiser's naval celebrations nothing less than a modern version of Rome's 'bread and games' or *Brot und Spiele*.[6]

A number of modern historians have followed this interpretation. George Mosse explained national German festivals as 'instruments of mass politics', employed to instigate national pride and unity. Late nineteenth-century 'circuses and monuments' were, in his view, central arenas for the 'nationalization of the masses'.[7] Mosse's interpretation was echoed by Hans-Ulrich Wehler in his seminal study of the *Kaiserreich*, and by Volker Berghahn in his analysis of the *Tirpitz-Plan*.[8] Both saw the Wilhelmine naval programme as a grand exercise by which the ruling elite had tried to deflect public attention away from the mounting socio-political crisis facing Germany. Wehler and Berghahn earned themselves the label of 'Kehrites' by drawing on Eckart Kehr's pioneering studies of the 1920s, which had explained the Imperial Navy as a tool of domestic politics, a powerful vehicle designed to orchestrate consensus and ensure the survival of the ruling elite.[9] The public staging of the navy appeared in this interpretation as a key component of the Wilhelmine version of 'bread and circuses'. Moreover, for historians such as Mosse the use of public ritual for the manipulation of 'the masses' presented one of the key continuities between the *Kaiserreich* and Hitler's Germany. The naval theatre served, in this reading, as evidence of the *Sonderweg*, the 'special path' that Wilhelmine Germany

---

[4] Juvenal, *Satires*, 10, 81.
[5] *Hamburger Echo*, 10 Sept 1904; *Hamburger Echo*, 26 May 1912; *Labour Leader*, 23 June 1911.
[6] *Vorwärts*, 27 June 1895.
[7] George L. Mosse, 'Caesarism, circuses and monuments', *Journal of Contemporary History* 6 (1971), pp. 167–82. See also his *Nationalisation of the Masses*, ch. 4 and 5.
[8] Berghahn, *Tirpitz-Plan*; Volker Berghahn, 'Der Tirpitz-Plan und die Krisis des preußisch-deutschen Herrschaftssystems', in Schottelius and Deist (eds.), *Marine und Marinepolitik*, pp. 89–115; Wehler, *Deutsches Kaiserreich*, pp. 96–121, 171–8; Wehler, *Deutsche Gesell-schaftsgeschichte*, vol. 3, pp. 985–90, 1129–45.
[9] Eckart Kehr, *Schlachtflottenbau und Parteipolitik 1894–1901* (Berlin, 1930); Eckart Kehr, *Der Primat der Innenpolitik*, edited by Hans-Ulrich Wehler, second edition (Berlin, 1970).

had taken in the late nineteenth century and which explained the rise of the Nazis in the 1930s.[10]

Undoubtedly, the tradition of interpreting public spectacle as a modern form of 'bread and circuses' is much stronger in German than in British historiography. Yet historians of modern Britain have also advanced this argument. John MacKenzie and others have presented imperial celebrations as instances of propaganda and manipulation 'from above'.[11] Denis Judd has explained Victoria's Diamond Jubilee of 1897 as 'a British version of the ancient Roman formula of "bread and circuses"'.[12] And James Scott Myerly has interpreted military ceremonies as instruments of discipline that instilled an acceptance of hierarchy and conformity into British society, which he saw marked by a 'fundamental conflict between workers and owners'. Public ritual served a ruling elite as a vehicle of social control and political dominance, Scott Myerly claims, neatly following the argument that Wilhelmine and Edwardian socialists had advanced against the naval theatre.[13]

One of the main objections to this interpretation, at least as far as Imperial Germany is concerned, has been brought forward by Geoff Eley.[14] He rejected the 'Kehrite' notion that naval enthusiasm had been created 'from above'. Rather, he argued, a new nationalist right, which was a key part of the unfolding of popular politics in the 1890s, acted as a catalyst for 'self-mobilization'. Instrumental in this were leagues such as the *Flottenverein*, which followed a dynamic of their own and developed into populist pressure groups, a 'radical right' that increasingly acted against government intentions. The popularization of the navy was thus not so much a product of government manipulation, but rather

---

[10] George L. Mosse, 'Caesarism, Circuses and Monuments'; *Nationalisation of the Masses*, chs. 4, 5. See also Patrick Brantlinger, *Bread and Circuses: Theories of Mass Culture as Social Decay* (Ithaca, 1983), p. 71.

[11] MacKenzie, *Propaganda and Empire*; MacKenzie, *Popular Imperialism and the Military*; Mangan, *Making Imperial Mentalities*; Schneer, *London 1900*, pp. 28–34.

[12] Denis Judd, *Empire: The British Imperial Experience from 1765 to the Present* (London, 1996), p. 133.

[13] Myerly, *British Military Spectacle*, esp. pp. 167–70; Myerly, ' "The Eye Must Entrap the Mind" ', pp. 105–31.

[14] Eley, *Reshaping the German Right*; Eley, 'Some Thoughts on the Nationalist Pressure Groups', in Paul Kennedy and Anthony Nicholls (eds.), *Nationalist and Racialist Movements in Britain and Germany before 1914* (London, 1981), pp. 40–67; Geoff Eley, *From Unification to Nazism: Reinterpreting the German Past* (London, 1986), esp. pp. 85–109 ('Army, State and Civil Society: Revisiting the Problem of German Militarism') and 110–53 ('*Sammlungspolitik*, Social Imperialism and the Navy Law of 1898'). For the more general critique of the 'Kehrite' position: Thomas Nipperdey, *Deutsche Geschichte 1866–1918*, vol. 2, *Machtstaat vor der Demokratie* (Munich, 1992), pp. 242–7.

an expression of the mobilization 'from below' through the leagues and *Vereine*.[15]

The naval theatre provides an apt opportunity to revisit this debate. It was here that 'above' and 'below' met, and that the power relations between governments, monarchs, 'the people' and a number of other actors were played out. In taking this public arena as a test case for the wider debate about 'bread and circuses', this chapter addresses three key questions. First, what was the role of the 'radical right', which Eley and others have seen as so instrumental in the creation of naval enthusiasm? How, in particular, does it compare to the influence of other actors who do not fall into the much-quoted, yet frustratingly imprecise, categories of 'above' and 'below'? Second, how did people make sense of the naval theatre? Are claims about 'manipulation' or 'self-mobilization' born out by their experiences? Third, was the naval theatre an arena of militarism, as contemporaries and historians of the 'manipulation' school have claimed? And how did the two countries compare in this respect? In bringing these questions together, the chapter suggests a revision of what 'bread and circuses' meant in the age of empire.

The 'radical right' and the local factor

As one would expect, the *Flottenverein* and the Navy League had a substantial interest in the naval theatre. Both in Britain and Germany their role was two-fold: that of promoters and that of participants. They boosted the publicity for the naval theatre by organizing trips to fleet

---

[15] Stig Förster has argued a similar case in *Der doppelte Militarismus. Die deutsche Heeresrüstungspolitik zwischen Status-quo-Sicherung und Aggression 1890–1913* (Stuttgart, 1985), pp. 75–207: a conservative form of militarism, to be found in the governing elite, stood in conflict with a second form of militarism instigated 'from below'. On the 'radical right' in Germany see Roger Chickering, *We Men Who Feel Most German: A Cultural Study of the Pan-German League, 1886–1914* (London, 1984); Marilyn S. Coetzee, *The German Army League: Popular Nationalism in the Wilhelmine Germany* (Oxford, 1990); Thomas Rohkrämer, *Der Militarismus der 'kleinen Leute'. Die Kriegervereine im Deutschen Kaiserreich. 1871–1914* (Munich, 1990); Dieter Düding, 'Die Kriegervereine im Wilhelminischen Reich und ihr Beitrag zur Militarisierung der deutschen Gesellschaft', in Jost Dülffer and Karl Holl (eds.), *Bereit zum Krieg. Kriegsmentalität im wilhelminischen Deutschland, 1890–1914* (Göttingen, 1986), pp. 99–121. On right-wing leagues in Britain: Geoffrey Searle, 'The "Revolt from the Right" in Edwardian Britain', in Kennedy and Nicholls, *Nationalist and Racialist Movements*, pp. 21–39; Ann Summers, 'The Character of Edwardian Nationalism: Three Popular Leagues', ibid., pp. 66–87; Wolfgang Mock, 'Entstehung und Herausbildung einer "radikalen Rechten" in Großbritannien 1900–1914', *Historische Zeitschrift*, Beiheft 8 (Munich, 1983), pp. 5–45; Arnd Bauerkämper, *Die "radikale Rechte" in Großbritannien. Nationalistische, antisemitische und faschiste Bewegungen vom späten 19. Jahrhundert bis 1945* (Göttingen, 1991).

reviews and ship launches.[16] During fleet reviews, the leagues sold guides and programmes, which combined practical information with commentary in support of increases in naval expenditure. 'Pens of the Navy' such as H. W. Wilson and Arnold White were given plenty of space in these publications.[17] Naturally, no such programme was without self-promotion. The *Navy League Guide to the naval review* (1897) asked:

Are you ready to help us strengthen the splendid fleet you have seen? Then join the Navy League. A strictly non-party organization to urge upon the Government of the day and the electorate the paramount importance of an adequate Navy as the best Guarantee of Peace. Members, £1 1s. Ladies, 10s. 6d. Associates 5s. or less.[18]

The prevalence of such advertising reflected the great potential of naval celebrations to raise support for the navy, which was the leagues' declared main purpose. As Admiral von Koester, the *Flottenverein*'s president, wrote to Tirpitz, launches of warships offered 'very good possibilities for the fostering and illustrating' of naval matters for the members of the league and the general public.[19] The naval leagues were keen not only to promote, but also to be part of this public theatre. From early on, the *Flottenverein* and the Navy League sought privileged forms of participation. After the turn of the century, representatives of the *Flottenverein* were given places in the stands for specially invited guests at ship launches.[20] Von Koester and Tirpitz agreed on the mutual benefit of this special treatment.[21]

However, the role of the *Flottenverein* and the Navy League should not be overestimated. While they were represented prominently at fleet reviews and ship launches, their actual influence was limited. Their

---

[16] Correspondence on the *Flottenverein*'s initiatives in promoting naval events and celebrations is recorded in BA-MA, RM3/9871. See also BA-MA, RM3/9967, RM3/9830-3 and PRO, ADM 1/8265: Agnes E. Weston to Secretary of the Admiralty, 26 June 1912.

[17] See the examples in BA-MA, RM3/10238, Bl. 58 ff. and *The Navy League Guide to the Naval Review* (London, 1897); H. W. Wilson (ed.), *Navy League Guide to the Coronation Review June 28, 1902* (London, 1902); *Navy League Guide to the Thames Review* (London, 1909).

[18] *Navy League Guide to the Naval Review* (1897), back cover. See also the *Flottenverein*'s guide for the 1911 Kiel fleet review, of which the *Reichsmarineamt* ordered ten issues to be printed on special paper for distribution on board the imperial yacht: BA-MA, RM3/10238, Bl. 54.

[19] BA-MA, RM 3/9959, Bl. 172: Koester to Tirpitz, 25 Aug 1911. Similarly in BA-MA, RM3/118, Bl. 139–40: Koester to Tirpitz, 26 Aug 1911.

[20] BA-MA, RM 3/9958-62 contains correspondence with local *Flottenverein* branches on this aspect. On the participation of the *Kriegervereine* and *Jugendwehr* see BA-MA, RM3/176, Bl. 73–4.

[21] BA-MA, RM 3/118, Bl. 139–40: Koester to Tirpitz, 26 Aug 1911; Bl. 141: Tirpitz to Koester, 19 Sept 1911.

initiative and, more importantly, their power to shape the naval theatre was relatively insignificant in comparison to the part played by the actors examined in the previous chapter: governments and naval administrations on the one hand; the mass media, entertainment and tourist industries on the other. The 1902 coronation review at Spithead offers a good example. More than one hundred excursion ships from throughout the UK took part. The vast majority of them were organized by tour operators such as Thomas Cook and Henry Lunn as well as a large number of shipping companies.[22] A further dozen or so were chartered by a variety of voluntary clubs and societies, amongst them the Oxford and Cambridge University Club, the Civil Service Co-operative Society and the Ripley Street Pleasant Sunday Afternoon Society, none of them forces of the 'radical right'. One single vessel was sent by the Navy League.[23] Similarly, out of the large number of pleasure steamers that attended the Kaiser's 1912 fleet review off Heligoland, only one had been chartered by the *Flottenverein*. It was, in a twist of irony, called *Vorwärts*.[24]

The subordinate role of the 'radical right' for the celebration of the navy becomes even more obvious when compared to the rich culture of civic and commercial pride that operated at the local level. The late nineteenth century saw the rise of local government, urban culture and commercial and industrial success both in Britain and Germany.[25] The role of local government expanded not only administratively and financially, but also in its public representation. This dynamic civil society developed a 'distinctive rhetoric of civic pride', centring on liberal and voluntarist ideas.[26] Towns such as Glasgow, Newcastle and Portsmouth, as well as Bremen, Hamburg and Kiel underwent a rapid industrial and commercial expansion; and they were busy expressing this new

---

[22] PRO, ADM 116/132, vol. 2. This included the North of Scotland & Orkney & Shetland Steam Company, Aberdeen; M. Langlands & Sons, Liverpool; the Belfast Steamship Company; J. T. Duncan Steamship & Sailing Ship Brokers, Cardiff, and the Aberdeen Steam Navigation Company.

[23] Ibid.

[24] BA-MA, RM3/10238, Bl. 19. *Vorwärts* was also the title of the Social Democrats' main party publication, quoted in the first paragraph of this chapter.

[25] Jan Palmowski, 'Liberalism and Local Government in Late Nineteenth-Century Germany and England', *Historical Journal* 45 (2002), pp. 381–409; Martin Daunton (ed.), *The Cambridge Urban History of Britain*, vol. 3, *1840–1950* (Cambridge, 2000); Harrison, *Transformation of British Politics*, pp. 114–32; P. J. Waller, *Town, City and Nation: England 1850–1914* (Oxford, 1983); E. P. Hennock, *Fit and Proper Persons: Ideal and Reality in Nineteenth-Century Urban Government* (London, 1973). See also the classic Kingsley Smellie, *A History of Local Government* (London, 1946).

[26] Palmowski, 'Liberalism and Local Government', p. 381.

role, largely by means of public display and ritual.[27] As much of their pride and prosperity depended on shipbuilding, shipping and trade, it was hardly surprising that these cities turned to naval celebrations as one of the most important avenues for self-representation.[28] The strong civic and urban culture made up of local government, business, education, as well as voluntary and private initiatives, became a major influence for the celebration of the navy and the sea. Festivities and functions, receptions and speeches, balls and dinners, visits and excursions: all these layers of celebration were organized and financed by local society. Schools regularly granted holidays to mark ship launches.[29] Children presented bouquets of flowers and pupils sang hymns. Local charities and citizens' committees organized gifts and entertainment for officers and sailors. Mayors gave speeches, hosted dinners and invited their important guests to visit local sights such as town halls, museums, theatres or universities.[30] The rise of the naval theatre can hardly be understood without taking this 'local organism' into account.[31]

The key role played by the 'local factor' is particularly well illustrated by the 1895 inauguration of the *Kaiser-Wilhelm-Kanal*. The Hamburg Senate decided early on that this should be a celebration of Hamburg as much as an imperial and naval pageant. As Johann Georg Mönckeberg, one of the most prominent Senators of the 1890s and 1900s, pointed out in his diary, this was a key event for the Senate, which occupied itself with the preparations for weeks.[32] It was important that the dignitaries and diplomats invited for the maiden voyage through the new canal should be publicly connected with Hamburg rather then simply pass through the city on their way to the canal's lock at Brunsbüttel. The Senate therefore invited close to 5,000 guests to a dinner on 19 June, the evening before the

---

[27] Jennifer Jenkins, *Provincial Modernity: Local Culture and Liberal Politics in Fin-de-Siècle Hamburg* (Ithaca, 2003); H. Glenn Penny, *Objects of Culture: Ethnology and Ethnographic Museums in Imperial Germany* (Chapel Hill, 2003), pp. 43–9; Maiken Umbach, 'A Tale of Second Cities: Autonomy, Culture and the Law in Hamburg and Barcelona in the Long Nineteenth Century', *American Historical Review* 110 (2005), pp. 659–92; Jörgen Bracker, 'Das Hanseatische Bürgertum und seine Repräsentanten', in Plagemann, *Übersee*, pp. 238–43.

[28] On Hamburg's industrial expansion and the resonance the navy found in the Hanseatic city see Richard J. Evans, *Death in Hamburg: Society and Politics in the Cholera Years, 1830–1910* (Oxford, 1987), pp. 28–33.

[29] *Glasgow Evening News*, 1 May 1911; *Daily Express*, 2 Feb 1911.

[30] For a flavour of such arrangements see BA, R901/ 2864: Programm für die Reise S. M. des Kaisers und Königs nach Wilhelmshaven, Helgoland, Bremen im März 1908; BA, R43/955, Bl. 98: Programm für die Reise Ihrer Majestäten nach Kiel im März 1911.

[31] 'Local organism' as a description of local civil society was first coined by George Dawson in his address at the opening of the first public library in Birmingham in 1861, cf. Hennock, *Fit and Proper Persons*, pp. 75–6.

[32] StA Hamburg, 622-1 Mönckeberg 21a, Bl. 285.

canal was to be inaugurated. The town hall's *Großer Saal* was restored especially for the occasion, 'at great cost' as Mönckeberg observed.[33] The newspapers noted approvingly that the rich decoration of the hall included the arms of those cities that had been part of the Hanseatic League. While dining in the hall, the guests would marvel at the imagery depicting Hamburg's central role in the nation's historic mission to conquer the the sea.[34]

To extend the city's role in the celebrations further the Senate commissioned the construction of an artificial island in the middle of the *Binnenalster*, which was to be visited by the Kaiser and his entourage. The original plan to erect an imitation of Frederick I's *Sanssouci* castle on the island had to be abandoned for engineering reasons. The final version instead evoked an eclectic combination of maritime themes. Called *Alsterinsel*, *Kaiserinsel* or *Aegir-Insel* in the press, it came complete with fake cliffs, a lighthouse and a triumphal arch made out of two massive whalebones.[35] At night, it was illuminated with the help of six light masts. During the Kaiser's visit it was the site of a series of firework displays and a Venetian carnival, providing a spectacle, the *Hamburger Nachrichten* noted, 'unlike anything the world has seen'.[36] After the festivities, the *Eintagswunder*, as *Die Zukunft* dubbed the island, was dismantled. The lights, fake rocks and whalebones were auctioned off. Two years later it emerged how much the spectacle had cost. For the festivities Hamburg's Senate had burdened the city's budget with 585,159 marks;[37] the island in the Alster had cost 160,000 marks.[38] It was the singularly most expensive stage prop the city had ever funded for a public celebration. Together with the dinner, reception, presentations and fireworks, the *Alsterinsel* was part of a strategy to encourage as many dignitaries as possible to spend as much time as possible in the city. It was a remarkable exercise in appropriating the naval theatre for local and civic agendas. Here and at numerous other occasions, the fleet appeared less as a

---

[33] Ibid. The *Hamburger Fremdenblatt* reported on 19 July 1897 that the renovation had cost 129,900 marks.

[34] *Hamburger Fremdenblatt*, 11 June 1895, Hauptblatt. Compare the section 'The renaissance of the Hanseatic League' in Chapter 4. On the 1895 celebrations see also Kai Detlev Sievers, 'Staatliche Feiern als dramatische Handlungen: Grundsteinlegung und Eröffnung des Nord-Ostsee-Kanals 1887 und 1895', *Mitteilungen des Canal-Vereins* 9 (1988), pp. 105–39 and the special issue *Kanaleröffnung 1895* of the *Mitteilungen der Gesellschaft für Kieler Stadtgeschichte* 79 (1995).

[35] The details are recorded in StA Hamburg, 331-3, S4875.

[36] *Hamburger Nachrichten*, 14 June 1895, Hauptblatt.

[37] *Hamburger Fremdenblatt*, 19 July 1897, Hauptblatt.

[38] *Die Zukunft*, 15 June 1895, p. 527; *Hamburger Fremdenblatt*, 12 July 1895, Zweites Beiblatt.

monarchical symbol and more as the expression of the key role played by the middle classes and the urban and industrial elite. As Hamburg's Burgomaster Burchard put it, launches of warships were public displays of the 'confident German bourgeoisie'.[39]

The 'local factor' played a similarly prominent role on the other side of the North Sea. The Lord Mayor and the Corporation of London were especially active in sponsoring and initiating many festivities celebrating navy, nation and the City. The most striking example was the fleet's visit to the Thames in July 1909, described at the opening of Chapter 1. It was on the Lord Mayor's invitation that the fleet came to town and staged the most widely attended maritime spectacle of this period.[40] And it was the Corporation that footed the bill for the festivities.[41] The dinners and visits, naval shows and parades celebrated London and the City as much as the navy and the nation. This sentiment was expressed in an artefact that the Corporation saw as particularly symbolic for the fleet's visit to London: Nelson's Monument, erected in the Guildhall in 1810. Not only did the official programmes and even the menu cards for the reception refer to the monument, but the seating arrangements in the Guildhall were made in such a way as to ensure that as many officers and ratings as possible could see it directly.[42] The monument evokes Nelson's triumphs and shows his tomb, flanked by Neptune, Britannia and her lion. The central figure, however, is an allegory of the City of London, overtowering Britannia and Neptune, and writing the names Nile, Copenhagen and Trafalgar on Nelson's tomb – an expression of the active role that the Corporation claimed for itself in the naval past. It was this role, as much as the navy and the nation, which was being celebrated in July 1909.[43]

[39] StA Hamburg, 132-1 I, 2282. The key role to which the Hanseatic cities aspired in the naval theatre was underlined by the privileges they acquired in the ceremonial of ship launches, documented in BA-MA, RM3/118, Bl. 41–8. In Hamburg this went as far as establishing a separate *Senatorentribüne*. This special stand, dedicated solely to the representation of the Hanseatic Senators, was situated close to the ritual epicentre marked by the launching platform. It was a most visible reminder of Hamburg's central role in the spectacle, of its civic, bourgeois and commercial pride. On the extent to which the Hanseatic cities were prepared to finance the celebrations accompanying ship launches see Chapter 1. Mark Russell, 'The Building of Hamburg's Bismarck Memorial, 1898–1906', *Historical Journal* 43 (2000), pp. 133–56 has emphasized the role of the 'local organism' similarly, see esp. p. 135.
[40] Hansard, Fifth Series, House of Commons, vol. 7, cl. 23 (28 June 1909).
[41] CLRO, Common Council Minutes and Reports 1909, report no. 54, p. 16.
[42] Ibid.: Plan Showing Arrangements of Tables in Guildhall on the Occasion of the Reception of the Men of the Fleet, Wednesday, 21 July, 1909.
[43] CLRO, Visit of the Men of the Fleet to the Guildhall, Wednesday, July 21, 1909, souvenir menu card. For another example see the role that the City claimed for itself at fleet reviews, documented in ADM 179/60, pp. 128–31. The Corporation even

The key part played by local, civic and commercial initiative, symbolized by Nelson's Monument in the Guildhall, was not limited to the capital or to the South of England. The expanding industrial cities of the North were equally keen to have their share in the public celebration of the navy. One of the most striking examples took place in August 1912 when Glasgow celebrated the centenary of the launch of Henry Bell's *Comet*, the first commercial steamship in British waters. The special guests invited for the occasion were representative of local and national, commercial and naval contexts: Prime Minister Asquith and the leading ranks of the Admiralty, including First Lord Winston Churchill, took part, as well as twenty-four MPs, a host of shipbuilders and shipping magnates, Scottish peers, knights and deputy lieutenants.[44] The initiative for the festivities lay with Glasgow City Chambers, the Lord Provost and a vast number of civic and commercial committees.[45] Early on, the Executive Committee chaired by the Lord Provost had resolved that the Royal Navy should be represented strongly in the festivities. After some lobbying, the Admiralty agreed to participate in a 'review' of naval and merchant vessels. It sent a detachment of eleven ships. Headed by HMS *Hercules*, the flagship of Vice-Admiral Sir John Jellicoe, the battleships, cruisers and destroyers assembled off Greenock in the Clyde and anchored next to the ocean liners, yachts, dredgers and barges which were also part of the festivities.[46] As the climax of the *Comet* Centenary, an official party headed by the Lord Provost inspected this fleet of civic, commercial and naval vessels on 31 August 1912, which was declared a general holiday in the towns on the Clyde. At the heart of the *Comet* celebrations was thus the symbolic merging of naval and national with local representation. It had been instigated and organized by the Glasgow City chambers rather than by radical leagues or central government.[47]

attempted to have the City represented with its own vessel in the royal procession through the lines of warships: PRO, ADM 1/7336B: Memorandum by Secretary of the Admiralty, 3 June 1897.

[44] Glasgow City Archives, G 2/1/8: 'Comet' Centenary, 1912. See also *London Illustrated News*, 7 Sept 1912, special supplement.

[45] The list of 'Public Bodies Co-operating in Celebration' in the official programme took up nine pages. It included a large number of county and town councils, the Clyde Navigation Trust, the Greenock Harbour Trust, Glasgow University, Glasgow Merchants' House, the Royal Technical College, the Glasgow Shipowners' Association, the Glasgow Trade House and the West of Scotland Iron and Steel Institute. See *Celebration of Centenary of Launch of Steamer Comet, Built for Henry Bell: Official Programme, 29th, 30th, and 31st August, 1912* (Glasgow, 1912), pp. 27–40.

[46] *Map of the River and Firth of Clyde from Glasgow to Greenock with Reference to "Comet" Centenary Celebration, August, 1912* (Glasgow, 1912).

[47] This is underlined by the correspondence and discussion documented in Glasgow City Archives, G 1/1/17: Lord Provost to Secretary of the Admiralty, 1 Aug 1912; *Minutes of*

The impressive variety of initiatives taken at local level defies categorization in the terms suggested by the debate about manipulation and self-mobilization. The 'local organism' was neither orchestrated by national governments nor mobilized by the 'radical right'. It does not fit neatly into the dichotomy of 'above' and 'below'. Rather, local civic and commercial culture was a driving force in itself. Even if the naval theatre was intended by the Admiralty and the *Reichsmarineamt* to be a modern form of 'bread and circuses', it was just as much shaped by other actors with different agendas. Of these, the naval leagues were much less significant than has been previously thought. Rather, it was the 'local organism' in combination with the forces of modern media, consumerism and transport, which gave the naval spectacle its expanding and socially inclusive character. At the heart of the naval theatre was not one source of agency, be it government initiative or the 'radical right', but a dynamic relationship between a number of actors, local and national, official and private, commercial and governmental, who shaped the celebration of the navy. None of them was in a position solely to determine the character of this public theatre.

Going to the games

How did wider audiences participate in this public theatre? Was it 'bread and circuses' for them? The 'general public', composed of vastly different backgrounds, interests and motivations, was to be found inside the perimeter of official sites as well as outside, at informal locations that were not usually controlled by police, nor paraded by soldiers.[48] Upholding the boundary between the crowds of spectators and the specially invited guests could be difficult. In 1897, the Portsmouth naval station introduced a policy of closing the dockyard at particular intervals in the hours before fleet reviews. 'So many persons tried to gain

---

the *Corporation of Glasgow*, Nov 1911–April 1912, pp. 1249–57, 2285–93. On the key role played by the 'local organism' see also the visit of the ships *Glasgow*, *Bristol* and *Lane*, documented in PRO, ADM 1/8215 and the *Glasgow Herald*, 29 April 1911, and Corporation of Liverpool, *Liverpool Naval Exhibition, 1892* (Liverpool, 1892). Local governments kept careful records detailing the etiquette and privileges observed at these occasions. Many of them were published by the local press, creating a ritual calendar. The newspapers in Barrow-in-Furness, for example, printed a 'Complete List of Previous Launches' at the occasion of each ship launch (see *North-Western Daily Mail*, 29 April 1911).

[48] For a detailed police report on such an informal space see StA Hamburg, 331-1I, no. 715, Bl. 13–7: Polizeibehörde, Abteilung IV (Polizeiwachtdienst), District III, Bez[irk] Stadt, 13 Oct 1899. See also StA Bremen, VIII.F.31, Nr. 22, Anlage 1, Bl. 33: AG 'Weser' to Polizei-Direktion, 18 April 1902. For the idea of 'the general public' see *Illustrated Chronicle* (Newcastle), 21 March 1912 and *Times*, 19 June 1905.

admittance', explained the Superintendent of the Dockyard Police, 'that I found it necessary to suspend the admission of ordinary visitors during the forenoon', lest control over the situation should be lost.[49] In December 1900, the head of police in Bremen instructed his subordinates 'to put up sufficient crowd barriers', since they had been overpowered by the masses at the last launch; so much so, in fact, that the invited guests had not been able to get through.[50] Amongst other dignitaries, the President of the Bremen *Bürgerschaft* had been forced to leave his motor-car and 'walk the last metres'.[51] In April 1902, Tirpitz wrote to the Bremen Senate and the Head of Police, demanding more rigorous law enforcement during launches.[52] In the hours before the launch of SMS *München* in April 1904, the crowds had become so overwhelming that the AG 'Weser' yard had to telephone the police headquarters, urging them to 'immediately' send more men to gain control over the masses of spectators.[53] At the 1904 combined army and navy parade in Hamburg, police and military proved 'powerless against the pushing masses' and were forced to call in the fire brigade to use water cannons against them.[54] Controlling the crowds was still a problem in January 1909 when the Bremen police introduced yet new measures to keep the masses of spectators separate from the space reserved for privileged participants at the core of naval celebrations.[55]

If keeping the audience physically within its boundaries was problematic enough, communicating with 'the crowd' was even more difficult. Dignitaries such as Hamburg's Burgomaster Mönckeberg flattered themselves that the masses of spectators could hear their ceremonial utterances:

When we arrived at Blohm & Voss in the imperial launch incredible masses of people had assembled there. The ironclad [*der Panzer*] was situated close to the floating dock, and the vast space around it was black with people. I had to climb a very steep staircase and stood high above the masses, so that I thought at first that one would not be able to hear me. The gigantic hull to the right of me must have

---

[49] PRO, ADM 179/55: Superintendent, Metropolitan Police H. M. Dockyard Portsmouth, to Commander-in-Chief Portsmouth, 2 July 1897.

[50] StA Bremen, VIII.F.31, Nr. 22, Bl. 1: Bericht Ostermann, Anmerkung Polizei Direktor, 1 Dec 1900.

[51] StA Bremen, VIII.F.31, Nr. 22, Bl. 7–8: Präsident der Bürgerschaft, 22 March 1902; Bericht des Schutzmann Niemann, 24 March 1902.

[52] StA Bremen, VIII.F.31, Nr. 22, Bl. 17: Staatssekretär RMA to Senatskommission, 2 April 1902.

[53] StA Bremen, VIII.F.31, Nr. 22, Anlage 3: Telephonische Mitteilung AG 'Weser', 30 April 1904, 3.30 Uhr.

[54] *Hamburgischer Correspondent*, 6 Sept 1904, Abend-Ausgabe.

[55] StA Bremen, VIII.F.31, Nr. 22, Anlage 8, Bl. 25; *Bremer Nachrichten*, 25 Jan 1909; *Bremer Nachrichten*, 9 July 1903, Erstes Blatt.

acted like a sounding board, so that people understood every word even at a far distance.[56]

Yet, given that these acts were performed in the open air and without the help of microphones, it is very unlikely that anyone apart from those in the inner circle would have been able to understand what was being said. The only way in which the more distant audiences could be informed was indirectly, through the guides and programmes sold in advance and through special announcements in the newspapers. Here, spectators were told what to expect and were advised how the masters of ceremony wished them to participate. Yet, they did not always go along with such instructions. Singing and cheering could erupt at points when protocol prescribed silence. Instead of orchestrated acclamation there could be unregulated noise and shouting. As the *Hampshire Telegraph* noted with disbelief at the launch of the *Orion* in 1910, the call to cheer the ship's patron went unheard, as the audience of around 40,000 spectators had started to talk amongst themselves.[57] There were thus clearly limits to the extent to which the audience could be 'educated' about how to behave at these occasions. Often enough, the ways in which spectators behaved stood in contrast to or even openly contradicted official intentions. Any strategy of 'bread and circuses' had to contend with important obstacles imposed by 'the masses' themselves.

This becomes particularly clear when first-hand accounts of those in 'the crowd' are considered. The police reports that have survived in German archives are particularly important here. They are part of the genre uncovered by Richard Evans, who has made the pub conversations of Hamburg workers famous.[58] Called *Vigilanzberichte* or *Straßenberichte*, they record the views and opinions of workers, shopkeepers and craftsmen as overheard by secret police. For the naval theatre, these sources are particularly insightful. In the days before any large public ceremony, undercover police officers visited pubs and other public places in order to glean the views and opinions of workers, shopkeepers and craftsmen. Their observations were recorded in reports intended to give the authorities a picture of popular sentiment and to warn them of potential disturbances. Yet, the sources used for this chapter extend significantly beyond such *Stimmungsberichte*. They also include the records kept by undercover police who were employed at naval celebrations themselves. Plain-clothes officers regularly stood amongst the crowds. Under

[56] StA Hamburg, 622–1, Mönckeberg 21a, Bl. 291.
[57] *Hampshire Telegraph*, 26 Aug 1910.
[58] Richard J. Evans, *Kneipengespräche im Kaiserreich. Die Stimmungsberichte der Hamburger Politischen Polizei 1892–1914* (Reinbek/Hamburg, 1989).

instructions to prevent any disturbances and to look out for potential anarchists and revolutionaries, these undercover officers watched the audiences rather than the spectacle. Afterwards they documented what they had seen and heard, recording if and how they had had to intervene. There could be a personal bias in this, since these reports testified not only about the behaviour of crowds, but also indirectly about whether the officers writing them had fulfilled their duty well. But, if treated with the necessary caution, these files provide a unique perspective into the views of ordinary participants, in particular working-class and lower middle-class audiences.[59]

The Labour politicians and Social Democrats who saw in the naval theatre a modern form of 'bread and circuses' were adamant that workers and comrades should abstain from going to fleet reviews and ship launches. Yet, while the *Labour Leader*'s 'Marxian' was proud that he had 'stayed at home and read *Don Quixote*' during the 1902 coronation fleet review,[60] there is little doubt that large numbers of workers went to see the naval theatre, in particular launches of warships. These were acts that struck a chord with many of them. It was here, as the socialist *Hamburger Echo* put it, that workers could see 'the fruit of their labour' draped in 'festive ornament'.[61] When the Hamburg police eavesdropped on pub conversations in the weeks before the opening of the Kiel Canal, they found that many amongst the working class and lower middle-class audiences felt that they had an economic interest in such public rituals. Police officer Bürow noted that there was an expectation in the pubs he had visited 'that shops, craftsmen and workers will make a decent profit out of the festivities'.[62] After the celebrations, officers recorded similar voices. 'Had it not been for this work, many people would walk around without employment', was the opinion of patrons frequenting the *Destillation Rudolf*, as reported by officer Sackmann on 21 June 1895. There was much hope, he wrote, that such public celebrations would be staged more frequently, so that more workers and artisans would be employed during the preparations.[63]

[59] See Evans, *Kneipengespräche*, pp. 7–39, for a detailed methodological discussion.
[60] *Labour Leader*, 16 Aug 1902, p. 257.
[61] *Hamburger Echo*, 11 June 1911, Hauptblatt. Shipyard workers were usually given half a day off work to watch launches. See *Hamburger Echo*, 19 Oct 1899 and Hansard, Fifth Series, House of Commons, vol. 8, cl. 239–40 (19 July 1909).
[62] StA Hamburg, 331-3, S4875: Bericht Bürow, 2 March 1895. Officer Graumann made similar observations six weeks later, see StA Hamburg, 331-3, S4875: Bericht Graumann, 13 April 1895.
[63] StA Hamburg, 331-3, S4875: Bericht Sackmann, 22 June 1895. See also Bericht Voigt, 2 March 1895.

Indeed, some workers showed open admiration for the high personages at the centre of public rituals. British newspapers noted that workers had spontaneously greeted Churchill and other Admiralty leaders with ovations and cheering at the launch of the *Iron Duke* in October 1912.[64] The Hamburg police even recorded a peculiar case of emperor worship. Police officer Szymanski reported:

On Wednesday, 23 May 1912, when His Majesty approached the imperial enclosure at the Vulcan yard for the ship launch, a man who had stood in a group of workers suddenly, without me being able to prevent this, kneeled down, took his cap off, crossed himself, and bowed repeatedly in front of His Majesty. An officer of the harbour police, who stood close, took the man aside who stated that he had only intended to show reverence to His Majesty. This was a custom in Bukowina, where he was from. He had not been aware that he was not allowed to practise this custom here.[65]

Yet, there were just as many instances in which officers recorded disagreement and opposition, both in pub conversations and at naval celebrations themselves. Workers repeatedly made fun of what they called *Spießbürger*, the petit bourgeoisie, and their eagerness to display enthusiasm for the naval theatre.[66] Patrons of workers' pubs were recorded as regarding the naval pomp and ceremony as a waste of money. Police officer Graumann reported that workers were lamenting the '*Mordskosten*' caused by ship launches and fleet reviews.[67] The sums spent on the celebration of the navy and the emperor stood in stark contrast to the fact that many workers were made redundant after ship launches. As officer Lehmann reported from August Knibbe's pub in April 1914, workers saw ship launches often as symbolic events marking the loss of jobs. If there was no new ship to be laid down, a launch meant that many of the workers would have to 'pack their bags'.[68]

Moreover, workers often understood ship launches as a solemn rather than celebratory occasion at which to commemorate friends and fellow workers who had died in accidents while working on the particular ship. When the *Imperator* was launched in 1912, there were many workers

---

[64] *Evening News and Southern Daily Mail*, 12 Oct 1912.
[65] StA Hamburg, 331-3, S18765: Bericht Szymanski, 24 May 1912. An incident with similar religious undertones, albeit less spontaneous, was recorded by the Kaiser in *Ereignisse und Gestalten*, p. 38–9.
[66] StA Hamburg, 331-3, S4875: Bericht Jochum, 11 June 1895; ibid.: Bericht Graumann, 11 June 1895. On Hamburg's social structure in the late nineteenth century see Evans, *Death in Hamburg*, pp. 52–4.
[67] StA Hamburg, 331-3, S4875: Bericht Graumann, 13 April 1895.
[68] StA Hamburg, 331-1, S1154: Bericht Lehmann, 11 May 1914, who had been recording conversations between Blohm & Voss workers in August Knibbe's pub on 9 April 1914.

who gave the occasion a distinct *Eigensinn*. They participated not in the way that protocol prescribed, but according to their own sense of occasion: they mourned for the ten fellow workers who had died and the hundred or so who had been injured during the building of the ship.[69] Such symbolic acts constituted a layer of appropriation that was independent from official ceremonial. By insisting on their own reading and creating alternative rituals, workers could give this public theatre a meaning that was radically different from official messages and outside the control of the supposed masters of ceremony.

While such acts of *Eigensinn* were mostly quiet displays of disagreement, public rituals could also be sites for the direct, organized expression of opposition. Hamburg police reports are replete with conversations between workers voicing their dissatisfaction with the conditions in shipyards, in particular at Blohm & Voss. Officer Noroschat wrote in 1907:

> On Monday, 14 October [. . .] I visited the pub owned by Hermann Drews. Five guests were present. A locksmith apprentice complained bitterly about the Blohm & Voss yard and said the following: I have to advise everyone never to enter these slave huts [*Sklavenbuden*].

Conditions at Blohm & Voss were 'just like at the army, but the treatment and the whole system is much worse'.[70] Other reports recorded workers lamenting 'the low payment and the treatment which workers receive' and the 'bad working conditions'.[71] *Schutzmann* Laatsch, who had repeatedly observed Blohm & Voss workers, reported: 'There is a large number of discontent elements [*unzufriedener Elemente*] at Blohm & Voss'.[72] Ship launches provided public sites where such discontent could be acted out. At the launch of the *Kaiser Karl der Große*, on 18 October 1899, for example, workers at Blohm & Voss staged a protest against the management, with the plain-clothes police too slow to intervene. Watched by the Kaiser and Hamburg's Burgomaster Mönckeberg, the workers took the sandwiches that had been prepared for them and threw them at the company's director.[73]

[69] *Deutsche Böttcher Zeitung* (Bremen), 1 June 1912. On the concept of *Eigensinn* see Alf Lüdtke, 'Organisational Order or *Eigensinn*? Workers' Privacy and Workers' Politics in Imperial Germany', in Sean Wilentz (ed.), *Rites of Power: Symbolism, Ritual and Politics since the Middle Ages* (Philadelphia, 1985), pp. 303–33 and Alf Lüdtke, *Eigen-Sinn. Fabrikalltag, Arbeitererfahrung und Politik vom Kaiserreich bis in den Faschismus* (Hamburg, 1993).
[70] StA Hamburg, 331-1, S1154: Bericht Noroschat, 15 Oct 1907.
[71] StA Hamburg, 331-3, S1154: Bericht Szymanski, 23 May 1908; Bericht Noroschat, 15 Oct 1907; Bericht Ranning, 16 Oct 1905; Bericht Kramer, 7 July 1905.
[72] StA Hamburg, 331-3, S1154: Bericht Laatsch, 6 Dec 1904; similar example on 17 Dec 1904.
[73] StA Hamburg, 331-3, S1154: Bericht Erxleben, 19 Oct 1899.

There were also symbolic gestures of defiance from parts of the audience towards particular political personalities, including the Kaiser. A striking example was recorded by Hamburg's *Politische Polizei* at the launching of the *Imperator*, then the largest and most luxurious ocean liner. Wilhelm II was closely associated with this symbol of the *Kaiserreich*'s power and progress. Scores of police and soldiers were lined up when he arrived for the christening of the *Imperator* at the Vulcan dockyard on 23 May 1912. Yet, when he entered the site, there was a quiet, but effective, show of opposition, which the police could do little to stop. Officers recorded: 'The workers of the Vulcan yard did not lift their hats nor did they cheer when His Majesty passed'.[74] Defying imperial protocol and social etiquette, the workers of the Vulcan yard put their disagreement on record in a public gesture that was aimed both at the emperor and the wider audience. They quite literally acted out their opposition against the Kaiser, despite the strong presence of uniformed and undercover police. Clearly, the naval theatre could, at least at a number of documented occasions, be a site for the enactment of a 'counter public' or a *Gegenöffentlichkeit*.[75]

There were thus significant limits to any official strategies aimed at the 'mobilization of the masses'. Not even the large numbers of police attending these occasions were in a position to completely control the behaviour of spectators. Strikingly diverse attitudes and forms of participation existed amongst the 'general public'. This could range from admiration and acclamation to disagreement and defiance. Certainly, there were the signs that are often quoted as indicators for 'naval enthusiasm': the cheering and waving, the lifting of hats and the children wearing sailor suits. Yet, there were also forms of behaviour that ran contrary to official intentions, and there were symbolic gestures of opposition. To attend public rituals did not necessarily mean agreement with those staging it or an acquiescence to their policies. In fact, in a number of cases significant

---

[74] StA Hamburg, 331-3, S18765: Bericht Szymanski, 24 May 1912, attachment. Not dissimilar was the ostentatious refusal of British workers to drink to the King's health during the 1911 coronation, as recorded by the *Labour Leader*, 30 June 1911.

[75] However, this never reached the scale or the degree of orchestration seen at Sedan celebrations, on which see Wolfgang Hardtwig, 'Nationsbildung und politische Mentalität. Denkmal und Fest im Kaiserreich', in Wolfgang Hardtwig, *Geschichtskultur und Wissenschaft* (Munich, 1990), pp. 264–301, here 287–90; Alon Confino, *The Nation as a Local Metaphor: Württemberg, Imperial Germany, and National Memory, 1871–1918* (Chapel Hill and London, 1997), chs. 2–4; Ute Schneider, 'Einheit ohne Einigkeit: der Sedantag im Kaiserreich', in Sabine Behrenbeck and Alexander Nützenadel (eds.), *Inszenierungen des Nationalstaats. Politische Feiern in Italien und Deutschland seit 1860/71* (Cologne, 2000), pp. 27–44 and Gerhard Birk, 'Der Tag von Sedan. Intentionen, Resonanz und Widerstand (1871–1895)', *Jahrbuch für Volkskunde und Kulturgeschichte* 25 (1982), pp. 95–110.

numbers of spectators attended in order to voice their dissatisfaction or opposition.

Technology and entertainment

Yet this does not explain why so many went to the naval theatre. Hundreds of thousands regularly attended ship launches, millions came to see fleet reviews. Critical observers invariably explained this high turnout by referring to the sense of spectacle and sensation that these occasions offered. What made the naval stage so 'seductive and intoxicating', wrote the *Hamburger Echo*, was that it appealed to people's liking for spectacle.[76] 'The gaping masses are easily swayed', it complained in September 1904, when a combined naval and military parade attracted over 500,000 spectators to Hamburg.[77] Naval and military displays seemed to have a magic, quasi-religious attraction for people, the *Echo* wrote in 1912, offering the Krishna cult in ancient India as a comparison. With an obvious dislike for such irrational motives, the *Echo* labelled the naval theatre *ein begafftes Spektakulum*, a 'gaped-at spectaculum'.[78]

The lust for sensation that critics found so objectionable needs to be examined more closely. It deserves to be taken seriously as a key attraction at work in the naval theatre. The first-hand accounts in diaries, notebooks, letters, reports and telegrams convey a strong sense of visual fascination: to see a dreadnought of unprecedented size slowly slip into the water; to watch hundreds of warships proceed to sea in battle formation; to view the fleet illuminated, with searchlights beaming and fireworks burning. 'It was a grand sight',[79] 'how vast to the eye',[80] 'it must have looked grand from the beach',[81] were typical descriptions. 'A magnificent sight' and 'a beautiful sight' was how George V put it in his

---

[76] *Hamburger Echo*, 11 Sept 1904, Erstes Beiblatt. See also *Hamburger Echo*, 9 Sept 1904, Hauptblatt.

[77] *Hamburger Echo*, 10 Sept 1904, Hauptblatt. For the number of spectators see the police estimate in StA Hamburg, 331-3, S12440 and *Hamburger Neueste Nachrichten*, 7 Sept 1904, Beiblatt.

[78] *Hamburger Echo*, 26 May 1912. For similar examples see *Labour Leader*, 16 Aug 1902 (leading article by Keir Hardie) and *Labour Leader*, 23 June 1911.

[79] Churchill Archives, BGGF, 1/62: Captain Sir Bryan Godfrey-Faussett, private diary, 24 June 1911. Admiral Dudley de Chair used the same words in his depiction of the 1914 fleet display *The Sea Is Strong* (London, 1961), p. 157.

[80] Frank Fox, *Ramparts of Empire: A View of the Navy from an Imperial Standpoint* (London, 1910), p. 100.

[81] RNM, 1997: James Colvill, 24 June 1911. Colvill was a junior officer on board HMS *Attentive*.

diary.[82] *Bild*, *Schauspiel*, *Anblick*, *Eindruck* are the recurrent terms that appear in German descriptions.[83] For the workers, shopkeepers and artisans whose conversations the police recorded, the sensation of *watching* was a prime reason why they and others went to reviews and launches. 'To see such a thing', the act of *beluken*, as one Hamburg worker called it idiomatically, was what made them go to naval and military displays.[84]

What exactly was the main attraction for spectators? For those at the heart of the naval theatre, the answer was clear: it was the ships themselves and the feats of engineering that they represented. Here is how the Kaiser described the experience:

A ship launch is both for the layman and the naval officer an imposing, I would say, a deeply moving act. The massive hull, the product of many considerations and calculations done by the devoted and restless work of the mind, and by many hundred straining hands, this construction is to be passed into its element.[85]

Lord Selborne, First Lord of the Admiralty, put it in similar, if more sober words: 'The launch of a battleship is always an interesting event, her mere passage into the water under the conditions imposed by modern science in itself conveying a profound impression'.[86] Such explanations should not be easily dismissed. There was indeed 'something strikingly impressive' about these displays of modern engineering.[87] The launching day marked the culmination point in the building process of a ship. A hull weighing tens of thousands of tons, sitting on a massive wooden cradle, was to slide into the water on greased slipways. Eduard Blohm, director of the Blohm & Voss shipyard, explained: 'The most dangerous moment comes when the hull has advanced approximately two thirds down the ways. If not enough water is displaced, the hull tries to tilt over its end'.[88]

---

[82] RA King George V's Diary, 26 June 1897; ibid., 16 Aug 1902; ibid., 7 Aug 1905.
[83] Moltke, *Erinnerungen*, 17 Sept 1912; Hopman, *Logbuch*, p. 373; Bogdan Graf von Hutten-Czapski, *Sechzig Jahre Politik und Gesellschaft*, vol. 1 (Berlin, 1936), p. 268; Groener, *Lebenserinnerungen*, p. 123; *Eulenburgs politische Korrespondenz*, vol. 3, p. 1510, nr. 1114: Eulenburg to Holstein, 22 June 1895; *Das Tagebuch der Baronin Spitzemberg. Aufzeichnungen aus der Hofgesellschaft des Hohenzollernreiches*, edited by Rudolf Vierhaus (Göttingen, 1960), p. 380. See also BA, R901/2865/1, vol. 3: Königlich Preußische Gesandtschaft in Mecklenburg und den Hansestädten to Bethmann Hollweg, 31 March 1912.
[84] StA Hamburg, 331-3, S12440, Bericht Ramming, 29 August 1904.
[85] Penzler, *Reden*, vol 2, p. 23 (address given after the launch of SMS *Kaiser Friedrich III*).
[86] *Times*, 21 Dec 1903 (after the launch of the *Hindustan*).
[87] *Portsmouth Evening News*, 10 Feb 1906 (at the launch of the *Dreadnought*).
[88] StA Hamburg, 622-1, Blohm, Nr. 2, p. 256. Similar: Dipl.-Ing. Willibald Vollrath, 'Von der Helling ins Wasser', *Die Flotte*, Nov 1909, pp. 164–5; *General-Anzeiger*, 5 April 1913: 'Stapellauf'; *Hamburger Nachrichten*, 18 June 1913: 'Die Technik des Stapellaufs'.

15. Technology and entertainment. Spectators at the launch of SMS *München* at the A G Weser yard, Bremen, 30 April 1904.

Massive drag chains, each weighing hundreds of tons, had to be in place to hold the hull in check when entering the water.[89] Ship launches could fail.[90] And they could end in tragedy. At the launch of the cruiser *Albion* in 1898, the backwash swept away a stage on which spectators had gathered, drowning fifty people.[91] When the *Imperator* was launched in June 1912, the launching cradle caught fire:

As a consequence of the immense compression [...] and the resulting high friction, the [launching] cradle starts to burn. But since all parts of it are pulled into the water with the hull, the fire is extinguished immediately.[92]

This sense of risk, excitement and visual fascination was at the heart of what made the naval theatre so 'seductive and intoxicating'.[93] Launches of warships and fleet reviews were events that allowed spectators a first-hand experience of the 'modern wonders' of technology.[94] Like the zeppelin and aeroplane, both of which were regularly included in naval displays, the navy was at the forefront of technological progress, provoking admiration and curiosity. The battleships of the Dreadnought era were icons of the rationality and efficiency of the machine age, evoking new experiences of space and time as well as novel forms of risk and 'the unknown'.[95]

The fascination with these symbols of modernity was heightened by the dramatic advances in shipbuilding. From 1898 to 1913, the length of capital battleships almost doubled and their displacement rose even at a

---

[89] The launch particulars recorded at shipyards provide ample evidence of the immense size of these operations. For a complete set see Cumbria Record Office, BDB 16/L/64–75: launch particulars of ships launched at Vickers, Barrow-in-Furness between 1889 and 1919. See also *Naval and Military Record*, 29 Aug 1907.

[90] In June 1913, the *Derfflinger* stubbornly refused to move down the ways, leaving admirals and dignitaries with an embarrassing non-event in front of tens of thousands of spectators. A comprehensive analysis of the *Derfflinger*'s failed launch is given in BA, R901, R901/2865/1: Blohm & Voss to RMA, 18 June 1913.

[91] *Times*, 21 June 1898 and 22 June 1898; *Schulthess*, p. 262.

[92] *Neue Hamburger Zeitung*, 1 June 1912.

[93] *Hamburger Echo*, 11 Sept 1904, Erstes Beiblatt. See also *Labour Leader*, 16 Aug 1902 (leading article by Keir Hardie) and *Labour Leader*, 23 June 1911. For examples of how the danger and fascination involved in ship launches was depicted in popular culture see Neudeck and Schröder, *Das kleine Buch von der Marine*, pp. 248–52 and Charles J. de Lacy, 'The Cost of Placing a Battleship in the Water', *Boy's Own Paper*, 15 Feb 1908, pp. 311–14.

[94] Bernhard Rieger, ' "Modern Wonders": Technological Innovation and Public Ambivalence in Britain and Germany, 1890s to 1933', *History Workshop Journal* 55 (2003), pp. 152–76.

[95] Stephen Kern, *The Culture of Space and Time, 1880–1918*, with a new preface (Cambridge, MA, and London, 2003); Michael Adas, *Machines as the Measure of Men: Science, Technology, and Ideologies of Western Dominance* (Ithaca and London, 1989). For a case study see Jan Rüger, 'Das U-Boot', in Geisthövel and Knoch (eds.), *Orte der Moderne*, pp. 259–69.

higher rate.[96] The ships travelling down the ways threatened to become too big for harbours and rivers. The backwash created when they entered the water posed an increasing risk to the safety of the audiences. Repeatedly, launching facilities and slipways had to be enlarged and security arrangements improved.[97] The strong sense of international competition that existed in shipbuilding was made all the more urgent by the unfolding of the Anglo-German naval race after the turn of the century. The escalation in the size, speed, and armament of ships was translated into ever more spectacular displays of technology and power. All of this was clearly on display when Prime Minister Asquith watched the 1912 fleet review. Returning from the event, which had for the first time included hydroplanes taking off from warships and landing on water, he told reporters: 'I have just come from witnessing a spectacle to which I suppose there has never been a parallel in the history of the world'.[98]

Nowhere was the visual fascination that the naval theatre provided more obvious than in the fleet illuminations. Already in 1887 the Admiralty had noted that the display of lights on a large scale was the most important element in achieving a 'general effect' on audiences.[99] It went to great trouble to secure this effect. The programme for the illuminations in 1887 had seventeen different sections, each a meticulous choreography of light display and fireworks. The spectacle took one hour, culminating in the hoisting of the illuminated letters 'V.R.' on each ship.[100] With the advent of the powerful steamships of the late nineteenth century, a new element was introduced into the illumination of the fleet, at once technological and creative. In what came to be known as 'the play of the searchlights', the electric searchlights of the modern battleships, designed to detect enemy vessels at night, were used like the floodlights in circuses or theatres. Again, this feature was pioneered in 1887. The Review Orders read like the choreography of a West End extravaganza:

---

[96] In Britain the length of capital warships rose from 390 feet (Canopus class) to 580 feet (Iron Duke class), the displacement from 12,950 to 25,000 tons. In Germany, the length rose from 377 feet (Kaiser Friedrich III class) to 580 feet (König class), the displacement from 10,474 to 26,575 tons. See NA (1914), plates 1–9, 31–7 and J. T. Sumida, 'The Royal Navy and Technological Change', in R. Haycock and K. Neilson (eds.), Men, Machines and War (Ontario, 1988), pp. 75–91.

[97] For the extensions of launch ways at Palmer and Armstrong see TWAS, Proceedings of the Tyne Improvement Commissioners 1911–1912 (Newcastle, 1912), pp. 566, 807–8. On the precautions taken against the increasing backwash see StA Bremen 4,14/1, VIII.F.31, Nr. 22 and StA Hamburg, 331-1I, 869 Stapellauf 'Vaterland', 3 April 1913.

[98] Daily Mail, 9 May 1912.

[99] PRO, ADM 1/6871: Commander-in-Chief Portsmouth to Secretary of the Admiralty, 31 May 1887.

[100] PRO, ADM 179/54: Programme for Illumination of Ships Taking Part in the Proposed Naval Review.

Three blasts on the siren to indicate that all ships are to search the shore with their searchlights outwards from the lines for ten minutes, then when the flagship inclines her lights upwards to do the same, the beams of their respective lights touching the beams of the lights of opposite ships thus to form an arch overhead.[101]

After the turn of the century, the 'play of the searchlights' became the most impressive part of naval performances, combining the show of power and technology with an artistic and playful element. In 1902, the creative minds at the Admiralty introduced colour into this nightly spectacle. Different makes of paint were tested before the Secretary of the Admiralty ordered the fleet to paint the protective glass of the searchlights with five different colours.[102] Judging by the response, the effect was spectacular. Observers spoke of the shining of 'streams of colour', and the Prince of Wales thought it was 'a beautiful effect'.[103] The press lauded the innovation in stagecraft. One correspondent wrote: 'Then the ships' funnels sent forth great clouds of smoke, and the searchlights being trained upon these produced a startlingly beautiful effect. The variations of the searchlights seemed endless.'[104] It was the Edwardian and Wilhelmine naval theatre that pioneered the decidedly modern genre of displaying power and technology through artificial light, a genre that was to become a standard feature of public rituals in the 1930s.[105]

Crucially, this display of technology and power could be experienced as a form of entertainment. The naval theatre was, as Henry Newbolt put it in his poem 'England', a 'game for man and boy'.[106] Fleet reviews and mock battles presented pictures of conflict and violence, but this was never divorced from a range of activities that involved mostly fun and amusement.[107] This is evident in most descriptions of the naval theatre. Reporting from Portsmouth in the days before the 1902 fleet review, the correspondent of the *Daily Express* felt 'haunted by a sense of holiday-making from the appearance of the crowds in the streets'.[108] At ship launches, too, a 'sense of holiday' was palpable.[109] Music, beer and 'well-stocked picnic baskets' were cited as main attractions.[110] At British launches, military and shipyard bands played 'popular waltzes' and 'lively

---

[101] Ibid.
[102] ADM 179/56, p. 312: Secretary of the Admiralty to Commander-in-Chief Portsmouth, 21 May 1902.
[103] RA King George V's Diary, 16 Aug 1902.
[104] *Naval and Military Record*, 21 Aug 1902. See also ADM 179/56, pp. 308–10, 802–5 and *Times*, 14 Aug 1902.
[105] Compare the section 'Technology, modernity and gender' in Chapter 4.
[106] Henry Newbolt, 'England', in Newbolt, *Island Race*, p. 78.
[107] Compare the section 'The rhetoric of rivalry' in Chapter 5.
[108] *Daily Express*, 15 Aug 1902.
[109] *Naval and Military Record*, 29 Aug 1907.   [110] Hopman, *Logbuch*, p. 29.

16. 'Illumination of a Warship in Kiel Harbour' (postcard). Note the illuminated crown and 'W' (for 'Wilhelm'), suspended between the two masts.

17. 'Greetings from Kiel'. Postcard depicting a searchlight display in
Kiel harbour.

airs' in the hours before the proceedings commenced, 'entertaining the
masses'.[111] The *Hamburgischer Correspondent* commented after the 1904
combined military and naval parade that the real spectacle had taken place
in the restaurants, pubs and shops.[112] For the inauguration of the Kiel
Canal a number of new brothels opened in Hamburg and Kiel. Surveying
the preparations for the festivities, the *Hamburger Echo* wrote in June 1895:
'The number of brothels in Kiel has risen by another three. In each of
them reside five girls who have to pay a rent of 12 to 18 marks per day and
room'.[113]

At the heart of the naval theatre there was, then, a peculiar combination
of popular entertainment, traditional pageantry and modern technology.
What defined its public appeal was partly an unprecedented visual and

---

[111] *Naval and Military Record*, 29 Aug 1907; *North-Western Daily Mail*, 22 Feb 1909;
Illustrated [Newcastle] Chronicle, 21 March 1912; *Evening News and Southern Daily
Mail*, 12 Oct 1912.

[112] *Hamburgischer Correspondent*, 5 Sept 1904.

[113] *Hamburger Echo*, 13 June 1895, Hauptblatt. See also *Vorwärts*, undated cutting, in StA
Hamburg, 331-3, S4875. For most of the ratings, the crucial aspect of fleet reviews was
the time off afterwards: RNM, 1980/115: Diary of petty officer Fletcher; RNM, 1988/
294: Diary of Robert Percival, p. 35.

genuinely modern spectacle that emphasized the novelty, efficiency and power of the vast machinery that was the navy. The 'language of modernism' that scholars have seen as created by the First World War was clearly pioneered earlier and perhaps most prominently here, in the naval theatre.[114] Yet this was never divorced from traditional pageantry, nor from popular forms of amusement and entertainment. This continuous ambiguity between 'modern' and 'traditional' impulses explains why the crowds were so keen 'to see these warships', as the Hamburg police officer Jochum put it in 1895.[115] The naval theatre offered unprecedented vistas of technology and power while simultaneously catering to the traditional 'ornamentalism' of pageantry and royal ritual.[116] It is mainly for this reason that fleet reviews and ship launches created such 'immense excitement'.[117]

A silent consensus?

Historians have pointed to the popular culture of entertainment and holidaymaking as evidence for the consensual and 'apolitical' character of public ritual.[118] If people enjoyed the naval theatre in a festive sense, was there not an underlying 'silent consensus' between the audiences and those staging this spectacle? The sources examined above shed considerable doubt on such a reading. Even if large parts of the audience cheered and enjoyed themselves, there were clearly others who expressed disagreement and opposition. Moreover, the public appearance of social harmony and political consensus that historians have stressed was all too orchestrated. Certainly, many of the spontaneous gestures such as the waving of handkerchiefs, the clapping and cheering, were genuine expressions of loyalty.[119] Yet, there is a danger here of taking such gestures at face value. Both locally and centrally, official strategies were in place

---

[114] Modris Ekstein, *Rites of Spring: The Great War and the Birth of the Modern Age* (London, 1989). On the critique of Ekstein's interpretation see Jay Winter, *Sites of Memory, Sites of Mourning: The Great War in European Cultural History* (Cambridge, 1995) and Jay Winter, Geoffrey Parker and Mary R. Habeck (eds.), *The Great War and the Twentieth Century* (New Haven, 2000).

[115] StA Hamburg, 331-3, S4875, Bericht Jochum, 16 June 1895.

[116] On the latter see David Cannadine, *Ornamentalism: How the British Saw Their Empire* (London, 2001).

[117] Heinrich Spies, *Das moderne England. Einführung in das Studium seiner Kultur. Mit besonderem Hinblick auf einen Aufenthalt im Lande* (Straßburg, 1911), p. 69.

[118] Paulmann, *Pomp und Politik*, p. 378; Vogel, *Nationen im Gleichschritt*, pp. 258–62.

[119] See BA-MA, RM 3/9958, Bl. 265 and GStA PK, Rep. 89, Nr. 32229, Bl. 7 for telegrams sent by members of the public to the navy or the Kaiser, congratulating and thanking them after ship launches and fleet reviews. RNM, 1986/422: J. H. P. Southby, 23 June 1911, has an evocative description of the enthusiasm shown by spectators.

that aimed at creating the image of popular support. Flag displays, swarms of cheering schoolchildren, the singing of anthems and burning of fireworks were standard features organized by city halls and special committees. It was regular practice for local administrations to publish notices in the press in advance, appealing to the public to show their enthusiasm and decorate the streets for visits and celebrations.[120] In Hamburg, the Senate's commission responsible for organizing the official side of ship launches and visits requested that all houses along the routes to be taken by dignitaries display flags. Similar appeals were made in British cities.[121]

The strong presence of police, both uniformed and undercover, helped further to stir positive responses from those who would otherwise have been less enthusiastic.[122] It also ensured that most forms of protest would be kept away from the centre of the celebrations. In Germany, police observed alleged anarchists and other 'suspicious individuals' in the weeks before naval events.[123] Whenever the monarch took part, additional special forces were detached from London or Berlin to 'regulate the crowds'.[124] Separate gates and routes ensured that there would be no overlapping between the workers' share in the ritual and that of the 'privileged persons'.[125] As the programme for the 1903 launch of the *Hessen* detailed: 'The workers of the Germania yard will find place next to Berth 1 and Berths 6 and 7. They will be cut off by fences from the route which the All Highest personages will take'.[126] At times, this separation was the object of bitter and sarcastic comment in the workers' press. 'It would of course be too bad if one of the well-dressed gentlemen or ladies

---

[120] StA Hamburg, 132-1I, 28 UA 1, Bl. 62: Note by the Senatskommission für die Reichs- und Auswärtigen Angelegenheiten to be published in newspapers.

[121] *Inside Asquith's Cabinet: From the Diaries of Charles Hobhouse*, edited by Edward David (London, 1977), p. 142.

[122] StA Hamburg, 331-3, S1154: Bericht Graumann, 29 May 1895.

[123] RM 3/188, Bl. 4: RMA to Direktor Carlson, Schichau-Werft, 19 Sept 1913, gives details of the standard police involvement. See also GStA PK, I. HA Rep. 77, Titel 872, Nr. 12, Bd. 1: Staatssekr. RMA Tirpitz an Staatsminister und Minister des Innern, Berlin, 17.10.1908; StA Hamburg, 331-3, S12440.

[124] PRO, MEPO 2/929: Undersecretary of State, Home Office, to Commissioner of Police of the Metropolis, 9 Feb 1906; StA Hamburg, 132-1 I, 2282, Bl. 97a: Resumée der Kommission; ibid., 331-3, S18765: Anordnung für die Anwesenheit des Kaisers; Polizei-Amt Altona to Vulkan, 10 May 1912.

[125] PRO ADM 179/52: Metropolitan Police at Portsmouth Base to Commander-in-Chief Portsmouth, not dated, but before 7 Aug 1909. See BA, R43/955: Situationsplan für den Stapellauf S. M. Linienschiff 'M' and the arrangements sketched in BA-MA, RM 31/1067, Bl. 213 and Bl. 228.

[126] BA-MA, RM 31/1067, Bl. 94–95: Programm für die Feier des Stapellaufes S. M. Linienschiff 'L', 18 Sept 1903.

were to be given a fright by the sight of a worker', wrote the *Hamburger Echo* in July 1911.[127]

Uniformed police were a visible deterrent, but workers particularly feared the secret police. There are reports of workers stating that they felt obliged to cheer and wave at these events – out of fear that they might otherwise be noted by the police. The workers in Hamburg mentioned in particular '*Angst vor der Criminalpolizei*' and a possible arrest for *lèse-majesté*.[128] The extent to which 'unruly elements' were closely monitored is illustrated by the case of Georg August Wilhelm Rutkowski, a worker at Blohm & Voss, who was to attend the Kaiser's visit to the shipyard on 16 December 1895. Hours before Wilhelm II was expected to arrive at the yard, Rutkowski mentioned to colleagues that he intended to speak to the Kaiser at the occasion. Plain-clothes detective Erxleben, instructed to spy on the yard's workers before the event, overheard this, followed Rutkowski and, pretending to be a fellow worker, entered into a conversation,

in which he explained to me that he had served in the 73rd infantry regiment and [that he had] injured his left arm permanently when he fell badly at a *Felddienstübung*. He had been dismissed without compensation and although he had written to the Kaiser a number of times he still had not received a response.[129]

Officer Erxleben suggested that Rutkowski write to the Kaiser again, as attempting to have a personal conversation with him would have 'an adverse effect'. Rutkowski then left the yard, being followed by undercover police to the nearby *Kaffeehalle*. When he mentioned to workers there that he would try to speak to the Kaiser, the police took him aside and told him that he would not be allowed back into the yard. Officer Erxleben followed Rutkowski for the next hours on his journey through Hamburg until the Kaiser had come and gone.[130] Such police surveillance meant that potential protest could in most cases be kept outside the boundaries of the official centre of the naval theatre. For this reason, strikes rarely affected launches of warships directly.[131] Similarly, when suffragettes tried in 1908 and again in 1909 to exploit the buzz around

[127] *Hamburger Echo*, 11 July 1911, Hauptblatt.
[128] StA Hamburg, 331-3, S1154: Bericht Graumann, 29 May 1895.
[129] StA Hamburg, 331-3, S5301: Bericht Erxleben, 17 Dec 1895.   [130] Ibid.
[131] In 1911 the launch of SMS *Friedrich der Große* had to be postponed because of labour disputes. Yet in most other cases, strikes had little impact. HMS *Falmouth* was launched in 1910 without the strike of boiler-makers and rivet-boys causing any disruption, and HMS *Queen Mary* was launched at Jarrow in the midst of the 1912 coal strike without any occurrences. See BA-MA, RM3/170, Bl. 23: Vulcan, Hamburg, to RMA; *Illustrated Chronicle*, 19 March 1912; *Scotsman*, 21 Sept 1910.

warship launches to further their cause, police made sure they would not reach the site of the spectacle. 'The police kept them in order', as the local newspaper put it.[132]

Yet the authorities went further in the staging of social harmony and political consensus. While 'suspicious elements' were observed and controlled, groups of 'official workers' were incorporated into the ritual itself. Socialist newspapers such as the *Hamburger Echo* called them *Mußpatrioten*, 'forced patriots', and *Staffage*, 'stage props'.[133] From the turn of the century, the official representation of workers was a standard feature at public naval displays both in Britain and Germany. Launches featured a designated space for *Arbeiterabordnungen* or an 'enclosure for workspeople'.[134] Careful selection ensured that these workers would be *brave deutsche Arbeiter*, as Wilhelm II put it.[135] The names of ticket holders for workers' enclosures were checked against lists of known agitators.[136] For the 1902 review, the Admiralty invited 206 selected workers on board one of the official ships sailing through the lines. This is how the Admiralty summarized the new feature:

It was with a view to giving the arrangements more of a national and representative character that it was thought very desirable to invite representatives (a stipulated proportion of whom must be foremen and workmen) from the leading gun-making, ship-building and manufacturing firms employed by the Admiralty. This idea was originated by Mr Arnold Foster [...]. A special steamer (the S. S. "Nubia") was chartered for their accommodation and partitioned off into three divisions, viz: (i) for Partners, Managers, etc. (ii) Foremen, etc. (iii) Working men, Employees. Different tickets were issued for each class to prevent mistakes occurring.[137]

Consider the display of social order on this special Admiralty steamer: with the different classes separated on different decks and the boundaries between them marshalled ('to prevent mistakes from occurring'), the *Nubia* was a floating image of the social ideal envisaged by the masters of ceremony in the Admiralty.

---

[132] *North-Western Daily Mail*, 22 Feb 1909. See also *Western Morning News*, 9 Nov 1908.

[133] *Hamburger Echo*, 15 Dec 1895, Hauptblatt; similarly: *Hamburger Echo*, 13 June 1895, Hauptblatt; 16 June 1895, Hauptblatt; 11 June 1903, Hauptblatt. The *Labour Leader* published similar claims on 16 Aug 1902 and 23 June 1911.

[134] *Jarrow Guardian*, 22 March 1912.

[135] *Ereignisse und Gestalten*, p. 39. See also his address to shipyard workers on 3 Aug 1900, recorded in Penzler, *Reden*, vol. 2, p. 224, where Wilhelm uses similar descriptions of the 'good worker', characterized by 'the good German spirit'.

[136] BA-MA, RM 3/176, Bl. 75–6: Regierungspräsident Kiel to RMA. In cases where workers were to be decorated, special investigations were conducted to ensure no Socialist members would be amongst them. This is particularily well recorded for the launch of the *Prinzregent*, see GStA PK: Rep. 89, Nr. 32228, Bl. 151 and Bl. 164: Staatssekretär RMA an Chef Marinekabinett, 13 Feb 1912.

[137] PRO, ADM 116/132.

The conversations recorded by the Hamburg police show that workers were keenly aware of such strategies aimed at creating an image of cohesion and consensus. In 1901, Hamburg police officer Graumann reported that many workers were wary that the naval theatre was designed 'to make the whole world think that the German people was as one for the creation of a strong fleet'.[138] Many of these workers attended ship launches, but they did not interpret their own participation as support for the Kaiser and a strong fleet.[139] If workers cheered or waved their caps, this could have a radically different motivation than the wish to express affirmation for those at the heart of spectacles. Officer Graumann reported a pub conversation on 29 May 1895 in which one worker had said:

One has to take into account that not only the patriotic public will take part in the celebration, but also the Social Democrats, who normally despise such festivities; they will be there in large numbers, mostly out of curiosity, and they will shout Hooray and Hey just like the best patriot, if only out of fear that they could otherwise be arrested by the *Criminalpolizei* for *lèse-majesté*.[140]

This conversation corroborates reports in the socialist, liberal and conservative press indicating that large numbers of workers and Social Democrats did attend the naval theatre. Yet it also suggests that, if they showed the signs that are often quoted as indicators of 'naval enthusiasm', they were largely motivated by fear rather than consent.

To describe the naval theatre as apolitical or as characterized by consensus neglects this strong element of orchestration and intervention: conflict was hidden, consensus was staged. Moreover, to see in this public theatre a genuine expression of popular sentiment underestimates the complex and contradictory ways in which people participated. Audiences went to see the naval theatre for a range of reasons. There is little doubt that many of them were fascinated by the technological and visual spectacle it offered. Yet they did not have to buy into the display of hierarchy and power; nor did they have to refrain from interpreting aspects of the spectacle politically and critically. Many Social Democrats and members of the Labour party went to see the naval theatre. Yet, the same party members who watched launches and reviews could agitate against naval enthusiasm in the Reichstag. This point was made by socialist newspapers and SPD party members.[141] It was also stressed by many of the workers who were monitored by Hamburg's police. There were reports in which

[138] StA Hamburg, 331-3, S1154: Bericht Graumann, 9 April 1901.
[139] StA Hamburg, 331-3, S4875: Bericht Jochum, 11 June 1985.
[140] StA Hamburg, 331-3, S1154: Bericht Graumann, 29 May 1895.
[141] *Hamburger Neueste Nachrichten*, 26 March 1909; *Hamburger Echo*, 26 March 1909; *Hamburger Echo*, 9 Sept 1904, Hauptblatt; *Hamburger Echo*, 10 Sept 1904, Hauptblatt.

workers emphasized that they found no fault with comrades and party members going to watch the naval games. And yet, at the same time they expected the party to attack the government about the exuberance and waste displayed on this public stage. It was very much possible to both enjoy the naval theatre and oppose those celebrated by it.

This was also true for those in the navy. For the lower ranks there did not have to be a contradiction between being proud of the show that the navy put on, and feeling profound dissatisfaction with those who most seemed to benefit from it. This is particularly well illustrated by the example of Robert Percival from North London. Percival was a stoker on board HMS *Lancaster* from 1910 to 1912. He was one of the ratings for whom fleet reviews primarily meant hard work.[142] From the early days of his appointment Percival kept a private diary, which – unlike midshipmen's journals – was neither seen nor censored by his superiors. It makes clear that there were numerous voices of discontent on the lower deck during naval celebrations. Percival described himself in his diary as a member of the working classes. He repeatedly stressed his intense dislike for the middle and upper classes. Indeed, the main emphasis in the diary is on the contrast between the lower deck keeping the ships running on the one hand, and the admirals 'going for the pleasure of the Elité' (*sic*) on the other:[143]

Much has been written of the glories and the mysteries of the sea, poets and novelists have woven yards of romance around it, but I am not writing this from any romantic point of view, but from the standing point of one, who, driven by economic pressure was forced to adopt it, as a means of livelihood; a captain who I had served under in a previous ship, once told the assembled ships company, that if we were not in the Navy, we would very likely be in the Workhouse, or Prison; apart from the insult contained in the assertion there was more truth in it than was meant to be conveyed [...]; thoughts like these in my mind, I must be excused if I fail to rapsodise [sic] about the Blue and Green of the Ocean.[144]

Percival upheld this critical perspective when it came to the 1911 royal review, yet combined it with a sense of pride and honour:

If anyone in the Engines branch cared to keep a careful record of the hours worked daily for a commission, it would make nice reading and would take the starch out of that song, the chorus of which says, 'Britons shall never be slaves'. But we were working with a will now, as we were going to be inspected, by no less a personage than King George V. Paint was used in a most reckless fashion to hide the blistered funnels and other evidences of our recent scrap. [...]. This was the biggest fleet

---

[142] See on this aspect NMM, JOD/193/1: Wilfried S. Mann, 9 July 1912.
[143] RNM, 1988/294: Diary of Robert Percival, p. 7.
[144] Ibid., pp. 9–10 (emphasis in original).

I had ever seen underway, and to the man in the street, no doubt, would be looked upon as a spectacle, but to the initiated, every smoking funnel meant <u>Work</u>.[145]

In Percival's diary, pride and honour come together with a deep sense of dissatisfaction and a strong antipathy towards the naval leadership and 'the Elite'. This is a striking example of the way in which public appearances and private views could coexist. Clearly, participants from a range of backgrounds found it possible to be part of the naval theatre without accepting or internalizing the social and political hierarchy that it embodied.

All this suggests that, even if there were clear strategies of 'bread and circuses' involved in the public staging of the navy, their success was limited by a number of factors. The most important of them was simply that those watching by no means had to believe in these displays of traditional order. This point was not only made by Socialists and radicals, but also by observers at the other end of the social and political spectrum. Baroness Spitzemberg, a keen supporter of the monarchy, judged the effect of public ritual on 'the masses' as very limited. Describing the scenes in Kiel in June 1911, where the Kaiser had been received by jubilant crowds, the Baroness observed that 'the same people [who show enthusiasm] vote *ultramontan* or Socialist'.[146] Many spectators who found the naval theatre entertaining and who showed no hesitation in cheering the Kaiser, would vote against the parties who were seen as supporting such public pomp. Hierarchies were displayed and enacted at these occasions, but they did not have to be internalized by those watching.

These findings suggest that some of the generalizations about popular sentiment in the 'age of the masses' have been overstated. There certainly was a 'pleasure culture of war' both in Britain and Germany, but this did not mean that audiences identified themselves as part of a 'warrior nation'.[147] It is similarly misleading to extrapolate from the popular literature celebrating the navy and the empire that there was a pervasive social and political consensus that could be characterized as an 'imperial mentality' or as 'popular imperialism'.[148] Nor does the idea of a 'folkloric

---

[145] Ibid., p. 33 (emphasis in original).

[146] *Tagebuch der Baronin Spitzemberg*, p. 529 (5 June 1911).

[147] Michael Paris, *Warrior Nation: Images of War in British Popular Culture, 1850–2000* (London, 2000).

[148] MacKenzie, *Imperialism and Popular Culture*; MacKenzie, *Popular Imperialism and the Military*; Mangan, *Making Imperial Mentalities*. See also John M. MacKenzie, 'Empire and Metropolitan Cultures', in Andrew Porter (ed.), *The Oxford History of the British Empire*, vol. 3 (Oxford, 1999), pp. 290–2.

militarism' seem very convincing in the light of the above.[149] Certainly, there was a widely shared taste for the combination of pageantry, technology and entertainment in the naval theatre, both in Britain and Germany. However, the liking for this spectacle that clearly existed in large parts of society should not be mistaken as a popular form of militarism that complemented or affirmed government strategies. As the above has made clear, there were varying and conflicting experiences amongst audiences. To attend public rituals did not necessarily mean agreement with those staging them or acquiescence in their policies. Many spectators found no difficulty in taking a position of critical distance whilst watching the naval theatre.

Militarism revisited

For most of the contemporary critics, who saw the naval theatre as a modern form of 'bread and circuses', it was the stage-masters, not the audiences, who were driven by militarism. The *Labour Leader* saw naval reviews and launches of warships as shows where 'militarism [. . .] blazed forth in all its barbaric magnificence'.[150] These were 'Armada displays' and pieces of 'naval agitation' showing a dangerous militarist and imperialist spirit.[151] In 1909, at the height of the naval race, the *Labour Leader* urged its readers not to fall for the militarist spectacle staged by the navy:

> Mammon's an admiral on the seas;
> How brave his Dreadnoughts show!
> The great armadas on the tide
> Will fill your hearts with pride
> And the pockets of Mammon and Co.
> They follow the standard, stir your souls
> To a patriotic glow!
> Do not think of the folly, nor count the costs;
> What matter if lives of your brothers are lost?
> There'll be pickings for Mammon and Co.[152]

The party organ of the SPD, the *Vorwärts*, derided the naval theatre similarly as 'militaristic pomp'.[153] The *Hamburger Echo* saw naval parades

---

[149] This is Jakob Vogel's characterization of the audiences at German and French army celebrations: Vogel, *Nationen im Gleichschritt*, pp. 265, 270–8, 288; Jakob Vogel, ' "En revenant de la revue". Militärfolklore und Folkloremilitarismus in Deutschland und Frankreich 1871–1914', *Österreichische Zeitschrift für Geschichtswissenschaften* 9 (1998), pp. 9–30; Jakob Vogel, 'Military, Folklore, Eigensinn: Folkloric Militarism in Germany and France, 1871–1914', *Central European History* 33 (2000), pp. 487–504.
[150] *Labour Leader*, 23 June 1911.
[151] *Labour Leader*, 18 June 1909.   [152] *Labour Leader*, 6 Aug 1909.
[153] *Vorwärts*, 24 May 1912; 23 June 1895; 27 June 1895; 8 Sept 1904.

and launches of warships as expression of 'insatiable militarism'[154] or as 'emanations of militarism'.[155]

Were these critics right: was the naval theatre a grand show of militarism? And how did the two countries compare in this respect? Any answer depends of course on the definition of 'militarism'. For the socialist and radical critics quoted above, the naval theatre was a show of militarism because it displayed the ever-increasing armaments expenditure that both countries' governments seemed committed to. This filled the pockets of 'Mammon and Co.', but left the masses impoverished. Moreover, it created an atmosphere of warmongering that could easily lead to international conflict. All this was made possible by the undue power that the military exerted over civil society. More than anything, the naval theatre symbolized the dominance of the military over civilians. As the *Hamburger Echo* wrote after the 1904 joint naval and military parade: 'Militarism is triumphant. Everything has to submit to it. The civilian pack is nothing but the obedient servant of militarism [*die gehorsame Dienstmagd des Militarismus*]'.[156]

A comparative analysis of militarism in Britain and Germany must begin here, with the relationship between the civil and military spheres of society. This aspect, which was in the focus of the older historiography on militarism,[157] has received new attention recently. Notably, Rainer Lepsius has argued that the negotiation of power between military sub-culture and civil society is crucial for an understanding of militarism.[158] A society's degree of militarization is, according to Lepsius, defined by 'the extent to which leading ideas and criteria of rationality taken from the military sphere are also structuring civil arenas of society'.[159] The following

---

[154] *Hamburger Echo*, 26 May 1912.
[155] *Hamburger Echo*, 11 Sept 1904, Erstes Beiblatt. Similar examples ibid., 4 May 1895, Hauptblatt; 29 May 1895, Hauptblatt; 8 April 1910, Erste Beilage; 5 Sept 1911, Hauptblatt and 5 March 1913, Hauptblatt.
[156] *Hamburger Echo*, Beiblatt, 4 Sept 1904. Similarly *Hamburger Echo*, 11 Sept 1904, Erstes Beiblatt. The SPD criticized naval pageants as shows of militarism regularly in the Reichstag. For an early example, see the speech by Schoenlank in December 1897: *Sten. Ber., IX. Legislaturperiode, V. Session, 1897/98*, vol. 1 (Berlin, 1898), p. 51. Such criticism combined what Nicholas Stargardt has identified as the liberal and pacifist 'ideas of militarism', see Nicholas Stargardt, *The German Idea of Militarism: Radical and Socialist Critics, 1866–1914* (Cambridge, 1994).
[157] For a survey see Volker R. Berghahn, *Militarism: The History of an International Debate 1861–1979* (Leamington Spa, 1981). See also Werner Conze and Michael Geyer, 'Militarismus', in Otto Brunner, Werner Konze, Reinhart Koselleck (eds.), *Geschichtliche Grundbegriffe*, vol. 4 (Stuttgart, 1978), pp. 1–47 and Gerhard Ritter, *Staatskunst und Kriegshandwerk*, vol. 1 (Munich, 1954).
[158] M. Rainer Lepsius, 'Militärwesen und zivile Gesellschaft', in Ute Frevert (ed.) *Militär und Gesellschaft im 19. und 20. Jahrhundert* (Stuttgart, 1997), pp. 359–70.
[159] Ibid., pp. 367–8.

analysis takes up this approach, albeit in a widened sense. It is not only crucial to assess to what extent military rationale influenced civil society, as Lepsius suggests. It is equally important to gauge the reciprocal movement: the degree to which civilians were able to influence the military.

The naval theatre was a particularly prominent stage on which this relationship was played out. It was here that the boundary between military and civil worlds was negotiated publicly.[160] Both in Britain and Germany civil maritime celebrations drew heavily on naval ceremonial and iconography. In display and rhetoric, the launches of passenger liners such as the *Mauretania* or the *Aquitania*, the *Imperator* or the *Vaterland*, imitated launches of capital warships. The same dignitaries gave speeches and performed the christenings, the same parading of troops took place, national anthems were played, scores of officers attended: all this under-lined that these were military as much as civil events. When the HAPAG liner *Deutschland* was launched in the presence of the Kaiser, the speech delivered by Chancellor Bülow sounded like one he could have given at the launch of a warship:

Germany has to be strong enough at sea to secure German peace, German honour and German well-being. We will not be deterred or defeated if we are forced to overcome obstacles on this path which fate has shown us. Nor if we have to pass difficult passages. We will strive towards the final aim [*Endziel*] with bravery, steadiness and energy. [...]. May God the Almighty bless this ship which carries our country's name [...]. Just as this ship shall be superior to other ships, as many as there might be crossing the seas, Germany shall always be for all Germans above everything else, above everything else in the world [*so möge immerdar für jeden Deutschen Deutschland über alles sein, über alles auf der Welt*]!

Bülow closed his speech with the three cheers for the Kaiser that were customary at launches of warships: 'We are united in the call which sums up what we are feeling, hoping and striving for: the leader [*Führer*] of this nation, His Majesty the Kaiser and King, *er lebe hoch!*'[161] The extent to which the Vulcan yard, which had built the liner, and the HAPAG line, which had ordered it, allowed military language and display to dominate the launch of a commercial passenger liner was remarkable.[162] Nor was this a solitary case. The launch of the *Imperator* in Hamburg in 1912 reflected a similar appropriation of naval ceremonial for a civil occasion. The structure of the ritual strictly followed naval custom. This included the separation between male and female tribunes, the setting up of an

---

[160] In what follows, 'military' will be used as including the navy.
[161] *Hamburgischer Korrespondent*, 5 Jan 1900.
[162] The details of the launch are recorded in StA Hamburg, 132-1 I, 2149.

Ablaufpavillon and the parading of military societies.[163] In his speech, Hamburg's Burgomaster Burchard employed the exact phrases that were used at launches of warships; he even ranked the new luxury liner alongside the capital battleships of the Imperial Navy, all under the command and foresight of the Kaiser.[164]

A similar encroachment of the military upon civil society took place in Britain. Launches of commercial ships followed naval ritual and they never took place without the Royal Navy being prominently represented. Liners such as the *Mauretania* and *Lusitania* were enlisted in a maritime race between the British and German shipping industries, a race in which the boundaries between commercial and military were blurred.[165] Indeed, Lord Tweedmouth, First Lord of the Admiralty, likened the launch of the *Mauretania* to that of the *Dreadnought*.[166] There was a range of other civil celebrations at which naval ritual and rhetoric was adopted. The 1913 'mercantile review' in the River Mersey provides a striking example. While this was part of a celebration of commercial shipping, much of its choreography followed naval practice. In calling this display a 'mercantile review', the Cunard Steam Ship Company, one of the main organizers and participants, consciously drew a parallel with the fleet reviews in the Solent. The ships were assembled in a parade and the King proceeded through their lines on board the royal yacht, just like at Spithead fleet reviews. The Admiralty was closely involved in the planning of this commercial imitation of naval ritual, and it ensured uniformity of display and procedures. Cunard employees, amongst them Captain W. T. Turner, the commander of the *Mauretania*, who did not have a rank in the Royal Naval Reserve, were each given naval uniforms. The aim was to create as close an image as possible to the Spithead fleet reviews.[167] There can be little doubt that

---

[163] StA Hamburg, 331-1I, 224/4: Notizen der Polizeibehörde, 21 May 1912. StA Hamburg 132-1 I, 2282, Bl. 88a: Werftskizze; Bl. 97a: Resumée der Kommission. Just as at naval launches, scores of decorations were handed out as part of the celebration: BA, R901/ 2865/1, vol. 3: Stapellauf des HAPAG Dampfers 'Imperator' 1912.

[164] StA Hamburg 132-1 I, 2282, Bl. 78.

[165] Part-financed by the Admiralty, the *Mauretania* and the *Lusitania* were built with the specific aim of challenging the German record of speed across the Atlantic. See Arnold Kludas, 'Der Wettkampf der Ozeanriesen: Deutsche Schiffe als Auslöser und Höhepunkt des großen friedlichen Wettrüstens vor 1914', *Jahrbuch der Schiffbautechnischen Gesellschaft* 79 (1985), pp. 67–76; Rieger, *Culture of Modernity*, pp. 228–9; Holger Afflerbach, *Das entfesselte Meer. Die Geschichte des Atlantik* (Munich, 2001), pp. 273–88.

[166] *Newcastle Daily Journal*, 21 Sept 1906. See also the speech by Sir William White at the launch of the *Mauretania* (ibid.).

[167] PRO, ADM 1/8361: Cunard Steam Ship Company, Liverpool, to Secretary of the Admiralty, 22 May 1913. Indeed, a number of newspapers enquiring at the Admiralty

this was a case where the rationale of military ceremonial governed a display organized by civilians.[168]

Clearly, then, in Britain and in Germany, a considerable militarization of civil public ritual existed in the decades before 1914.[169] Military rationale and representation strongly influenced civil celebrations in both countries. Yet how far did civilians reach into the military sphere? Here the comparison produces a stark Anglo-German contrast. While in Britain both parliament and government were regularly represented at fleet reviews, there were no displays of civil government at these occasions in Germany. What the public got to see was the ceremonial meeting of the Kaiser and the navy, a public staging of the close relationship between the naval forces and their 'All Highest' commander, which carefully excluded any representation of civilians.[170] A similar difference can be seen when the scenes on board are considered. At British fleet reviews, civilians were present on most warships. The orders specifically allowed officers and midshipmen to bring guests to the review. Even for the 1914 test mobilization, the review orders detailed: 'Guests may be allowed to visit ships at Spithead at the discretion of Commanding Officers, but care is to be taken that they are not in conspicuous positions should H. M. pass the ship they are on board'.[171]

The considerable influence of civil society on naval ritual is underlined by first-hand accounts. Consider the experience on board HMS *Attentive*, as described by the young officer James Colvill in his diary on 24 June 1911:

Review Day. Not very fine in the morning but cleared up into a beautiful sunny afternoon with a decent breeze. All the guests got on board about noon, Daddy,

mistook this 'review' of commercial ships for a fleet review of the Spithead type. See PRO, ADM 1/8361: Review of the Home Fleet, Applications to take Photographs, 26 Feb 1913.

[168] For another example see the centenary of the launch of the *Comet* in Glasgow, analysed above. This civic and urban celebration, called 'a great nautical demonstration' by the Lord Provost of Glasgow, was consciously designed as a naval demonstration, with an assembly of warships and a speech by Churchill, then First Lord of the Admiralty. Cf. Glasgow City Archives, G 1/1/16: Lord Provost to Mrs Winston Churchill, 19 April 1912. For the sailing events in Cowes and Kiel, at which military and civilian merged similarly, see Chapter 1, n. 137.

[169] This assessment stands in contrast to the scholarship that seems to view 'militarism' as a wholly un-British phenomenon. The *Oxford Companion to British History*, ed. John Cannon (Oxford, 1997), has no entry on 'militarism'. Hew Strachan, 'Militär, Empire und *Civil Society*: Großbritannien im 19. Jahrhundert', in Frevert (ed.), *Militär und Gesellschaft*, p. 93, finds 'militarism' a term 'too loaded and overburdened with meaning' to apply it to Britain. Nor does Steve Attridge, *Nationalism, Imperialism, and Identity in Late Victorian Culture: Civil and Military Worlds* (Basingstoke, 2003) offer any clues about the power relations between civil and military parts of society, despite the title.

[170] See the section 'Maritime theatre' in Chapter 1.

[171] NMM, Caird Library: Home Fleet Order No. 766, Memorandum: Assembly of the Home Fleets at Spithead, July 1914, art. xviii: guests.

18. Visitors on the flagship during the coronation review at Spithead, 16 August 1902.

Georgie and Bobbie amongst them. Dressed ship at noon. Took Georgie and Bobbie round the ship while Daddy talked to Hawkesworth the clerk to whom I introduced him. We manned ship at 1pm and fired the Royal Salute of 21 guns when the [royal] yacht entered the lines.[172]

Clearly, this experience was as much about entertaining families and friends as it was about naval representation (compare illustration 18).[173] During fleet reviews, it was standard procedure on board British ships to offer drinks and snacks and to sell programmes and souvenirs to guests.[174] This strong civil flavour was unthinkable at German fleet reviews. Here, ships cleared, guns were 'ready for action' and no civilians were allowed on board.[175] A similar difference existed with regard to the

[172] RNM, 1997: James Colvill, 24 June 1911.
[173] See also NMM, JOD/27: Richard Webb, 9 July 1912.
[174] PRO, ADM 179/55: Review Orders, Diamond Jubilee Naval Review 1897, art. 74.
[175] BA-MA, RM 2/106, Bl. 285: Anlage zum Flottentagesbefehl Nr. 87 vom 12. Aug. 1911; Anordnungen für das Zeremoniell bei Besichtigung der Hochseeflotte durch S. M. den Kaiser am 5. Sept. 1911.

wearing of uniforms.[176] While the regulations were strictly enforced in Germany, there was a remarkably relaxed atmosphere about this at Spithead, to the extent that Admiral John Fisher was able to wear a yachting suit for a naval review instead of his uniform.[177] Tolerated by the authorities, scores of naval officers regularly watched the naval theatre wearing civilian clothes rather than uniform.[178] Clearly, fleet reviews in Britain were influenced by civil culture to a considerable degree. While the Royal Navy had a strong impact on civil celebrations, it did also allow for civil culture to have an effect on naval ritual. In Germany, by contrast, the navy showed a strong determination to resist any such influence. Here, public ritual signalled that the military world was keen to exercise its power in civil society, but that it would not allow any intrusion of civilians' ideas into its own realm.

Gender and militarism

This finding about Anglo-German difference is confirmed by an analysis of the gender relations at the heart of the naval theatre.[179] Fleet reviews and ship launches featured strong displays of masculine and military identities in both countries. Numerous symbolic exchanges between men and women were made whenever ships visited 'their' city or county. So-called 'ladies' presentations' were regular features at ship launches and naval visits, occasions at which selected women representatives offered gifts to the officers and men of the navy that emphasized traditional gender roles.[180] All this displayed women as 'waiting on the shore' with complaisance and passive admiration, while men would defend the nation on the oceans.[181] At the heart of the spectacle was, as the Lord

---

[176] On this point see also Naubert, *Land und Leute*, p. 555.
[177] *Naval and Military Record*, 17 June 1909.
[178] PRO, ADM 179/52: Commander-in-Chief Portsmouth to Admiral Superintendent, 27 July 1909.
[179] On the role of gender for the differentiation between nineteenth-century military and civilian spheres see Ute Frevert, *Die kasernierte Nation. Militärdienst und Zivilgesellschaft in Deutschland* (Munich, 2001); Frevert, 'Das Militär als "Schule der Männlichkeit". Erwartungen, Angebote, Erfahrungen im 19. Jahrhundert', in Frevert (ed.), *Militär und Gesellschaft*, pp. 145–73; 'Einleitung', in Frevert (ed.), *Bürgerinnen und Bürger. Geschlechterverhältnisse im 19. Jahrhundert* (Göttingen, 1988), pp. 11–16.
[180] For an example see the presentation of a centrepiece, given by 'the ladies of Glasgow' to the officers of HMS *Glasgow* in April 1911 as 'an expression of their love for the Navy as a whole' (*Glasgow Herald*, 29 April 1911). The organization of the presentation and the visit of HMS *Glasgow* are documented in PRO, ADM 1/8215.
[181] On the late eighteenth and early nineteenth-century background see Margarette Lincoln, *Representing the Royal Navy: British Sea Power, 1750–1815* (Aldershot, 2002), ch. 6. For an anthropological analysis of the gender relations involved in ship launches see Rodgers, 'The Symbolism of Ship Launching'. Just how much the navy symbolized a

Provost of Glasgow put it at the launch of the *Agamemnon*, the wish to 'admire the action of the heroic men of our navy'.[182] Similar ideas about the navy as an exclusively male institution existed in Imperial Germany. They were expressed, amongst other ways, in Wilhelm II's memorial for the navy, inaugurated in Kiel in June 1900. As Wilhelm explained to the Imperial Chancellor in 1899, he intended the sculpture to be a memorial for the officers and ratings who had died 'in the course of duty'.[183] Yet, it was more than a commemoration of the dead. The Kaiser described the monument, showing Jesus on the Cross with a praying woman at his feet, holding a child, as a 'visible sign' of what was at the heart of the Imperial Navy: the separation between men and women. Both he and the priest of the Kiel station who blessed the monument emphasized this in their inaugurating speeches. The monument was intended to symbolize the place of man and woman in the Wilhelmine gender order.[184]

Yet, while such ideas about the navy as a male realm can be found in both societies, it is remarkable how much more active and prominent a role women played in naval ceremonies in Britain. In the Royal Navy, it had become customary to have female patrons launch warships in the early nineteenth century. This role was expanded by the presentations and social functions created around ship launches. Women were guests of honour, they regularly gave speeches, at times highly political ones.[185] Women not only smashed the bottle at launches, but also cut the cord holding back the vessel and gave the ceremony significance by pronouncing the only public words that were said during the launching.[186] The female launch patron clearly played an elevated role. This stood in stark contrast to German launching ceremonies. Here, the role of the female launch patron was restricted to breaking the bottle. In Germany there was no cutting of the cord: at most occasions, the male dockyard director initiated the launch by giving instructions or pulling a lever. The launching speech was, without exception, delivered by senior male figures. Lunches or dinners after launches were predominantly male affairs, and

bulwark of male dominance was clearly on display during the *Dreadnought* hoax of 1910, analysed in Chapter 2. It was specifically male pomp and self-importance that the Bloomsbury literati intended to mock. Virginia Woolf came away from the episode with a 'new sense of the brutality and silliness of men', as Quentin Bell put it in *Virginia Woolf*, vol. 1 (London, 1972), p. 158.

[182] *Glasgow Leader*, 29 June 1906.
[183] BA-MA, RM 2/85, Bl. 94: Wilhelm II to Reichskanzler, Abschrift, 13 Nov 1899.
[184] *Die Einweihung der Kruzifixgruppe vor der Marine-Garnisonkirche in Kiel* (Berlin, 1900), p. 3 (speech given at the inauguration of the memorial, 20 June 1900). See also BA-MA, RM2/85.
[185] For an example see *Naval and Military Record*, 27 March 1912 on the speech given by the Duchess of Sutherland after the launch of HMS *Ajax* on 21 March 1912.
[186] This is also stressed by Rodgers, 'Symbolism', part 3.

the idea of the female launch patron giving a speech at one of these social events would have been unthinkable. There was thus, in addition to the language of might and masculinity that enveloped these occasions, a much reduced role for the female patron. This alone gave the impression of a male and military ritual that was resistant to female influence and an opening towards civil society

Just how closely knit male and military representation was at these occasions was underlined by the spatial gender demarcation that characterized the Wilhelmine naval theatre. Launches of capital warships featured a special ladies' stand, removed from the ritual core marked by the launch platform. This *Damentribüne* offers important clues about gender relations and militarism in Wilhelmine Germany. It was only in the clearly defined zone of the *Damentribüne* that women were allowed into the inner circle of participation. The 'ladies of the invited guests' (*Damen der eingeladenen Gäste*) and 'ladies of the honorary guests' (*Damen der Ehrengäste*) needed a special ticket to gain access. These tickets had a different colour from those for male guests and were issued as *Damenkarten* to their husbands.[187] Married couples arriving at the entrance thus had to show their differently coded tickets and were separated, women taking up a seat on the *Damentribüne*, men 'taking up position' (*Aufstellung nehmen*) with the officers in uniform. This *Herrengesellschaft* made up of officers and 'invited gentlemen' was situated close to the ship, often between the women's stand and the launching platform.[188] Programmes and invitations informed the guests that there would be a separate women's stand and that only men would be allowed into the reception after the launch, the *Herren-Imbiß*. Both at government and private yards the strict separation between 'noble and distinguished men' and 'the ladies', as Burgomaster Mönckeberg put it,[189] was minutely planned and strictly adhered to.[190]

This demarcation had striking visual and symbolic effects. It suggested a gendered difference between active and passive participation. The

---

[187] BA-MA, RM 31/93, Bl. 16; Bl. 116; Bl. 117: Programm für den Stapellauf S. M. Gr. Kreuzer A, 22 March 1900; Bl. 191: Beitrag zum Stationstagesbefehl; BA-MA, RM 31/1067, Bl. 97: Germaniawerft Kiel-Gaarden to Kaiserliches Kommando Kiel, 10 Sept 1903; StA Hamburg, Blohm & Voss, 836.

[188] HA Krupp, WA 16 R 87, Werksalbum: Stapellauf 'Schleswig-Holstein', 17 Dec 1906; BA-MA, RM 31/93, Bl. 16 and Bl. 58: Skizze für Stapellauf Kl. Kreuzer A auf Germaniawerft Kiel, 21 Nov 1899; BA-MA, RM3/129; StA Hamburg, 132-1I, Nr. 3391, p. 2; StA Hamburg, 132-1 I, Nr. 2282.

[189] StA Hamburg, 662-1 Mönckeberg 21a, Bl. 284.

[190] For the imperial yard at Kiel this is documented in BA-MA, RM 31/93; for the Germania yard in HA Krupp, FAH 3 B 181 and FAH 4 C 55; for Hamburg in StA Hamburg, 132-1 I, Nr. 3391 and 2282.

'invited gentlemen' were free to interact with officers and soldiers, while their wives had to sit separately.[191] The men, positioned close to the ship and launching platform, could feel themselves active participants and watched as such by 'the ladies'. Naturally, this gender separation applied only to the invited guests and not to the wider audiences situated around them. To the outside observers, the role of the 'invited ladies' emphasized the degree to which this was a male and military ritual, a ritual that allowed the participation of women only as passive onlookers in a separate and controlled space. Photographs of the launch of SMS *Schleswig-Holstein* in December 1906 show naval and military batallions, honorary guards, an army band and detachments of the *Kriegervereine* and *Kampfgenossen* all positioned around the hull, together with the officer corps and those few invited male guests who did not have the privilege to wear uniform (illustration 20). This was, as one of the participants described it, the image of a 'shining *Herrengesellschaft*'.[192] The numerous ladies who watched from the *Damentribüne* with due distance were assigned the role of quietly affirming the male ritual. Similarly, newsreels showing the launch of SMS *Prinzregent Luitpold* in 1912 show ladies in their best dresses (launching invitations prescribed *Promenadengarderobe*), watching the male spectacle from the *Damentribüne*. At the end of the ceremony the main actors leave, followed by parading soldiers, officers and the 'invited gentlemen', all watched by the women in their special stand, waving as the male and military procession passes by.[193]

This Wilhelmine gender spectacle becomes all the more remarkable when it is compared with Britain. The British launching ceremonial as practised from the 1870s onwards did not involve any such gender separation.[194] Here, women and men stood together in the same stands and there was much less of a distinction between male and female, civilian and military. In the face of profound challenges to traditional gender roles and ideas of masculinity, the Wilhelmine ceremonial thus forcefully reserved an inner ritual core purely for military and male representation. It marshalled a strict boundary not only between men and women, but also between military and civil worlds. Both German fleet reviews and

---

[191] For a depiction of this effect see *Neue Stettiner Zeitung*, 25 July 1903, Abendausgabe. This gender demarcation was not upheld as strictly at launches of commercial vessels. Yet at particularly grand occasions such as the launch of the ocean liner *Imperator* in 1912, a similar separation could be observed. See StA 132-1I, 2282, Bl. 97a: Resumée der Kommission.

[192] HA Krupp, WA 16 R 87, Werksalbum: Stapellauf 'Schleswig-Holstein', 17 Dec 1906.

[193] BA-FA, SL 22821.

[194] On the gender demarcation in early nineteenth-century naval ritual see Lincoln, 'Naval Ship Launches', p. 469.

19. Launch of SMS *Kaiser Wilhelm der Große*, 1 June 1899. Note the *Damentribüne* on the left.

launching ceremonies enacted a close relationship between weaponry, war, power and masculinity, and they demonstrated publicly that civil/ female influence had no place in this *Männerbund*.[195]

---

[195] The idea of the *Männerbund* was first introduced by the ethnologist Heinrich Schurtz in *Altersklassen und Männerbünde* (Berlin, 1902) and taken up prominently by Hans Blüher in *Die Rolle der Erotik in der männlichen Gesellschaft* (Jena, 1917). Best translated as 'male brotherhood', it became associated with 'closed' male circles such as the Prussian army's officer corps and the Kaiser's 'Liebenberg circle'. The term has also been applied to male society in ancient Sparta, to orders such as the Teutonic Knights, and to the SA and SS in Nazi Germany. See Jürgen Reulecke, 'Das Jahr 1902 und die Ursprünge der Männerbund-Ideologie in Deutschland' and Klaus von See, 'Politische Männerbund-Ideologie von der wilhelminischen Zeit bis zum Nationalsozialismus', both in Gisela Völger and Karin von Welck (eds.), *Männerbande – Männerbünde. Zur Rolle des Mannes im Kulturvergleich*, vol. 1 (Cologne, 1990), pp. 3–10, 93–102. See also Thomas Rohkrämer, 'Das Militär als Männerbund? Kult der soldatischen Männlichkeit im Deutschen Kaiserreich', *Westfälische Forschungen* 45 (1995), pp. 169–87; Nicolaus Sombart, 'The Kaiser in His Epoch: Some Reflexions on Wilhelmine Society, Sexuality and Culture', in Röhl and Sombart, *Kaiser Wilhelm II*, pp. 287–311; Nicolaus Sombart, 'Männerbund und politische Kultur in Deutschland', in J. H. Knoll and J. H. Schoeps (eds.), *Typisch deutsch. Die deutsche Jugendbewegung* (Opladen, 1988), pp. 155–76; Kohut, *Wilhelm II and the Germans*, p. 106; Marschall, *Reisen und Regieren*, pp. 46–51.

20. The gender divide enacted. Launch of SMS *Schleswig-Holstein*, 17 December 1906. The *Damentribüne* is situated in the foreground on the left.

What does this mean for the long-standing debate about militarism in Germany? The Imperial Navy has always played a central role in this controversy.[196] Both in his seminal history of the *Kaiserreich* and in his more recent *Deutsche Gesellschaftsgeschichte* Hans-Ulrich Wehler has argued that there was a peculiar form of militarism which played a strong part in the German *Sonderweg*.[197] According to Wehler, German militarism developed into a mass phenomenon after 1871, ubiquitous in everyday life. In its pervasiveness and comprehensiveness this *Sozialmilitarismus* was unique and fundamentally different from other European countries.[198] The above findings partially support Wehler's assessment. On the public stage, the German navy displayed substantially stronger militarist tendencies than the Royal Navy. Britain and Germany were clearly not 'marching in step', as Jakob Vogel has suggested with regard to France and Germany.[199] The way in which the Kaiser's fleet was celebrated showed a determination to keep civilian rationale outside the navy, which was lacking in Britain. There was a well guarded boundary between civil and military in the Wilhelmine naval theatre, which mirrored the constitutionally safeguarded role of the navy as exempt from direct civilian control. This was a form of militarism that was instigated by the naval leadership, the army and the emperor, and which can be seen as peculiar when compared to Britain. In the naval theatre, however, this was not matched by *Sozialmilitarismus* or a 'militarism from below' in any pervasive sense.[200] The military and male actors at the centre of these rituals may well have been 'ready for war'.[201] They certainly portrayed themselves as such in their speeches. Yet, if their audiences believed or internalized such displays is an entirely different matter. It is a crucial (if simple) differentiation: watching displays of military power and hierarchical order was not the same as believing in them.

---

[196] For Emilio Willems, *A Way of Life and Death: Three Centuries of Prussian-German Militarism* (Nashville, 1986), p. 89, the navy even symbolized the 'epitome of German militarism'.

[197] For an introduction to the *Sonderweg* debate see Evans, *Rethinking German History*, ch. 3.

[198] Wehler, *Deutsche Gesellschaftsgeschichte*, vol. 3, pp. 880–5. Similar: Isabel V. Hull, *Absolute Destruction: Military Culture and the Practices of War in Imperial Germany* (Ithaca, 2005), ch. 4. For the critique of Wehler's portrait of the *Kaiserreich* see David Blackbourn and Geoff Eley, *The Peculiarities of German History: Bourgeois Society and Politics in Nineteenth-Century Germany* (Oxford, 1984); Evans, *Rereading German History*, pp. 12–22; Thomas Nipperdey, 'War die wilhelminische Gesellschaft eine Untertanen-Gesellschaft?', in Nipperdey, *Nachdenken über die deutsche Geschichte* (Munich, 1990), pp. 208–24.

[199] Vogel, *Nationen im Gleichschritt*, esp. pp. 270–8

[200] On the idea of militarism 'from below' see also Förster, *Der doppelte Militarismus*; Rohkrämer, *Der Militarismus der 'kleinen Leute'* and Hull, *Absolute Destruction*, ch. 4.

[201] Dülffer and Holl, *Bereit zum Krieg*.

Panem et circenses

This, in turn, emphasizes a point that has surfaced throughout this chapter and which relates to wider questions about 'bread and circuses' in the age of empire. The diverse ways in which people experienced the naval theatre defy categorization in any one-dimensional fashion. Observers such as Hamburg's Burgomaster Burchard were right when they noted that the spectators found this 'powerful spectacle' fascinating and appealing.[202] However, the same commentators were mistaken when they concluded that the 'appetite for pageantry' that they saw amongst 'the masses' represented any particular political allegiance. Audiences could enjoy the naval theatre without having to agree with or support those celebrated in it. Just as it would be naïve to assume that the public staging of the navy was not informed by the wish to influence, it would be cynical to see these rituals as mere exercises in the manipulation of the masses. Even if there were official strategies designed to employ the naval theatre as a modern form of 'bread and circuses', this chapter has shown the strong limits to such strategies.

Nor were the audiences that went to see the celebration of the navy in any substantial way mobilized by the 'radical right'. In the naval theatre the influence of leagues such as the *Flottenverein* was subordinate to factors that do not fit into the dichotomy between 'above' and 'below', which has characterized so much research. Two of them have been stressed in this and the previous chapter. First, the influence of the media, entertainment and tourist industries, which discovered the naval theatre as a key attraction in the 'age of the masses'; second, the rich texture of local government, society and business, which organized and financed much of the festive culture on display in the naval theatre. Both of these shaped the naval theatre independently from any central governments and radical leagues.

Taken together, these factors suggest a revision of how historians understand Wilhelmine and Edwardian public ritual and the 'mobilization of the masses' in the imperial age. As Geoff Eley himself has pointed out, 'the fixing of the argument into the "manipulation" versus "self-mobilization" dichotomy [. . .] has rather prevented new questions from being fruitfully generated and pursued'.[203] By focusing on government propaganda and the role of the 'radical right', historians have neglected the complex power relations that characterized this public arena and that

---

[202] BA-MA, RM 3/129, Bl. 52 (launch of the *Hamburg* in Stettin, 25 July 1903).
[203] Geoff Eley, 'Is there a History of the *Kaiserreich*?', in Eley (ed.), *Society, Culture, and the State in Germany, 1870–1930* (Ann Arbor, 1996), p. 13.

have remained hidden behind the metaphor of *panem et circenses*. On closer examination, Juvenal's dictum points to a decidedly more ambivalent relationship between stage masters and audiences than most of those who employ this phrase would allow. As far as the example of Imperial Rome is concerned, Paul Veyne has demonstrated that the games were neither 'simply charity', nor merely a vehicle in the orchestration of 'the masses'.[204] Rather, they constituted a theatrical acknowledgement of the considerable power exercised by the Roman populace. This power was expressed directly in the circus, where opposition could be shown and where hostility between the emperor and the spectators developed regularly. Recent studies by Ancient historians have given further emphasis to Veyne's interpretation. Rather than a distraction from it, the circus was part of politics. It involved a 'constant struggle between emperor and people as to how power was to be distributed, and (more formally) where sovereignty lay'.[205]

It is in this sense that the naval theatre ought to be interpreted: not merely as a function of propaganda or manipulation, but as an arena in which power was in flux. At its heart was not one source of agency, be it government initiative or the 'radical right', but the tension between a number of actors, local and national, official and private, commercial and governmental. What this public theatre signified for wider audiences remained a contentious issue, even at the sites of celebration, where alternative rituals and open gestures of defiance could be staged by groups of spectators. While there was a strong sense of entertainment and spectacle, this was never isolated from fundamental political questions about power and sovereignty, entitlement and participation, questions that were embodied particularly powerfully by the navy. To interpret the public staging of the navy as a distraction from politics is therefore misleading: it *was* politics. While the naval theatre certainly showed the willingness of governments and monarchs to impress and influence their audiences, it reflected just as much the rise of 'the masses' and the increasingly vociferous projection of their entitlement to participation.

---

[204] Paul Veyne, *Le pain et le cirque* (Paris, 1976). See also the abridged English version, *Bread and Circuses: Historical Sociology and Political Pluralism*, translated by Brian Pearce (London, 1990), esp. pp. 398–416.

[205] Thomas Wiedemann, *Emperors and Gladiators* (London, 1992), p. 169. See also Brantlinger, *Bread and Circuses*, esp. pp. 21–23 and 69–73; Keith Hopkins, *Death and Renewal: Sociological Studies in Roman History*, vol. 2 (Cambridge, 1983), pp. 14–20.

4   Nation, navy and the sea

When Michel Foucault described ships as 'the greatest reserve of the imagination', he thought of their symbolic power as 'heterotopias': as vessels that symbolically unite spaces or sites that would otherwise be seen as incompatible.[1] There can be few arenas in which this quality was more at work than in the naval theatre that unfolded in and between Britain and Germany in the late nineteenth century. Here, the fleet was a powerful cultural symbol, a 'heterotopia' which played a particularly important role in the imagination of 'the nation'. The question of how this maritime stage served to reconcile otherwise divergent ideas of nationhood and belonging is examined in this chapter. It brings together the local, regional, national and imperial contexts that are essential for an understanding of the identity politics involved in the public staging of the navy. Monarchy, empire and military tradition, but also gender, technology and geography, merged in the representation of the navy and the sea. In unravelling this staging of 'the nation', this chapter argues that the celebration of the navy was a theatre of identity as much as it was one of power and might.

Steel and water

Conflicting ideas about what constituted 'the nation' existed both in the United Kingdom and in Imperial Germany. In the case of the *Kaiserreich*, founded only in 1871, this tension was felt particularly acutely. The new construct of a unified German state faced competing ideas of tradition, loyalty and belonging. The 'persistent struggle between cohesion and fragmentation', which James Sheehan has stressed as a key theme of nineteenth-century German history, continued after 1871.[2] Indeed, Bismarck's *kleindeutsche* foundation challenged traditional ideas of German nationhood

---

[1] Michel Foucault, 'Of Other Spaces', *Diacritics* 16 (1986), pp. 25, 27.
[2] James J. Sheehan, 'What is German History? Reflections on the Role of the Nation in German History and Historiography', *Journal of Modern History* 53 (1981), p. 22.

as much as it offered a solution to them. Not only did the German-speaking parts of the Austro-Hungarian Empire pose a reminder of the *großdeutsche* alternative that had been at the heart of much thinking about German nationhood, but challenges to the Prussian-dominated idea of a *kleindeutsche* nation-state also existed within the new *Kaiserreich*. The states that formed Imperial Germany continued to exert considerable power as separate entities, both culturally and politically. Some of them – Bavaria, Baden, Württemberg and Saxony in particular – had sided with Austria against Prussia only five years before unification.[3] A number of recent studies have explored regional and local Germany in the late nineteenth century and its relationships with the more distant vision called *Kaiserreich*.[4] The picture that emerges shows a Germany that was, despite unification, deeply fragmented. This fragmentation was reinforced by a high degree of regional autonomy, especially where culture and education were concerned. Alon Confino concludes that:

in spite of the unification of the nation-state, German nationhood continued to exist as a patchwork of regions and states, a mosaic of divergent historical and cultural heritages sanctioned by the nation-state's federal system. While the regional states lost their sovereignty, they maintained their pre-unification structure including a head of state, symbols, a Landtag (regional parliament), a government, a bureaucracy, and peculiar laws.[5]

Two factors posed further obstacles to the development of a sense of unified German identity. First, confessional division. While Prussia and

---

[3] On regional particularism see Volker Sellin, 'Nationalbewußtsein und Partikularismus in Deutschland im 19. Jahrhundert', in Jan Assmann and Tonio Hölscher (eds.), *Kultur und Gedächtnis* (Frankfurt, 1988), pp. 241–64; Wolfgang Hardtwig, 'Nationsbildung und politische Mentalität. Denkmal und Fest im Kaiserreich', in Wolfgang Hardtwig, *Geschichtskultur und Wissenschaft* (Munich, 1990), pp. 264–301.

[4] Celia Applegate, *A Nation of Provincials: The German Idea of Heimat* (Berkeley, 1990); Confino, *The Nation as a Local Metaphor*; Abigail Green, *Fatherlands: State-Building and Nationhood in Nineteenth-Century Germany* (Cambridge, 2001). The case of Hamburg is particularly well documented. One of the key themes that emerged from Richard Evans's *Death in Hamburg* were the frictions between the Hanseatic city, Prussia and Imperial Germany. His findings have since been expanded into the cultural arena, in particular by Jenkins, *Provincial Modernity*; Glenn Penny, *Objects of Culture*; and Russell, 'The Building of Hamburg's Bismarck Memorial'. For other regional and local examples see James Retallack, '"Why Can't a Saxon be More Like a Prussian?" Regional Identities and the Birth of Modern Political Culture in Germany, 1866–7', *Canadian Journal of History* 32 (1997), pp. 26–55; James Retallack, 'Saxon Signposts: Cultural Battles, Identity Politics, and German Authoritarianism in Transition', *German History* 17 (2000), pp. 455–69; Dieter K. Buse, 'Urban and National Identity: Bremen, 1860–1920', *Journal of Social History* 26 (1993), pp. 521–37; Georg Kunz, *Verortete Geschichte. Regionales Geschichtsbewußtsein in den deutschen Historischen Vereinen des 19. Jahrhunderts* (Göttingen, 2000).

[5] Confino, *The Nation as a Local Metaphor*, p. 14. Green, *Fatherlands*, p. 334 comes to a similar conclusion.

the German Emperor were staunchly Protestant, roughly a third of the Kaiser's subjects, mostly in the West and in the South, were Catholic. And although Catholicism in itself did not necessarily imply an opposition to the *kleindeutsche* nation-state,[6] its loyalty to a supra-national institution was not easily reconciled with the Prussian-Protestant national project. What made matters worse was the *Kulturkampf*, a conflict that went beyond the question of what role the Catholic Church should play in German public life. As Helmut Walser Smith has argued, the *Kulturkampf* amounted to a 'strategy for nation-building', an attempt to impose by state means a Protestant-Prussian vision of 'the nation', which ultimately failed.[7] It left a divisive legacy for ideas of German nationhood, which had reverberations long after the conflict between the Prussian state and the Catholic Church had been laid to rest. The *Kulturkampf* represented to many Catholics the experience of a German state interfering deeply into their private affairs, it contributed substantially to the politicization of Catholicism which could additionally be charged with regional and particularist agendas, and it showed the limits that existed in Imperial Germany to the state's attempts at imposing its will upon cultural affairs.[8] As a result, confessional allegiances continued to present one of the most powerful sources of division in Imperial Germany. In 1907, twenty years after the *Kulturkampf* had been abandoned by Bismarck, the theologian Adolf Harnack found that a strong sense of confessional division still permeated German public life:

In numerous and important questions of life [. . .], our nation is at the outset divided into two camps, and this state of affairs, starting from the centre, works its way into the periphery of our existence, deep into the smallest and most everyday

---

[6] As Dieter Langewiesche, 'Nation, Nationalismus, Nationalstaat: Forschungsstand und Forschungsperspektiven', *Neue politische Literatur* 40 (1995), pp. 214–6 has convincingly argued.

[7] Helmut Walser Smith, *German Nationalism and Religious Conflict: Culture, Ideology, Politics, 1870–1914* (Princeton, 1995), p. 14.

[8] David Blackbourn, *Marpingen: Apparitions of the Virgin Mary in Nineteenth-Century Germany* (Oxford, 1993); Ronald J. Ross, *The Failure of Bismarck's Kulturkampf: Catholicism and State Power in Imperial Germany, 1871–1887* (Washington D.C., 1998); Eleonore Föhles, *Kulturkampf und katholisches Milieu in den niederrheinischen Kreisen Kempen und Geldern und der Stadt Viersen* (Viersen, 1995); Anderson, *Practicing Democracy*, ch. 4. On the continuing impact of confession in the nineteenth century: Olaf Blaschke, 'Das 19. Jahrhundert: ein zweites konfessionelles Zeitalter?', *Geschichte und Gesellschaft* 26 (2000), pp. 38–75 and Olaf Blaschke (ed.) *Konfessionen im Konflikt. Das zweite konfessionale Zeitalter zwischen 1800 und 1970* (Göttingen, 2001). See also Ellen L. Evans, *The Cross and the Ballot: Catholic Political Parties in Germany, Switzerland, Austria, Belgium and The Netherlands, 1785–1985* (Boston, 1999) and Christopher Clark and Wolfram Kaiser (eds.), *Culture Wars: Secular-Catholic Conflict in Nineteenth-Century Europe* (Cambridge, 2003).

aspects of our lives. Everywhere one confronts confessional prejudice; everywhere one encounters the fence, indeed the wall of confession.[9]

A second source of fragmentation was nurtured through the identity politics driven by the 'minor' German royal courts and their governments. Wilhelm II repeatedly found that the monarchs and princes in Bavaria, Württemberg and Baden, 'these Southerners', as he called them,[10] were at pains to stress their own independent identities. Indeed, they were 'busy inventing traditions of their own', as David Blackbourn has put it.[11] Philipp Eulenburg's correspondence and the diary of Baroness Spitzemberg provide ample evidence for the difficulties and differences between the Hohenzollern and the Southern German courts.[12] These differences did not go unnoticed by outside observers, either. Vincent Corbett, British Consul General at Munich, wrote to Edward Grey in March 1913 about the visit of the Bavarian Prince Regent and Princess Ludwig to Berlin:

It is a curious fact and illustrative of the eminently conservative traditions of the minor German Courts that Princess Ludwig is now, at the age of 64 and after 45 years as a German Princess, visiting both Berlin and Dresden for the first time.[13]

Such royal politics went hand in hand with the promotion of regional ideas of 'the nation' that states such as Bavaria had been keen to foster before unification and that continued after 1871. Successive Berlin governments were painfully aware of this. Bernhard von Bülow, foreign secretary from 1897 and imperial chancellor between 1900 and 1909, was deeply concerned about such challenges to national unity. 'Bülow's prolific correspondence before 1897', writes Katharine Lerman, 'reveals an acute awareness of the divisions between Germans, the new and unfinished nature of the Bismarckian Empire'.[14] Vital for Germany's future was, in the Chancellor's view, the 'nurturing of the national idea', a continuous strengthening of the ties between the Southern

---

[9] Adolf Harnack, 'Protestantismus und Katholizismus in Deutschland', *Preußische Jahrbücher* 127 (1907), p. 295.

[10] *Philipp Eulenburgs politische Korrespondenz*, vol. 3, p. 1902, doc. 1377: Eulenburg to Bülow, 4 July 1898.

[11] Blackbourn, *Populists and Patricians*, p. 49. On the traditional fragmentation of the German nobility, see also the classic work by Norbert Elias, *Die höfische Gesellschaft* (Darmstadt, 1969).

[12] *Tagebuch der Baronin Spitzemberg*, pp. 344–5 (13 and 29 June 1896) and pp. 408–9 (16 June 1902).

[13] PRO, FO 371/1650: Corbett to Grey, 7 March 1913.

[14] Katharine A. Lerman, 'Bismarck's Heir: Chancellor Bernhard von Bülow and the National Idea, 1890–1918', in John Breuilly (ed.), *The State of Germany: The National Idea in the Making, Unmaking and Remaking of a Modern Nation State* (London, 1992), p. 109.

German states and the *Reich*.[15] The Imperial Foreign Office closely observed how far a sense of separatism was alive or even growing in cases ranging from Bavaria to Hanover. It also intervened directly when it thought that too strong an emphasis was being placed on the public representation of independent identities in the German states. The diplomatic row between Munich and Berlin created in February 1900 by the unwillingness of the Bavarian government to display flags on the birthday of the German emperor provides a case in point.[16]

All of this underlines the contested character of German nationhood *after* the foundation of the *Kaiserreich*. It makes sense to take 1871 not so much as the end point of 'German unification', but as the beginning of a long process of nation-building in which culture and politics were inseparably linked.[17] On this basis, the current chapter aims to contribute to the understanding of what Geoff Eley has identified as 'one of the outstanding issues for historians of the *Kaiserreich*', namely 'the making of German identity between the 1860s and World War I'.[18] It addresses in particular the relation between local and national projections of identity, between, as Eulenburg put it, *Lokalpatriotismus* and *deutschem Nationalgefühl*.[19]

The naval theatre offered an ideal stage for the projection of national identity. Naval celebrations brought together representations of the wider German nation and the empire with the strong local and regional interest in these rituals. The Imperial Navy itself presented a uniquely well-suited vehicle for a national emphasis. Unlike the army, which remained fragmented in structure, the navy was an imperial institution. It unequivocally represented the new united Germany.[20] The naval theatre thus presented a central site for the display of German unity, an arena in

[15]   Ibid, p. 108. For a similar assessment by Tirpitz see his *Erinnerungen*, pp. 27, 34.
[16]   PA-AA, R 2856 Bayern 64. The row started in February 1900 when Bavarian authorities ordered that the flags shown at university buildings in Würzburg in honour of the Kaiser's birthday be removed, since this was against official regulations. In response to inquiries from Berlin the Munich government declared that according to Bavarian law, public buildings were only to show flags at the birthday of the Bavarian King and Prince Regent, not however at the birthday of the German Kaiser.
[17]   Blackbourn, *History of Germany 1780–1918*, p. 259.
[18]   Eley, 'Is there a History of the *Kaiserreich*?', p. 9.
[19]   *Philipp Eulenburgs politische Korrespondenz*, vol. 3, p. 1902, doc. 1377, n. 3.
[20]   Steinberg, *Yesterday's Deterrent*, pp. 31–59; Michael Salewski, 'Selbstverständnis und historisches Bewusstsein der deutschen Kriegsmarine', in Michael Salewski, *Die Deutschen und die See* (Stuttgart, 1998), pp. 170–90; Gerhard Bidlingmaier, *Seegeltung in der deutschen Geschichte* (Darmstadt, 1967), esp. p. 81. For the regionally fragmented character of the German army see Stig Förster, 'The Armed Forces and Military Planning', in Roger Chickering (ed.), *Imperial Germany: A Historiographical Companion* (Westport and London, 1996), pp. 454–88, here 473.

which the patchwork of identities could be symbolically reconciled and where 'the nation' could be experienced as an 'emotional community' by large audiences.[21]

This potential was not lost on the Kaiser and the *Reichsmarineamt*. Tirpitz and August von Heeringen, the head of the *Nachrichtenbureau*, stressed the fleet's cultural value as a vehicle that could unite Germans across traditional divisions. They saw the navy as a *volkseinende Kraft*, literally as 'a power that could unite the people': the fleet would bring together 'North and South' and was of central importance for 'national cohesion'.[22] While such statements were undoubtedly informed by the desire to convince 'North and South' of the necessity of naval expansion and to unite them in their support for a strong navy, they did show that the Imperial Fleet was thought of by its architects not only in strategic, but also in cultural and symbolic terms. Indeed, Tirpitz saw the sea as a *Kulturgebiet*, a 'cultural space', in relation to which the fleet had an important role beyond its naval function.[23] This role lay predominantly in the promotion of national unity and the celebration of 'Germanness'.[24]

If unification in 1870/71 had been reached through 'iron and blood', could the cultural nation-building that followed be driven by 'steel and water', by the navy and its public celebration?[25] Wilhelm II clearly thought so. In 1902, Count Paul Wolff Metternich, German Ambassador in London, reported to Berlin an account of a discussion between Prime Minister Arthur Balfour and the Kaiser, who was on a visit to the United Kingdom:

His Majesty then pointed out to the Prime Minister how necessary a fleet was for Germany. Whereas England formed a political entity complete in itself [*ein staatlich in sich abgeschlossenes Ganzes*], Germany resembled a mosaic in which the individual pieces were still clearly distinguishable and had not yet blended together. This could be seen in the army which, though inspired by the identical patriotic spirit, was still made up of contingents from the various German states.

---

[21] Etienne François, Hannes Siegrist and Jakob Vogel, 'Die Nation. Vorstellung, Inszenierung, Emotionen', in Etienne François, Hannes Siegrist and Jakob Vogel (eds.), *Nation und Emotion. Deutschland und Frankreich im Vergleich. 19. und 20. Jahrhundert* (Göttingen, 1995), pp. 13–35, 23.

[22] Deist, *Flottenpolitik und Flottenpropaganda*, pp. 211–2, 264–5.

[23] Tirpitz, *Erinnerungen*, p. 16.

[24] Such thinking reflected a wider Wilhelmine discourse about the sea as a source of culture and unity. Friedrich Ratzel wrote in *Das Meer als Quelle der Völkergrösse. Eine politisch-geographische Studie* (Munich and Leipzig, 1900) that the sea was *volksverbindend*: it united a people into an organic whole, which he saw as the prerequisite for 'cultural achievements'. Compare the section 'The sea: culture and contest' in Chapter 5.

[25] For Bismarck's original dictum see Horst Kohl (ed.), *Die politischen Reden des Fürsten Bismarck*, vol. 2 (Stuttgart, 1892), p. 30.

However, the young German Empire needed institutions that embodied the unitary *Reichs* idea. The Navy was such an institution. The Kaiser was its only commander. The Germans from all counties [*Gauen*] rushed towards it, and it was a constant living example of the unity of the *Reich*. For this reason alone, the navy was necessary and found a warm supporter in His Majesty.[26]

There were numerous other occasions at which the Kaiser declared how central the navy was to the strengthening of national unity and the 'imperial idea'. His speeches and declarations were impregnated with a language in which the navy was 'binding together' the various German 'tribes' into one indivisible people. The fulfilment of German unification was to be represented by a strong fleet, and it was in celebrating this fleet that unity and nationhood would be projected to domestic and foreign audiences.[27]

What were the strategies involved in staging the navy as the 'living example of the unity of the *Reich*', as the Kaiser explained it?[28] Launches of warships provide a particularly apt set of case studies here. It was at these events that 'a piece of the nation' was 'put on to the water', as Wilhelm II put it after the launch of the *Kaiser Karl der Große* in 1899.[29] In unravelling the strong national investment in these rituals, the speeches that were invariably delivered before the christening of warships are particularly pertinent. Given by dignitaries ranging from local mayors to army generals and occasionally the Kaiser himself, the speeches received high priority in the preparation of launches, not least because they were usually quoted verbatim in the press. They proclaimed the purpose and mission of each new vessel and stated the values that it was to represent at sea. And they charged the ship with metaphors in which technology, masculinity and heroism merged with ideas of tradition and identity. Three recurrent themes can be identified in the speeches given at launches of capital warships between 1897 to 1914.[30] They mirror the *Leitmotive* that dominated the celebration of the navy in Wilhelmine Germany: first, the idea of an 'imperial mosaic' that bound the German states together and which was safeguarded by the Kaiser and his navy;

[26] PA-AA, R 5772: Metternich to Bülow, 9 Nov 1902.
[27] Steinberg, *Yesterday's Deterrent*, pp. 31–60; Elisabeth Fehrenbach, *Wandlungen des deut-schen Kaisergedankens 1871–1918* (Munich, 1969), p. 170–3; Kohut, *Wilhelm II and the Germans*, ch. 9.
[28] PA-AA, R 5772: Metternich to Bülow, 9 Nov 1902.
[29] Penzler, *Reden*, vol 2, p. 176.
[30] The following is based on an analysis of the ninety-one speeches given at launches of battleships, battlecruisers and light and heavy cruisers in this period. The original texts of these speeches can be found in the *Nachrichtenbureau*'s files (BA-MA, RM 3/9958–9960) and the *Marinekabinett*'s extensive collection of ceremonial files (BA-MA, RM 2/1618–1630). On the editing and censoring of these speeches see Chapter 1.

second, the example of the Hanseatic League as evidence of a German naval tradition; third, the Prusso-German military past, and in particular the victories over France as the founding myth of the German nation-state and an *Ersatz* tradition for the navy. What these three themes had in common was that they merged diverse locally and regionally defined senses of belonging with visions of the past and ideas about the future aimed at providing a sense of legitimacy for both the navy and the *kleindeutsche* nation.

The Kaiser and the imperial mosaic

Under Wilhelm II an elaborate catalogue of symbolic acts, designed to tie regional and local Germany to the national representation of the fleet, was introduced into the naval theatre. Capital battleships were named after monarchs and princes from all over the *Kaiserreich*. New names such as *Prinzregent Luitpold*, *König Albert* or *Markgraf* suggested a link between the Southern German royals and the navy. In 1903, the Kaiser estab-lished by decree a new line of names, aimed to foster a sense of imperial unity.[31] Most notably, the decree prescribed that light cruisers, which had so far been given the names of classical goddesses and female protagonists of the *Nibelungen*, now had to be named after German cities. Instead of *Freya*, *Medusa* or *Ariadne*, light cruisers were now given names such as *Straßburg*, *München* or *Nürnberg*. Twenty-five such 'city cruisers' were launched between 1903 and 1914. In addition, twenty new battleships took the names of regional states or provinces, amongst them the *Thüringen*, *Elsass*, *Westfalen*, *Posen*, *Hessen*, *Lothringen*, *Schwaben* and *Nassau*.

The selection of a name for a new warship was followed by numerous public acts that tied the respective state, royal family or city to the navy. The launches of the newly invented 'city-cruisers' involved the mayors of the chosen cities travelling to the coast, giving speeches and acting as the patrons of 'their' cruiser. Similarly, royals were invited to be present at the launches of battleships carrying their or their region's name. Thus SMS *Schwaben* was launched by the King of Württemberg, SMS *König* by Duke Albrecht of Württemberg, SMS *König Albert* by Princess Mathilde of Saxony, and SMS *Thüringen* by the Duchess of Saxony-Anhalt. The dignitaries giving speeches at the launches of these floating emblems of local and regional Germany were asked to stress the 'honour' and

---

[31] On this and the following see BA-MA, RM 3/40: Namengebung von Schiffen, 1899–1914. Compare also Albert Röhr, *Handbuch der Marinegeschichte* (Oldenburg, 1963), pp. 170–1.

'prestige' bestowed on their state or city in becoming the patron of the new ship. Employing a standard figure of speech, the Grand Duke of Baden said at the launch of SMS *Nassau*: 'The inhabitants of this *Land* [i.e. Baden] will feel with joyful pride the honour that one of the proudest ships of our Imperial Navy will in future carry the name of their *Heimat* over the seas'.[32] Beyond the launching ceremony, cities were encouraged to form a special link with 'their' ship by presenting gifts and organizing visits. Captain and crew responded by visiting cities and sending telegrams.[33]

These symbolic acts were aimed at cultivating a link between local, regional and national senses of belonging. In celebrating the fleet as a force that brought these different 'Germanies' together, it helped that any mention of the multiple sources of friction between them was carefully avoided. Instead, North and South, *Heimat* and nation, the German *Stämme* and royal families, were portrayed as united in the national naval project. The rhetorical strategies deployed in this process varied. Speaking at the launch of SMS *König*, Duke Albrecht of Württemberg said:

Our *Land* [i.e. Württemberg] lies far away from the sea, in the South of the *Reich*, but our affection for the Imperial Navy is warm; and lively is the wish that the fleet may develop strongly and powerfully. This is proven by the substantial number of Württembergers who stand in the ranks of the navy.[34]

Represented by these *Landsleute*, Württemberg participated in the naval display of a unified Germany. The speaker at the launch of SMS *Westfalen* referred to the 'reconciliation of historical, confessional and economic antagonisms'. He evoked the Kaiser's slogan of '*ein* Reich, *ein* Volk, *ein* Gott' and called upon the ship and its crew to be 'hard like Westphalian steel and tough like Westphalian oak'.[35] It was the dominant strategy in these speeches to identify such local links with the navy and the nation. The mayor of Danzig declared his city 'the cradle of German warship building', which joined in the imperial naval programme 'with pride and joy'.[36] Hamburg's Burgomaster Burchard claimed that the *Hansestadt*, with its shipbuilding industry and trading tradition, was 'in one with the

---

[32] BA-MA, RM 3/9958, Bl. 211: launch of SMS *Nassau*, 7 March 1908.
[33] The commander of the *Bremen* and the Bremen Senate continued to exchange telegrams during the war, see StA Bremen, Senatsregistratur, 3-M.2.q, Nr. 73.
[34] BA-MA, RM 3/9959, Bl. 300: launch of SMS *König*, 1 March 1913. The name of the ship was chosen to represent the King of Württemberg, as the correspondence in BA-MA, RM 3/118, Bl. 146–7 shows.
[35] BA-MA, RM 3/9958, Bl. 270: launch of SMS *Westfalen*, 1 July 1908.
[36] BA-MA, RM 2/1620, Bl. 56: launch of SMS *Danzig*, 22 Sept 1905.

nation' and 'especially enthusiastic' about the creation of a strong navy.[37] At times the metaphorical unity between local identities and the greater naval and national project seemed rather stretched. The mayor of Cologne spoke of the 'breath of the sea' that was felt in Cologne (five hundred kilometres inland) and the Grand Duke of Baden claimed that the 'roar of the ocean' was heard in his *Heimat* (even further removed from the sea).[38]

A particularly striking example of how the regional and the national were tied together in the naval theatre can be seen in the 1912 launch of the *Prinzregent Luitpold*. With the *Wittelsbach* having been launched in 1900 and the *München* in 1904, this was the third capital warship with a Bavarian namesake. Its launch at Krupp's Germania yard in Kiel was one of the biggest spectacles of its kind. The Kaiser had ordered the highest possible protocol for the occasion, adding a *Großer Empfang* to the already elaborate launching ceremony.[39] He was to attend the launch himself. Prince and Princess Heinrich and Prince Adalbert of Prussia were to accompany Prince Ludwig and Princess Therese of Bavaria. The three naval administrations were represented by Tirpitz, von Holtzendorff and von Müller. An additional twenty-nine flag officers were invited.[40] The whole *Ostseestation* was mobilized for the occasion: 26,623 officers and ratings were involved in the day's programme. In addition to the massive display of naval might and honour, the local *Kriegervereine* and *Jugendwehr* were present.[41] A host of Bavarian dignitaries and high civil servants, amongst them Count von Lerchenfeld-Köfering, the Bavarian envoy at Berlin, and Freiherr von Würtzburg, honourable chairman of the Bavarian branch of the *Flottenverein*, were invited. The arrangement of the ceremonial site was carefully geared towards tying as much Bavarian representation into the spectacle as possible. Bavarian flags were displayed next to the Imperial German colours on the launching platform, on the *Kaiserpavillon* and on specially erected poles.[42] On a ceremonial level, remarkably, the Kaiser remained in the background. He made his entry at 11.30 a.m. and, after the inevitable parade, proceeded with his entourage to the *Kaiserpavillon*, where he waited for the Bavarian guests to arrive.

---

[37] BA-MA, RM 3/129, Bl. 52: launch of SMS *Hamburg*, 25 July 1903.
[38] BA-MA, RM 3/9959, Bl. 48: launch of SMS *Cöln*, 5 June 1909; BA-MA, RM 3/9958, Bl. 211: launch of SMS *Nassau*, 7 March 1908.
[39] BA-MA, RM 31/1068, Bl. 136: Chef Marinekabinett to Stationschef Kiel, 5 Feb 1912; ibid., Bl. 191: Flottentagesbefehl Nr. 22, Kiel, 15 Feb 1912; StadtA Kiel, Bestand Stadt Kiel, I, 3, 21557, Bl. 87: Stationstagesbefehl No. 44, 12 Feb 1912, Anlage zum Stapellauf; ibid., Bl. 91: Stapellauf 'Ersatz Odin'.
[40] BA-MA, RM 31/1068, Bl. 65.   [41] *Kieler Zeitung*, 19 Feb 1912.
[42] BA-FA, BSL 22821: Stapellauf des Linienschiffes *Prinzregent Luitpold*, 1912.

The Bavarian royals arrived half an hour later. Upon entering the inner square of the launching site, Princess Therese was presented with a bouquet of flowers in Bavarian blue and white. Led by Tirpitz and Krupp von Bohlen und Halbach, she and Prince Ludwig climbed the launching platform. From here, Ludwig delivered his speech. He had been to launches of warships before, he declared, but the present one was a unique occasion. Unique because of the Kaiser's presence as well as of the choice of the name, 'a name that is dear to every Bavarian and every German: the name *Prinzregent Luitpold*'. Carefully avoiding any allusion to the time before 1871, Ludwig managed to praise both his father and German unity:

His Royal Highness, the Prince Regent of Bavaria, who, unimpeded by his great age, looks back at the four decades of the new German Empire, is one of the few amongst us who in their mature years lived through those important events that have opened this new chapter in the history of the German people. His heart, beating with warmth for everything that concerns the greatness and health of the *Reich*, is full of belief and hope for the *Reich*'s future which is guaranteed by the co-operation of the German royals and states who are allied in loyalty.[43]

Looking back at the 'four decades of the new German Empire' conveniently excluded any reference to the time before 1871, during which the German royals and states had been anything but 'allied in loyalty'. This particularly avoided any mention of the war of 1866 when Bavaria had sided with Austria against Prussia. The symbolic uniting of North and South in the naval theatre required a decidedly selective memory.

The *Reichsmarineamt* went to great lengths to ensure that the event was filmed and shown as soon as possible in Bavarian cinemas. In a series of coded telegrams exchanged between Berlin, Essen, Kiel and London (where Krupp von Bohlen was staying at the time), Tirpitz's office ensured that Bavarian cinematographers would be given access to the launch. As Steinike, the director of the Germania yard, wired to the Krupp head office, the *Nachrichtenbureau* was 'for domestic political reasons [*aus innerpolitischen Gründen*] very keen that the pictures will be shown in Southern Germany as quickly as possible'.[44] In another feat of orchestrated publicity, the *Marinekabinett* sent an imperial telegram to the Bavarian Prince Regent. Such telegrams, announcing the successful launch and expressing best wishes, were routinely issued to the semi-official Wolff newsagency. Prepared well in advance, but publicized with perfect timing, they suggested an immediacy that was not lost on the

[43] BA-MA, RM 3/176, Bl. 138–40.
[44] HA Krupp, FAH 4 C 55: Steinike, Germaniawerft Kiel, to Muehlon, Essen, 3 Feb 1912. On propaganda and publicity see Chapter 2.

press. Reported widely in the papers, the Kaiser telegraphed to the ailing Prince Regent:

The new battleship *Ersatz Odin* has just been launched after pithy words [*markige Worte*] by H. R. H. Prince Ludwig. It was christened *Prinzregent Luitpold* by H. R. H. Princess Therese of Bavaria. May the proud ship tie another bond between mountain and sea [. . .], between the inhabitants of beautiful Bavaria and our navy.[45]

The theme of bonding North and South continued after the launch, when scores of Prussian officers were given Bavarian decorations and vice versa.[46] During the lavish dinner given in honour of the House of Wittelsbach on the same evening, Wilhelm II gave a short speech, addressed to Ludwig of Bavaria:

Everyone who concerns himself with art knows the beautiful medium of mosaic and adores the wonderful pictures formed by it. From a distance, one sees a colourful and complete image [*farbenprächtiges Gesamtbild*]; at close inspection, however, one realizes that this artwork consists of many individual pieces, each of them of a different form and colour, unique in itself. The nature of our *Reich* is the same. From a distance it resembles a powerful and complete entity [*mächtiges Ganzes*], but it consists of individual *Stämme*, all of them proud of their particularity, and loyal to their own traditional dynasties whose colourful flags they have been following for centuries. In guarding over the German *Reichspanier* they have a common bond.[47]

Wilhelm II used this metaphor of the 'imperial mosaic', the *Mosaikbild des Reiches*, at a number of other occasions, most notably in his 1902 conversation with Balfour cited above. Imperial Germany resembled a mosaic, a patchwork of identities and traditions. In the naval theatre, this patchwork was symbolically bound together, *festgeschart*, as the Kaiser put it, for the protection of the empire.

---

[45] BA-MA, RM 2/1628, Bl. 72: Wilhelm II to Prinzregent Luitpold, 17 Feb 1912. A similar rhetoric was employed in the telegram sent by Wilhelm II to Ludwig of Bavaria after the launch of the cruiser *München* in 1904: 'It is an outstanding pleasure that you launched the cruiser which carries the name of the beautiful Capital of Bavaria. I take your warm interest in the development of the German fleet as new evidence for the patriotic sentiment [*vaterländische Gesinnung*] binding South and North together' (PA-AA, R 2249, Wilhelm II to Prinz Ludwig, 1 May 1904).

[46] In preparation, the *Reichsmarineamt* had located as many Bavarian officers as possible and secured their attendance, see BA-MA, RM 3/176, Bl. 174–7. Tirpitz and von Müller were awarded the *Prinzregent Luitpold Medaille*. See BA-MA, RM 3/176, Bl. 158–9 and RM 31/1068, Bl. 148–75.

[47] *Schulthess' Europäischer Geschichtskalender*, Neue Folge, Jahrgang 1912 (Munich, 1913), p. 40. The *Münchener Neueste Nachrichten*, the main Munich newspaper, went along with this rhetoric of bonding. It published the texts of speeches and telegrams under the headline '*Vom Fels zum Meer*' and concluded that the launch had been 'invigorating evidence of German unity and national self confidence' (*Münchner Neueste Nachrichten*, 18 Feb 1912, Morgen-Blatt, title page).

Such imagery of binding and bonding was a recurrent feature in the whole spectrum of launching speeches. They spoke of the navy as providing the *Bindeglied*, the *Glied* or *Band* for German unity. North and South, the *Stammesbrüder von Nord und Süd*, were 'bound together' or 'tied to each other' in the navy, typically through 'bands of steel'.[48] This symbolism also integrated those parts of the *Reich* whose 'Germanness' seemed particularly contested, such as Alsace, Lothringen and Posen. They were bound to the Empire through 'a new tie', they were 'strongly united with us', claimed the speakers at the launch of the *Posen*, the *Elsass* and others.[49] The vehicle that was to facilitate this unity was the Imperial Navy in which 'all German hearts beat as one'.[50] Merging regional and national representation, the naval theatre thus provided a powerful cement for the 'mosaic of empire'. As Dresden's mayor put it at the launch of SMS *Dresden*:

> If there is something that could truly strengthen the ties even further by which the great period of 1870 and 71 has bound the German *Stämme* together, something that could make this bond even more durable, then it has to be the creation of a German navy.[51]

These evocations of unity and bonding hardly ever failed to mention the guiding father figure that stood behind the navy and the nation: the Kaiser. In the naval theatre, Wilhelm II appeared as the creator of the navy who held together the 'imperial mosaic' of otherwise divergent German 'tribes' and who would defend German unity against future enemies. A range of procedures was designed to emphasize the emperor as the *Übervater* of the navy and the nation. The choreography of launching ceremonies was structured in such a way that put representations of the emperor at their centre.[52] The same was true for the rhetoric of these rituals. Even when the Kaiser did not attend himself, the monarchical and

---

[48] BA-MA, RM 3/9959, Bl. 109: launch of SMS *Thüringen*, 27 Jan 1909; RM 3/129, Bl. 52: launch of SMS *Hamburg*, 25 July 1903; RM 3/9958, Bl. 166: launch of SMS *Dresden*, 5 Oct 1907; RM 3/9959, Bl. 48: launch of SMS *Cöln*, 5 June 1909; RM 3/9959, Bl. 18: launch of SMS *Mainz*, 23 Jan 1909. A visual representation of this idea can be seen in the decoration of the ceiling of the *Aula* in the naval academy in Mürwik, showing the crests of the German states and Hanseatic cities, united by the Imperial eagle and Germany's naval mission. Compare Stefan Bölke, *Die Marineschule Mürwik. Architekturmonographische Untersuchung eines Repräsentationsbaus der Kaiserlichen Marine* (Frankfurt 1998), plates 33, 34.

[49] BA-MA, RM 3/9959, Bl. 9: launch of SMS *Posen*, 12 Dec 1908; RM 3/9959, Bl. 37: launch of SMS *Von der Tann*, 20 March 1909; RM 3/127, Bl. 137: launch of SMS *Elsass*, 26 May 1903; *Danziger Neueste Nachrichten*, 27 May 1903, Erste Beilage.

[50] BA-MA, RM 3/9959, Bl. 48: launch of SMS *Cöln*, 5 June 1909.

[51] BA-MA, RM 3/9958, Bl. 166: launch of SMS *Dresden*, 5 Oct 1907.

[52] See the section 'Launching the Imperial Navy' in Chapter 1.

imperial message was unmistakable. Not a single launching speech passed without multiple references and reverences to the emperor. Launching patrons invariably opened their speeches with a formula thanking the Kaiser for the honour and stressing that the naming of the ship took place 'by the command of His Majesty'. Addressing the ship itself, speakers called upon its braveness in battle – and its loyalty to *Reich* and *Kaiser*. In the words of Helmuth von Moltke, every new warship's mission was 'to fight and wrestle for our German fatherland, for our emperor and master'.[53] 'Loyal to your emperor, loyal until death' was a formula used frequently: *Treu deinem Kaiser, Ihm getreu bis in den Tod*.[54] Speeches closed with three cheers for the Kaiser, followed by the band playing the imperial hymn at the moment the ship entered the water.[55]

This orchestrated reverence ensured that the Kaiser appeared as the source of the navy, as its commander and visionary. Parliament and government remained unmentioned. By effectively controlling the content of speeches, Tirpitz's press office made sure that this focus on the emperor was adhered to. During the weeks leading up to a launching ceremony, the *Nachrichtenbureau* sent extensive instructions to the chosen speaker, reminding him of the standard phrases to be used, and pointing out ways in which praise for the Kaiser could be linked to the specific name of the ship that was to be launched. Even when the imperial chancellor Bethmann Hollweg was to deliver the speech at the 1911 launch of SMS *Kaiser*, Tirpitz's office gave polite yet clear instructions. Carefully underlining the word 'Kaiser', Karl Hollweg, director at the *Nachrichtenbureau*, wrote to the Imperial Chancellory:

Without doubt you will find an opportunity to refer to the unparalleled development of our navy in the last 40 years; a navy which owes its greatness to the initiative of His Majesty, the Kaiser, and which would be impossible without a strong *Kaisertum*, in which the strength of the united *Reich* is expressed.[56]

The chancellor's ghost-writers obliged. The result was a speech that eulogised at once *Kaisertum*, Imperial Navy and German nationhood. In the presence of Wilhelm II and the empress, who was to christen the ship, Bethmann said:

---

[53] BA-MA, RM 3/9959, Bl. 115: launch of SMS *Moltke*, 7 April 1910.
[54] BA-MA, RM 3/9958, Bl. 270: launch of SMS *Westfalen*, 1 July 1908; RM 2/1620, Bl. 56; RM 3/129, Bl. 52: launch of SMS *Hamburg*, 25 July 1903; similarly RM 2/1626, Bl. 174: launch of SMS *Scharnhorst*, 22 March 1906.
[55] *MVBl* 31 (1900), pp. 397–8: Das Zeremoniell bei Stapelläufen.
[56] BA-MA, RM 3/9959, Bl. 112: Hollweg, Vorstand Nachrichtenbureau, to Vortragender Rat in der Reichskanzlei, von Oppen, 27 Feb 1911 (emphases in original).

By order of Your Majesty the ship awaiting its launch today, on the birthday of Kaiser Wilhelm, will be christened *Kaiser*. *Kaiser* – the word around which the dreams of German greatness and German longing swirl. *Kaiser* – the bounty of bloody battles forty years ago. *Kaiser* – the man in our midst who gave us a German fleet [...]. Loyalty to the *Kaiser* in the hearts of your crew will be the compass by which you will be steered, so that you may plant loyalty in the hearts of all the Germans out there. May you raise your head high in the battle with the elements, just as the *Kaiser* stands elevated above the arguments of the day.[57]

Bethmann's speech demonstrated the versatility of the fleet as an instrument for the merging of regional, national, civic and naval with monarchical representation. The Kaiser, the united German nation and the imperial navy appeared as one entity, bound together through loyalty, past experience of war and the longing for German greatness in the future.

The renaissance of the Hanseatic League

The second *Leitmotiv* that featured prominently in the Wilhelmine naval theatre was the example of the Hanseatic League, the *Hanse*. As Tirpitz put it, the imperial navy and the German nation were destined to 'pick up the lost thread of the *Hansa*', demonstrating to themselves and to the world that there was a long tradition of Germany's mission on the sea.[58] As a national fleet the Imperial Navy had of course very little 'tradition'. Its history was 'still young', as Burgomaster Burchard put it at the launch of the *Hamburg*.[59] It had only been in 1848 that plans for a unified German fleet had been set up for the first time by the revolutionary Frankfurt parliament, a fact which remained largely unmentioned in the Wilhelmine naval theatre.[60] Nor was there much of a Prussian naval tradition. The Great Elector of Brandenburg had founded a small Prussian fleet and something close to a colonial settlement in Africa in the late seventeenth century, but this had remained inconsequential, especially by comparison with Prussian military history.[61] It was in response to this absence of a strong naval tradition that the history of

---

[57] BA-MA, RM 3/9959, Bl. 116: launch of SMS *Kaiser*, 22 March 1911.
[58] Tirpitz, *Erinnerungen*, p. 22.
[59] BA-MA, RM 3/129, Bl. 52: launch of SMS *Hamburg*, 25 July 1903.
[60] On the German navy before the 1890s see Lawrence Sondhaus, *Preparing for Weltpolitik: German Sea Power before the Tirpitz Era* (Annapolis, 1997).
[61] For one of the occasions at which the Great Elector was evoked as a historical example see the launch of the *Großer Kurfürst* in May 1913, documented in BA-MA, RM 3/9960, Bl. 12.

the Hanseatic League was discovered and re-invented as the period in which the foundations of German sea power had been laid. Simultaneously, the 'historical memory of the brilliant times of the *Hansa*' was paraded as a key motivation for the bonding of the German *Stämme* in the greater naval and national project.[62]

This was part of a wider renaissance that the *Hanse* underwent in the Wilhelmine period. A movement can be seen in architecture and public iconography, in museums and schools, in academia and learned societies, which sought to connect the Wilhelmine present with the Hanseatic past.[63] The new Hamburg *Rathaus*, inaugurated in 1897, the naval academy in Mürwik and the restoration of parts of the historical centres of Lübeck and Bremen all featured strong references to the medieval and Hanseatic past.[64] A flood of books, academic and popular, emphasized the Germanness of the *Hanse*.[65] Amongst the most prolific authors were Walther Stein, Dietrich Schäfer, Theodor Lindner and Ernst Robert Daenell.[66] Highly influential in the Wilhelmine re-narration of the Hanseatic past was also the *Verein für Hansische Geschichte*.[67] Its main activity lay in the editing of documents, the publishing of articles and monographs, and the organizing of conferences and lecture series, all on the subject of the *Hanse*. The journal *Hansische Geschichtsblätter*, begun by the *Verein* in 1871, was one of the prime platforms for the scholarly

---

[62] BA-MA, RM 3/9958, Bl. 166: speech by the mayor of Dresden at the launch of SMS *Dresden*, 5 Oct 1907. For a similar example see *Überall* (1901), p. 272.

[63] For a good survey see Dirk Schümer, 'Die Hanse', in Etienne François and Hagen Schulze (eds.), *Deutsche Erinnerungsorte*, vol. 2 (Munich, 2001), pp. 369–86.

[64] Jenkins, *Provincial Modernity*, pp. 288–93; Bölke, *Marineschule Mürwik*, ch. 13.

[65] The Senates of Hamburg, Bremen and Lübeck collaborated in a joint project that aimed to publish an official history of the Hanseatic League. This endeavour is documented in StA Hamburg, 132-5/2 HG VI b (2). For the prominence of the Hanse in Wilhelmine schoolbooks see Hermann de Buhr, 'Darstellung und Funktion der Hanse in den deutschen Schulbüchern der letzten hundert Jahre', *Geschichte in Wissenschaft und Unterricht* 29 (1978), pp. 693–701.

[66] Walther Stein, *Zur Entstehung und Bedeutung der Deutschen Hanse* (Lübeck, 1911); Walther Stein, *Beiträge zur Geschichte der deutschen Hanse bis um die Mitte des 15. Jh.* (Giessen, 1900); Theodor Lindner, *Die deutsche Hanse. Ihre Geschichte und Bedeutung dargestellt für das deutsche Volk* (Leipzig, 1899); Dietrich Schäfer, *Die deutsche Hanse. Mit 99 Abbildungen* (Bielefeld und Leipzig, 1903); Ernst Robert Daenell, *Geschichte der deutschen Hanse in der zweiten Hälfte des 14. Jh.* (Leipzig, 1897); Ernst Robert Daenell, *Die Blütezeit der deutschen Hanse*, 2 vols (Berlin, 1905). See also Harry Denicke, *Von der deutschen Hansa. Eine historische Skizze* (1884) and Walther Vogel, *Kurze Geschichte der Hanse* (Munich and Leipzig, 1915).

[67] On the origins of the *Verein* see Wilhelm Mantels, 'Der Hansische Geschichtsverein', *Hansische Geschichtsblätter*, vol. 1 (Leipzig, 1874), pp. 3–8. Amongst its members were the Kaiser and a range of Wilhelmine luminaries, but the bulk of the membership was made up by historians, archivists, librarians and teachers, as well as local politicians and bureaucrats.

discussion of the Hanseatic past. When it started a second journal in 1908, the *Verein* announced that its main aim was to show that 'the nature and content [*Wesen und Inhalt*] of the *Hanse* is its representation of Germany at sea'.[68]

The fact that the renaissance of the Hanseatic past blatantly served the politics of the present was evident in the writing of most of the Wilhelmine historians of the *Hanse*. In his 1899 monograph *Die deutsche Hanse*, Theodor Lindner, Professor of History at the University of Halle, offered a narrative of how 'the Germans' had discovered the *Hanse* in the nineteenth century:

When the German *Volk* was burning in longing for new greatness, for a powerful fatherland, it directed the views back to its past and found in it solace and hope, the guarantee [*Bürgschaft*] of a new future. It was most of all the *Hanse* that radiated like a guiding star in dark night. What the ancestors had accomplished could not be denied to the descendants, because their flesh and blood was still the same. In a time in which the sea belonged to all peoples but the Germans, they were taught by the image of the *Hanse* what was needed most of all. The desire for a German fleet stood at the top of the national wishes.[69]

Lindner's depiction mirrored all of the main ideas that played a strong role in the Wilhelmine renaissance of the Hanseatic League. The German nation had come to itself in the nineteenth century and, looking for examples of past greatness, it turned almost naturally to the *Hanse* as a 'guiding image'. A bond of 'flesh and blood' united the Hanseatic past and the German present. This bond also carried a 'debt to the future': what had been Hanseatic greatness in the past was to be reclaimed by the Imperial Navy in the years to come. German nationhood and the claim to the sea were thus inseparably linked in the Hanseatic example. Often enough, this was associated with Anglo-German rivalry. Many of the authors writing about the *Deutsche Hanse* saw in 'England' the main reason why the League had been doomed. Friedrich Schulz employed a standard explanation in his monograph *Die Hanse und England*, published in 1910:

The *Volk* that was able to throw the greater political power on to the scales had to be the one to whom victory would fall. The *Hanse*, facing the purposeful and

---

[68] *Abhandlungen zur Verkehrs- und Seegeschichte* 1 (1908), preface, p. iv. The *Abhandlungen* were edited by Dietrich Schäfer, professor of history at Berlin University and one of the most enthusiastic advocates of Hanseatic history. On his connection with the Pan-German League (*Alldeutscher Verein*) see Chickering, *We Men Who Feel Most German*, p. 146.

[69] Lindner, *Die deutsche Hanse*, p. 203.

energetic national politics [*nationale Politik*] pursued by England, lacked the backing of a powerful state.[70]

Similar formulations can be found recurrently in the writing of scholars such as Theodor Lindner and Dietrich Schäfer. In the *Hanse*, they discovered the German nation as a competitor of Britain, a power that was both role model and rival. That the Hanseatic League had ultimately found itself outwitted by this opponent was an occurrence, they suggested, that would not be repeated: the main difference between past and present Anglo-German rivalries was that the Wilhelmine incarnation of the *Hanse* was backed by a strong nation-state, an expanding navy and a visionary emperor.[71]

Presenting the *Hanse* as the origin of the Wilhelmine mission on the sea required a considerable bending of historical facts. The Hanseatic League had been neither a state, nor a nation or a people, but a trading alliance between various cities along the North Sea and the Baltic Sea. If anything it had been supra-national. It consisted of cities that were located in or surrounded by different principalities, cities that were neither united by one cultural or lingual background, nor by the belief in a shared national character or mission. What brought them together was a common interest in trade and commerce. Furthermore, the Hanseatic League had never had an easy relationship with the princes, kings and emperors, 'German' or not, who had been influential in Northern Europe. Even as ardent an advocate of the Wilhelmine re-invention of the *Hanse* as Theodor Lindner conceded that the League had never been part of the medieval Holy Roman Empire, the 'first *Reich*' which the Kaiser and many of his contemporaries identified as the origin of a German imperial tradition.[72] As Lindner wrote, the *Hanse* and successive medieval and early modern emperors had 'little to do with each other'.[73] In fact, the rise of the sovereign and centralized monarchical state in early modern Europe had been a key factor in the demise of the Hanseatic League.[74] On a number of scores, the historical link between the *Hanse* and the Wilhelmine *kleindeutsche* nation-state therefore looks decidedly weak.

---

[70] Friedrich Schulz, *Die Hanse und England* (Berlin, 1910), p. 194.

[71] Ibid, passim. Similar: Dietrich Schäfer, 'Deutschland zur See', in Dietrich Schäfer, *Aufsätze, Vorträge und Reden*, vol. 2 (Jena, 1913), pp. 24–101, here p. 55; Schäfer, *Die deutsche Hanse*, p. 135; Lindner, *Die deutsche Hanse*, pp. 207–8; Neudeck and Schröder, *Das kleine Buch von der Marine*, p. 2.

[72] Fehrenbach, *Wandlungen des deutschen Kaisergedankens*, pp. 107–15.

[73] Lindner, *Die deutsche Hanse*, pp. 200–1.

[74] Heinz Duchhardt, 'Die Hanse und das europäische Mächtesystem des frühen 17. Jahrhunderts', in Antjekathrin Grassmann (ed.), *Niedergang oder Übergang? Zur Spätzeit der Hanse im 16. und 17. Jahrhundert* (Cologne, Weimar, Vienna, 1998), pp. 11–24.

Notwithstanding such complexities, the Wilhelmine re-narration of the medieval past cultivated the Hanseatic League as the origin of Imperial Germany's mission on the sea. It was as if the *Hanse* was reborn in the Wilhelmine present. At the same time, 'the nation' was narrated back into the history of the Hanseatic League, suggesting that this had been 'the German people' and not a group of city-based traders. The Kaiser's navy was thus presented as the logical continuation of the *Hanse*'s attempt at establishing Germany as a major sea power. While lending the Imperial Navy an *Ersatz* tradition, the Hanseatic League offered a convenient metaphorical link between local identities and the more distant *Reich*. In order to stress this link, the Northern cities that had been at the core of the *Hanse* were given special status in the naval theatre. New cruisers were launched carrying the names of Hamburg, Bremen and Lübeck, of Danzig, Rostock and Stralsund. Just as these cities had been 'powerful members of the *Hansa*, loyal to the alliance and reliable in battle', they were now presented as similarly loyal and reliable components of the Imperial Navy and the *Reich* it embodied.[75] Even cities such as Cologne or Dresden trumpeted their Hanseatic credentials in the naval theatre.[76]

It was through the co-operation of the three *Hansestädte* Hamburg, Bremen and Lübeck with the Imperial Naval Office that the re-invention and glorification of the Hanseatic League reached its climax. A series of occasions celebrated both the Imperial Navy and the Hanseatic past of the three cities. This included the opening of the Kiel Canal in 1895 and the launching of the *Hansa* in 1898, the *Hamburg* and the *Bremen* in 1903, and the *Lübeck* in 1904, as well as numerous dinners, visits and parades. The bond between the navy and the Hanseatic cities was symbolized by a crest donated by the cities, depicting their arms in unity with the Imperial Eagle. Costly gifts for the crews of the *Hansa*, *Bremen*, *Hamburg* and *Lübeck* further strengthened this 'close relationship'. For the string of functions and festivities that celebrated the Hanseatic past, the otherwise thrifty cities were prepared to fund unprecedented expenses.[77] The imagery and rhetoric employed at these occasions merged *Reich*, *Hanse* and navy into one. After the launch of the *Hansa*, in which Hamburg, Bremen and Lübeck had been given special representation, Tirpitz sent telegrams to the Burgomasters of the three cities:

---

[75] BA-MA, RM 3/9959, Bl. 182: launch of SMS *Stralsund*; Bl. 257–8: launch of SMS *Rostock* 12 Nov 1912.
[76] BA-MA, RM 3/9958, Bl. 285: launch of SMS *Rheinland*, 26 Sept 1908; Bl. 166: launch of SMS *Dresden*, 5 Oct 1907; RM 3/9959, Bl. 3: launch of SMS *Kolberg*, 14 Nov 1908; Bl. 48: launch of SMS *Cöln*, 5 June 1909.
[77] See Chapters 1 and 3.

The cruiser just launched successfully at the Vulcan yard has by the All Highest order been given the name *Hansa*. The whole navy is proud that one of the new ships carries again this glorious name that expresses the close relationship between the fleet and the Hanseatic cities.[78]

In Bremen, this telegram was read out in the Senate and Burgomaster Pauli responded to Tirpitz that he may convey to His Majesty their 'joyful satisfaction' that the name of the *Hanse* would now 'continue to live' in the spirit of the 'blossoming fleet of the new empire'.[79] It was as if the *Hanse* had been reborn in the new fleet.

What made the public celebration of the Hanseatic past so popular with the three cities, as well as with the navy and the Kaiser, was that the *Hanse* was uniquely well suited to represent diverse interests and traditions in one unifying metaphor. In the Wilhelmine re-invention of the *Hanse* a cluster of identities and interests – local and national, civic and naval – were united. In a two-way process, the celebration of the *Hanse* lent a much needed sense of tradition and historical legitimacy to the navy while it represented and reinforced the interests of the Hanseatic cities. It stressed their central role in trade and shipping, their historical privileges and peculiarities, yet it also reconciled them with the *Reich*. Moreover, the *Hanse* could be paraded as proof of the necessity for a strong emperor. In the Wilhelmine reading of the past, the decline of the *Hanse* in the seventeenth century was explained by the absence of a powerful German Kaiser. Now, however, with Germany united under one emperor and equipped with a growing Imperial Navy, there was the dawn of a new era, a 'time of blossoming' [*Blütezeit*] as many speeches put it. It was under the *Flottenkaiser* that the navy and the nation would, in Tirpitz's words, pick up the 'thread of sea power' where the Hanseatic League had left it.

Military tradition and a violent future

The third *Leitmotiv* evoked by the Wilhelmine naval theatre as a source of unity was military tradition. Just like the example of the Hanseatic League, the military past was to offer the navy an *Ersatz* tradition, it served as a source of national identification, and it paraded the blessings of a strong German Kaiser. In 1903, a new line of ship names was

---

[78] StA Bremen, 2-M.6.b.4.e.3, Nr. 20: Tirpitz to Pauli, Erster Bürgermeister Bremen, 12 March 1898.

[79] Ibid. For the similar and similarly well-publicized exchange of telegrams between Hamburg's Burgomaster Burchard and the Kaiser, see StA Hamburg, 132-1I, 3391, Bl. 22–5 and *Hamburger Correspondent*, 27 July 1903.

introduced that stressed these themes. Battle-cruisers (*große Kreuzer*) had until then been named after Germanic gods and protagonists of the *Nibelungen*, such as *Hildebrand* or *Odin*. Now they were to be given the names of past army leaders and generals. Quite literally, the old Germanic *Nibelungen* heroes were superseded by the more worldly ones of 'iron and blood'. Between 1903 and 1914, nine such 'hero cruisers' were launched with names such as *Blücher*, *Yorck*, *Scharnhorst*, *Gneisenau*, *von der Tann* and *Moltke*. The descendants of these military demi-gods were invited to become patrons of the new ships. Countess Blücher von Wahlstatt christened the *Blücher*; Countess Yorck was made the patron of the *Yorck*; Count von Schlieffen gave the speech at the launch of the *Gneisenau*; Helmuth von Moltke spoke at the launch of the *Moltke*; and Count Waldersee did so at the launch of the *Roon*, to name but a few.

Almost all the heroes after whom the new battle-cruisers were named were Prussian, a fact which received little attention in the launching speeches. Instead, Prussian victories were presented as German ones. This re-narration of the past was reinforced by the choice of military heroes, who were predominantly taken from the 'wars of liberation' against Napoleonic France and the 'wars of unification' leading up to 1871. *Befreiung* and *Einigung* were the key themes, rather than Prussian dominance and expansion. The 'awakening of the nation' and the 'bonding of army and people' during the Napoleonic era were called upon, notwithstanding the fact that many Southern Germans had fought with rather than against Napoleon for much of that time.[80] Again and again, the generals of 1870/71 were mythologized as having equipped the nation with the instruments by which it was united.[81] The Wilhelmine fleet and Germany's mission on the sea were portrayed as the logical continuation of unification achieved 'on the battlefield' by the Prussian-German army. 'The German fleet', declared Helmuth von Moltke in 1910, 'would be unthinkable had not the fragmented forces of the German tribes [*Stämme*] been forged by blood and iron'. It was therefore only fitting that the navy carried the names of those men 'who had put an end to Germany's inner conflicts, who had raised the proud construction of the *Reich*'.[82]

---

[80] Particularly strong in BA-MA, RM 2/1626, Bl. 173: launch of SMS *Scharnhorst*, 22 March 1906; and in RM 3/9959, Bl. 3: launch of SMS *Kolberg*, 14 Nov 1908.

[81] For examples see BA-MA, RM 2/1622, Bl. 97: launch of SMS *Roon*, 27 June 1903; RM 2/1626, Bl. 172–4: launch of SMS *Scharnhorst*, 22 March 1906; RM 3/9959, Bl. 9: launch SMS *Posen*, 12 Dec 1908; ibid., Bl. 18: launch of SMS *Mainz*, 23 Jan 1909; ibid., Bl. 114: launch of SMS *Moltke*, 7 April 1910; ibid., Bl. 151: launch of SMS *Goeben*, 28 March 1911; ibid., Bl. 166: launch of SMS *Friedrich der Grosse*, 10 June 1911.

[82] BA-MA, RM 3/9959, Bl. 115: launch of SMS *Moltke*, 7 April 1910.

Wilhelmine naval mythology thus retrospectively portrayed 1870/71 as the result of Prussian army tradition – and the Imperial Navy as a key product of unification. The pasts of the various German states were co-opted into this teleological representation of Prussian military tradition. Avoiding any mention of the part played by the armies of Bavaria, Württemberg or Saxony in the Napoleonic wars or in the Prussian-Austrian war of 1866, their traditions were presented as consistent with Prussian-turned-German military history. In the naval theatre, there was a quasi-mythical unity of German kings and princes, generals and soldiers as a 'brotherhood in arms' that had been forged in past battles and would stand together against future challenges.[83]

The fact that the naval theatre employed Prussian-German military tradition so heavily in its rhetoric and iconography made it embarrassingly obvious just how little of a victorious past the Imperial Navy itself had. Indeed, the *Reichsmarineamt* and the Kaiser rarely ever considered that a high-ranking naval officer would be able to offer the symbolic qualifications necessary for a launching patron. Instead, it mostly asked Prussian generals to deliver the speeches at these occasions, evoking the army's past victories for the guidance of the navy. The fleet was to embody Frederick the Great's qualities 'on the waves of the sea', it was to imitate the heroic deeds of a long tradition of generals and Field Marshals.[84] Officers and ratings were to carry themselves like Moltkes and Blüchers. 'Always devotedly ready for the splendour of the Empire [*Allzeit treu bereit für des Reiches Herrlichkeit*]. I want to pass these beautiful words by Moltke on to you, proud ship', was what General von der Tann-Rathsamshausen proclaimed at the launch of the *Von der Tann*.[85] Generalfeldmarschall von Haesseler told the crew of the *Scharnhorst*: 'Just as this hero [...] has fought to the last breath for Prussia's victory, your fluttering flag shall symbolize Germany's protection and honour'.[86]

This projection of military values and army tradition on to the navy created a strong sense of expectation. The incessant recalling of past military victories suggested that the Imperial Navy would repeat on the sea what the Prussian army had achieved on land. Time and again, the

---

[83] A particularly striking example can be seen in the launch of the *König* in March 1913, at which, in the presence of the Kaiser and numerous Southern German dignitaries, Duke Albrecht of Württemberg declared that the German dynasties had been 'brothers in arms' in the past. See BA-MA, RM 3/9959, Bl. 300: launch of SMS *König*, 1 March 1913. For similar examples see RM 3/9959, Bl. 3: launch of SMS *Kolberg*, 14 Nov 1908 and RM 3/9958, Bl. 270: launch of SMS *Westfalen*, 1 July 1908.

[84] BA-MA, RM 3/9959, Bl. 166: launch of SMS *Friedrich der Grosse*, 10 June 1911.

[85] BA-MA, RM 3/9959, Bl. 37: launch of SMS *Von der Tann*, 20 March 1909; ibid., Bl. 152: launch of SMS *Goeben*, 28 March 1911.

[86] BA-MA, RM 2/1626, Bl. 174: launch of SMS *Scharnhorst*, 22 March 1906.

navy was summoned to follow the victorious path of Prusso-German armies, to achieve its own Leipzig, Waterloo or Sedan. In order to be victorious in future, it was to embody the qualities that the Prussian army had shown in the past: *Opferwilligkeit* and *Kampfeslust*.[87] At the launch of the *Von der Tann*, the new ship was urged to 'use its dashing weapon [*schneidige Wehr*]', just like von der Tann had done 'on the blood-soaked battlefields'.[88] At the launch of the *Friedrich der Große* the navy was told:

You shall always be ready for battle, ready to use your arms and to let the thunder of your guns roar, when the hour of decision nears; always ready for attack, just like the army of your patron who told his soldiers: the Prussian cavalry is always the first to attack! These royal words shall be your motto, they shall be the whole navy's motto in battle.[89]

While the use of such martial language and an overarching expectation of future naval victories was recurrent, the speeches given in the naval theatre remained remarkably imprecise as to the exact purpose of the Imperial Navy. 'Honour' and 'Germanness' were most frequently referred to. The warships were to represent *deutsche Kultur* and *deutsches Wesen*, *Macht*, *Kraft* and *Ehre*.[90] The fleet was to be ready to fight for 'Germany's greatness and honour' and its 'vital interests', its *Lebens- interessen*.[91] However, exactly what constituted 'German honour' and 'German greatness' was never elaborated upon. As the Hamburg Senator and Burgomaster Burchard put it 1903, the fleet reflected the

complete feeling [*Vollgefühl*] of German strength and diligence, of national self- confidence [...]. The *Reich* is young, it is stretching its powerful limbs [*markigen Glieder*], and with its ships it is growing beyond the seas.[92]

This urging forward, the Wilhelmine *Vorwärtsstreben*, was embodied in the navy. A strong 'belief in the future' carried the fleet forward, the mayor of Straßburg declared. A 'believing and daring future [*gläubig*

---

87 BA-MA, RM 3/129, Bl. 53: launch of SMS *Hamburg*, 25 July 1903; RM 3/9958, Bl. 166: launch of SMS *Dresden*, 5 Oct 1907; RM 2/1626, Bl. 173: launch of SMS *Scharnhorst*, 22 March 1906; RM 3/9959, Bl. 166: launch of *Ersatz Heimdall*, 10 June 1911; ibid., Bl. 37: launch of SMS *Von der Tann*, 20 March 1909; ibid., Bl. 109: launch of SMS *Thüringen*, 27 Jan 1909; ibid., Bl. 300: launch of SMS *König*, 1 March 1913; ibid., Bl. 115: launch of SMS *Moltke*, 7 April 1910; RM 3/9958, ibid., Bl. 285: launch of SMS *Rheinland*, 26 Sept 1908.
88 BA-MA, RM 3/9959, Bl. 37: launch of SMS *Von der Tann*, 20 March 1909.
89 BA-MA, RM 3/9959, Bl. 166: launch of SMS *Friedrich der Große*, 10 June 1911. Similar: ibid., Bl. 3: launch of SMS *Kolberg*, 14 Nov 1908.
90 BA-MA, RM 3/9959, Bl. 9: launch of SMS *Posen*, 12 Dec 1908; ibid., Bl. 18: launch of SMS *Mainz*, 23 Jan 1909; ibid., Bl. 115: launch of SMS *Moltke*, 7 April 1910.
91 BA-MA, RM 3/9959, Bl. 37: launch of SMS *Von der Tann*, 20 March 1909; RM 3/9958, Bl. 285: launch of SMS *Rheinland*, 26 Sept 1908.
92 BA-MA, RM 3/129, Bl. 52: launch of SMS *Hamburg*, 25 July 1903.

kühne Zukunft]' lived in the ships filled with 'youth and manly strength'.[93] More than anything, the Imperial Navy symbolized the youth, strength and expansion of Germany. Helmuth von Moltke claimed at the launch of the *Moltke* that the rapidly expanding navy embodied the 'youthful strength of united Germany'.[94] Germany had 'begun a new path in her development', the fleet and the *Flottenkaiser* would ensure that the *Reich* would 'go forward without hindrance'.[95] The way in which the naval theatre cultivated the impression of a young Germany reaching beyond traditional limits recalled Max Weber's inaugural lecture in which he had explained German unification as a *Jugendstreich* which the nation had better refrain from, unless it wanted to use it as the 'starting point for a German world position [*Weltmachtposition*]'.[96]

While a powerful sense of moving forward dominated the rhetoric of Wilhelmine warship launches, there was no clear indication as to the ultimate aim of such progression. Similarly, any restraints or limitations on the unfolding of the glorious new era remained unmentioned. This mirrored some of the main characteristics of Wilhelmine *Weltpolitik*: its impulsiveness and heady rhetoric, its lack of clearly defined goals, of an overall idea or 'great aim', as Tirpitz noted.[97] While the naval theatre obsessively evoked national unity, the nature of 'overseas' and Germany's mission 'beyond our shores' remained unexplored. The space in which the new ships and their representation of 'the nation' were to operate was recurrently described as 'out there', 'on the waves' or as 'wherever you are sent'. Rather than offering any clear idea about Germany's mission on the sea or any guidance as to the rationale behind German imperialism, it was 'the nation' that dominated these speeches. Indeed, it seemed as if the navy was much more about German unity than about colonial expansion, as if the projection of the *Reich*'s identity, prestige and 'honour' on to the sea was more important than any concrete formulations of ideas of imperialism and colonialism.[98]

---

[93] BA-MA, RM 3/9959, Bl. 171: launch of SMS *Straßburg*, 24 Aug 1911.
[94] BA-MA, RM 3/9959, Bl. 114: launch of SMS *Moltke*, 7 April 1910.
[95] BA-MA, RM 3/9959, Bl. 166: launch of SMS *Friedrich der Große*, 10 June 1911; RM 3/9958, Bl. 166: launch of SMS *Dresden*, 5 Oct 1907; RM 3/129, Bl. 53: launch of SMS *Hamburg*, 25 July 1903; RM 3/9959, Bl. 114: launch of SMS *Moltke*, 7 April 1910.
[96] Max Weber, *Gesammelte politische Schriften*, edited by J. Winckelmann, third edition (Tübingen, 1971), p. 23.
[97] Tirpitz, *Erinnerungen*, p. 156.
[98] On the imperial imagination and the cultural production of 'the foreign' that went on in other arenas see Alexander Honold and Klaus R. Scherpe (eds.), *Mit Deutschland um die Welt. Eine Kulturgeschichte des Fremden in der Kolonialzeit* (Stuttgart, 2004); Birthe Kundrus (ed.), *Phantasiereiche. Zur Kulturgeschichte des deutschen Kolonialismus* (Frankfurt, 2003) and Sara Friedrichsmeyer, Sara Lennox and Susanne Zantop (eds.), *The Imperialist Imagination: German Colonialism and its Legacy* (Ann Arbor, 1998).

Beyond mirroring aspects of Wilhelmine *Weltpolitik*, the speeches analysed here illustrate what Dieter Langewiesche has described as the 'Janus-face of modern nations'.[99] Cultivating unity, tradition and imperial strength within Germany went hand in hand with the projection of force and power abroad. In the naval theatre, the summoning of *Einheit* was recurrently accompanied by the evocation of past wars and victories. France served as a prime source of identification: it was in the wars against 'the French' that the divergent German 'tribes' had come together in defending 'the nation'. In future, such threats might come from abroad, and it was against such threats that the nation and the *Reich* had to stand in unity. The *Nachrichtenbureau* ensured that any direct mention of Britain was avoided wherever possible, but there remained the odd reference to 'the rival across the North Sea' or comparisons between 'old and young nations' competing over the oceans.[100] In short, these rituals can be seen as exercises in the construction of the Wilhelmine nation, driven by a two-sided dynamic: while Imperial Germany was put on stage as united by tradition and common experience, this was never divorced from representations of aggression and violence, whether they were seen in the past or the future.

While ideas of 'the nation' remained heavily contested in Wilhelmine Germany, the naval theatre thus was employed as a stage for cultural nation-building. Relying on careful selection and a degree of historical amnesia, the close to one hundred speeches given at these occasions celebrated the navy as a metaphor that was at once local, regional, national and imperial.[101] Avoiding allusions to past conflict and fragmentation, the naval theatre presented the *kleindeutsche* nation and the blessings of Hohenzollern Kaiserdom and Prusso-German military tradition as closely intertwined. It projected the image of a nation that was united by 'steel and water' in the present as much as it had been brought together by 'iron and blood' in the past. Speaking at the launch of the *Nassau*, the Grand Duke of Baden portrayed the fleet as 'a sword-carrying *Germania*' that held 'the imperial crown as a shield over the German land'. Evoking the 'imperial mosaic', he exclaimed that the Kaiser and the navy had united 'the land's interior and the sea'.[102]

---

[99] Langewiesche, 'Nation, Nationalismus, Nationalstaat', p. 192.   [100] See Chapter 5.
[101] Confino, *The Nation as a Local Metaphor*.
[102] BA-MA, RM 3/9958, Bl. 211: launch of SMS *Nassau*, 7 March 1908.

Island nation

National identity was just as contentious an issue in the United Kingdom as it was in the *Kaiserreich*.[103] After the first Act of Union, new manifestations of 'Britishness' had developed alongside, and in competition with, English, Scottish and Welsh ideas of nationhood. Yet, the four 'subnations' had continued to exert a strong influence.[104] With the incorporation of Ireland into the United Kingdom and the expansion of the empire, questions of nationhood were complicated further. Mounting Anglo-Irish tensions and the fierce debate about Home Rule meant that by the end of the century this was 'already a disunited kingdom'.[105] The conflict about Home Rule was the strongest factor, but by no means the only one. In parallel to the continuing crisis about the future of Ireland, the awakening of Scottish and Welsh nationalism produced a growing articulation of uncertainty about British identity.[106] Notions of nationhood were similarly challenged from outside the United Kingdom. The empire, an important source of a shared vision of 'Britishness', seemed heavily stretched. The South African War in particular exposed the 'weary titan'.[107] It severely tested the imperial construct, and simultaneously galvanized particularist and anti-imperialist movements, especially in Ireland.[108] Threats to the British command of the sea also undermined

---

[103] J. G. A. Pocock, 'British History: A Plea for a New Subject', *Journal of Modern History* 47 (1975) pp. 601–28; Hugh Kearny, *The British Isles: A History of Four Nations* (Cambridge, 1989); Norman Davies, *The Isles* (London, 1999); J. C. D. Clark, 'English History's Forgotten Context: Scotland, Ireland, Wales', *Historical Journal* 32 (1989). See also David Armitage, 'Greater Britain: a Useful Category of Historical Analysis?', *American Historical Review* 104 (1999), pp. 427–45 and Raphael Samuel, 'Four Nations History', in Samuel, *Island Stories*, pp. 22–40.

[104] Colley, *Britons*; Kearny, *British Isles*, pp. 230–62; Robbins, *Nineteenth-Century Britain*, pp. 1–28; Keith Robbins, *Great Britain: Identities, Institutions and the Idea of Britishness* (London, 1998), pp. 262–94; Clark, 'Protestantism, Nationalism, and National Identity', pp. 275–6; Adrian Hastings, *The Construction of Nationhood: Ethnicity, Religion and Nationalism* (Cambridge, 1997), pp. 1–95.

[105] Peter Clarke, *Hope and Glory: Britain 1900–1990* (Harmondsworth, 1996), p. 1.

[106] Kearny, *British Isles*, ch. 10; John S. Ellis, 'Reconciling the Celt: British National Identity, Empire, and the 1911 Investiture of the Prince of Wales', *Journal of British Studies* 37 (1998) pp. 391–418; Paul Readman, 'The Place of the Past in English Culture *c.* 1890–1914', *Past & Present* 186 (2005), pp. 147–99; Elfie Rembold, *Die festliche Nation. Geschichtsinszenierungen und regionaler Nationalismus in Großbritannien vor dem Ersten Weltkrieg* (Berlin, 2000).

[107] Joseph Chamberlain coined the phrase of the 'weary titan' staggering 'under the vast orb of its fate' at the colonial conference in 1902; see James L. Garvin and Julian Amery, *The Life of Joseph Chamberlain*, vol. 5 (London, 1969), p. 30. The financial and military weakness that the war uncovered is analysed in detail by Aaron L. Friedberg, *The Weary Titan: Britain and the Experience of Relative Decline, 1895–1905* (Princeton, 1988).

[108] Donal Lowry, ' "The Boers were the Beginning of the End"?: The Wider Impact of the South African War', in Donal Lowry (ed.), *The South African War Reappraised*

senses of national identity, closely connected as they were to naval superiority in this period. All this meant that a strong sense of unresolvedness characterized the issue of nationhood in the United Kingdom of the late nineteenth century, a kingdom that was increasingly struggling to accommodate its four nations and define their common purpose.

The cultural relevance of the navy and the sea for the processes in which these challenges were negotiated has been continuously neglected by historians. The debate about national identity in the British Isles, with Linda Colley as one of the most influential recent protagonists, has focused on religion, state formation and conflict.[109] Neither the interest in 'institutions and the idea of Britishness' (Keith Robbins) nor the analysis of the symbols involved in the 'making and unmaking of British identity' (Raphael Samuel) have extended to an examination of the navy's cultural role.[110] This is all the more surprising, given that the naval theatre was a particularly prolific arena for cultural nation-building. Indeed, the Royal Navy was one of the most important agents of national sentiment in the Victorian and Edwardian era. While the army was bound, by tradition as well as recruitment, to regional allegiances, the navy offered itself ideally for a British, unionist and imperial emphasis.[111]

Consequently the Admiralty discovered the naval theatre as an ideal arena for the cultural construction of 'the nation'. From the turn of the century, it developed a conscious policy that aimed to symbolically accommodate Ireland, Wales and Scotland in the public staging of the navy. This began with the choice of names for new ships. The Admiralty dropped the custom of naming cruisers after classical gods. Instead, the new generation of cruisers launched from 1901 were named after selected counties and cities of the United Kingdom. Edward Fraser, the contemporary naval historian who had such a keen interest in public ritual, observed that the new naming policy was aimed at providing a link

(Manchester, 2000), pp. 231–6; Geoffrey Searle, ' "National Efficiency" and the "Lessons" of the War', in David Omissi and Andrew S. Thompson (eds.), *The Impact of the South African War* (Basingstoke, 2002), pp. 194–211.

[109] Colley, *Britons*; Colley, 'Britishness and Otherness'. For a critique of Colley see J. C. D. Clark, 'Protestantism, Nationalism, and National Identity, 1660–1832', *Historical Journal* 43 (2000), pp. 249–79.

[110] Robbins, *Great Britain: Identities, Institutions and the Idea of Britishness*; Robbins, *Nineteenth-Century Britain*; Robbins, 'National Identity and History'; Samuel, *Patriotism*; Samuel, *Island Stories*. Recent studies on Englishness have overlooked this role similarly: Colls, *Identity of England*; Colls and Dodd, *Englishness*; so has the scholarship on royal rituals and public pageants: Cannadine, 'Context, Performance and Meaning of Ritual'; Cannadine and Price, *Rituals of Royalty*; Colley, *Britons*, ch. 5; Kuhn, *Democratic Royalism*, pp. 1–14, 57–81; Williams, *Contentious Crown*, pp. 230–62.

[111] Colin Matthew has stressed this point in his introduction to the *Short Oxford History of the British Isles: The Nineteenth Century* (Oxford, 2000), p. 22. See also Max Jones, *The Last Great Quest: Captain Scott's Antarctic Sacrifice* (Oxford, 2003), ch. 6.

between local, regional and national loyalties in the navy.[112] What he failed to notice, however, was that the names were consciously selected in order to represent all four nations of the United Kingdom. More than a third of the new city and county cruisers had Scottish, Welsh or Irish associations, carrying names such as *Glasgow*, *Dublin*, *Donegal*, *Antrim*, *Carnarvon*, *Argyll* and *Shannon*.

The new naming practice triggered a set of local and regional, civic and naval events, symbolically displaying the link between ship and county or city. Correspondence between the Admiralty and local authorities shows how local civic and central naval initiative went hand in hand at these occasions. Visits by the newly commissioned ships were in high demand. As the Lord Provost of Glasgow wrote, the Corporation felt that the *Glasgow* 'should in some way be identified with the City after which it is named'. He suggested that the cruiser should be sent to the Clyde so that gifts could be exchanged between the crew and the citizens of Glasgow.[113] Almost all cities and counties represented by the new class of ships hosted such visits. The Admiralty actively encouraged these symbolic meetings between the navy and the 'local nation'. It ensured publicity and public funding, and even set up a special ceremonial for these occasions.[114] When the *Glasgow* was sent to visit its patron city in April 1911, an internal Admiralty memorandum noted that the event was 'for show purposes'.[115] The ship's captain reported after the visit:

On arrival, the Lord Provost and members of the Corporation paid an official visit which I afterwards returned at the City Chambers. In the afternoon the ship was open to the public, and between 15,000 and 16,000 came on board. On Friday, 15 officers including myself, and 200 men, accompanied by the band [...] marched to the City Chambers, where [...] the gifts [...] were presented. In the afternoon, between 300 and 400 guests attended an 'At Home' on board, and in the evening, the ship was again open to the public and large numbers came on board. [...] It is calculated that during the ship's short stay, quite twenty-five thousand people visited the ship, and I was greatly struck by their orderly behaviour. On Thursday, although it was raining in torrents, people stood for hours in a queue – quite half a mile long – waiting to get on board.[116]

---

[112] NMM, Fraser, Box 49.

[113] PRO, ADM 1/8215: Lord Provost of Glasgow to First Lord of the Admiralty, 22 Aug 1910.

[114] PRO, ADM 1/8215: Memo M Branch, 23 Aug. 1910; PRO, ADM 198/3, 326: Presentations to Ships of County Class: Ceremonial to be Observed in Future.

[115] PRO, ADM 1/8215: Memorandum, Naval Branch, April 1911.

[116] PRO, ADM 1/8215: Captain HMS *Glasgow* to Commander-in-Chief Portsmouth, 1 May 1911.

21. The navy as a local and national metaphor. Programme for the launch of HMS *Superb* in Newcastle, 7 November 1907.

Not all of these visits were greeted with such enthusiastic attendance. However, there can be little doubt that these were major public spectacles, designed as symbolic displays of unity between the navy and the 'local nation'. When the cruisers sailed from their bases to their patron cities, exchanging gifts and promising future visits, they linked divergent parts on the mental map of the United Kingdom, providing an 'ever-lengthening chain', as the *Glasgow Herald* put it, between local, regional and national senses of belonging.[117]

In a similar vein, ship launches became carefully structured towards representing the unity of the United Kingdom's four nations. This was most visible in 1912 when the Admiralty changed the ceremonial of ship launches. Until then, one of the hymns sung during the service before the christening of warships had been: 'May England's sons, her destined crew / Be men of might, brave hearts and true'.[118] In a move towards greater inclusion, the nationality of 'her destined crew' was changed – from English to British. As the First Lord of the Admiralty announced in the House of Commons on 17 July 1912: 'In consequence, with the permission of the holder of the copyright, the phrase "May England's sons" will [. . .] be altered to the phrase, "May Britain's sons"'.[119] The change in terminology demonstrated how keenly aware of the navy's public role the Admiralty was, stating publicly that a redefined sense of Britishness should govern the celebration of the fleet. In this, it responded to numerous complaints that had demanded a stronger representation of Scotland and Ireland in the Royal Navy.[120]

The conflation of 'English' and 'British' in much of the navy's nomenclature had drawn particular criticism in the press and in letters sent to editors. As one reader had pointed out, if 'the name of our country is Great Britain, then, of course, the Navy must be "British" (the possessive of Britain), quite apart from what nationality predominates in that Navy, be they Scots, English, Irish'.[121] In April 1911, the St Andrews Society of Edinburgh had even demanded that the Admiralty change 'the so-called White Ensign, which is the English Flag with a Union Jack in the canton,

---

[117] *Glasgow Herald*, 29 April 1911. For a similar example see *Daily Record*, 2 May 1911.
[118] See the section 'Going down the ways' in Chapter 1 for an analysis of the religious aspect of ship launches.
[119] Hansard, Fifth Series, House of Commons, vol. 41, cl. 366 (17 July 1912). For the full text of the hymn by L. M. Sabine Pasley see *Service to be Used at the Launching of Ships of His Majesty's Navy* (London, 1902).
[120] See Jan Rüger, 'Nation, Empire and Navy: Identity Politics in the United Kingdom 1887–1914', *Past & Present* 185 (2004), pp. 159–87 for a detailed account.
[121] *Daily Express*, 26 July 1909.

thereby ignoring the true position of Scotland and Ireland as partners in the Union'.[122] While the navy was not prepared to change its revered flag, it went out of its way to accommodate the United Kingdom's four nations in public representation. It was not only by substituting 'British' for 'English' in official terminology that it appealed to non-English sentiment. Entire launches were dedicated to the celebration of Scotland and Ireland as part of the wider nation.

The launch of the *Hibernia* at Devonport on 17 June 1905 provides a case in point. A range of iconographic and ceremonial elements were aimed at signifying 'Irishness'. Contemporaries noted how 'shamrock and other Irish emblems entered largely into the scheme of decoration'.[123] Lady Ormonde had travelled from Ireland to perform the ceremony accompanied by other Irish aristocrats, amongst whom the papers noted Lady Mayo and Lady Donegal. Before the christening, Lady Ormonde presented, 'on behalf of the Irish ladies', a special Union Jack to the ship. Other gifts, it was announced, would follow after the commissioning of the *Hibernia*: a ship's bell and a bracket of old Celtic design, a silver challenge shield, and three centrepieces for the messroom tables, all 'made by the people of Ireland'. Giving the ship the ancient name for Ireland, Lady Ormonde broke a bottle of Irish whiskey – instead of the customary bottle of wine – on the *Hibernia*'s bows. Other launches with Irish themes followed, as did naval visits and presentations. Together with innovations such as allowing the wearing of a sprig of shamrock in the navy, these changes were part of a strategy to accommodate Irish sentiment and promote unionism.[124] The naval theatre thus served as a key arena for the symbolic uniting of the four nations of the United Kingdom. Consciously appealing to Scottish, Irish and Welsh sentiment in display and ceremonial, it was a powerful vehicle aimed at 'reconciling the Celt' when Anglo-Irish tensions were at an all-time high.[125]

One of the key ideas employed in this staging of unity was insularity. The 'island nation' was a powerful trope in Victorian and Edwardian Britain. Evoked in cultural as much as in political discourses, it served as

[122] PRO, ADM 1/8257: St Andrews Society, Edinburgh, to Secretary of the Admiralty, 21 April 1911.

[123] *Times*, 19 June 1905; NMM, Fraser, Box 50.

[124] PRO, ADM 12/1357: Wearing of Shamrock, 10 March 1900. Three days before, the Queen had ordered that all ranks of the army should wear a sprig of shamrock on St Patrick's Day.

[125] Ellis, 'Reconciling the Celt'.

an important *Leitmotiv* in British identity politics.[126] In addition, the shoreline was invested with national symbolism, notably in the case of the 'white cliffs of Dover', a signifier of the border between 'home' and 'foreign' that was exploited in literature, art and popular culture long before the First World War.[127] Any threat to these 'natural' boundaries, whether through imagined invasions, technological innovation or 'disfigurement' through advertising, inspired passionate debate.[128] The importance of insularity as a source of self-understanding was also underlined during the public debate provoked by Rudyard Kipling's poem 'The Islanders' in 1902. Kipling had attacked the British as 'islanders' who were obsessed with gentlemanly ideals and country sports, instead of endorsing conscription and military efficiency. The outraged responses to his poem showed how strongly established insularity was as a source of national identification. Countless readers wrote to *The Times*, where the poem had first appeared, to assert that 'island race', 'islanders' and 'insular needs' were ideas that carried decidedly positive connotations. Insularity was, as one reader put it, at the heart of the 'character of the British people'.[129]

---

[126] Robert Shannan Peckham, 'The Uncertainty of Islands: National Identity and the Discourse of Islands in Nineteenth-Century Britain and Greece', *Journal of Historical Geography* 29 (2003), pp. 499–515; Stephen Daniels, *Fields of Vision: Landscape Imagery and National Identity in England and the United States* (Cambridge, 1993), pp. 114–38; Cynthia F. Behrmann, *Victorian Myths of the Sea* (Athens, Ohio, 1977); Keith Robbins, 'Insular Outsider? "British History" and European Integration', in Keith Robbins, *History, Religion and Identity in Modern Britain* (London, 1993), pp. 45–57. See also Diana Loxley, *Problematic Shores: The Literature of Islands* (Houndmills, 1990) and Gillian Beer, 'The Island and the Aeroplane: The Case of Virginia Woolf', in H. K. Bhabha (ed.), *Nation and Narration* (London, 1990), pp. 265–90.

[127] It seems surprising how little attention historians have paid to the political and cultural role of 'natural boundaries' and the sea in Britain. This stands in stark contrast to Continental European history, see Peter Sahlins, *Boundaries: The Making of France and Spain in the Pyrenees* (Berkeley, 1989); Peter Sahlins, 'Natural Frontiers Revisited: France's Boundaries since the Seventeenth Century', *American Historical Review* 95 (1990), pp. 1435–43; Peter Schöttler, 'The Rhine as an Object of Historical Controversy in the Interwar-Years: Towards a History of Frontier Mentalities', *History Workshop Journal* 39 (1995), pp. 1–21.

[128] Alfred M. Gollin, 'England Is No Longer an Island: The Phantom Airship Scare of 1909', *Albion* 13 (1981), pp. 43–57; I. F. Clarke, *Voices Prophesying War: Future Wars 1763-3749* (Oxford, 1992); Keith M. Wilson, *Channel Tunnel Visions 1850–1945: Dreams and Nightmares* (London, 1994); Daniel Pick, *War Machine: The Rationalisation of Slaughter in the Modern Age* (New Haven, 1993), ch. 10: 'Tunnel Visions'. On the cliffs of Dover, see Paul Readman, 'Landscape Preservation, "Advertising Disfigurement", and English National Identity, c. 1890–1914', *Rural History* 12 (2001), pp. 61–83.

[129] *Times*, 6 Jan 1902; ibid., 7 Jan 1902; ibid., 8 Jan 1902. See also the strong reaction in *Punch*, 15 Jan 1902, pp. 42, 52, a publication that had linked Britishness and insularity for decades (compare illustration 22). For Kipling's interpretation of the debate see

"COMPASS'D BY THE INVIOLATE SEA."

(*On the Diamond Jubilee Day.*)

A QUEEN sat on the rocky brow
Which looks o'er the broad British sea
War-ships in hundreds ranged below,
To grace our Diamond Jubilee.

Punch counted them, and cried, "Hooray
This sight well crowns a glorious day!"
Britannia silent sat and gazed
On those grim warders of her isle,

Flags flaunted, beacons brightly blazed!
Responsive then to *Punch's* smile,
"All's well," she cried, "old friend, whilst we
Are 'compass'd by the inviolate sea.'"

22. Celebrating insularity. 'A queen sat on the rocky brow / Which looks o'er the broad British sea / War-ships in hundreds ranged below / To grace our Diamond Jubilee. / *Punch* counted them, and cried, "Hooray / This sight well crowns a glorious day!" / Britannia silent sat and gazed / On those grim warders of her isle, / Flags flaunted, beacons brightly blazed! / Responsive then to *Punch's* smile, / "All's well," she cried, "old friend, whilst we / Are 'compass'd by the inviolate sea'"' (*Punch*, 19 June 1897).

If the Victorians and Edwardians were busy constructing their nation 'as an island',[130] the naval stage must be seen as a key arena for this celebration of insularity. Part of the 'lure of the sea', certainly in the case of the tourism attracted by the cliffs of Dover, was to experience the natural boundaries of one's country.[131] The public rituals performed by the navy emphasized these boundaries. Just as in poetry, literature and popular culture, the fleet was employed in the naval theatre as a tool of delimitation. The warships were signifiers that hovered around the nation's boundaries, vessels that constantly marked the beginnings and ends of the country. The navy thus described the country's 'natural' boundaries. During fleet reviews, vast audiences occupied the shoreline to marvel at the 'nation's bulwark' commanding the space that set the country apart from others. Importantly, the way in which the naval theatre evoked the 'island nation' left open exactly what island and what nation this referred to. This sense of openness acknowledged that there were competing claims about nationhood within the United Kingdom. As Keith Robbins has put it:

Of course there had never been 'one Island', except for rhetorical purposes. The 'Eastern Atlantic Archipelago' – viewed from the United States – was made up of a cluster of islands ranging in size from Ireland and England/Scotland/Wales as a whole to the Northern Isles (Orkney and Shetland), Anglesey and the Isle of Wight, not to mention the Isle of Man and the Channel Isles. They were all in a sense 'British Isles', but quite in *what* sense was becoming contentious.[132]

The 'island nation' or 'island race' was as geographically imprecise as ideas of 'the nation' were contested in the British Isles. In the naval theatre, this was a strength: precisely because it remained ambiguous, the idea of the 'island nation' could appeal to different senses of belonging and identification.

Already in 1887, when Victoria's reign was celebrated with an unprecedented naval spectacle, the 'island status' of Britain was a central theme in the commemorative literature. The long ballad *The Ocean Throne: Verse for the Celebration of the Fiftieth Year of the Reign of Victoria* by John Huntley Skrine merged praise for the Queen with the evocation of the navy and the sea as guardians of the 'island home' that was Britain:

Rudyard Kipling, *Something of Myself and Other Autobiographical Writings*, ed. Thomas Pinney (Cambridge, 2000), pp. 129–30. The poem can be found in *Rudyard Kipling's Verse: Inclusive Edition, 1885–1918* (Edinburgh, 1922), p. 347.

[130] Peckham, 'Uncertainty of Islands', p. 505.
[131] Alain Corbin, *The Lure of the Sea* (Berkeley and Los Angeles, 1994); Alexa Geisthövel, 'Der Strand', in Geisthövel and Knoch, *Orte der Moderne*, pp. 121–30; Rob Shields, *Places on the Margin: Alternative Geographies of Modernity* (London, 1991), pp. 73–116.
[132] Robbins, 'Insular Outsider', p. 51.

> Britons of the island home,
> Narrow nest in girdling foam:
> Britons reared the broad earth o'er
> Whom one island mother bore.[133]

Nationhood was inseparable from insularity, the sea and the navy. Perhaps the most popular author who celebrated this theme was Henry Newbolt. His collection of ballads *Admirals All* sold fourteen editions between 1897 and 1898 alone. In the poem that gave the collection its name, nation and territory appeared demarcated by the 'realm of the circling sea'. Central in this 'Song of Sea Kings', as the subtitle went, was the idea that the sea and the navy defined the British:[134]

> Admirals all, they said their say
> (The echoes are ringing still).
> Admirals all, they went their way
> To the haven under the hill.
> But they left us a kingdom none can take –
> The realm of the circling sea –
> To be ruled by the rightful sons of Blake,
> And the Rodneys yet to be.

Admirals All was followed by the equally best-selling *The Island Race* in which the navy again encapsulated the intertwined issues of national identity and insularity. 'Yarnder lumes the Island, yarnder lie the ships' was the catch-phrase of 'Drake's Drum', one of the most prominent poems in the collection.[135] Clearly, it was in the navy that the most visible symbol of the 'island race' existed.

The Admiralty was therefore eager to project insularity as a source of the nation's freedom and identity. In February 1902, the First Lord of the Admiralty, the Earl of Selborne, gave a speech at a Unionist dinner at Oxford that drew strongly on the topos of the 'island nation'. Imperial and national unity were underpinned, he suggested, by what he called 'our insular prejudices'. Insularity encapsulated national unity: the holding together of the United Kingdom's four nations and the coming together of its social classes was best expressed in the island image. Selborne closed his speech by exclaiming: 'But we were islanders, and therefore would say, "Oh that my countrymen had one hand, that I might

---

[133] Huntley Skrine, *Ocean Throne*, p. 19. Similar: Nassau Strachey, *Sea-Power of England*, p. 1.

[134] Henry Newbolt, *Admirals All* (London, 1897), p. 7.

[135] Henry Newbolt, 'Drake's Drum', in Newbolt, *Island Race*, p. 40. A similar conflation of navy and 'island race' featured in Newbolt's 'England', ibid., p. 78.

grip it." (Cheers).'[136] Despite domestic conflict and foreign challenges, Selborne suggested, the people in the United Kingdom shared a common bond as 'islanders'. Such rhetoric drew on a well established tradition that saw insularity as a source of freedom, both politically and economically. Insularity was constructed here as a 'natural' explanation as to why the British were not only predisposed to the sea and all things naval, but also why they were prone to dislike any form of foreign rule or tyranny.[137] In contrast especially to Continental nations, the 'island nation' had resisted absolute rule, it was the home of the 'bold and free', as Newbolt had it in 'Admirals All'.[138] The naval theatre took such arguments and projected them in one powerful image in which navy, nation and island merged with other themes that were central in the late nineteenth-century constructions of Englishness and Britishness.

The floating empire

The naval stage played an important role not only for the construction of the nation, but also of the empire. Fleet reviews, ship launches and a range of other displays celebrated the navy as a symbol of imperial unity and strength. This naval staging of the empire expanded remarkably between the 1880s and 1914. It can be seen in the increasing frequency and scale of displays, in their expanding costs, and in the transformation of old and the invention of new ceremonies designed to foster imperial sentiment. It was here that the 'remarkable transoceanic construct of substance and sentiment'[139] called the empire was most visibly put on stage for audiences at home and abroad. While historians have neglected the relevance of the naval theatre for the staging of the empire, contemporaries were in no doubt about it. Sir George Sydenham Clarke wrote in 1898 that the representation of the navy was 'one of the principal factors

[136] *Times*, 24 Feb 1902.
[137] As Kathleen Wilson, *The Island Race: Englishness, Empire, and Gender in the Eighteenth Century* (London, 2003), p. 5 has shown, the trope of the island emerged in eighteenth-century Britain 'not only as a metaphor, but also as an explanation for English dominance and superiority'. This drew on authors of the Enlightenment who had seen island populations as naturally inclined towards the 'rule of freedom'. Montesquieu, for example, argues in *The Spirit of the Laws* that 'island peoples are more inclined to liberty than continental peoples'. See *The Spirit of the Laws*, edited by Anne M. Cohler, Basia C. Miller and Harold S. Stone (Cambridge, 1989), part 3, ch. 5, p. 288. See also Peckham, 'Uncertainty of Islands', pp. 502–3 and David Armitage's interpretation of the sea as a source of the ideological construction of empire in *The Ideological Origins of the British Empire* (Cambridge, 2000), ch. 4.
[138] Newbolt, 'Drake's Drum', p. 40.   [139] Cannadine, *Ornamentalism*, p. 122.

in promoting and maintaining the unity of the Empire'.[140] The Admiralty itself was adamant that the naval theatre should be exploited for the fostering of imperial sentiment. During the South African War, it intro-duced new measures that emphasized the navy as an agent of empire. An element of imperial representation was now to be part of all launches of warships. Imperial delegates were to be invited to these spectacles, and 'colonial wine' was to be used for the christening of warships instead of the 'foreign wine' that had been used traditionally.[141] The change was welcomed by commentators such as Edward Fraser who wrote that this had 'a distinct value [...] as a matter of sentiment' and formed 'a graceful recognition of the unity of the Empire which cannot fail to be fully appreciated in our colonies'.[142] The first ship to be christened with 'imperial wine' was the *Good Hope*, launched in February 1901 as a floating symbol of imperial unity. Its name had been changed at the last minute as 'a compliment to the people of the Cape Colony'.[143] At the end of the South African War, Joseph Chamberlain stressed the ship's sym-bolic value when he chose it for his passage to South Africa to implement the peace treaty. The *Good Hope*'s departure from Britain to the Cape was staged as a spectacle of victory and imperial unity, shown in cinemas in the British Isles and the colonies.[144]

The example of the *Good Hope* was followed in the years up to 1914 by an armada of warships carrying imperial names, each designed to foster the link between mother country and colony. The Admiralty chose the new King Edward VII class of battleships specifically as agents of imperial sentiment. As McKenna, the Secretary of the Admiralty, wrote in December 1910, it was 'desirable' that 'the Imperial idea [...] runs through the naming of this class of battleships'.[145] Speaking at the launch of the *Hindustan*, the First Lord of the Admiralty, Lord Selborne, explained the identity-fostering purpose of the King Edward VII class:

The idea of the class was to group round the 'Sovereign' the component parts of the Empire. We began with those two great colonies that had done so much for us fighting side by side in South Africa – the 'Dominion' and the 'Commonwealth'. We then passed on to that wonderful colony, smaller than the other two, which sent no fewer than ten separate contingents of men, he meant 'New Zealand'; and

[140] George Sydenham Clarke, *Russia's Sea-Power: Past and Present of the Russian Navy* (London, 1898), pp. 132–3. Although the book was primarily about Russian sea power, it was the Royal Navy that Clarke was concerned with in this passage.
[141] PRO, ADM 12/1369: Colonial Wine for Use at Launches of HM ships, 11 Jan 1901.
[142] NMM, Fraser, Box 50; *Times*, 16 Feb 1901.   [143] *Times*, 22 Feb 1901.
[144] NFTVA, 25/11/1902 Hepworth: Departure of Mr Chamberlain for South Africa.
[145] PRO ADM 1/8220: Secretary of the Admiralty to High Commissioner for New Zealand, 1 Dec 1910.

then to the gem of the British Empire [...], 'Hindustan'. The last three ships of the class would be the 'Africa', and then, coming home, they would have the 'Hibernia' and the 'Britannia'.[146]

In this idea of the empire grouped around the sovereign as well as 'Hibernia' and 'Britannia', the image of the imperial family was paramount. Britain and Ireland resembled imperial parents, around which the sons and daughters of empire were assembled. Invoking the South African victory as shared by the empire created the sentiment of an imperial comradeship in arms, symbolized in the cruisers and battleships, the 'empire's bulwark'.

In order to sustain such imagery, the Admiralty went as far as renaming ships that were already in service. When New Zealand commissioned its first 'own' battle-cruiser in 1910, the Admiralty was keen to give the ship a name connected to the colony, and decided that it ought to be called the *New Zealand*. Unfortunately, that name already existed in the King Edward VII class, and in looking for a new name for the old *New Zealand* McKenna found that it was 'not very easy' to find one 'that could be directly connected with the Dominion'.[147] The High Commissioner for New Zealand and the Governor-General suggested 'Maori', but the Admiralty was not prepared to name a warship after an indigenous people. Instead, faced with impatient questions in Parliament and in the press, their Lordships invented, with the King's blessing and some creativity, the *Zealandia*.[148]

The ceremonies in which these 'ambassadors of empire'[149] were launched reflected the enormous attention paid to imperial themes. Colonial representatives were regularly asked to perform the christening ceremony. When the *Hindustan* was launched in 1903, Lord Selborne explained that the Admiralty had suggested the Duke and Duchess of Connaught as patrons for the ship 'because of their close connection with India', a connection which 'prompted his Majesty to designate her [the duchess] to launch the *Hindustan*'.[150] As a standard feature, telegrams were exchanged between colony and mother country, creating a sense of simultaneity in the celebration of the new ship and the imperial bond it was intended to symbolize. These telegrams, in which colonial representatives and British officials assured each other of their common spirit, were published both in the British and colonial press. Thus the governor

---

[146] *Times*, 21 Dec 1903.
[147] PRO, ADM 1/8220: Secretary of the Admiralty to High Commissioner for New Zealand, 1 Dec 1910.
[148] PRO, ADM 1/8220: High Commissioner for New Zealand to Secretary of the Admiralty, 6 Dec 1910.
[149] *The Standard of Empire*, 3 Nov 1911.   [150] *Times*, 21 Dec 1903.

of Natal, 'on behalf of the Colony', wished 'every success' to the *Natal*.[151] When the *Dominion* was launched, Lord Grey, the Governor-General, telegraphed from Canada to Britain: 'We are also smashing bottles in sympathy'.[152] Once commissioned, 'imperial' cruisers and battleships continued to be publicly associated with the colony whose name they carried. Colonial representatives made visits and presented gifts to 'their' warship, visits which the Admiralty ensured would be paid for by public funds and publicized in the press.[153] These occasions came close to imperial pilgrimages, with the ships as floating shrines where visitors left tokens of their bond with the mother country.[154] By 1911, the imperial celebration of warships had reached such heights that critics warned that the exuberant ceremonial was triumphing over substance. The *Sydney Morning Herald* felt bound to remind its readers that 'the whole formality of the launch of a ship, and its attendant ceremonial observances of patriotic rejoices, are the merest preliminaries to the real business at hand'.[155]

Fleet reviews offered the most effective type of spectacle by which the naval theatre celebrated the empire. It was here that the full imperial armour could be displayed, on a dazzling scale and with huge media attention. A large part of the rising cost of naval reviews was directly attributable to expanding imperial representation. In explaining why the 1902 review had been on a much larger scale than that of 1897, an Admiralty memorandum pointed out that the aim to include as many representatives and troops from the colonies as possible had led to a substantial increase in expenditure. It was, in particular, 'owing to the presence of the following: Indian Princes; Colonial Premiers; Distinguished Indian Guests; Distinguished Colonial Guests' that the review had been so much more expensive than the previous event.[156] It was the political will to stage these naval celebrations as 'great imperial festivals' that made them such costly affairs.[157]

---

[151]   PRO, ADM 1/7854: Telegram, Governor of Natal, 29 Sept 1905. Compare the extensive coverage in the *African World*, 7 Oct 1905.

[152]   *Times*, 21 Dec 1903.

[153]   PRO, ADM 198/4, 69: Secretary Admiralty to Commander-in-Chief, Nore, 16 April 1907. For examples of such visits see *Sydney Morning Herald*, 25 Oct 1911 on the presentation of a plate 'on behalf of the Australian people to the officers and men of HMS *Commonwealth*'; and *Times*, 28 Nov 1905 on the presentation of a ship's bell by the Natal government to HMS *Natal*.

[154]   When Frank Fox, Australian journalist and author, came to Britain to see the fleet in 1909 he described himself as 'pilgrim from the outer marches of the Empire' (Fox, *Ramparts of Empire*, p. 98).

[155]   *Sydney Morning Herald*, 28 Oct 1911.   [156]   PRO, ADM 116/132.

[157]   John E. C. Bodley, *The Coronation of Edward the Seventh: A Chapter of European and Imperial History* (London, 1903), p. 319.

PUNCH, OR THE LONDON CHARIVARI—June 26, 1897.

SPITHEAD. JUNE 26.

Britism Lion (taking the Young Lions out to see the Great Naval Review). "LOR' LOVE YER, MY LADS, THIS IS THE PROUDEST MOMENT OF MY LIFE!"

23. The spectacle of empire. 'British lion (taking the Young Lions out to see the Great Naval Review), "Lor' love yer, my lads, this is the proudest moment of my life!"' (*Punch*, 26 June 1897).

In June 1909, a new type of such festivals was introduced. As part of the Imperial Press Conference, the Admiralty ordered for the first time a fleet assembly designed exclusively for imperial delegates and the press. As the *Naval and Military Record* pointed out: 'The assembly of a fleet at Spithead for the special benefit of representatives of the Empire's Press is a new feature in our history'.[158] Journalists and politicians from throughout the empire came to see the spectacle of 144 warships assembled in seven lines, in total eighteen sea miles long. The carefully designed programme of naval entertainments included torpedo attacks and sham fights.[159] There was no training purpose in the assembly, nor was it followed by manoeuvres or exercises. The 40,000 officers and men involved in the display were employed solely to put on an impressive show of naval might and imperial unity. At the height of the Anglo-German naval race this was a demonstration to rivals on the Continent and to the 'imperial family'. 'United We Stand' was the official message.[160]

---

[158] *Naval and Military Record*, 17 June 1909.   [159] PRO, ADM 179/52.
[160] *Naval and Military Record*, 17 June 1909.

The image of imperial unity projected by the naval theatre was not lost on the colonial delegates and journalists whom the Admiralty invited to attend. One of them, E. S. Cunningham, stated: 'There is a strong feeling of regret that the advantage of such a sight could not be shared by all the peoples of the Empire. Seeing even one division of the fleet would bring the more distant parts of the Empire into closer touch'.[161] Cunningham was not alone in believing that witnessing the navy's spectacle would bring the empire together. For Frank Fox, chief reporter for the Melbourne *Age*, the display also symbolized the imperial bond. 'How vast to the Australian eye that power', he wrote in his account of the fleet assembly: 'We had seen the ramparts of the Empire – wonderful as manifestations of human energy and human genius, more wonderful as manifestations of pride of race'.[162] Fox's account illustrates how imperial sentiment was offered an ideal symbol in the navy. The navy was the empire's safeguard and global link, and it was clad in a striking imagery of heroism and adventure, steel and guns. The naval theatre showed the empire's 'bands of steel', 'imperial warriors' that stretched 'hands across the sea'.[163] It brought home and made visible the empire, offering an icon, at once modern and romantic, for the imagination of a shared imperial vision.

The fleet itself brought this vision to the colonies. The long voyages of imperial cruisers and squadrons, as well as the imperial tours undertaken by royals, quite literally connected the empire. Historians have shown that the tour of the empire, undertaken by the Duke and Duchess of York in 1901, was designed to display 'a thousand miles of loyalty'.[164] As an official publication had it, the voyage and the festivities accompanying it spun the 'web of empire'.[165] One of the most spectacular examples of the touring of the naval theatre to the colonies took place in 1913, when the Australian Navy was inaugurated. The symbolic value of the departure, passage and arrival of the ships that were to be the heart of Australia's new navy was not lost on the authorities. The Admiralty, the Colonial Office, the Australian High Commissioner and the Australian Commonwealth Government were acutely aware of the unique opportunity for naval,

---

[161] *The Age* (Melbourne), 15 June 1909.   [162] Fox, *Ramparts of Empire*, pp. 100, 102–3.
[163] *Sunday Special*, 17 Aug 1902. For a similar example see *Glasgow Herald*, 3 July 1911.
[164] Phillip Buckner, 'The Royal Tour of 1901 and the Construction of an Imperial Identity in South Africa', *South African Historical Journal* 41 (2000), pp. 324–48; Judith Bassett, ' "A Thousand Miles of Loyalty": The Royal Tour of 1901', *New Zealand Journal of History* 21 (1987), pp. 125–38.
[165] *The Web of Empire: Diary of the Indian Tour of T. R. H. the Duke and Duchess of York* (London, 1901).

national and imperial advertising.[166] The preparations for this naval rite of passage were accordingly wide-ranging. Before the *Australia* and the *Sydney* departed from Britain they were the subject of an array of celebrations. On 31 June, George V, accompanied by the Prince of Wales, visited the *Australia* for a farewell. After receiving a royal salute and inspecting the ship he knighted Rear-Admiral Sir George Patey, 'Australia's Admiral', on the quarterdeck. This was the first time since the days of Drake that a British monarch had knighted an admiral on board a warship. The rare ritual was duly noted as a special honour.[167] It was followed by the visit of 600 Australians living in Britain who, on invitation by the Admiralty and the High Commissioner, arrived by special train to join the officers and crew for a ceremonious goodbye.[168]

In organizing these events, the Admiralty and the High Commissioner for Australia drew on experiences gained earlier that year when the *New Zealand* had left Britain for service in the Southern hemisphere.[169] Cinematographers and journalists were allowed on board to ensure that the farewell for the *Australia* and the image of the bond between mother country and colony would be disseminated all over the empire. Anxious that a continuous flow of articles should keep readers interested in the voyage of the *Australia* and the *Sydney*, a member of the High Commissioner's staff, F. M. Cutlack, was recruited as official reporter.[170] As the Australian Secretary of External Affairs wrote to the Navy Office, Cutlack's job was 'to follow the first enthusiasm' created by the departure and maintain public interest and suspense.[171] On their way to Sydney the Australian ships visited South Africa, an occasion that was consciously designed as a celebration of the 'sisterhood' of the two colonies and their imperial commitment.[172] When the ships finally arrived in their home waters in October 1913, they were welcomed in a string of festivities including balls, banquets and dinners, parades, marches and sham fights,

---

[166] The arrangements are detailed in NAA, MP472/1, 16/13/8787 and MP472/1, 16/13/7920.
[167] NAA, MP472/1, 16/13/7920: High Commissioner to Naval Secretary, 4 July 1913; PRO, ADM 12/1517: Inspection of HMAS *Australia* by the King, 8 April 1913.
[168] NAA, MP472/1, 16/13/7920: High Commissioner to Naval Secretary, 17 June 1913.
[169] PRO, ADM 1/8319: Visit of H. M. the King to the *New Zealand*, 5 Feb 1913.
[170] NAA, MP472/1, 2/13/10293: Secretary, External Affairs, to Secretary, Defence, 5 Feb 1913.
[171] NAA, MP472/1, 2/13/10293: Secretary, External Affairs, to Secretary, Defence, 12 Mar 1913. In Britain, Cutlack's reports were published in *The Times* and the *Morning Post*; in Australia in the *Sydney Morning Herald*.
[172] On the preparation of the visit see NAA, MP472/1, 16/13/8787: Prime Minister, Commonwealth of Australia, to Prime Minister of South Africa, 26 June 1913.

fireworks, illuminations and a Venetian carnival.[173] Newspapers and magazines sold special 'naval issues' and the cinemas showed pictures such as 'The King's Navy', promising 'magnificent pageants of imperial naval power'.[174] Deliberately papering over any contradictions between British and Australian ideas of 'the nation', the naval festival stressed the unity of the imperial family. One souvenir postcard showed the Union Jack and the Southern Cross draped around the *Australia* with the caption: 'One King, One Fleet, One Nation'.[175]

The example of the Australian fleet's 'coming home' in 1913 underlines the central role that the navy played as a cultural instrument in the decades before the First World War. While Britain's position as a world power began to decline, the Royal Navy's symbolic value increased remarkably. Merging regional, national and imperial identities, the naval theatre provided an important stage for processes of cultural nation-building, at a time when shared visions of nationhood were contested both from within and without the United Kingdom. With its careful accommodation of otherwise conflicting identities, the celebration of the navy projected the symbolic merging of immediate, mostly locally defined senses of belonging, and the more distant vision called Great Britain, the United Kingdom or the British Empire. It was here, on the naval stage, that a shared bond between the four nations in the British Isles and the wider empire could be imagined and experienced.

Sailor King and *Flottenkaiser*

National and imperial were inseparable from monarchical representation in the naval theatre. These were, after all, the *Royal* Navy and the *Kaiserliche Marine*, with the monarchs as their titular heads. The naval theatre celebrated the monarchy as much as the fleet and the nation. In the *Kaiserreich*, this reflected the close personal involvement of Wilhelm II with the navy. The records of the Imperial Navy Office and the Naval Cabinet reveal how intensely Wilhelm II concerned himself with the public staging of his navy. He demanded to be personally involved in the preparations of every launch of a capital warship in Germany. The date and programme of each launch and a plan of the dockyard

[173] NAA, MP472/1, 16/13/8794 has a complete list of festivities, co-ordinated by a special naval committee set up by the Prime Minister's office. For a flavour of 'Sydney en fête' see *Sydney Mail*, 8 Oct 1913.
[174] *Sydney Morning Herald*, 6 Oct 1913.
[175] NAA, A1861, 3058: Set of Souvenir Postcards by Charles E. Turner. For a more detailed analysis of the voyage and its use for the politics of Australian nationhood and imperial sentiment see Rüger, 'Nation, Empire and Navy'.

arrangements had to be submitted for the Kaiser's approval. He wanted to be kept continuously informed about the preparations in the days leading up to each event.[176] When he did not attend a launch personally, a range of regulations and representations ensured that he would be projected as the *Übervater* behind the navy. Each launching speech was required to refer to the Kaiser: at the beginning when the speaker thanked him for the honour and emphasized that the launch took place 'on the orders of His Majesty'; and again at the end of the speech when three cheers were given for the Kaiser. After each launch, Wilhelm II was to be notified by telegram and copies of these self-congratulatory messages, conveying the loyal greetings of his navy, were to be given to the press.[177]

Although consecutive British monarchs did not interfere with naval ceremonial in any way that would have resembled the Kaiser's master-minding of public ritual, a strong will to link the Crown and the navy publicly was evident in Britain, too.[178] A number of features, such as the singing of the national anthem and the three cheers for the monarch at the end of ship launches, ensured that these rituals featured strong royal representation. The names chosen for warships also reflected a strategy to promote the monarchy in the naval theatre. While this was part of a well established repertoire of symbolic acts that linked the monarchy and the navy,[179] contemporaries noted innovations even here. The *Naval and Military Record* observed in 1911:

---

[176] The *Allerhöchster Kabinettsorder* of 1900 stated unequivocally that a plan showing the arrangements and processional routes had to be submitted to the Kaiser before each launch. A check-list at the *Reichsmarineamt* reminded officials to ask His Majesty for permission at various stages in the preparation of a launch. See *MVBl* 31 (1900), p. 397 and BA-MA, RM 3/117, Bl. 1–2.

[177] GStA PK, I Rep 89, Nr. 32225, Bl. 1–10 has a good selection of these telegrams. More can be found in BA-MA, RM2/1619–1629. This personal involvement can also be seen in the attendance of ship launches. Victoria attended three, Edward VII two, and George V not a single launch of a capital warship until 1914. Wilhelm II, in contrast, attended thirteen such launches, three of which he performed himself, not counting the launching of ocean liners, yachts and smaller naval vessels that he visited. Considering that one and a half as many capital warships were launched in Britain than in Germany during this period, this meant that between 1897 and 1914 every ninth capital ship of the German navy was launched in the presence of the Kaiser, whereas not even every fiftieth involved monarchical presence in Britain.

[178] One of the few cases in which the Crown directly interfered with the Admiralty's planning of ship launches took place in February 1906 when the launch of the *Dreadnought* was being prepared. Edward VII insisted that he himself would launch the new battleship, a precedent that broke with the tradition of female launch patrons. See PRO, ADM 1/7873: Private Secretary to First Lord of the Admiralty to Commander-in-Chief Portsmouth, 5 Feb 1906.

[179] Rodger, 'Queen Elizabeth and the Myth of Seapower'.

In selecting the name for the new ship the King followed a precedent set as recently as eight years ago; for although the Navy has had scores named after reigning Sovereigns, all save one have lacked the distinguishing numeral. Thus we have had Edwards and Henrys [...], we have had a Victoria, a Royal William, a William and Mary [...] and so on, but not until 1903, when the King Edward VII was launched, did we have a ship which was distinguished by the numeral as well as the name of the reigning Sovereign.[180]

Both in Germany and Britain, the naval theatre was thus a prominent stage for the display of the link between the monarch and the navy. A special expression existed in both countries for this relationship: *Flottenkaiser* and 'Sailor King'. Used by the press, the navy and the royal courts alike, these labels evoked a romanticized, pre-modern idea of the unity between monarch and navy.

Yet what kind of monarchy was enacted in the naval theatre? And how did the two countries compare in this respect? An answer is best sought in a close reading of fleet reviews. In Britain, these rituals were consciously designed to allude to the triumphal processions of ancient and medieval kings. The maritime procession at the heart of the Spithead spectacles was led by the Trinity Yacht, heralding the entry of the monarch and imitating the precursors customary in ancient and medieval ritual.[181] While the royal yacht passed the lines of warships, the salutes and the cheering of the crews acknowledged the monarch's status. Afterwards, this acknowledgement was symbolically returned through the gifts that the monarch offered the fleet by ordering the signal 'splice the mainbrace' (rum to be dished out on all vessels) and granting the crews an afternoon ashore as a holiday. In addition, there was regularly a pardoning of offenders undergoing punishment on board.[182] All this was part of an iconography that suggested a continuity from Roman and medieval emperors to British monarchs.[183] However, in the course of the

---

[180] *Naval and Military Record*, 11 Oct 1911.

[181] Ernest Kantorowicz, 'The King's Advent and the Enigmatic Doors of Santa Sabina', in Ernest Kantorowicz, *Selected Studies* (New York, 1965), pp. 37–75; Klaus Tenfelde, 'Adventus. Zur historischen Ikonologie des Festzugs', *Historische Zeitschrift* 235 (1982), pp. 45–84; Winfried Dotzauer, 'Die Ankunft des Herrschers. Der fürstliche "Einzug" in die Stadt (bis zum Ende des alten Reiches)', *Archiv für Kulturgeschichte* 55 (1973), pp. 245–88.

[182] PRO, ADM 179/56, Bl. 8–9: Secretary of the Admiralty to Commander-in-Chief Portsmouth, 6 June 1902, conveying the King's wishes for the naval review.

[183] On the tradition of the reciprocal exchange of gifts as acknowledgement of authority: Marcel Mauss, *The Gift*, translated by W. D. Halls, with a foreword by Mary Douglas (London, 1990), first published in 1950, pp. 50–5. On the symbolic gifts made during Roman and medieval triumphal entries: Ernest Kantorowicz, *Laudes Regiae: A Study in Liturgical Acclamations and Medieval Ruler Worship* (Berkeley, CA, 1946), pp. 75–6; Tenfelde, 'Adventus', pp. 52–5.

nineteenth century the royal pageantry in the Solent was adapted to acknowledge the changing constitutional situation in Britain. As early as 1853, Parliament was given a ceremonial role in fleet reviews. The Houses of Parliament were represented by two separate vessels in the procession that followed the royal yacht through the lines of assembled warships.[184] By the late nineteenth century a strong parliamentary representation was a well established tradition. The royal reviews at Spithead now reflected the wider constitutional arrangement between monarchy, parliament and government.

The 'order of procession' observed at the Jubilee naval review of 1897 was a typical example. Preceded by the Trinity Yacht, the royal yacht sailed through the lines of warships, greeted by the fleet's salutes. It was followed by two yachts for Her Majesty's guests. Then came the *Enchantress*, the Admiralty Yacht, carrying the leading cast of the naval administration and other parts of government, followed by two vessels for their guests and the press. The third group in the naval procession was comprised of the Houses of Parliament, each on a separate steamer.[185] With the Crown, government and Parliament all separately represented, the procession offered a maritime image of the British constitution. Rather than merely royal rituals, British fleet reviews were symbolic meetings between navy, monarch, government and Parliament that indicated a sharing of power between them. Parliament took these occasions seriously, so much so that in 1911, when the two steamers hired for the Lords and the Commons proved too large for the procession, angry debates took place.[186] Moreover, there were ceremonial occasions at which the two chambers 'inspected' the fleet without the monarch.[187] All this underlined that the navy was ultimately answerable to Parliament. The naval theatre thus mirrored the constitutional situation in which the British monarchy found itself at the end of the nineteenth century.[188]

---

[184] *Times*, 12 Aug 1853. See also Wilson, 'Previous Naval Reviews', pp. 19–20.

[185] PRO, ADM 179/55: Review Orders, art. 92–3; ibid. LC 2/146: Admiralty Report on the Naval Review at Spithead on Saturday, 26 June 1897.

[186] Hansard, Fifth Series, House of Commons, vol. 26 (14 June 1911).

[187] Such 'Parliamentary inspections', as they came to be known, took place in 1900 and 1912. Strictly speaking, only the monarch or the Admiralty could 'inspect' the fleet, see Chapter 1. As a Treasury memorandum noted in 1912, 'talk about Members of Parliament "inspecting" the fleet is of course absurd' (PRO, T 1/11642, 15 June 1912).

[188] There were two occasions, at Torbay in 1910 and at Weymouth in 1912, at which the British monarch deviated from this format. Billed as 'private' inspections, they showed an image of the 'Sailor King' that emphasized training and functionality. Rather than ceremoniously holding a review, the king actually joined the navy and observed a number of special manoeuvres. See PRO, ADM 179/35: Inspection of the Fleet by His Majesty the King at Weymouth, 7 to 11 May 1912.

24. The crew of HMS *Lord Nelson* cheering Edward VII during the fleet review at Spithead, 31 July 1909.

A remarkably different image of monarchy was on display in Wilhelmine Germany. Government and, even more so, parliament played a negligible role in the ritualized meetings of Kaiser and his fleet. Certainly, groups of parliamentarians were occasionally invited to visit naval stations and ships, but they were never publicly represented through the navy.[189] The idea of the members of the Reichstag on their own steamer following the *Hohenzollern* through the lines of the Fleet while salutes were being fired would have been an anathema. At no point did the German navy consider staging a 'Parliamentary inspection'. Nor was the German government directly represented at fleet reviews. There was no equivalent to the Admiralty Yacht which, at British reviews, followed the *Victoria and Albert* through the lines of the fleet. Neither the Reichstag nor the government thus received anything close to the ceremonial attention their British counterparts enjoyed. Instead, the naval theatre powerfully displayed the Kaiser's 'All Highest Command',

---

[189] Two such visits on a larger scale took place. Twenty-four members of the Reichstag and the Bundesrat visited the fleet at Kiel in June 1907, another forty in June 1908: *Marine-Rundschau*, July 1907, p. 937–8; *Marine-Rundschau*, June 1908, pp. 779–80. See also Fischer, 'Die Faszination des Technischen' and Deist, *Flottenpolitik und Flottenpropaganda*, pp. 98–9.

his constitutionally safeguarded *Kommandogewalt*.[190] Above all, German reviews projected a close personal relationship between Wilhelm II and *his* navy. They displayed the almost comrade-like unity between forces and emperor encapsulated in the idea of *Flottenkaiser*, the naval equivalent to the *Heereskaiser*. It was the tangible, physical merging of fleet and Kaiser that lay at the heart of German naval reviews.

This conclusion is supported by an analysis of the choreography of Wilhelmine fleet reviews. There were three main phases: approach, passing and unification. During the approach, the Kaiser's yacht and fleet sailed towards each other at slow speed. Upon meeting, the fleet fired the imperial salute, the highest *Ehrenbezeigung* of the Imperial Navy. The *Hohenzollern* and the fleet then passed each other, the fleet arranged either in one long line (*in Kiellinie*) or in squadrons. After the fleet had acknowledged the command of the 'All Highest Warlord', Wilhelm II responded by leaving the royal yacht and boarding the flagship, where he took position at the bridge while the Imperial Standard was hoisted. All this demonstrated that he had actively taken over the command of the fleet. Almost all reviews ended with the Kaiser proceeding to sea with the fleet, carrying out exercises and manoeuvres.[191] What spectators observed at these events was, in essence, a symbolic uniting of the fleet and its highest commander. This enactment of the *Flottenkaiser* stood in remarkable contrast to the way in which the 'Sailor King' was displayed in the British naval theatre. It rested on a fundamentally different interpretation of the role of monarchy in relation to the armed forces, government and parliament.[192]

Considered more closely, the annual rendezvous between the Kaiser and his navy offers an important insight into the nature of Wilhelm II's reign. The Kaiser was, in a formal sense, in a powerful position. The Imperial Constitution of 1871 had enshrined a wide-ranging military

---

[190] On the Kaiser's *Kommandogewalt* and its public representation see Deist, 'Kaiser Wilhelm in the Context of his Military and Naval Entourage', pp. 169–92.

[191] Compare the section 'Maritime Theatre' in Chapter 1.

[192] Wilhelm II's interpretation of the role of Parliament was neatly encapsulated in a letter to Queen Victoria, written in the run-up to the fleet review that the Kaiser was to attend in August 1889. He informed the Queen that he understood 'that the Houses of the British Parliament have resolved to assist at the Naval Review' and he agreed that the review should therefore be brought forward by one day (RA VIC/I57/36: Wilhelm II to Victoria, 23 June 1889). Clearly, what he saw as a 'mark of kindness shown to us by the Representatives of the whole British nation' (ibid.) was just as much a mark of the power exercised by these representatives *vis-à-vis* the Crown: not only did Parliament play an active part in the fleet review, it was also in a position to request a change in its timing.

prerogative for the monarch. It was he, not parliament, who deter-
mined the strength, structure and distribution of the forces. And it was
he, the 'All Highest Warlord', who had the supreme command over
the army and the navy. A range of institutions through which the
Kaiser exercised his command bolstered this prerogative. The Kaiser
had his own military and naval cabinets, separate from the government ministries. The *Immediat-System* ensured that the army's and
the navy's leading officers had direct access to the Kaiser and he
to them, again circumventing civil government and parliamentary
control.[193]

John Röhl has argued that these formal powers together with important informal influences allowed the Kaiser to establish a 'personal
rule' after Bismarck's abdication in 1890. Apart from asserting his
constitutional rights, the Kaiser had skilfully played on the 'kingship
mechanism', a term coined by Norbert Elias to describe the informal
power wielded by monarchs in court societies. Applied to Wilhelmine
Germany, it described the many registers of favour and patronage
that the emperor employed to secure loyalty, not least at public rituals.
It was by exercising this informal power and by using the constitutionally enshrined prerogative that the Kaiser had begun to install his
'personal rule', appointing ministers willing to outmanoeuvre or manipulate parties and parliament.[194] Röhl's critics have seen this argument
as placing too much emphasis on personalities and too little on the
realities of the German political system, which imposed practical limits
to whatever the Kaiser's intentions might have been. There is little
evidence that the Kaiser managed to control the executive or install
an alternative system of 'personal rule'. Indeed, there were cases when
the Kaiser was isolated and could not exercise much power at all, as
seen in the 1908 scandal around the *Daily Telegraph* interview.[195]

---

[193] Deist, 'Kaiser Wilhelm in the Context of his Military and Naval Entourage'; Berghahn,
Tirpitz-Plan, p. 23 ff; Steinberg, *Yesterday's Deterrent*, pp. 76–7, 197.

[194] John C. G. Röhl, 'Introduction', in Röhl and Sombart, *Kaiser Wilhelm II*, pp. 14–9; John
C. G. Röhl, 'Kaiser Wilhelm II., Grossherzog Friedrich I. und der "Königsmechanismus"
im Kaiserreich', *Historische Zeitschrift* 263 (1983), pp. 539–77; John C. G. Röhl, 'Der
"Königsmechanismus" im Kaiserreich', in John C. G. Röhl (ed.), *Kaiser, Hof und Staat.
Wilhelm II. in der deutschen Geschichte* (Munich, 1987), pp. 116–40. For the earlier debate
about 'personal rule', which Röhl revised, see Erich Eyck, *Das persönliche Regiment Wilhelms
II. Politische Geschichte des deutschen Kaiserreichs von 1890 bis 1914* (Zurich, 1948); Fritz
Hartung, 'Das persönliche Regiment Kaiser Wilhelms II.', *Sitzungsberichte der deutschen
Akademie der Wissenschaften zu Berlin* 3 (1952), pp. 4–20 and Ernst Rudolf Huber, 'Das
persönliche Regiment Kaiser Wilhelms II.', in Ernst-Wolfgang Böckenförde (ed.), *Moderne
deutsche Verfassungsgeschichte (1815–1918)* (Cologne, 1972), pp. 282–303.

[195] See the excellent article by Geoff Eley, 'The View from the Throne: The Personal Rule
of Kaiser Wilhelm II', *Historical Journal* 28 (1985), pp. 469–85. For a less convincing

Against such objections, however, Röhl has recently reasserted his interpretation.[196] What, then, does the naval theatre reveal about this debate? Can the Kaiser's parades and reviews be seen as examples of the 'kingship mechanism'? The annual fleet reviews held for the Kaiser's entertainment provide telling case studies of the relationship between the emperor, the naval leadership and the public. And they complicate our understanding of how the Kaiser 'ruled'. It is often forgotten that, despite his formal constitutional prerogative, the reality of being 'All Highest Warlord' was more ambiguous than the Kaiser's frequent rhetorical use of the title suggested. Wilhelm's public appearances could be deceptive, both for himself and his audience. Indeed, the naval theatre was aimed at hiding the strong contrast between Wilhelm II's official title and the realities of 'being in command'. It was crucial for the naval leadership to make Wilhelm appear to be in control of naval affairs. Tirpitz noted in 1903 that it was essential that the Kaiser was given the *impression* that he was in command: 'This is the sad and depressing thing about this talented monarch: that he values the appearance more than the essence. Not the *subject* itself is crucial for him, but the question of whether he makes an appearance as the only master [*Meister*]'.[197] The Kaiser was just as open to manipulation as leading politicians and bureaucrats were to the trappings of the 'kingship mechanism'. Indeed, much of the naval programme spearheaded by Tirpitz rested on persuading the Kaiser that this was the navy that he had always wanted. Christopher Clark has shown that Tirpitz, while lamenting Wilhelm II's superficiality, knew how to exploit it. Clark comes to the persuasive conclusion that 'the truth of the matter was surely that it was Tirpitz who had seized control over the essentials of the naval programme, leaving Wilhelm with the mere appearance of control'.[198]

The fleet reviews and naval manoeuvres watched by the 'All Highest Warlord' must be seen as skilful exercises in this 'managing of the Kaiser'.

critique of Röhl, suggesting a shift from 'personal rule' to the responsibility of 'the elite', see Wolfgang J. Mommsen, *War der Kaiser an allem schuld? Wilhelm II. und die preußisch-deutschen Machteliten* (Berlin, 2002). On the *Daily Telegraph* affair see Kohlrausch, *Monarch im Skandal*, pp. 243–63; Peter Winzen, *Das Kaiserreich am Abgrund. Die Daily-Telegraph-Affäre und das Hale-Interview von 1908* (Stuttgart, 2002) and Terence F. Cole, 'The Daily-Telegraph Affair', in Röhl and Sombart, *Kaiser Wilhelm II*, pp. 249–68.

[196] John C. G. Röhl, *Wilhelm II. Der Aufbau der persönlichen Monarchie* (Munich, 2002), p. 974. 'Personal rule' looms also large in Annika Mombauer and Wilhelm Deist (eds.), *The Kaiser: New Research on Wilhelm II's Role in Imperial Germany* (Cambridge, 2003).

[197] Cited in Berghahn, *Tirpitz-Plan*, p. 352.

[198] Christopher Clark, *Kaiser Wilhelm II* (Harlow, 2000), p. 138. See also Volker Berghahn's analysis of Tirpitz's *Immediatvorträge* in *Tirpitz-Plan*, pp. 332–54 and Lamar Cecil's interpretation of the relationship between Tirpitz and the Kaiser in *Wilhelm II: Prince and Emperor*, pp. 313–6.

These rituals projected Wilhelm's idea of his official role, while hiding its considerable limits behind this facade. They aimed to convey a strong impression of the Kaiser being personally in control as the highest commanding officer of the Imperial Navy. This was reinforced by the Kaiser boarding the flagship after fleet reviews to 'take command'; by the orchestrated camaraderie between him and officers; and by the famous *Manöverkritik*, the 'post-mortem' after the mock manoeuvres, in which he treated the navy's leadership to his criticism. Fleet reviews thus provided an important public arena in which the Kaiser's *Kommandogewalt* was – literally – acted out. This was an elaborate theatre, designed to display the Kaiser as the 'All Highest Warlord' in front of his entourage, the naval leadership, government, parliament, and the wider domestic and foreign public. Behind the scenes these occasions were felt to be painful lessons in the deception of appearances. While Wilhelm II inspected his navy passionately and demonstratively, the reality was that the navy had the Kaiser on parade just as much.

Technology, modernity and gender

In the naval theatre, the traditional imagery of the *Flottenkaiser* and the 'Sailor King' merged with distinctly modern tropes of nationhood, especially through the representation of technology. Nationalism and technology, closely intertwined from the late nineteenth century onwards, entered a powerful relationship in the celebration of the fleet. Like the aeroplane and the zeppelin, both prominent in this public theatre, the navy was at the forefront of technological advance.[199] The warships launched in the decades before the First World War had little in common with the traditional image of the 'age of sail'. Gone were the wooden vessels that had dominated the idea of a fleet for centuries. The modern battleships of the Dreadnought era were 'monsters of steel' with compact superstructures, funnels instead of tall masts and large guns mounted on turrets. These ships were the embodiment of technological innovation and scientific progress, icons of the rationality and efficiency of the machine age. When Helmuth von Moltke visited the German navy in 1910 he was captivated by the character of warships as 'machine organisms':

---

[199] Peter Fritzsche, *A Nation of Fliers: German Aviation and the Popular Imagination* (Cambridge, MA, 1992); Guillaume de Syon, *Zeppelin! Germany and the Airship, 1900–1939* (Baltimore, 2002); Robert Wohl, *A Passion for Wings: Aviation and the Western Imagination, 1908–1918* (New Haven and London, 1994). The special effects which zeppelins and aeroplanes produced in the naval theatre was often noted by contemporaries. For an example see NMM, JOD/193/1: Wilfried S. Mann, 9 July 1912.

We were all on board the *Nassau* and viewed every part of this gigantic ship. It is most interesting to admire the sum of intelligence that is expressed in this complex mechanism. A ship like this has its own brain and its own nerves, just like a human being. The electric connections control every limb; and the ship moves its gigantic guns to the right and the left, upwards and downwards, and starts its machines with the same ease by which we stretch a leg or move an arm.[200]

The fascination for modern warships expressed by Moltke was not only for *what* these 'monsters of steel' could do, but *how* they did it. These high-tech organisms operated with an efficiency and rationality that provoked admiration as well as anxiety. They were 'sites of modernity' in that they expressed a new relationship between individual and machine, offered new experiences of space and time, and involved new forms of risk.[201] The fascination invoked by warships was thus part of the wider enthusiasm for modern technology that characterized the Wilhelmine and Edwardian period. Baroness Spitzemberg observed this craze even amongst the conservative nobility. 'Aristocratic boys', she lamented, were 'dreaming day and night' of *Technik*, rather than being interested 'in hunting, in horses and dogs'. A whole generation was in the grip of this *Zeitgeist*, as she called it.[202]

Importantly, warships were not only icons of modern technology, they also made it possible to represent power in new ways. It is here that the light displays mentioned in the last chapter played a key role. The powerful electric searchlights of warships, the *Marinescheinwerfer*, had been invented to make naval battle at night possible. Yet these symbols of modern technology and naval might were also instruments of stagecraft. They were used with striking effect in what came to be known as 'the play of the searchlights'. In the evening of naval celebrations, the 'long fingers' of light beams moved over warships, the sea and the shoreline. What made this techno-spectacle particularly effective was that it involved the audiences. This was the case as early as 1887. The orders that choreographed the Queen's jubilee fleet review detailed that the ships were to train their searchlights not only on to the ships and their guns, but also on the shore and the watching

---

[200] Moltke, *Erinnerungen*, p. 357 (22 July 1910).

[201] Compare the section on 'Technology and entertainment' in Chapter 3.

[202] *Tagebuch der Baronin Spitzemberg*, p. 565. On German and British responses to modern technology see Joachim Radkau, *Technik in Deutschland. Vom 18. Jahrhundert bis zur Gegenwart* (Frankfurt, 1989), esp. pp. 22–39; Thomas Rohkrämer, *Eine andere Moderne? Zivilisationskritik, Natur und Technik in Deutschland, 1880–1933* (Paderborn, 1999); Rieger ' "Modern wonders" '; Rieger, *Technology and the Culture of Modernity*; Pick, *War Machine*, esp. pp. 175–8.

masses.[203] This made the audience visible in the darkness, literally casting them as 'one crowd', united by its experience of light and power. The popular press and illustrated magazines celebrated this effect. It was, as journalists noted, not only the 'great black hulls' that were 'suddenly springing out of the blackness', but also the masses watching on shore.[204] Photographs and illustrations attempted to reproduce the 'play of the searchlight' and reports elaborated on it, employing a language and imagery that reinforced the sense of the merging of fleet, crowd and power into one dynamic entity. A picture in the *Illustrated London News* showed a mass of spectators cast out of the darkness by the strong floodlights, with the headline running: 'Revealed by the searchlights: friends, not enemies: searchlights of the fleet playing on the crowd'.[205] This 'playing on the crowd' became a standard feature of the naval theatre. It offered an experience, aided by the surrounding darkness and the novelty of strong floodlights, that suggested a merging of navy and nation in a display of light and technology. In the naval theatre modern technology thus offered new forms for the representation of the intertwined issues of power and identity. This was all the more effective since it coincided with innovations in the reproduction of images: photography and film captured this spectacle and reinforced its visual impact.[206]

At the same time, the naval theatre addressed the anxieties provoked by these 'modern wonders'. Indeed, it seemed to reconcile the deep contradictions and challenges that modern technology brought about. The 'gigantic bodies' of warships that Hamburg's Burgomaster Mönckeberg admired[207] were vessels of imagined chivalry and tradition as much as they were high-tech symbols of efficiency and progress. The naval theatre played heavily on romanticized notions of adventure and the triumph of the human spirit over the elements.[208] What made this spectacle so fascinating was that it brought together the new possibilities, the *Machbarkeit* offered by modern technology, with older ideas of adventure,

---

[203] PRO, ADM 179/54: Programme for Illumination of Ships Taking Part in the Proposed Naval Review, 1887.

[204] *The Sphere*, 9 Aug 1902.

[205] *Illustrated London News*, 24 July 1909 (illustration by H. W. Koekkoek). Similarly *Daily News*, 19 July 1909.

[206] It was not unusual for contemporaries watching naval displays to comment on the expected impact these spectacles of technology would have when reproduced in film and photography; see only NMM, JOD/193/1: Wilfried S. Mann, 9 July 1912. For a more detailed analysis of film and modern technology see Rieger, *Technology and the Culture of Modernity*, ch. 4.

[207] StA Hamburg, 622-1, Mönckeberg 21a, Bl. 291.

[208] On the 'permanent struggle against the sea' see David Blackbourn, *The Conquest of Nature: Water, Landscape and the Making of Modern Germany* (London, 2006), p. 121.

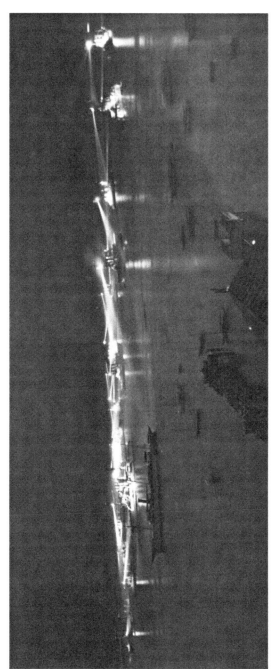

25. Searchlight display performed by the Imperial Navy in Kiel harbour.

heroism and chivalry.[209] It combined the traditional 'story of the sea' with the unprecedented possibilities offered by new technology.

The symbolic value of the navy was all the more important for cultural nation-building since it had strongly gendered associations.[210] Both in Britain and Germany the naval theatre forcefully emphasized that the working of this armada of steel and technology was a male prerogative. The 'one vast machine' that was the navy was an exclusively male dominion, a realm of masculinity in which 'guns and men' came together.[211] In Germany, the exclusively male speakers at ship launches invoked an arsenal of masculine characteristics. Ships and men alike were to display bravery, discipline, stamina, will-power and the readiness to die for the *Vaterland*. Indeed, the language employed at these occasions suggested that, above all, the officers and ratings ought to prove their masculinity. *Mannesmut* (male bravery) and *deutsche Manneszucht* (German manly discipline) were recurrent phrases.[212] It was not unusual for speeches to depict warships as male bodies, resembling the physique of heroes: 'May you, muscular and beautiful, be prepared and ready for action, like an armed man'.[213] Warships were called upon to go into battle like men and return home like heroes, decorated with wounds and honour.[214] Warships were metaphors of masculinity:

Thus you proud weapon have been given the most noble essence [*edelster Saft*] and the presence of a body which makes you beautiful and terrible. A believing and daring future lives in you, conferred upon you by the spirit that created you and by the youth and manly power that will guide your course through luck and danger.[215]

The pervasive language of might and masculinity underlined that these modern war machines were a male domain, carefully set apart from

---

[209] Detlev Peukert emphasized this cloaking of modernity in traditional language for the Wilhelmine period in *Die Weimarer Republik. Krisenjahre der Klassischen Moderne* (Franfurt, 1997), p. 179. Recent research has also stressed the reconcilability of traditional and modern language in evocations of the past: Readman, 'The Place of the Past in English Culture'.

[210] For the relationship between gender and nation see Ida Blom, Karen Hagemann and Catherine Hall (eds.), *Gendered Nations: Nationalisms and Gender Order in the Long Nineteenth Century* (Oxford, 2000) and Nira Yuval-Davis, *Gender and Nation* (London, 1997).

[211] *Daily Express*, 19 July 1909; *Official Programme of the Coronation Review, Spithead, June 24th, 1911: All About the Ships: All About the Guns and Men* (London, 1911).

[212] BA-MA, RM 3/9959, Bl. 116; BA-MA, RM 3/9959, Bl. 9; BA-MA, RM 3/9959, Bl. 116; BA-MA, RM 3/129, Bl. 52; BA-MA, RM 3/9959, Bl. 151.

[213] BA-MA, RM 3/9959, Bl. 82.

[214] BA-MA, RM 3/9959, Bl. 151; BA-MA, RM 2/1626, Bl. 172.

[215] BA-MA, RM 3/9959, Bl. 171. For similar examples see: BA-MA, RM 3/127, Bl. 148 and BA-MA 3/9959, Bl. 166.

26. 'All about the guns and men'. Official programme, coronation review, 1911.

female characteristics or associations. In Imperial Germany this was further emphasized by the gendered space in which these rituals took place. As the last chapter has shown, a strict demarcation between men and women was at the core of warship launches, a demarcation that was informed not only by ideas about separate gender spheres, but also about the division between military and civilian society. The separation of 'the ladies' from the male participants, who were in the majority, was minutely planned and strictly adhered to, both at government and private yards. It was a key mechanism by which the Wilhelmine naval theatre constructed 'the nation' along gender lines. While this demonstrative demarcation between men and women was a uniquely Wilhelmine phenomenon, the naval theatre projected a strongly gendered image of 'the nation' in both countries. At a time when traditional gender images were profoundly contested, it celebrated the 'hegemonic masculinity' that was expressed in the navy.[216] In this gendered theatre, the display of modern technology merged with images of masculinity and evocations of 'the nation'. The ships were 'sea fighters', they resembled the nation's 'sinews of steel'.[217] The fleet was a creature with 'hard and clear eyes' and the 'joyful calm of a man who knows his duties and who approaches the grand test of world history'.[218]

Both in Britain and Germany the navy was thus a cultural symbol that brought together some of the most important sources of the nineteenth-century construction of the nation: monarchy, empire, technology, gender, war and geography. What made this amalgamation so powerful was the international dimension inherent in the celebration of the navy and the sea. As the next chapter demonstrates, the naval theatre was at once a national and an international stage. Images of conflict and rivalry were, directly or indirectly, always present. The lines of warships were, after all, designed to deter the enemy. The fleet resembled a 'front of steel' or an

---

[216] John Tosh, 'Hegemonic Masculinity and the History of Gender', in Stefan Dudink, Karen Hagemann and John Tosh (eds.), *Masculinities in Politics and War: Gendering Modern History* (Manchester, 2004), pp. 41–60. For an illuminating case study see Lucy Delap, '"Thus Does Man Prove His Fitness to Be the Master of Things": Shipwrecks, Chivalry and Masculinities in Nineteenth- and Twentieth-Century Britain', *Cultural and Social History* 3 (2006), pp. 45–74. On the wider challenges to traditional gender roles: Sally Ledger, 'The New Woman and the Crisis of Victorianism', in Sally Ledger and Scott McCracken (eds.), *Cultural Politics at the Fin de Siècle* (Cambridge, 1995), pp. 22–44; Leonore Davidoff, *Worlds Between: Historical Perspectives on Gender and Class* (Cambridge, 1995); Michael Roper and John Tosh (eds.), *Manful Assertions: Masculinities in Britain since 1800* (London, 1991).

[217] *Illustrated London News*, 17 July 1909; *Naval and Military Record*, 17 June 1909 and 22 July 1914.

[218] *Presse-Stimmen*, pp. 11–12 (*Tägliche Rundschau*, reporting from the 1911 Kiel fleet review).

'impenetrable wall of armour'.[219] The ships were 'iron bodies', 'bulwarks' or 'ramparts', forming 'long drawn out avenues of steel, bristling with big guns'.[220] They were easily paraded as symbols of invincibility and preparedness for war. Moreover, such performances were known to be received not only 'at home', but also 'abroad'. The naval stage could therefore hardly fail to reinforce ideas of 'overseas' and 'otherness'. It projected 'the nation' not least in opposition to others.

In the naval theatre, displays of power and deterrence were thus intertwined with representations of identity and nationhood. This was all the more potent since the naval theatre brought together local, regional and national contexts in its celebration of the navy and the sea. It celebrated the fleet as both a local and a national metaphor.[221] One of the main reasons why the naval theatre developed such strong popular appeal and symbolic power has to be seen in its ability to publicly reconcile otherwise divergent senses of identification and nationhood. Monarchy, empire, race, gender, technology and war came together with evocations of international competition and rivalry. Its capability to symbolically merge these national signifiers made the naval theatre a unique arena for cultural nation-building. Long before the North Sea turned into a theatre of war in 1914, it was a theatre of power and identity, a maritime 'parade ground of the nations', watched by domestic and foreign audiences alike.[222]

---

[219] Ibid., pp. 11–12 (*Tägliche Rundschau*); p. 21 (*Lübecker Generalanzeiger; Leipziger Illustrierte Zeitung*); p. 15 (*Der Tag*) and p. 18 (*Kölnische Volkszeitung*).

[220] *Illustrated London News*, 9 Oct 1909; *Illustrated [Newcastle] Chronicle*, 31 March 1911; *Naval and Military Record*, 17 June 1909 and 22 July 1914.

[221] Confino, *The Nation as a Local Metaphor*.

[222] Georg Friedrich List had described the sea as the 'Paradeplatz der Nationen' in 1843, in an essay that combined economic, political and cultural arguments in its praise for the sea as the space where German unity would be found – and displayed to others. See *Das Zollvereinsblatt*, no. 2, 8 Jan 1843, pp. 17–20: 'Die deutsche Flagge'.

5 The Anglo-German theatre

Traditionally, historians have narrated the growing rivalry between Britain and Germany in strategic, diplomatic and economic terms. This was perhaps most famously the case in Paul Kennedy's seminal studies *The Rise of the Anglo-German Antagonism* and *The Rise and Fall of the Great Powers*. For Kennedy and many other scholars the source of antagonism was located in the socio-economic development of the two countries, and in the diplomatic and strategic decisions taken by their leaders.[1] Dissatisfied with this predominantly political focus, a number of historians have since explored the cultural dimension of the two countries' relations. Their interest lies with Anglo-German comparison, exchange and transfer, with stereotypes and ideas about 'the other'.[2] Yet this enquiry has been left disconnected from the world of power and politics, as if to confirm diplomatic historians in their view of culture as a separate phenomenon and a source of subordinate influence. As a result, the political and the cultural histories of the Anglo-German relationship continue to be written in isolation from one another.

This chapter aims to bring together these two divergent strands of historiography. In the naval theatre, culture and politics were inseparable. The public staging of the navy was part of the imperial game, the struggle between great powers over spheres of influence and the domination of the sea. This was an eminently political arena, closely watched and participated in by the governments of both countries. And yet it was about entertainment, leisure and consumption. This was, as previous chapters

---

[1] Kennedy, *Rise of the Anglo-German Antagonism*; Kennedy, *Rise and Fall of the Great Powers*; Massie, *Dreadnought*; Schöllgen, *Imperialismus und Gleichgewicht*; Stevenson, *Armaments and the Coming of War*; Hildebrand, 'Zwischen Allianz und Antagonismus'.

[2] Muhs, Paulmann and Steinmetz, *Aneignung und Abwehr*; Reinermann, *Kaiser in England*; Blaicher, *Deutschlandbild*; Wendt, *Britische Deutschlandbild*; Firchow, *Death of the German Cousin*; Epkenhans, 'Aspekte des deutschen Englandbildes'; Christiane Eisenberg, 'Pferderennen zwischen "Händler-" und "Heldenkultur". Verlauf und Dynamik einer englisch-deutschen Kulturbegegnung', in Hartmut Berghoff and Dieter Ziegler (eds.), *Pionier und Nachzügler? Vergleichende Studien zur Geschichte Englands und Deutschlands im Zeitalter der Industrialisierung* (Bochum, 1995), pp. 235–58.

have demonstrated, a game that was played and enjoyed by vast audiences who appropriated the naval theatre for their own interests. Strategic and diplomatic developments merged with popular culture and mass media. The public collision of these intensely political and cultural aspects was precisely what made the naval theatre so potent for Anglo-German relations. In unravelling the intertwined cultural and political dimensions of the Anglo-German stage, this chapter suggests a revision of how the relations between the two countries should be approached. The peculiar character of the naval theatre makes it necessary to understand the rivalry between the two countries not just as a strategic conflict, but also as a cultural one: the Anglo-German antagonism was a dramatic game played out for domestic and foreign audiences, a game in which important cultural issues were bound up with strategic and diplomatic developments.

A stage between the nations

In 1895, at the inauguration of the Kiel Canal, Bogdan Count von Hutten-Czapski observed that such celebrations had a decidedly 'international character': the Kaiser's fleet review and the ceremonial opening of the strategically important canal were consciously designed to impress observers and journalists from abroad.[3] Those on the fringes of the naval theatre also noted this international dimension. Hamburg workers described the inauguration of the canal in pub conversations in April 1895 as a 'theatrical piece' given for 'the foreign powers'.[4] Undercover officer Graumann reported two months later from the *Wirtschaft Knegendorf*:

One guest said that all the celebrations of the canal opening served the sole purpose of *showing the foreign nations what Germany can achieve*; one could also see that the celebration did not have the character which it should have had, a so-called people's celebration [*eine sogenannte Volksfeier*]; no, this was nothing but a military show with which one wanted to impress others.[5]

British observers also commented on the international dimension inherent in the naval theatre. *The Times* wrote in 1909 that 'no amphitheatre ever presented such facilities of view for a display of naval strength as the sheet of water enclosed by the shores of Hampshire and the Isle of Wight'.

---

[3] Bogdan Graf von Hutten-Czapski, *Sechzig Jahre Politik und Gesellschaft*, vol. 1 (Berlin, 1936), p. 269.
[4] StA Hamburg, 331–3, S4875: Bericht Graumann, 13 April 1895, Wirtschaft Tillmann.
[5] StA Hamburg, 331–3, S4875: Bericht Graumann, 28 June 1895, Wirtschaft Knegendorf, emphasis added.

The rituals staged in this amphitheatre, the author continued, were intended for foreign as much as domestic audiences.[6] The '*Armada* display at Spithead', wrote the *Labour Leader* of the Spithead review of the same year, represented a 'theatrical climax', designed to impress 'the public both at home and abroad'.[7]

What turned the naval theatre into such a powerful stage between the nations was the coming together of imperial competition and naval rivalry with the transformation of media and popular culture. The unfolding of the 'age of the masses' in the late nineteenth century meant that the international audiences who participated in this theatre were expanding rapidly. It was no longer only a few dignitaries and statesmen who could afford to watch naval ceremonies in other countries. A surprisingly large number of Wilhelm II's subjects followed his lead in travelling to Britain to marvel at the Royal Navy's spectacular displays. As early as 1897, German steamers sailed across the North Sea to Spithead, carrying German tourists eager to watch a review of the British fleet. HAPAG, the Hamburg shipping line, was at the forefront of this naval tourism. It even managed to secure special berths close to the lines of warships allocated by the Admiralty.[8] In 1902, HAPAG sent the *Auguste Victoria* to Spithead, a tourist steamer with four decks, an additional promenade deck and 180 cabins.[9] Such naval tourism became so popular that newspapers started to organize 'readers' trips'. In 1909, the *Berliner Morgenpost* offered its readers such an *England-Reise* of seven days for 195 marks, all inclusive.[10]

The naval theatre even began to feature in tourist guides. The most remarkable example was *Das moderne England*, published in 1911 by the Berlin Anglicist Heinrich Spies. This was easily the most comprehensive and well-researched guide to contemporary Britain available in Imperial Germany. Combining travel advice with observations about British everyday life, it was intended as an 'introduction to the study of English culture'. Amongst much valuable information, his readers (mostly well educated middle-class travellers and students) found a section in which Spies commented on 'an especially interesting sight': the launch of a warship. This was a public event that, wherever it took place in Britain, created 'immense excitement' and was watched without fail 'by a colossal crowd'. Spies recommended this public spectacle to German travellers

---

[6]   *Times*, 1 June 1909. For similar examples see *Berliner Morgenpost*, 5 Sept 1911 and
       Times, 6 Sept 1911.
[7]   *Labour Leader*, 18 June 1909.
[8]   PRO, ADM 179/55: List of Merchant Vessels allotted special berths.
[9]   PRO, ADM 116/132, vol. 2: Hamburg American Line to Admiralty, 11 April 1902.
[10] *Berliner Morgenpost*, 22 July 1909, Erste Beilage.

for its entertainment value and as a peculiarly telling site of 'English culture'.[11] Inspired by such advice, German tourists brought home souvenirs from visits to Britain and had stories to tell which – whether true or invented – showed that a new Anglo-German significance was ascribed to the public staging of the navy. Under the headline 'The German Invasion' and accompanied by a rather self-satisfied commentary, the *Tägliche Rundschau* published a reader's letter:

I visited an elderly English gentleman who had seen the grand fleet display in the Thames. Full of pride he showed me a coin that he had bought as a souvenir of this memorable day. It was a small, gold-plated coin of aluminium, which showed the heads of the King and the Queen, saying: 'Our beloved King and Queen'. [. . .] However, when I had a closer look, I discovered to my great surprise, hidden on the rim of the coin, in small, but clearly readable letters the meaningful inscription: *Made in Germany!*[12]

In a similar vein, British tourists were increasingly noted at German naval events. During the 1911 review at Kiel, the *Frankfurter Zeitung* wrote that most foreigners in the audience seemed to be *Engländer*.[13] The correspondent of the *Leipziger Illustrierte Zeitung* overheard a chat between '*englische Herren*' who seemed astonished by the powerful display of German naval might. Their envious comments, wrote the correspondent, should be reason for 'wrathful joy [*ingrimmige Freude*]' amongst German readers.[14]

While such firsthand experience of the other country's naval theatre remained the privilege of affluent travellers, growing media coverage meant that vast numbers of the public experienced the international dimension of the naval game at home. The foreign coverage of fleet reviews and ship launches rose steadily in the three decades before the First World War. In 1887, at Victoria's Jubilee review, only one international newspaper had asked the Admiralty for admission.[15] In 1911, fifty foreign correspondents were accredited.[16] Yet even more important than the press was the cinema for the internationalization of the naval theatre. As the result of a globalized trade dominated by French and American firms, copies of the footage of naval displays were shown at cinemas all over Europe,

---

[11] Spies, *Das moderne England*, p. 69.
[12] *Tägliche Rundschau*, 13 Aug 1909. See the section 'The naval game' in Chapter 2 on British toy dreadnoughts 'made in Germany'. On the wider context: Sidney Pollard, '"Made in Germany" – die Angst vor der deutschen Konkurrenz im spätviktorianischen England', *Technikgeschichte* 53 (1987), pp. 183–95 and Maiken Umbach, 'Made in Germany', in François and Schulze, *Deutsche Erinnerungsorte*, vol. 2, pp. 405–18.
[13] *Frankfurter Zeitung*, 7 Sept 1911, Abendblatt.
[14] *Leipziger Illustrierte Zeitung*, in *Presse-Stimmen*, p. 22.
[15] PRO, ADM 1/6871: Press Tickets Issued 13 July 1887.
[16] PRO, ADM 116/1159: Coronation Naval Review, Saturday 24th June, 1911, Foreign Press.

North America and parts of Asia. As Charles Urban, one of the central figures in the Edwardian cinema business, pointed out in 1907, naval topics ranked high amongst the most popular 'cinematograph film subjects of present-day events'. Films of 'naval demonstrations' and the 'launching of war vessels' were in especially high demand.[17] German naval events were shown in British cinemas as early as 1896, when the opening of the Kiel Canal was included in the programme of Edison's Vitascope.[18] From then until 1914, a large number of films and newsreels brought the German navy to British audiences and vice versa.[19]

This international dimension was further enhanced when, in the years before 1914, it became increasingly common for large cinematographic firms to send operators from different countries to cover the same naval events. The London, Berlin and Paris branches of companies such as Pathé or Éclair would each send a team to the same review at Portsmouth, thereby ensuring that the pictures could be shown in all three countries in the shortest possible time.[20] This came in response to the strong rise in demand for footage of foreign naval celebrations. When applying for permission to film the 1911 naval review, Gaumont, the French film distributor, emphasized that it was 'firmly established in every large continental city' where it saw 'a great demand of a thoroughly representative series of films'.[21] Pathé Frères claimed that 'more than 10 million people all over the world' would see its images of the review.[22] And Eclair Film wrote in 1913 that its pictures of naval displays were 'shown throughout the entire world' to an estimated audience of thirty-eight million.[23]

---

[17] Urban, *Cinematograph*, pp. 22–3.

[18] Compare Lange-Fuchs, *Kaiser, Kanal und Kinematographie*, p. 104, where Edison's programme of 23 April 1896 is reprinted. These were the first moving pictures ever taken of a public naval celebration. They were the product of a peculiar Anglo-German collaboration between the chocolate tycoon Stollwerck and the cinematographer Birt Acres. See Loiperdinger, 'Wie der Film nach Deutschland kam' and Lange-Fuchs, *Kaiser, Kanal und Kinematographie*.

[19] Of those that have survived, two examples are particularly notable: the footage of the British naval mock-fights performed at the 1907 review, shown at German cinemas under the title 'Torpedoangriff' (NFTVA, title ref. 12180, Charles Urban, 1907) and the pictures of the launch of the *Kaiser* at Kiel in 1911, released in Britain by Pathé (NFTVA, title ref. 578339, Pathé, 1911). See also NFTVA, title ref. 486514: 'The battleship Odin with all her guns in action' (British Mutoscope and Biograph Company, 1900) and NFTVA, title ref. 534620: 'The *Von der Tann*' (Pathé, 1914). Further examples in West, *Our Navy*, p. 48.

[20] PRO, ADM 1/8319: Eclair Film Co., London, to Secretary of the Admiralty, 15 May 1913.

[21] PRO, ADM 116/1157: Gaumont Co. to Secretary of the Admiralty, 5 April 1911.

[22] PRO, ADM 116/1157: Pathé Frères Cinema Ltd. to Secretary of the Admiralty, 3 June 1911.

[23] PRO, ADM 1/8319: Eclair Film Co. to Secretary of the Admiralty, 15 May 1913.

All this meant that the display of naval might in one country could for the first time be seen and experienced by mass audiences in another. Millions in Germany could watch the Royal Navy perform a review or launch the latest dreadnought. And millions in Britain could watch the latest *Schlachtschiff* being launched or the Imperial Navy being reviewed by the Kaiser. As the *Frankfurter Zeitung* wrote in 1911, the naval theatre now took place 'in the face of all of Europe'.[24] This had important repercussions. Whatever the intentions of those organizing them, naval displays could no longer be restricted to domestic consumption. The largest cinematographic companies operating in Germany and Britain were French. Their distribution networks were decidedly international. Their cameramen could be denied access to the naval theatre, but their market power reached much further than the *Reichsmarineamt*'s influence. When they were not allowed to film naval displays themselves, they simply bought pictures from local German firms and marketed them internationally under their own label. News and entertainment had become so internationalized that it was impossible for the *Reichsmarineamt* to limit the consumption of and participation in the naval theatre to the domestic market. More than any other force it was mass media and popular culture that turned the naval stage into an international theatre in which the rivalry between powers was a fascinating and entertaining game.

Deterrence and the performance of power

Against this backdrop, admirals and naval authors discovered the naval theatre as a stage between the nations. What dominates in their descriptions is the observation that naval displays were occasions at which an *image* of power could be created. 'Effect', 'impression', 'vision', *Bild* and *Schauspiel* were recurrent terms. A 'grand picture' was what Admiral Hopman thought the Imperial fleet had created on the international stage with its review in 1911.[25] Julian Corbett, the naval historian, wrote that the 1902 Spithead review would spread 'forth a breathing image of the mystery of its [the navy's] power'.[26] Such observations about the 'picture', 'image' or 'spectacle' of sea power attested to the

---

[24] *Frankfurter Zeitung*, 7 Sept 1911, Abendblatt ['*im Angesicht von ganz Europa*'].
[25] Hopman, *Logbuch*, p. 374.
[26] In H. W. Wilson (ed.), *Navy League Guide to the Coronation Review June 28, 1902* (London, 1902), p. 7. See also Churchill's depiction of the 'spectacle of British sea-power' in *A History of the English-Speaking Peoples*, vol. 4, *The Great Democracies* (London, 1956), p. 293.

character of the naval theatre as an arena of deterrence. Deterrence was, of course, a central concern in the age of navalism and imperialism. Its importance was stressed by the key protagonists in this naval game. For Sir John Fisher, impressing and intimidating were what naval strategy in the Dreadnought era was all about. In a 1903 memorandum he wrote: 'The word intimidate is used since the history of the world points to intimidation being the greatest safeguard against hostile operations'.[27] As he put it in a letter in February 1905, the prime concern of naval policy was deterrence:

Because if you "rub it in" both at home and abroad that you are ready for instant war with every unit of your strength in the first line (...) then people will keep clear of you.[28]

Across the North Sea, deterrence was similarly at the heart of naval policy. The Imperial Navy's publicly stated *raison d'être* was one of deterrence. This was to be a *Risikoflotte*, a fleet whose very existence would pose too high a threat for the Royal Navy to consider attacking Germany. Beyond this, however, the Imperial Fleet's purpose was more offensive. It was to contest British naval hegemony, and especially the British command of the North Sea. The aim was to gain diplomatic concessions from the dominating naval and imperial power that seemed to stand in the way of German expansion. In Tirpitz's words, the waters between the two countries were to be turned into the 'lever of Germany's world policy'.[29] The emphasis was on *posing* a threat, on exercising power without having to go to war. As Wilhelm Widenmann, German naval attaché at London, put it in 1912, by threatening Britain exactly at the point where it was

[27] PRO, ADM 116/942: 'Invasion and Submarines', appendix A. For Fisher's interest in displays of deterrence compare his correspondence with Julian Corbett held at Churchill Archives Centre, Churchill College, Cambridge, FISR 1/1–15; *Fear God and Dread Nought: The Correspondence of Admiral of the Fleet Lord Fisher of Kilverstone*, edited by Arthur J. Marder, vol. 1 (London, 1952), p. 278; Sumida, *In Defence of Naval Supremacy*, p. 259 and Lambert, *John Fisher's Naval Revolution*, pp. 73–94. For a behind-the-scenes view on Fisher's approach to naval demonstrations see *The Navy and Defence: The Autobiography of Admiral of the Fleet Lord Chatfield* (London, 1942), pp. 79–80.
[28] *Fear God and Dread Nought*, vol. 2, p. 51: Fisher to unknown recipient, 22 Feb 1905. On the tradition of deterrence see Andrew Lambert, 'The Royal Navy 1856–1914: Deterrence and the Strategy of World Power', in Keith Neilson and Elizabeth Jane Errington (eds.), *Navies and Global Defense: Theories and Strategy* (London, 1995).
[29] Alfred von Tirpitz, *Politische Dokumente. Der Aufbau der deutschen Weltmacht* (Stuttgart, 1924), p. 346. For the background see the concise treatment by Kennedy, 'Maritime Strategieprobleme' and Michael Salewski, 'Die wilhelminischen Flottengesetze. Realität und Illusion', in Salewski, *Die Deutschen und die See*, pp. 119–25. Steinberg, *Yesterday's Deterrent* and Berghahn, *Tirpitz-Plan* remain the best in-depth studies.

most vulnerable, the German fleet was to be a *Machtmittel im Frieden*, an instrument of power in times of peace.[30]

So important seemed the effect of deterrence in the decades before the First World War that politicians and admirals were prepared to sacrifice crucial elements of their fleet's fighting capabilities for the creation of 'a bold front'. Nicholas A. Lambert writes:

Statesmen thought of navies and sea power in terms of deterrence and prestige rather than fighting capability; this was just as true in 1914 as it was in 1880. From this perspective numbers of warships (and their cost) were more important than combat effectiveness.[31]

Jon Sumida too has emphasized the primacy of deterrence in British naval policy. His research shows that the Admiralty compromised essential elements such as fire control in favour of promoting strong deterrence effects. Sumida concludes:

In having to choose between capital ships with larger guns and more effective fire control, the Admiralty was in effect confronted by the conflicting requirements of deterrence and war fighting; its decision in favour of the former amounted to the putting up of a bold front at the cost of operational capability.[32]

Such concerns with deterrence, which were at the heart of both British and German naval policy, were strongly informed by contemporary theories about sea power. Percival Hislam wrote in *The North Sea Problem*: 'The command of the sea can be held in peace as long as our naval supremacy is so great and unquestionable as to compel peace by the simple threat of its employment in war'.[33] The notion of compelling peace by the threat of war was also central in the writings of Alfred Thayer Mahan, by far the most influential naval theorist of this period.[34] One of the key metaphors that he and many other navalists used, the 'fleet in being', encapsulated the importance of deterrence. Even if permanently inactive, and even if considerably smaller than its adversary, a fleet held in a strategic location could 'lock up' a greater rival. Power could be exercised without having to engage the enemy directly. The

---

[30] Widenmann, *Marine-Attaché*, p. 305. See Steinberg, *Yesterday's Deterrent* and Steinberg, 'Copenhagen Complex' for a more detailed analysis of this point.
[31] Lambert, *Sir John Fisher's Naval Revolution*, p. 15.
[32] Sumida, *In Defence of Naval Supremacy*, p. 338.
[33] Percival A. Hislam, *The North Sea Problem* (London, 1913), p. 96.
[34] A. T. Mahan, *The Influence of Sea Power Upon History, 1660–1783* (London, 1890). On Mahan see John B. Hattendorf (ed.), *The Influence of History on Mahan: The Proceedings of a Conference Marking the Centenary of Alfred Thayer Mahan's 'The Influence of Sea Power Upon History, 1660–1783'* (Newport, RI, 1991) and Jon Tetsuro Sumida, *Inventing Grand Strategy and Teaching Command: The Classic Works of Alfred Thayer Mahan Reconsidered* (Washington, 1997).

command of the sea was thus as much about being able to project the 'silent pressure' of deterrence as about actual fighting capabilities.

It is here that the naval theatre played a key role: it provided the stage on which the command of the sea could be claimed in front of domestic and foreign audiences. Creating a visual and emotional impression of threat was critical. For deterrence to work, it had to be felt. The public celebration of the navy did just that: it displayed the instrument of deterrence in front of mass audiences at home and abroad. Indeed, Julian Corbett saw fleet reviews as the prime occasion for projecting the 'silent pressure of sea power'.[35] This theatre of deterrence was all the more important since there were few other ways in which the command of the sea could be claimed in times of peace. In his seminal article in the *Encyclopaedia Britannica* of 1911, Sir Cyprian Bridge differentiated between an absolute and a relative form of the command of the sea. The 'absolute command of the sea', he wrote, was a 'condition [. . .] existent only in time of war'. It was only in battle that it could be proven who really ruled the waves.[36] In times of peace, by contrast, the command of the sea was relative. It was 'an attribute', in flux and open to challenges.[37] Naval mastery could not be tested or ascertained in peace, it could only be claimed or postulated. And the more one nation's 'relative command of the sea' was contested, the more it had to be displayed and asserted symbolically. The fleet was, as Bridge put it, the 'visible sign of sea-power'.[38] Its primary role in times of peace was to *demonstrate* sea power, to *perform* it on the stage between the nations. This, in turn, explains why admirals and naval authors were so concerned with the 'image' and 'impression' that the fleet would make at these occasions rather than its actual fighting capabilities.[39]

The press coverage of fleet reviews underlines the degree to which the celebration of the navy was considered to be about deterrence. As the *Kieler Zeitung* put it, the naval theatre was to have a powerful effect 'to the outward' [*nach außen hin*].[40] The *Berliner Morgenpost* wrote in 1911 that fleet reviews were exercises in 'sabre-rattling', with the message being: 'we are ready'.[41] Fleet reviews were about 'displaying naval strength', explained *The Times* in 1909, they were 'an exhibition' aimed

[35] In Wilson, *Navy League Guide to the Coronation Review*, p. 7.
[36] *Encyclopaedia Britannica*, vol. 24 (Cambridge, 1911), p. 530. See also Cyprian A. G. Bridge, 'The Command of the Sea', in Cyprian A. G. Bridge, *Sea-Power and Other Studies* (London, 1910), pp. 73–84.
[37] *Encyclopaedia Britannica*, vol. 24, p. 530.   [38] Ibid., p. 560.
[39] For another example see Vizeadmiral a. D. Hoffmann, 'Die britische Flottenparade', *Vossische Zeitung*, 14 July 1912, who talks of the Royal Navy's '*mise-en-scène* [*in Szene setzen*]' and the 'stage [*Bühne*] at Spithead'.
[40] *Kieler Zeitung*, 6 Sept 1911, Erstes Blatt; *Frankfurter Zeitung*, 7 Sept 1911, Abendblatt.
[41] *Berliner Morgenpost*, 5 Sept 1911.

27. The performance of deterrence. 'Flottenparade vor dem Kaiser' by
Willy Stöwer, 1912. Stöwer was the Kaiser's favourite naval painter.
The vessels are shown much closer to one another than they would have
been in reality. *U1*, Germany's first commissioned submarine, is seen
in the foreground, about to be passed by the imperial yacht *Hohenzollern*,
with Wilhelm II on the bridge.

at potential enemies.[42] The *Naval and Military Record* defined their
purposes as 'giving a picture of our naval strength' for those who doubted
'that we are, and intend to remain, the supreme Sea Power'.[43] The
importance of theatricality and stagecraft for the demonstration of sea
power is particularly well illustrated by an article in *The Times* in
September 1911. Commenting on the review of the French fleet at
Toulon, it wrote: 'It is felt that France has reasserted her claim to be
regarded as the leading Power in the Mediterranean and has succeeded in
solidifying her North African Empire'.[44] It was *felt* that France's position
had been reasserted, and that this had been effected by staging a large-
scale naval show: both points demonstrated that the naval stage was
perceived to be about creating images and impressions for foreign
audiences.

[42] *Times*, 1 June 1909.   [43] *Naval and Military Record*, 29 July 1914 and 10 June 1909.
[44] *Times*, 6 Sept 1911.

A huge aesthetic effort was invested in this international theatre. Newspapers commented on the 'art of stage direction' evident in these spectacles and discussed the impression they had made on foreign observers. Admirals appeared as directors, putting on good or disappointing shows. The 'pictures' or 'scenes' of naval might, the arrangement and choreography, the numbers and categories of ships, the main actors and their movements, the show's timing, its employment of new features, the strategy of bluff and the pretence of power – all this was part of the naval theatre, reviewed in the papers and noted by political observers. The Spithead spectacles were 'colourful bunting, masquerade, bluff', wrote the *Vossische Zeitung* at the occasion of the 1911 review.[45] 'Delcassé is not bluffing!' was the headline in the *Berliner Lokal-Anzeiger* three months later, when the Toulon fleet review stirred the imagination of France's neighbours.[46] British and German naval attachés closely observed and reported the other country's strategies of 'bluffing' and 'creating impressions'.[47] In 1912, the *Naval and Military Record* acknowledged that a strong sense of false advertising was at the centre of British reviews. Over the last years, it wrote,

whenever a demonstration of naval power was required, the Admiralty provided a review of a vast amount of warships riding at anchor. All were declared ready for war, but many of them were in fact *fit only for show*.[48]

This was a remarkable observation. It underlined the central role that deterrence played in this international spectacle: warships were floating symbols for the representation of power. So important was the image they created, that the Admiralty displayed vessels which were not ready to fight other warships. They were stage props, 'fit only for show', in a theatre of power that was designed to demonstrate superiority to domestic and foreign audiences.

---

[45] *Vossische Zeitung*, 26 June 1911.

[46] *Berliner Lokal-Anzeiger*, 5 Sept 1911, Erstes Blatt, Morgenausgabe. In a second article (*Berliner Lokal-Anzeiger*, 5 Sept 1911, Zweites und Drittes Blatt, Abendausgabe), the newspaper explained what it saw as Delcassé's strategy: he could have presented all ships of the *Danton* type at the review, however, he did not want to follow Germany's example by sending vessels on to the stage which were, in reality, unfit for battle.

[47] Widenmann, *Marine-Attaché*, p. 303. When Captain Heath, British naval attaché in Berlin, reported from a visit to Wilhelmshaven and Bremen in 1908, he stressed that the Germans were employing tricks in order to create the illusion of 'being in the lead': 'A good deal of work has been prepared for the *Ersatz Oldenburg* in the shops', he wrote, 'but my guide explained that the official laying of the keel was delayed as long as possible "*in order to make a record*"'. Cf. N.A. Report 46/08, 'Visits to Wilhelmshaven and Bremen, 20 October 1908', printed in E. L. Woodward, *Great Britain and the German Navy* (Oxford, 1935), pp. 489–90 (emphasis added).

[48] *Naval and Military Record*, 8 May 1912 (emphasis added).

These findings suggest a revision of the way in which historians con-
ceptualize sea power in the age of empire. Indeed, naval historians may
need to extend their vocabulary and think of sea power in cultural terms.
If performance and imagery were just as important as – and indeed at
times more important than – operational capabilities, then ideas such as
the 'command of the sea' and 'naval mastery' need to be re-evaluated.
Ever since Alfred Thayer Mahan, naval historians have studied sea power
in the context of strategy, geography and socio-economy. In the classic
Sea Power: A Naval History, published in 1960, E.B. Potter followed
Mahan stringently:

The elements of sea power are by no means limited to combat craft, weapons, and
trained personnel but include the shore establishment, well-sited bases, commercial shipping, and advantageous international alignments. The capacity of a
nation to exercise sea power is based also upon the character and number of its
population, the character of its government, the soundness of its economy, its
industrial efficiency, the development of its internal communications, the quality
and numbers of its harbours, the extent of its coastline, and the location of the
homeland, bases, and colonies with respect to communications.[49]

Forty-five years later, naval historians still study sea power in this limited
sense. The vast majority of them focus on naval battles, strategy, administration and technology.[50] Indeed, naval history 'continues to be written
mainly as one of operations in wartime'.[51] Even N. A. M. Rodger, who
has been influential in widening the scope of naval history, seems to
follow an essentially Mahanian approach. In the introduction to the
second volume of his *Naval History of Britain*, he describes the 'four
parallel streams' on which his study is based:

policy, strategy and naval operations; finance, administration and logistics,
including all sorts of technical and industrial support; social history; and the
material elements of sea power, ships and weapons.[52]

---

[49] E. B. Potter, 'Preface', in E. B. Potter and Chester W. Nimitz (eds.), *Sea Power: A Naval History* (London, 1960), p. vii. Paul Kennedy, *The Rise and Fall of British Naval Mastery*, p. 5, summarizes Mahan's approach and 'virtually all other variants upon it that one encounters in books upon sea power' in six main points: '(i) geographical position; (ii) physical conformation; (iii) extent of territory; (iv) number of population; (v) national character and (vi) character and policy of governments'.

[50] Recent examples: Sumida, *In Defence of Naval Supremacy*; Lambert, *Sir John Fisher's Naval Revolution*; Hobson, *Imperialism at Sea*; Christian Roedel, *Krieger, Denker, Amateure: Alfred von Tirpitz und das Seekriegsbild vor dem Ersten Weltkrieg* (Stuttgart, 2003); Robert K. Massie, *Castles of Steel: Britain, Germany, and the Winning of the Great War at Sea* (New York and London, 2003).

[51] Gough, 'The Royal Navy and the British Empire', p. 339.

[52] N. A. M. Rodger, *The Command of the Ocean: A Naval History of Britain 1649–1815* (London, 2004), p. lxiv.

Should there not be a fifth factor, namely the cultural elements of sea power? Sea power was an idea that was constructed and imagined, enacted and performed in a range of public arenas and discourses. It is time that historians explored this culture of sea power, in particular for the imperial age, when deterrence and the representation of power became arguably more important than the actual fighting of sea battles. Indeed, the dreadnought fleets of Britain and Germany were of debatable value for the new forms of naval warfare that came about in the early twentieth century. Their real value was a symbolic one: they were platforms for the theatrical demonstration of sea power.

The sea: culture and contest

In the naval theatre, the performance of sea power was not only about deterrence, but also about important cultural issues that were bound up with the sea and its mastery. The retired officer Lothar Persius wrote in 1909 that the Wilhelmine naval programme had 'pushed Germany on to the world stage with an entirely new ambition and claim'. What was to be represented and claimed on this stage was not only power, but also prestige, tradition and cultural influence.[53] In his many speeches given at naval ceremonies, the Kaiser stressed in a similar fashion that 'the naval game' was about honour, culture, tradition and identity.[54] Indeed, Tirpitz defined the sea as a *Kulturgebiet*, a 'cultural space'.[55] A host of issues were to be represented and negotiated in this space, issues that went beyond strictly strategic or naval matters.[56] If this *Welttheater* was as much about culture and identity as it was about power, it was particularly so between Britain and Germany. The rapid building of the Imperial Navy 'laid open' the North Sea not only in a strategic sense, as Percival Hislam put it, but also in a cultural sense.[57] An intense cultural competition developed over those stretches of water 'between Heligoland and the Thames' that the 'Tirpitz Memorandum' of June 1897, the birth certificate of the German navy, described as the Anglo-German amphitheatre.[58] Politicians, academics and journalists concerned themselves with the

---

[53] *Welt am Montag*, 8 Nov 1909, in PA/AA, Deutschland 138, vol. 41.
[54] For a poignant example see his speech at the swearing-in of naval recruits at Wilhelmshaven on 4 January 1892, in A. O. Klaußmann (ed.), *Kaiserreden. Reden und Erlasse, Briefe und Telegramme Kaiser Wilhelms des Zweiten* (Leipzig, 1902), p. 238.
[55] Tirpitz, *Erinnerungen*, p. 16.   [56] Ibid., pp. 95–6, 134.
[57] Percival A. Hislam, *The Admiralty of the Atlantic: An Enquiry into the Development of German Sea Power, Past, Present and Prospective* (London, 1908), p. 145.
[58] 'Allgemeine Gesichtspunkte bei der Festlegung unserer Flotte nach Schiffsklassen und Schiffstypen, Juni 1897', German original and English translation in Steinberg, *Yesterday's Deterrent*, pp. 208–9.

question of how to bring German culture 'on to the sea', how the North Sea could be 'made German' and denied as a cultural space to the British.[59] The convergence of two important ways of thinking about international relations gave further impetus to the discovery of the sea as a space for cultural competition: Social Darwinism and navalism. There is an impressive range of academic writing on Social Darwinism and its impact on the imperial age.[60] However, ideas of a 'struggle for survival' between nations are seldom considered in relation to the sea. This is surprising, given that the popularization of Social Darwinist thought occurred in parallel with the rise of navalism. Navalism, closely associated with the writings of Alfred Thayer Mahan, can best be described as the belief that, in the age of imperialism, great powers had to be naval powers. It was only by having access to the sea and its 'highways', and by being able to project power overseas through a strong navy, that nations could gain and sustain world power status.[61] Social Darwinist ideas charged this vision with a sense of existential struggle. If races or nations were engaged in a struggle for survival, the sea was, in the age of navalism, the obvious arena for this struggle. Indeed, in Social Darwinist readings, the sea itself was the source of a nation's well-being. The sea was, as Frank Bullen, the *Daily Mail*'s naval correspondent, put it, the 'reservoir of health'.[62] For Sir Charles Dilke and Henry Spenser Wilkinson, Britain and her empire derived 'their nourishment and their strength' from the sea.[63]

The key metaphor of German *Weltpolitik*, the *Platz an der Sonne*, was charged with similar ideas that brought together navalism and Social Darwinism. 'We do not want to put anyone into the shadow, but we also demand our space in the sun', was how von Bülow, the foreign secretary, captured Germany's ambitions on the world stage in his famous Reichstag speech in December 1897.[64] Bülow's phrase turned into a powerful, if somewhat vague, motto that was closely associated

---

[59] Peter Overlack, 'An Instrument of "Culture": The Imperial Navy, the Academics and Germany's World Mission', in Andrew Bonnell, Gregory Munro and Martin Travers (eds.), *Power, Conscience and Opposition: Essays in German History in Honour of John A. Moses* (New York, 1996), pp. 3–24; Steinberg, *Yesterday's Deterrent*, pp. 38–9. For a prime example see the section on 'The renaissance of the Hanseatic League' in Chapter 4.

[60] See Mike Hawkins, *Social Darwinism in European and American Thought 1860–1945: Nature as Model and Nature as Threat* (Cambridge, 1997) for a survey.

[61] Mahan, *The Influence of Sea Power Upon History*; Kennedy, *Rise and Fall of British Naval Mastery*, pp. 5–9; Hobson, *Imperialism at Sea*.

[62] Frank T. Bullen, *Our Heritage the Sea* (London, 1906).

[63] Sir Charles Dilke and Henry Spenser Wilkinson, *Imperial Defence* (London, 1892), pp. 42–3.

[64] *Sten. Ber., IX. Legislaturperiode, V. Session, 1897/98*, vol. 1 (Berlin, 1898), p. 60 (6 Dec 1897); *Graf Bülows Reden nebst urkundlichen Beiträgen zu seiner Politik*, collected and edited by

with the sea as a strategic, but also as a cultural space. In June 1900, Wilhelm II declared that Germany had reached 'the place in the sun', but needed a strong fleet to secure it permanently. This place, he made clear, was to be found on the sea. It was here, he explained at a dinner marking the end of the annual regatta on the river Elbe, that 'the rays of sunshine' would have 'their fertilizing impact' on the German nation.[65] Shortly before the international crisis that would lead to war began to unfold in July 1914, Bülow wrote:

The sea has become a factor of more importance in our national life than ever before in our history, even in the great days of the German *Hansa*. It has become a vital nerve which we must not allow to be severed if we do not wish to be transformed from a rising and youthfully vigorous people into a decaying and ageing one.[66]

Such statements reflected an increasing trend to conflate navalism with Social Darwinist ideas. The sea was thought of not only as a space of naval rivalry, but also as the location of a wider contest between nations, in which health and fitness, culture and character were the keywords. Particularly influential for this conceptualization of the sea was Friedrich Ratzel, often seen as the founder of human geography.[67] It was Ratzel who put the term *Lebensraum* on to the scholarly map of the late nineteenth century. One of the most fundamental laws explaining the evolution of animals, plants and human beings alike, he contended, was the competition for space. If they wanted to grow and expand, peoples (*Völker*) had to extend their boundaries, they had to reach out into new *Lebensraum*, literally 'living space'.[68] Ratzel applied these

Johannes Penzler, vol. 1 (Berlin, 1907), p. 8; Bernhard Fürst von Bülow, *Deutsche Politik*, edited and introduced by Peter Winzen (Bonn, 1992), pp. 35–6. On the context of Bülow's metaphor: Peter Winzen, *Bülows Weltmachtkonzept. Untersuchungen zur Frühphase seiner Außenpolitik 1897–1901* (Boppard, 1977); Gerd Fesser, *Reichskanzler Fürst von Bülow. Architekt der deutschen Weltpolitik* (Leipzig, 2003), pp. 52–81 and Joachim Radkau, *Das Zeitalter der Nervosität. Deutschland zwischen Bismarck und Hitler* (Munich, 1998), pp. 375–88.

[65] Klaußmann, *Kaiserreden*, p. 349 (speech held aboard the *Victoria Luise*, 19 June 1900).

[66] Bernhard von Bülow, *Imperial Germany* (London, 1914), written and published before the outbreak of the war. See also G. von Schulze-Gaevernitz, *England und Deutschland*, second edition (Berlin, 1908), p. 39.

[67] On Ratzel see Mark Bassin, 'Imperialism and the Nation State in Friedrich Ratzel's Political Geography', *Progress in Human Geography* 11 (1987), pp. 473–95; Gerhard H. Müller, *Friedrich Ratzel (1844–1904). Naturwissenschaftler, Geograph, Gelehrter. Neue Studien zu Leben und Werk und sein Konzept der "Allgemeinen Biogeographie"* (Stuttgart, 1996); R. P. Beckinsale, 'Friedrich Ratzel', *Dictionary of Scientific Biography*, vol. 11 (New York, 1975), p. 309; Mark Bassin, 'Friedrich Ratzel 1844–1904', in *Geographers: Biobibliographical Studies*, vol. 11 (1987), p. 128.

[68] Friedrich Ratzel, 'Der Lebensraum. Eine biogeographische Studie', in K. Bücher et al. (eds.), *Festgaben für Albert Schäffle zur siebzigsten Wiederkehr seines Geburtstages am 24. Februar 1901* (Tübingen, 1901), pp. 101–89.

thoughts to the sea in *Das Meer als Quelle der Völkergrösse*, published in 1900.[69] The sea had two major roles to play for the flourishing of nations. First, it was the space in which nations competed for access to new *Lebensraum*, space which Ratzel saw represented by colonies and overseas possessions. Second, the sea was the source not only of power and wealth, but also of a nation's identity and culture. Ratzel called it the *Wesen* (character) and *Seele* (soul) of a people.[70] The sea was the purest form of nature, the *reinste Natur*, to which humankind could find exposure. There was a retroactive impact (*Rückwirkung*) from 'the great characteristics of the sea to the spirit of humankind'.[71] New 'youth and fertility' passed from the sea to the people engaging with it, not only in a physical but also in a mental and cultural sense. Exposure to the sea was a pre-condition for 'cultural achievements'. People that lived in landlocked areas were only 'half-cultivated'.[72] Clearly, for Ratzel, who represented a highly influential strand of late nineteenth-century scholarship that brought together geography, biology and evolutionary theory, the sea and its command raised fundamental issues that went far beyond those traditionally associated with the navy. It was in the contest on and the conquest of the sea that nations proved themselves, their identity and 'cultural value'.[73]

Such concepts about the sea as a cultural space of the imperial age, charged the naval theatre with an added urgency, a seemingly existential importance.[74] The sea was the location of a nation's struggle for survival in which it would either flourish or vanish. This was 'the great alternative', as Henry Spenser Wilkinson, professor of military history, put it.[75] The sea gave access to *Lebensraum* and health, it was the source of culture and progress. The naval theatre was a prime arena in which the struggle over this space was imagined and anticipated. It was here that nations

---

[69] Friedrich Ratzel, *Das Meer als Quelle der Völkergrösse. Eine politisch-geographische Studie* (Munich and Leipzig, 1900).

[70] Ibid., pp. 39–40.   [71] Ibid., p. 40.   [72] Ibid., pp. 55–6.

[73] On the relationship between nature and identity on land see Blackbourn, *The Conquest of Nature*; Thomas M. Lekan, *Imagining the Nation in Nature: Landscape Preservation and German Identity 1885–1945* (Cambridge, MA, 2004); Readman, 'Landscape Preservation'; Stephen Daniels, *Fields of Vision: Landscape, Imagery and National Identity in England and the United States* (Cambridge, 1991); John M. MacKenzie (ed.), *Imperialism and the Natural World* (Manchester, 1990).

[74] For an example of the popularization of such thought see C. R. L. Fletcher and Rudyard Kipling, *A School History of England* (Oxford, 1911), pp. 235–6.

[75] Henry Spenser Wilkinson, *The Great Alternative* (London, 1894). For further examples see Behrman, *Victorian Myths of the Sea*, esp. pp. 111–5.

won or lost the 'test of war' in times of peace.[76] Reporting the fleet display on the Thames in July 1909, the *Daily Mirror* wrote that the sight of 'the fleet that stirs our blood and dazzles us with the splendour of its strength' taught one lesson: 'you must advance or perish'.[77] Frank Bullen wrote about the sea as 'our heritage': 'I say that I do not blame the Germans; if they succeed in their efforts to destroy Great Britain's place among the nations, it will only be because Britons have become unworthy to hold that place'.[78] The *Auswärtiges Amt* noted the use of similar Navalist-Social-Darwinist rhetoric during the 1909 imperial conference, which culminated in a grand fleet review. Metternich reported to von Bülow that Lord Roberts, one of the main speakers, had declared the North Sea the site of a 'gigantic struggle'.[79] This struggle was not just a strategic and military one. As the German Ambassador wrote to Bethmann Hollweg, the confrontation was on a deeper, cultural level. He quoted Winston Churchill, who had told the Royal Academy in May 1909 that the fleet was not just a military instrument, it was an expression of 'English civilization'.[80]

Wrapped up with such narratives was another factor that contributed to the increasingly important cultural role of the sea: the strong link between national identity and the sea. Much of contemporary discourse about the nation was permeated by naval and maritime imagery.[81] Chapter 4 has demonstrated how centrally 'the nation' featured as a theme on the naval stage. In both countries the navy and its public rituals served a strong cultural purpose as a carrier of national pride, tradition and unity. This was all the more important as naval celebrations combined some of the most potent sources of national identification, amongst them monarchy, geography and the past, but also aspects of gender, technology and vio-lence, in one powerful display. Given the strong links between nationhood and the sea, it is hardly surprising that naval challenges were understood as directed against a nation's culture and identity. When the German Ambassador, Paul Metternich, reported from the 1909 Imperial Press

[76] Harold F. Wyatt, *God's Test by War* (London, 1912). For further examples see the pamphlets and articles collected in Harold F. Wyatt and L. G. H. Horton-Smith (eds.), *The Passing of the Great Fleet* (London, 1909).
[77] *Daily Mirror*, 19 July 1909.   [78] Bullen, *Our Heritage the Sea*, p. 330.
[79] PA-AA, R 5583: Metternich to Bülow, 10 June 1909.
[80] PA-AA, R 5590: Metternich to Bethmann Hollweg, 5 May 1909.
[81] See the comprehensive list of naval metaphors in Hans Wilderotter, '"Unsere Zukunft liegt auf dem Wasser". Das Schiff als Metapher und die Flotte als Symbol der Politik des wilhelminischen Kaiserreichs', in Hans Wilderotter and Klaus-D. Pohl (eds.), *Der letzte Kaiser* (Gütersloh, 1991), pp. 55–78.

Conference, which featured a grand naval review, he came to the conclusion that the whole event had not produced any direct, political result.
Rather, its explicit purpose had been a cultural one: to bolster imperial and
national unity and a feeling of shared identity and solidarity between the
mother country and the colonies. Such displays of shared cultural values
were all the more important, Metternich continued, as 'centrifugal tendencies' in the colonies had become increasingly palpable. It was as
regrettable as it was alarming for Anglo-German relations, he concluded,
that such demonstrations of national and imperial unity seemed to require
the parading of the German fleet as a 'hostile other'.[82]

All this helps to explain why the 'great game for mastery in the North
Sea'[83] was as much a cultural phenomenon as it was a political one. The
rapid transformation of the media and popular culture; the translation of foreign relations and naval rivalry into a fascinating spectacle,
watched by mass audiences internationally; the imagination of the sea as
a space of cultural conflict; the situation of the naval stage at the intersection of national and international contexts; its role as a stage for
the performance of power and deterrence as well as nationhood and
difference: these factors made the celebration of the navy a key arena in
which international relations were acted out for domestic and foreign
audiences.

The theatre of antagonism

This was by no means an exclusively or uniquely Anglo-German theatre.
The tourists who came to see the celebration of the Royal Navy were not
only from Germany but from all over the world. Indeed, during the
launch of the *Thunderer* in February 1911 the *Daily Express* observed
that 'one could hear the babble of foreign tongues on all sides'.[84]
Moreover, other countries were just as busy celebrating their navies and
their claim to the sea as Britain and Germany. In 1898, Sir George
Sydenham Clarke wrote that the well choreographed fleet visits between
Russia and France 'touched the imagination of the masses as no diplomatic correspondence could have done'.[85] The US was also keen to
employ the navy as a cultural tool, most spectacularly in the case of the
'world tour' of the Great White Fleet from December 1907 to February

---

[82] PA-AA, R 5636 Metternich to Bülow, 28 June 1909; ibid.: Militär-Attaché, London, 28
June 1909, betrifft: Die Presskonferenz in London und die Landesverteidigung.
[83] Clarke, *Hope and Glory*, p. 56.   [84] *Daily Express*, 2 Feb 1911.
[85] Clarke, *Russia's Sea-Power*, pp. 132–3.

1909.[86] In Japan, naval matters were similarly bound up with cultural issues, as Naoko Shimazu has shown.[87] Yet in no other countries did the naval theatre develop such a strong bi-national character as it did between Britain and Germany. Between 1897 and 1914, the largest number of foreign correspondents present at Spithead fleet reviews were German.[88] From the turn of the century, it was standard procedure for the press in Britain to cover the Wilhelmine naval theatre in full-length articles. The *Daily Telegraph* sent a reporter to cover the launch of a German warship as early as 1897.[89] With the unfolding of Anglo-German naval rivalry, editors became more and more eager for their correspondents to be given direct access to fleet reviews and ship launches in Germany. They incessantly lobbied the naval leadership in Berlin as well as the local authorities in Bremen, Hamburg, Kiel and Danzig. When denied access, British journalists and photographers regularly managed to get around official restrictions. As one correspondent wrote to the Schichau dockyard:

It may interest you to know that I have seen every launch in your yard that I had any wish to see, for the last 12 years, and you must also be aware that if a person wishes to see the launch, there are many ways open to attain that end.[90]

In 1908, the *Daily Mail*'s correspondent, the aptly named F. W. Wile, was categorically refused access to ship launches of the Imperial Navy. Yet he managed to outwit the *Reichsmarineamt* and the *Admiralstab*. Lieutenant-Commander Karl Boy-Ed of the *Nachrichtenbureau* had to admit that

Mr. Wile was nonetheless [at the ceremony] in the dockyard. He answered my astonished question, how he had managed to get access, by showing me a yellow ticket for gentlemen [*Herren-Karte*]. He had acquired the ticket from Frau Loheyde, the wife of the hotel-owner.[91]

---

[86] James R. Reckner, *Teddy Roosevelt's Great White Fleet* (Annapolis, 1988).

[87] Naoko Shimazu, 'The Making of a Heroic War Myth in the Russo-Japanese War', *Waseda Journal of Asian Studies* 25 (2004), pp. 83–96. See also her forthcoming *Japanese Society at War: Death, Memory and the Russo-Japanese War* (Cambridge) as well as J. Charles Schencking, *Making Waves: Politics, Propaganda, and the Emergence of the Imperial Japanese Navy, 1868–1922* (Stanford, 2005) and J. Charles Schencking, 'The Imperial Japanese Navy and the Constructed Consciousness of a South Seas Destiny', *Modern Asian Studies* 33 (1999), pp. 767–96.

[88] PRO, ADM 1/8049: Cowes Review 1909, Press applications; ibid., ADM 116/1159: Coronation Naval Review, Saturday 24th June, 1911, Foreign Press.

[89] *Daily Telegraph*, 27 Sept 1897.

[90] PRO, FO 634/14: Frank Dunsby to C. Carlson of Schichau Yard, Danzig, 14 June 1910.

[91] BA-MA, RM 3/9958, Bl. 218: Memo by Boy-Ed, Nachrichtenbureau, 12 March 1908; ibid., Bl. 225: Boy-Ed to Wile, 12 March 1908; ibid., Bl. 236: Nachrichtenbureau to Hochseeflotte Kiel, 30 March 1908. For another example in which the *Daily Mirror* studiously tried to gain access to the Wilhelmine naval theatre, see BA-MA, RM 3/10237, Bl. 275.

The inventiveness of British correspondents and the eagerness of their editors to have first-hand accounts of the Wilhelmine naval theatre reflected the increasingly Anglo-German focus of this stage.[92] Left-wing critics agreed that there was a distinct Anglo-German character in the way the navy was being staged. When the *Labour Leader* described the 1909 royal fleet review as an 'Armada display at Spithead' that was designed to impress 'the public both at home and abroad', it was certain that, as far as foreign audiences were concerned, the display was directed above all at Germany. It was for 'the German people', wrote the *Labour Leader*, that this spectacle appeared to have been staged, and it hoped that the German press would laugh at the 'mixture of swagger and funk' that had been given at Spithead.[93] Across the North Sea, the *Hamburger Echo* observed that launches and reviews had turned into displays of Anglo-German rivalry and antagonism. The launch of the *Imperator* in May 1912, the *Echo* wrote, had been 'a welcome opportunity to get at the hated English'.[94] It was not only critics, but also those at the centre of these rituals who found that the celebration of the navy had turned into a theatre of Anglo-German antagonism. 'You can always fall back on "our cousins across the seas" for a topic', was what the chairman recommended to Lady Randolph Churchill at the launch of the *Benbow* in 1913, when she asked for advice about what to say in her speech.[95] At the launch of the *Dreadnought*, a Portsmouth priest called for the new ship to penetrate German steel plates.[96] The Kaiser, perhaps predictably, saw the celebration of the navy as an almost exclusively Anglo-German contest.[97]

The 'official mind' in the foreign offices and naval administrations also treated this as an arena in which the two countries were acting out their rivalry. Politicians, diplomats and officers closely observed and interpreted the other country's naval displays. From the turn of the century, the German embassy in London sent reports about all large naval

---

[92] That the rivalry between the two countries was being played out in, and intensified through, the naval theatre was one of the recurrent observations in the press. See *Berliner General-Anzeiger*, 5 Aug 1907; *Die Flotte*, Oct 1907: 'Flottenparaden'; *Deutsche Tages-Zeitung*, 6 Aug 1907: 'Swinemünde – Solent'; *Daily Express*, 19 July 1909; *Breslauer General-Anzeiger*, 26 Sept 1909; *Tägliche Rundschau*, 9 Sept 1911: 'Flottenvergleiche'; *Berliner Tageblatt*, 16 July 1914.
[93] *Labour Leader*, 18 June 1909.   [94] *Hamburger Echo*, 26 May 1912.
[95] GBRC, UGD 100/1/15/3: 'Lady Randolph's Visit to the Clyde', *The Citizen*, undated. For a similar example at the launch of HMS *Dreadnought* see *Portsmouth Evening News*, 12 Feb 1906.
[96] *Portsmouth Evening News*, 12 Feb 1906.
[97] BA, R 901/22418: Stapellauf des englischen Schiffes Vanguard, 4 Nov 1909. See also BA-MA, RM 2/160–202 for Wilhelm II's marginalia, frequently interpreting naval events to this end.

celebrations and their reception in the British press. It also sent dispatches about British reactions to German naval displays.[98] After 1906, the diplomatic protocol of inviting naval attachés to each other's launching ceremonies disintegrated.[99] Rows erupted with predictable regularity between London and Berlin over the question of whether attachés should be allowed to witness warship launches. By 1908, the two countries denied each other's diplomats access as a matter of course.[100] A memorandum by the German naval attaché at London laid the blame for this state of affairs squarely on the British who, he reported, had been refusing him access to launching sites and dockyards for some time.[101] Whether true or not, these allegations indicated the level of distrust that had begun to characterize the naval theatre. The fact that both countries denied the other access to launching sites and dockyards underlined that this stage had acquired a distinctly Anglo-German focus – in particular since both London and Berlin made a point of continuing to invite the diplomats of allied countries to these occasions. This introduced a strong element of mutual distrust into a widely publicized spectacle at a time when most diplomats saw the need for confidence-building measures between the two countries.

The Anglo-German character of this theatre was also reflected in the speeches given at warship launches – and in the way the *Nachrichtenbureau* edited them. Britain was the only foreign power mentioned, and mentioned regularly, in the draft speeches that were submitted to Tirpitz's public relations office. While many of dignitaries acting as launch patrons suggested they would talk of Britain as the prime foreign recipient of this public theatre, the *Nachrichtenbureau* insisted that any such wording be avoided. Without fail, the press officers in Berlin reminded speakers

---

[98] PA-AA, R5769–5797 and BA, R 901/22418. A similar recording went on at the *Reichsmarineamt* and the *Marinekabinett*, see BA-MA, RM 3/9686–98 and ibid., RM 2/160–202.

[99] Naval manoeuvres, in contrast, had always been off limits for foreign diplomats. British attachés were instructed by the Foreign Office not to accept offers to visit German manoeuvres. Otherwise, based on the principle of reciprocity, German attachés would have had to be given access to British naval manoeuvres, too. See Marder, *Anatomy*, p. 464, n. 20. On the background see Lothar Wilfried Hilbert, 'The Role of Military and Naval Attachés in the British and German Services with Particular References to those in Berlin and London and their Effect on Anglo-German Relations, 1871–1914', Ph.D. thesis, University of Cambridge (1954) and Klaus-Volker Giessler, *Die Institution des Marineattachés im Kaiserreich* (Boppard, 1976).

[100] BA-MA, RM 2/1618, Bl. 42 Chef Marinekabinett to Werft Wilhelmshaven, Kiel and Staatsekretär RMA, 21 Feb 1908. Similarly BA-MA, RM 3/9958, Bl. 199: Tirpitz to Werft Wilhelmshaven, 5 March 1908; ibid., Bl. 271: Schmidt to Vulcan Yard, Stettin and Marinestation der Ostsee, 10 July 1908. For the tightening of access for attachés in Britain see the memo in PRO, ADM 1/8047, 21 May 1909.

[101] BA-MA, RM 2/1618, Bl. 43: Marine-Attaché, London, 18 Feb 1908.

and their ghostwriters that Britain should not be referred to. They crossed out any direct jibes at the rival across the North Sea and suggested alternative wording. Describing a new warship as 'a strong weapon against England' was rather unfortunate, the *Nachrichtenbureau* wrote to General von Tann-Rathsamshausen. In polite, but clear terms they explained why he ought to revise his speech and leave out any mention of Britain:

> The *Nachrichtenbureau* has the honour of drawing most humbly Your Excellency's attention to the necessity of keeping a certain restriction with naming war-like purposes for our ships, especially since the launches create a lot of attention in England. The *Bureau* has taken the liberty to make, most obediently, the following suggestions for altering [the speech].[102]

This was a remarkable statement, all the more so since no similar statement was ever made with regard to any other country. The *Nachrichtenbureau* wrote that the public parading of the fleet created 'a lot of attention in England'. Yet the nature of Anglo-German rivalry required that, for the time being, any direct mentioning of the main rival was to be avoided.

What made this Anglo-German theatre so powerful was that it brought domestic politics and foreign affairs to a public collision. Historians have for some time been locked in a debate about this issue. Ever since Eckart Kehr's seminal work on the *Primat der Innenpolitik*, they have debated whether the naval race should be understood as motivated mostly by foreign or domestic policy considerations. This dichotomy is misleading. The *Reichsmarineamt* itself acknowledged, not least in its censorship policy, that a separation between the two contexts was impossible. As the *Vossische Zeitung* wrote about the 1909 Spithead review, what characterized this arena was that the navy and the issues connected to it were 'put on to the stage' simultaneously for national and international purposes.[103]

This intersection of the foreign and the domestic is crucial in order to understand the effect of the Anglo-German theatre on the relations between the two countries. Both the Admiralty and the *Reichsmarineamt* depended on the naval theatre as a site that appealed directly to the political mass market, circumventing parliament and party politics. There were two reasons why this was so important for the naval leadership in both countries. First, voters were taxpayers and had to foot the bill for the rapid

---

[102] BA-MA, RM 3/9959, Bl. 28: Nachrichtenbureau to Tann-Rathsamshausen, 15 March 1909, emphasis added. Compare Chapter 1 on the editing and censorship of launching speeches.

[103] *Vossische Zeitung*, undated cutting in BA-MA, RM 3/10222.

PUNCH, OR THE LONDON CHARIVARI.—January 8, 1908

POKER AND TONGS;

OR, HOW WE'VE GOT TO PLAY THE GAME.

KAISER. "I GO THREE *DREADNOUGHTS.*"

JOHN BULL. "WELL, JUST TO SHOW THERE'S NO ILL-FEELING, I RAISE YOU THREE."

28. John Bull and the Kaiser play the naval game. 'Poker and Tongs' (*Punch*, 8 January 1908).

naval expansion in both countries. If they were fundamentally opposed to increases in naval spending, they would vote for parties that opposed further expenditure – hence the need to promote and parade the fleet, and to bolster national identification with the navy. Second, extra-parliamentary pressure, amplified by radical leagues and the popular press, could be decisive for intra-governmental battles over the naval budget, as well as for Parliament's vote on it. Playing to these modern forces in order to exert pressure on other parts of government and on parliament was a tactic employed both by the *Reichsmarineamt* and the Admiralty. It was clearly on display during the 1909 naval votes. The tabloids rallying under the slogan 'We want eight and we won't wait', and the uncertainty over the full extent of German naval building combined to exert strong pressure on Cabinet and Parliament. Rather than checking this pressure and encouraging more realistic expectations, the Admiralty was happy to benefit from the heated debate and secure a vote for eight new ships. In July 1909, Metternich, the German Ambassador in London, wrote to von Bülow at the Foreign Office in Berlin:

As Sir John Fisher has conceded to the German naval attaché in London, it took a little naval scare to carry with him the part of the Liberal Party and those ministers who had inclined against a naval increase.[104]

Yet, while attempting to exploit the modern mass market, the Admiralty and the *Reichsmarineamt* ran the risk of being overtaken by it. It was relatively easy to appeal to the mass electorate, the media and the populist leagues. Yet it was much more difficult, and sometimes plainly impossible, to tone down public excitement. With the unfolding of the naval race, the British and German governments found that the naval theatre developed its own, barely controllable, dynamic. If anything united the Foreign Office and the *Auswärtiges Amt*, it was their struggle to come to terms with the new power of mass politics and the international role of the media. German and British diplomats complained to one other about the fabrications and distortions in the other country's press.[105] They lamented the way in which the popular press and mass media in the two countries spurred each other on in their obsession with the sea and naval rivalry.[106] Tirpitz wrote to the *Auswärtiges Amt* in 1903 that, 'in view of the continuous agitation in the press', it was desirable to exert a calming influence.[107] Indeed, it became an aim of foreign policy to exert a 'soothing influence on our Press and public opinion', as Grey put it to Goschen in 1909.[108] However, such attempts were almost always unsuccessful. The *Nachrichtenbureau*'s failure to control the coverage of the naval theatre has been examined above. The Foreign Office was in no better a position. When urging F. W. Wile, the *Daily Mail*'s correspondent in Berlin, to take a more neutral stance towards German naval news, the Foreign Office was told that the owner of the *Mail*, Lord Northcliffe,

---

[104] PA-AA, R 5789: Metternich to Bülow, 16 July 1909. This is underlined by the analysis in Phillips Payson O'Brien, 'The Cabinet, Admiralty and the Perceptions Governing the Formation of British Naval Policy: 1909, 1921–1922, 1927–1936', Ph.D. thesis, University of Cambridge (1992), pp. 112–5. Similar: Hobson, *Imperialism at Sea*, p. 327.

[105] *BD*, vol. 6, doc. 181, p. 274, enclosure: Heath to Goschen on conversation with Prince Henry of Prussia and Admiral Lans; ibid., doc. 182, p. 276: Grey to Goschen, 9 June 1909, reporting from a meeting with Metternich; ibid., doc. 185, p. 279: Goschen to Grey, 23 July 1909, reporting from a meeting with Bülow. The influence of the press in Germany during 1909 is further discussed ibid., doc. 157, pp. 246–7: Goschen to Grey, minutes; ibid., doc. 160, p. 250: Goschen to Grey, 23 March 1909.

[106] *GP*, vol. 17, doc. 5371, p. 574: Bernstorff to Bülow, 17 May 1903; PA-AA, R 2283, Foreign Office to Auswärtiges Amt, 28 Feb 1908; ibid., R 65772, Tirpitz to Staatssekretär des Auswärtigen Amtes, 30 Jan 1903; *BD*, vol. 6, doc. 168, pp. 258–9: Findlay to Grey, 31 March 1909; ibid., doc. 181, p. 274: minute by Eyre Crowe.

[107] PA-AA, R5772: Tirpitz to Staatssekretär des Auswärtigen Amtes, 30 Jan 1903.

[108] *BD*, vol. 6, doc. 152, p. 239: Grey to Goschen, 3 Feb 1909. Similarly doc. 168, p. 258: Findlay to Grey, 31 March 1909 and doc. 172, pp. 263–4: Findlay to Grey, 14 April 1909.

was of the opinion that 'the *Daily Mail* representative in Berlin is not expected to get his political inspiration from His Majesty's Embassy'.[109]

While serving the domestic market was a necessity for the Admiralty and the *Reichsmarineamt*, they came to realize that this could have disastrous effects on the foreign arena. In the naval theatre, it was rarely possible to raise support at home without fostering antagonism abroad. In 1909, the Foreign Office acknowledged that the Imperial Conference and its crowning glory, a grand fleet assembly, had been hugely successful in raising imperial awareness in Britain and the colonies. At the same time it noted that the display had had a disastrous effect on relations with Germany. Sir Edward Goschen sent nervous despatches from Berlin. He reported about the 'feeling aroused in Germany' by the naval demonstration, and informed London that 'the naval review held at Spithead has not failed to add some fuel to the flame'.[110] Indeed, Edward VII himself was sceptical about the wisdom of some of the naval displays that the Admiralty urged him to participate in. In December 1908, when Admiral Fisher suggested to Buckingham Palace that the King hold a fleet review at Spithead in the coming summer, the response was notably hesitant. Sir Frederick Ponsonby, Edward VII's private secretary, noted:

H. M. was inclined to think that such a demonstration would be a mistake while Europe was in its present disturbed state. It might be taken as a menace to Germany and would certainly be misconstrued.[111]

Across the North Sea, there were similar concerns. Von Hutten-Czapski was alarmed at the impression 'such shows' left in Britain.[112] Admiral Hopman maintained that the 1911 'show piece' [*Schaustellung*] had been unwise for the same reason.[113] As early as 1904, Count Reventlow, a naval critic, called upon Tirpitz and the Kaiser to refrain from staging large naval displays. These were 'mere rituals' that raised alarm in Britain at a time when the Imperial Fleet was by no means ready for a conflict

---

[109] R. Pound and G. Harmsworth, *Northcliffe* (London, 1960), p. 301: Wile to Northcliffe, 29 April 1907.

[110] PRO, FO 371/674, pp. 375–83: Goschen to Grey, 15 June 1909; ibid., ADM 12/1466: Imperial Press Conference in London. Copy despatch from Sir E. Goschen, 29 June 1909.

[111] RA X.5/11: Note by Ponsonby, Dec 1908. See also RA X.5/12: Fisher to Ponsonby, 12 Dec 1908. It was only after Fisher's persistent lobbying that Edward VII eventually agreed to hold a royal review – in a year when two other major naval assemblies were already taking place. In the event, it was not only the German, but also the British press who 'misconstrued' the fleet assemblies of 1909 as directed against Germany. For a poignant example see *Daily Telegraph*, 21 July 1909: 'A leaf from Germany's book'.

[112] Hutten-Czapski, *Sechzig Jahre*, vol. 1, p. 269.   [113] Hopman, *Logbuch*, p. 374.

with the Royal Navy. Rather than celebrate the fleet, it was therefore paramount to employ the 'art of silence [*die Kunst des Schweigens*]'.[114] In bringing the contradictory demands of domestic politics and foreign affairs to a public collision, the naval theatre constituted a powerful factor that contributed to the deterioration in Anglo-German relations. Tirpitz himself lamented this repeatedly. In his correspondence with naval dock-yards, he wrote that he wished less public fuss could be created around launches of warships, so that they would not increase tension with Britain.[115] Tirpitz instructed his public relations department to actively censor speeches that mentioned Britain as the rival against which the fleet was being built. He even attempted to tone down the coverage in the British press, urging correspondents to pay less attention to the spectacular displays of the Imperial Fleet.[116] This anxiety about the effect of the naval theatre on Germany's relations with Britain betrayed the fundamental flaw in the 'Tirpitz Plan'. In order to raise support at home, the Imperial Navy had to be staged and celebrated publicly. Yet, in the foreign arena exactly the opposite was needed. Naval muscle-flexing had to be avoided during the *Gefahrenzone*, those years in which the German Navy would not be strong enough to confront the Royal Navy. Launches and fleet reviews, however, attracted precisely such attention. The naval theatre thus brought the fundamental paradox facing Tirpitz and the Imperial Navy to a head: how could the navy be publicized and promoted when at the same time that very publicity was feared with regard to its effect on relations with Britain? In the age of modern, international mass media, domestic and foreign ramifications were inseparable.

Making alliances

The naval theatre was a source of antagonism in another sense. Behind the scenes, the foreign offices in London and Berlin were keen to engage in détente and ease Anglo-German tension.[117] Yet, the naval stage created

---

[114] Graf Ernst Reventlow, 'Die deutsche Flotte im englischen Parlament', *Münchner Neueste Nachrichten*, 18 Aug 1904. The Kaiser found the article so offensive that he wrote in the margins of his copy: 'This impertinent boy needs a good spanking' (*'Dieser vorlaute Knabe muss mal gehörig eins auf den Kasten kriegen'*), qtd. in Kohut, *Wilhelm II and the Germans*, p. 137.

[115] BA-MA, RM 3/118, Bl. 141: Tirpitz to Großadmiral von Koester, 19 Sept 1911; HA Krupp, FAH 4 C 55: Schreiben vom 26. Mai 1909. See also his conversation with attaché Heath, reported by the latter in *BD*, vol. 6, doc. 165, p. 256: Heath to Goschen, 30 March 1909.

[116] BA-MA, RM 3/9958: Nachrichtenbureau to Bashford, 5 March 1908; ibid., Bl. 199: Tirpitz to Werft Wilhelmshaven, 5 March 1908.

[117] Friedrich Kießling, *Gegen den großen Krieg? Entspannung in den internationalen Beziehungen, 1911–1914* (Munich, 2002).

the opposite effect: an image of two alliances facing each other with increasing inflexibility. As early as 1895, Friedrich von Holstein, the *éminence grise* of the German Foreign Office, observed that fleet visits were used to impress foreign and domestic audiences of the strategic alliance between countries. While the festivities marking the inauguration of the Kiel Canal were coming to an end, Holstein wrote in a letter to Eulenburg:

I have just read in the *Wolff* [news bulletin] that the squadrons of Russia and France arrived at Kiel *together*, sailing in one line. I had been prepared for such a demonstration. It confirms my view that the international celebration of the Canal opening is creating a lot of damage. French chauvinism had been in decline, out of lack of inspiration. But in the last three months it has reawoken. And for the Russians the celebrations are an opportunity for demonstrations which they make all the more as such demonstrations are seen by the French as a pay-back for the 'alliance'.[118]

Holstein was not alone in his assessment. Politicians, diplomats, officers and journalists alike stressed the central role of the naval theatre in making international allegiances visible and 'felt' on the world stage. This was part of the new theatricality at work in late nineteenth-century international relations.[119] Paul von Hintze, German naval attaché to St Petersburg from 1903 to 1911, wrote to Wilhelm II and Tirpitz in April 1907 with a comprehensive analysis of this phenomenon. He noted that it had lately become customary to demonstrate political tendencies towards other countries by means of maritime displays. The British, he wrote, with their 'at once simple and great policy' were especially successful at displaying international alliances in the naval theatre.[120]

The trend witnessed by Hintze had gained momentum around the turn of the century. Thus the Spithead review of 1902 celebrated not only the coronation of Edward VII, but also the new British-Japanese alliance. Meticulous planning behind the scenes ensured that Japanese and British ships were illuminated in a synchronized manner, even using the same coloured lights.[121] The effect was not lost on reporters and commentators, who spoke of 'a special honour' for the Japanese guests.[122] With the

---

[118] *Philipp Eulenburgs politische Korrespondenz*, vol. 3, doc. 1113, p. 1509: Holstein to Eulenburg, 17 June 1895 (emphasis in original).

[119] See also Paulmann, *Pomp und Politik*, ch. 3.

[120] *Paul von Hintze. Marineoffizier, Diplomat, Staatssekretär. Dokumente einer Karriere zwischen Militär und Politik, 1903–1918*, edited by Johannes Hürter (Munich, 1998), doc. 29, pp. 201–3: Hintze to Wilhelm II, 1 April 1907. See also the conversation with Bodo von dem Knesebeck, the Hohenzollerns' *Vizeoberzeremonienmeister*, recorded in *Tagebuch der Baronin Spitzemberg*, p. 339 (27 Oct 1895).

[121] PRO, ADM 179/56: Minute, Commander-in-Chief Portsmouth, 13 Aug 1902.

[122] *Standard*, 18 Aug 1902; *Daily Chronicle*, 15 Aug 1902.

making of the Anglo-Russian alliance came a host of similar public demonstrations. In 1912, the Admiralty organized a symbolic act in co-operation with the Foreign Office and a banker involved in Anglo-Russian affairs. A church bell, taken by the British forces during the Crimean War from the monastery of Solovetsky and since then used in the Portsmouth dockyard church, was ceremoniously returned to Russia.[123] As the correspondence between the Moscow Embassy, the Foreign Office and the Admiralty makes clear, this was designed as 'a sign of friendship and sympathy'.[124] When the British naval attaché presented the war relic at Archangel, a former 'trophy of war', as *The Times* put it, was turned into a symbol of 'Anglo-Russian friendship'.[125]

Nowhere were such demonstrations more striking than in the case of the Anglo-French Entente. On paper, this was nothing more than a colonial agreement, signed in April 1904, about the two countries' spheres of influence in Morocco and Egypt. Together with further agreements over territories and claims in Asia, Africa, the South Pacific and Newfoundland, this meant that the two countries had removed the most important sources of friction between them. However, this did not mean that they had formed an alliance. The treaties of 1904 did not involve either of the two countries in any obligations beyond giving each other diplomatic support in carrying out the agreements in relation to Morocco and Egypt.[126] While Anglo-French diplomatic and military co-operation grew in secret negotiations, mostly under the increasing impression of a German threat, there continued to be until 1914 opposing views about whether the Entente should develop into an alliance or not. As Sir Edward Grey, the British foreign secretary, noted on numerous occasions, much of British public opinion as well as parliament and parts of government would find a full alliance unacceptable, in particular if it bound Britain to support France in a war against Germany.[127] As a result, the nature of the Entente remained open-ended and non-binding.

---

[123] PRO, ADM 179/66, pp. 175–89.
[124] PRO, ADM 179/66, pp. 182–3: Sir George Buchanan, Moscow Embassy, to Foreign Office.
[125] *Times*, 10 Aug 1912.
[126] As P. M. H. Bell has written, as 'the foundation for a lasting partnership between two countries', these agreements looked 'distinctly dubious', see P. M. H. Bell, *France and Britain 1900–1940: Entente and Estrangement* (London and New York, 1996), p. 30. On the background also P. J. V. Rolo, *Entente Cordiale: The Origins and Negotiations of the Anglo-French Agreements of 8 April 1904* (London, 1969) and Christopher Andrew, *Théophile Delcassé and the Making of the Entente Cordiale: A Reappraisal of French Foreign Policy, 1898–1905* (London, 1968).
[127] *BD*, vol. 7, doc. 617, p. 602: Nicholson to Grey, 2 Nov 1911 and marginalia by Grey, 16 Nov 1911. See also Bell, *France and Britain 1900–1940*, pp. 39–40.

On the public stage, however, the colonial agreement of 1904 was transformed into the Entente Cordiale. The naval theatre was of central importance to this. It offered a prime vehicle for displaying the Entente and demonstrating Franco-British power. Here, the limited and non-committal character of the Entente could be hidden behind spectacular displays and ostentatious gestures. This cultural construction of the Entente accelerated with the interventions staged by Germany, in particular the Moroccan crises of 1905 and 1911. While behind the scenes the British reluctance to enter into a fully-fledged alliance was obvious, the Entente Cordiale was being celebrated publicly on an unprecedented scale. Again, the audiences were both domestic and international. It was as much Germany, attempting to undercut the Franco-British *rapprochement*, as the French and in particular the British public which were to be impressed with the significance of Franco-British friendship and co-operation.

The visit of the French fleet to Portsmouth in August 1905 provides a striking example.[128] A squadron of the Royal Navy had visited Brest a month earlier. On that occasion, commentators and cartoonists had already stressed the importance of the naval theatre for the public 'making' of the Entente.[129] Now, however, this was to be taken to a new level. A special committee was set up to coordinate the week of Anglo-French celebrations.[130] A range of activities, including balls and receptions, entertainment and sporting events, cinema visits and variety shows, were aimed at facilitating fraternization between French and British sailors. The streets of Portsmouth were decorated with the French *Tricolore* and the Union Jack. Photographs and postcards documenting the event show banners that read 'Vive la France' and 'Entente Cordiale'. A host of souvenirs and memorabilia, amongst them bilingual programmes and coloured handkerchiefs, bore witness to the detailed planning. The week of Anglo-French celebrations was seen by local residents as one of the largest naval celebrations of this period.[131] 'It is unlikely that any group of foreign sailors had ever had a welcome

---

[128]   The details of the visit, which lasted from 7 to 14 August 1905, are recorded in PRO, ADM 179/58.

[129]   For a good example see *Daily Mirror*, 10 July 1905: cartoon by W. K. Haselden.

[130]   PRO, ADM 179/58: Admiralty to Commander-in-Chief Portsmouth, confidential, 23 May 1905.

[131]   Portsmouth City Records Office, 207A (souvenirs); 16A/139/1–11: Agnes Frances Hewett, 7 to 9 Aug 1905. The collection of postcards (185/1981/C) is especially strong on the French visit of 1905. Portsmouth Central Library has further souvenirs and programmes, such as *Visit of the French Fleet 1905: Illustrated Guide with Special Chart* (Portsmouth, 1905).

to British shores to compare with that', concludes Gordon Brook-Sheperd.[132]

A number of features ensured that the event would be seen as more than a normal fleet visit. Edward VII set an example by his presence and active participation. He involved himself closely in the drawing up of the programme, hoping that the visit would have a strong 'theatrical effect',[133] and he made a point of receiving the senior French officers at Cowes. The Admiralty also pulled out all the stops. For the dinner given by the Prince of Wales in honour of the French Fleet, the Admiralty Plate was taken out of its sanctum at Greenwich and carried by special couriers under guard to Portsmouth.[134] In preparing for the event, the Admiralty and government made a special point of inviting both French and British reporters not only to the fleet display and on board ships, but also to banquets and balls. Journalists were given special blue leather passes granting them unprecedented access for the entire week to what the Admiralty called 'the Fêtes'.[135] This was part of a conscious publicity policy. In stark contrast to other visits, the public was encouraged to board French and British ships. At the end of the week of Anglo-French celebrations, the Superintendent of the Metropolitan Police at Portsmouth Dockyard reported: 'It is computed that 160,000 persons visited during the five days [...] and I think this a low estimate'.[136] At future Anglo-French summits and visits, the 1905 spectacle was remembered and heralded as the beginning of the 'Entente spirit', most notably during Poincaré's visit in 1913.[137] At a time when international tensions were running high (in March 1905 the Kaiser had landed at Tangier, proclaiming Germany's determination to safeguard its interests in Morocco), the naval theatre had offered one of the few ways in which Anglo-French co-operation and friendship could be displayed internationally while the future role of the Entente remained in question.[138]

---

[132] Gordon Brook-Shepherd, *Uncle of Europe: The Social and Political Life of Edward VII* (London, 1975), p. 251.

[133] Brook-Shepherd, *Uncle of Europe*, p. 251. The King's role in the preparation of the spectacle is stressed in *DDF*, vol. ser. 2, vol. 6, doc. 264: Cambon to Delcassé, 28 March 1905. For the wider role that Edward VII played in the orchestration of the Entente see Roderick McLean, *Royalty and Diplomacy in Europe, 1890–1914* (Cambridge, 2001), ch. 2.

[134] PRO, ADM 179/58, p. 277: Secretary Admiralty to Commander-in-Chief Portsmouth, confidential, 3 Aug 1905.

[135] NMM, Caird Library: *Visit of the French Fleet, 1905, Press Pass*.

[136] PRO, ADM 179/58, p. 287: Superintendent Metropolitan Police, H. M. Dockyard, Portsmouth, to Admiral Superintendent, Portsmouth, 16 Aug 1905.

[137] PRO, ADM 179/537; *Times*, 24 and 25 June 1913.

[138] The effect of the demonstration was strengthened by the sudden appearance of a German torpedo boat just after the naval review. According to London and Berlin newspapers, the uninvited German vessel passed the Anglo-French fleet assembly at

Nor was this the last spectacle that combined the celebration of the navy with displays of Franco-British friendship. Notably, there was a distinctly pro-French element to the Trafalgar centenary in October 1905. Official, semi-official and private initiatives were aimed at turning the centenary of the naval victory over France into a celebration of Anglo-French friendship. The *Tricolore* was hoisted next to the Union Jack during the festivities at the Royal Albert Hall on 21 October, and the audience was instructed to sing not only 'God Save the King', but also the *Marseillaise*.[139] In the days before the event, the British and Foreign Sailors' Society, like many other organizations, had presented a gift to 'the French nation'. In an accompanying letter, the Society asked the Council of Paris if 'you will accept for Paris and the French nation this message of peace and goodwill in the shape of a piece of Nelson oak'. The piece of victorious oak, afterwards exhibited in the *Musée Municipal* of Paris, bore the inscription:

This simple oak block from HMS *Victory* is in memoriam of the brave French sailors who fell with our immortal heroic, and never-to-be-forgotten Admiral Lord Nelson, on that fateful day, October 21, 1805. This precious memento is presented to France in the reign of his Majesty King Edward VII, who was crowned by the French nation with his proud title, *Le Roi Pacificateur*, E. R. VII.[140]

This was a remarkable re-narration of the past, which commemorated those 'brave French sailors' as having died *with* Nelson, rather than fighting him. The French recipients played along with this reading. The president of the *Conseil Municipal*, M. Brousse, hailed the present as a 'brotherly manifestation under the patronage of the *Roi Pacificateur*'. Without a hint of irony, he wrote that the French nation would keep this relic of the British victory over France as a symbol of the 'intimate union' between the two countries.[141]

great speed, flying a huge German flag. While the latter was an invention, the incident itself was not. According to internal *Reichsmarineamt* documents, it was explained by poor weather and the absence of the Southampton pilot, who had been expected to meet torpedo boat *G110* (acting as the company ship to Wilhelm II's sailing yacht 'Meteor') on the way to Cowes. Accident or not, the press had a field day with the Kaiser's torpedo boat gatecrashing the Anglo-French party. See BA-MA, RM 31/V: Bericht Kommandant H. M. Torpedoboot "G. 110" and news cuttings ibid.

[139] For a local example consider the shipbuilding town of Jarrow, where the *Tricolore* was also hoisted next to the Union Jack on 21 October. After a speech by the Mayor and a rendering of Kipling's 'Recessional', the band played the *Marseillaise*, followed by 'God Save the King'. See CUL, Vickers 1129: *Palmer Record*, No. 11, Feb 1906, p. 103.

[140] *Times*, 16 Oct 1905: 'The Nelson Centenary Celebrations'.

[141] Ibid. On the 'Nelson myth' and its uses for Anglo-French and Anglo-Japanese relations see MacKenzie, 'Nelson Goes Global', pp. 159–60. This aspect is curiously absent in Marianne Czisnik, *Horatio Nelson: A Controversial Hero* (London, 2005).

Many more such occasions followed until 1914, combining the celebration of nation, monarchy and the past with the emphatic evocation of
the Entente.[142] One of the most spectacular was the Franco-British
Exhibition of 1908. Its mastermind, Imre Kiralfy, a producer of naval
shows and historical spectacles,[143] saw the public demonstration of the
'Entente spirit' as the main aim of the exhibition. The twenty-seven
palaces and pavilions housing displays of art, architecture, agriculture
and engineering were carefully divided into French and British areas. An
artificial lake with close to a mile of navigable water united the ensemble
symbolically, open to visitors from 14 May to 31 October 1908.[144] On the
covers of the official catalogues and guides, Britannia and Marianne were
holding hands in front of the panorama of the exhibition.[145] The *Franco-
British Exhibition Illustrated Review* wrote after the exhibition that the 'bi-
national character' of the exhibition had 'proved absolutely and brilliantly
successful':

This was, indeed, its most distinctive feature, and the leading idea which led to its
initiation. It was intended to promote the *Entente Cordiale* between France and
Britain, and it has done so.[146]

Given all this public celebrating of Franco-British friendship, it is hard
to avoid the impression that the Entente was constructed culturally in
more substantial ways than it was built diplomatically. While diplomats

[142] This extended to representations of the naval theatre in art. In 1912, the French government commissioned M. E. Louis Gillot to paint a picture of the 1911 Coronation Naval
Review. The painting was presented to the George V by Ambassador Cambon in 1913, in
an act carefully designed to combine the celebration of the Entente with naval and royal
representation. Cf. PRO, ADM 179/60, p. 367: Buckingham Palace to Commander-in-
Chief Portsmouth, 29 Feb 1912; *Times*, 11 June 1913 and 26 July 1913. For the celebration of the Triple Entente during the Czar's visit to Cherbourg and Cowes in 1909 see
PRO, ADM 179/57.
[143] B. Gregory, 'The Spectacle Plays and Exhibitions of Imre Kiralfy, 1887–1914', Ph.D.
thesis, Manchester University (1988). See also MacKenzie, *Propaganda and Empire*,
pp. 97–120.
[144] For a detailed analysis see Paul Greenhalgh, 'Art, Politics, and Society at the Franco-
British Exhibition of 1908', *Art History* 8 (1985), pp. 434–52. See also Paul Greenhalgh,
Ephemeral Vistas: The Expositions Universelles, *Great Exhibitions and World's Fairs,
1851–1939* (Manchester, 1988), pp. 210–3. The 'White City' of Anglo-French attractions at Shepherd's Bush, West London, also housed a stadium for the fourth Olympic
Games, which were held at the same time.
[145] *Franco-British Exhibition, London, 1908: Official Guide* (Derby and London, 1908);
Franco-British Exhibition, London, 1908: Official Catalogue (Derby and London, 1908).
[146] F. G. Dumas (ed.), *The Franco-British Exhibition Illustrated Review 1908* (London,
1908), p. 4. With an estimated attendance of between 8.4 and 10.5 million, the
exhibition was seen as an unparalleled success. See Greenhalgh, 'Art, Politics, and
Society', p. 434 and John E. Findling (ed.), *Historical Dictionary of World's Fairs and
Expositions, 1851–1988* (New York, 1990), p. 205.

and politicians were unclear what exactly, apart from a colonial agreement, the Entente Cordiale was, it was ostentatiously celebrated in front of domestic and foreign audiences. The actual character of the Entente was secondary; what counted was as persuasive as possible an image of a close alliance. This again underlines the degree to which culture and politics were intertwined in the international relations of the decades before 1914. They resembled, to borrow Umberto Eco's expression, a 'prestige game' that was being played out on the stage between the nations. This game was 'won by the country that best tells what it does, independently of what it actually does'.[147] Power and prestige had to be narrated in order to be effective. And the more alliances were contested, the more they had to be 'made felt'. The naval theatre offered a prime arena for this game. It was here, as much as in secret diplomacy, that alliances were made.

Across the North Sea, the Dual Alliance was being celebrated in a similar fashion. In direct response to Franco-British demonstrations of the 'entente spirit', the Wilhelmine naval theatre staged the bond between Austria and Germany. The fleet review off Kiel in September 1911 offers a good example. This was the biggest naval display the Imperial Navy had ever arranged. It was organized, as the naval authorities stressed, 'to honour the Austrian successor to the throne'.[148] However, more than a dynastic celebration, this was a show of solidarity between Austria-Hungary and Imperial Germany during the Second Moroccan Crisis. The *Kölnische Zeitung* wrote:

In this serious hour, while high politics are still taking unknown paths, the German Kaiser is at Kiel with the Archduke and heir to the throne, the representative of the Austro-Hungarian monarchy, who is allied with us. They are at Kiel in order to review our complete naval forces [...]. This naval display, a particularly telling demonstration at this moment, is the greatest and most important ever unfolded in front of the All Highest Warlord. And this is also true in terms of the fighting power of the squadrons.[149]

Austro-German friendship, trust and the readiness and reliability of the Dual Alliance were to be shown to a European audience. The German naval attaché in Vienna acknowledged this in a dispatch to the Kaiser's Naval Cabinet in July 1911, during the preparations for the spectacle.[150]

[147] Umberto Eco, 'A Theory of Expositions', in Umberto Eco, *Travels in Hyperreality*, translated by William Weaver (San Diego, 1986), p. 296.
[148] BA-MA, RM 2/106, Bl. 72: Marinekabinett to RMA, 31 July 1911.
[149] *Kölnische Zeitung*, in *Presse-Stimmen*, p. 19.
[150] BA-MA, RM 2/106, Bl. 162: Marineattaché Wien to Chef Marinekabinett, 20 July 1911.

Journalists and diplomatic observers also commented on the Austro-German character of the event, signalled amongst other features by the shared display of Austrian and German flags.[151] After the review, the Kaiser and the Archduke decorated swarms of Austrian and German officers.[152] Admiral Count Montecuccoli, Commander-in-Chief of the Austro-Hungarian navy, stayed for a further three days to inspect important naval establishments. As a rare privilege, he was given unprecedented access to German dreadnoughts under construction, to U-Boats and to the fortifications in Heligoland.[153] This was a public staging of the Dual Alliance that used the naval theatre for the performance of solidarity and deterrence.

In sharp contrast, visits between the British and German fleets failed to cloak the antagonism between the two countries. The Anglo-German fleet visit of 1905 was described by leading German newspapers as anything but a symbolic fraternization. As the *Berliner Tageblatt* saw it, this was the 'visit of a rival'.[154] Nor was the position much different during the 1914 visit of the Royal Navy to Kiel. Some historians refer to this event as signalling a growing element of détente between the two countries.[155] The opposite was the case. The documents show that the visit only superficially concealed the fundamental rivalry between the two navies, a rivalry that had shaped much of the preparations leading up to the visit. Erich von Müller, German naval attaché in London, drew up special recommendations in the weeks before. These were endorsed by the Kaiser who ordered that officers and men should be instructed to be 'sharply' on their guard. The memorandum predicted that intelligence officers would be 'incognito' on board the visiting British warships, instructed by the Admiralty to spy on the German navy, 'for the proper assessment of a possible enemy'. The aim of the German hosts, Müller concluded, should be to make this task as difficult as possible for the British visitors. Anything else would mean 'shooting oneself in the foot [*sich in das eigene Fleisch schneiden*]'.[156]

---

[151] *Kölnische Zeitung*, in *Presse-Stimmen*, p. 19.
[152] BA-MA, RM 2/106, Bl. 206–8 has the details.
[153] BA-MA, RM 2/106, Bl. 203: Programm für den Besuch des österreichischen Marinekommandanten Admiral Grafen Montecuccoli.
[154] *Berliner Tageblatt*, 27 Aug 1905.
[155] This is especially evocative in Massie, *Dreadnought*, p. 853.
[156] BA-MA, RM 5/1175, Bl. 40–2: Müller to Tirpitz, ganz geheim, 4 June 1914, with marginal notes and instructions by Wilhelm II, 10 June 1914. For the implementation of the instructions during the Royal Navy's visit see Georg von Hase, *Die zwei weissen Völker! Deutsch-englische Erinnerungen eines deutschen Seeoffiziers* (Lepizig, 1923), pp. 24–6. For another example of the mistrust underlying such occasions, see PRO, ADM 1/8097 on Wilhelm II's visit to the Royal Navy's installations in Malta in 1909.

Such concerns with espionage at naval events were not new. Tirpitz had been worried about British intelligence gathering at these occasions as early as 1900.[157] Yet it is doubtful whether naval celebrations posed a risk of intelligence gathering significant enough to warrant such extensive security measures. Most of the time, the relevant information could be gained from a thorough reading of official and specialist publications as well as press reports.[158] The bluffing and camouflaging, the policing and counter-spying, point to a veritable fixation with espionage.[159] Rather than a reaction to any real threat of informants gaining crucial information, these were demonstrative acts of exclusion. Inquisitive British journalists were told by the *Nachrichtenbureau* that the measures against British observers at ship launches were taken in response to similar British gestures. Boy-Ed wrote to J. L. Bashford, correspondent of the *Daily Telegraph* in Germany, that 'we follow your nation's example, who believes without doubt that she is acting rightly with this procedure'.[160]

It therefore seems clear that the naval theatre offered a key international stage on which the public face of the two alliances that characterized European relations in the decade before 1914 were created. While important efforts took place behind the scenes to built détente and trust between the opposing powers, this was never effectively translated into public displays.[161] Whatever the complex realities of foreign policy and alliance negotiations were, the naval theatre offered demonstrations of 'us' against 'them'. It was here that the Entente Cordiale and the Dual Alliance were proclaimed, visibly and effectively, to domestic and foreign audiences. The theatrical displays of loyalty and unity, charged with national pride and deterrence, thus contributed crucially to the perception that two alliance systems were facing each other in Europe.[162]

---

[157] Compare the section 'Secrecy and publicity' in Chapter 2.

[158] British naval attachés, who, since they were excluded from these events, based their reports on the German press and private conversations, clearly felt that these sources were good enough for detailed reports to the Admiralty. See the digests in PRO, ADM 12/1466 which show that, out of the six reports sent between January and March 1909, two were solely on the subject of warship launches.

[159] This effect was underlined by the *Berliner Lokal-Anzeiger*, 23 July 1909, Zweite Ausgabe, Mittagsblatt: 'Spione bei der englischen Flottenparade'. The obsession with spies at naval displays was repeatedly caricatured in the press. A good example: *Kladderadatsch*, Nr. 32, 8 Aug 1909. See also David French, 'Spy Fever in Britain, 1900–1915', *Historical Journal* 21 (1978), pp. 355–70.

[160] BA-MA, RM 3/9958, Bl. 203: Boy-Ed to Bashford, 5 March 1908.

[161] Kießling, *Gegen den großen Krieg*, pp. 95–106, 274–6.

[162] For the ways in which army parades and commemorations could play a similar role, see *DDF*, Ser. 2, vol. 10, doc. 190 (25 Aug 1906) and Brook-Shepherd, *Uncle of Europe*, p. 262 and p. 277.

Englands Selbstmord.

Bericht eines Engländers aus dem Jahre 3000: Der Stapellauf ging glatt vonstatten, aber infolge der enormen Wasserverdrängung versoff unser geliebtes Vaterland!

29. England's suicide by ship launch. 'Report by an Englishman in 3000: The launch went successfully, but as a result of the enormous backwash our beloved country has sunk' (*Ulk*, 18 August 1912).

The rhetoric of rivalry

This effect was amplified by the way in which the naval theatre developed its own rhetoric and choreography of rivalry. When the *Daily Telegraph* sent a special correspondent to Kiel to witness a ship launch, he was duly impressed – and amused – by the peculiarly German ritual. He reported back to London that the launch had taken place amid curiously 'much naval ceremony'; and he could not help noting the strong contrast with the way these things were done in Britain:

Rear-Admiral Tirpitz in the presence of Countess William Bismarck, Prince Henry of Prussia, and other distinguished persons, addressed the new man-of-war in the imaginative fashion of Teutons on such occasions, saying: 'By command of His Majesty the Emperor, proud ship, shalt thou bear the name of the greatest German statesman of our century [. . .]'. That is all very picturesque and gallant, nor need we refuse our sympathy to so striking a performance; albeit, it is our British custom to do the thing more quietly, possibly because the launching of a great battleship is a very common incident in these islands.[163]

The 'Teutons' came across here as newcomers who were understandably eager to celebrate their new ships with great pomp and circumstance, while in Britain there was restraint and quiet superiority. Indeed, launching warships in an understated manner was an outer expression of British naval strength and tradition, the *Telegraph* suggested.

These comments were made in 1897, when the German naval programme was in its infancy. A decade later and the launching of a warship, if it had ever been a quiet affair in Britain, had turned into one of the most widely attended and ceremonious public rituals that the Edwardians knew. A veritable race for records developed in the choreography of this increasingly Anglo-German theatre. The choreographers on both sides of the North Sea responded to each other in developing new stage-props and innovations. In drawing up the regulations for ship launches and fleet reviews, the Kaiser and his naval leadership were keen to distinguish these rituals from the spectacle that the Royal Navy was putting on at Spithead and elsewhere. When the Kaiser read in March 1902 that for the first time the coronation of a British monarch was to be celebrated with a fleet review, he wrote '*echt englisch!*' next to the article.[164] Two months later, during the elaborate preparations for the spectacle at Spithead, he declared in another marginal note that, in contrast to the Royal Navy, the Imperial Navy did 'not exist for

---

[163] *Daily Telegraph*, 27 Sept 1897.
[164] BA-MA, RM 2/164, Bl. 111: Marginalia to *Naval and Military Record*, 20 March 1902.

ceremonial, but for war'.[165] The Kaiser's fleet reviews were designed to symbolize this Anglo-German contrast by focusing on exercise and training.[166] It was this emphasis on functionality, in turn, that led British observers to judge that 'except in the matter of weather' there was 'a great sameness' in Wilhelmine fleet reviews.[167]

Buckingham Palace and the Admiralty watched the unfolding of the Wilhelmine naval theatre closely – and did not hesitate to alter the choreography of their own displays in response.[168] In 1910, George V introduced the custom of 'private inspections' of the fleet, clearly inspired by the model of Wilhelm II's fleet reviews, which emphasized the unity between the *Flottenkaiser* and his navy.[169] And when Blohm & Voss invented a curious 'double ritual' in 1912, it was swiftly copied by British dockyards. The innovation lay in combining the launching of one ship with the keel laying of another in the same berth: while the *Seydlitz* was being christened, the keel plate for the next hull was already suspended over it. As soon as the launch was over, this plate was ceremoniously laid down. Eduard Blohm observed that this theatrical innovation, which emphasized speed and efficiency, had impressed the audience a great deal.[170] In Britain, a similar ceremony was introduced a year later at the launch of the *Benbow*. This is how the *Glasgow Herald* reported the invention that drew inspiration from the precedent set by Blohm & Voss in Hamburg:

Immediately after the launch and before the *Benbow* had been taken round to the firm's fitting-out basin, the keel of the new and larger battleship *Ramillies* was laid on the same berth. A large section – over 100 feet in length and weighing about 300 tons – had been suspended from the gantry cranes above the hull of the *Benbow*, and just as the vessel was clear of the ways this section was lowered into position on the keel-blocks on which the *Benbow* was built – this ceremony also to the strains of 'Rule Britannia' from the band. At the same time the name and yard number of the *Benbow* were removed from the berth and those of the *Ramillies* put in their place. [. . .]. The keel was put fully into position and work on the *Ramillies* was thus started before the hull of the *Benbow* had been removed from the end of the ways.[171]

---

[165] BA-MA, RM3/9688, Bl. 54–5: Marginalia to *Daily Telegraph*, 8 May 1902.
[166] See the section 'Maritime theatre' in Chapter 1. [167] *Times*, 30 Aug 1910.
[168] For an example of admiration for the stagecraft involved in Wilhelmine ship launches see PRO, FO 371/1651, p. 322: British Consulate General, Hamburg, to Sir Edward Grey, 16 June 1913. For critical observations about German tactics aimed at 'creating records' and impressing the audience see N.A. Report 46/08, in Woodward, *Great Britain and the German Navy*, pp. 489–90.
[169] See Chapter 1.
[170] StA Hamburg, 622–1/2: Eduard Blohm, Werfterinnerungen 1877–1939, p. 257.
[171] *Glasgow Herald*, 13 Nov 1913. See also *Scotsman*, 13 Nov 1913.

In the naval theatre, the Anglo–German antagonism was manifested in a race for records in stagecraft. Who could project speed and efficiency more impressively? Who could display threat and deterrence towards the other more convincingly? The headlines used in the coverage of ship launches and fleet reviews reflected this sense of competition: 'Latest and greatest. Launch of the *Monarch*';[172] 'World's largest battleship successfully launched. Surpassing any ship in any of the world's navies';[173] 'Still more powerful and more dreadful';[174] 'World's record battleship. Invincible and unsinkable';[175] 'Two hundred of the most complete sea fighters ever known. The greatest congregation of ships ever assembled';[176] 'No naval parade has been more powerful, none had a bigger impact, also with regard to the foreign arena, than this one'.[177] In 1910, the *Naval and Military Record* complained that it was hardly possible to have an objective or neutral discussion any more, since there was 'a tendency in writing and speaking about naval affairs to describe every other new ship as "revolutionary"'.[178] Philipp Eulenburg lamented in 1912 that the Germans were obsessed with achieving records in the speed, size and armament of their ships. Instead of engaging in a debate on what the fleet was actually for, they were chasing for *Weltrekorde*, world records.[179]

The most common rhetorical tool that accompanied this race was the evocation of war in the name of peace. *Si vis pacem, para bellum* – 'if you want peace, prepare for war' ran the slogan, resuscitated from Roman military writing.[180] Employed in speeches, articles and books, it was used widely both in Britain and Germany. *The Navy League Guide to the Coronation Review* explained what it saw as the 'true lesson to be derived from the naval review': 'The imposing armada which has been assembled for our inspection in the home waters [. . .] is the embodiment of the time-honoured maxim, *if you wish for peace, be prepared for war*'.[181] At a reception given for 1,000 guests after the launch of the *Queen Mary*, Captain H. B. Pelly explained that the *raison d'être* for the new warship and the navy as a whole was encapsulated in the dictum 'if you wish for

[172] *Illustrated Chronicle* (Newcastle), 31 March 1911.
[173] *Jarrow Guardian*, 22 March 1912.   [174] *Portsmouth Evening News*, 12 Oct 1912.
[175] *Portsmouth Evening News*, 10 Feb 1906. For a similar example see *Daily Record and Mail* (Glasgow), 2 May 1911.
[176] *Naval and Military Record*, 22 July 1914.
[177] *Kieler Zeitung*, 6 Sept 1911, Erstes Blatt.   [178] *Naval and Military Record*, 24 Aug 1910.
[179] *Philipp Eulenburgs politische Korrespondenz*, vol. 3, doc. 1554, p. 2203: 'Die deutsche Flotte' (April 1912).
[180] Vegetius, *Epitoma rei militarism*, book 3, prologue, is usually regarded as the earliest quotation.
[181] *The Navy League Guide to the Coronation Review* (London, 1902), p. 33.

peace you must prepare for war. (Applause)'.[182] The motto was employed in the same fashion at the launch of the *Dreadnought*; and similarly at the dinner given at the 1909 fleet visit to the Thames.[183] Churchill declared at the Royal Academy in the same year that 'the best way to make war impossible, is to make victory certain'.[184] His speech was met with praise in the British press, and alarm in the *Auswärtiges Amt*.

The idea of preparing for war in the name of peace featured just as prominently in the Wilhelmine naval theatre. At the launch of the *Yorck* in 1904, Generaloberst von Hahnke said that the 'old wisdom *si vis pacem, para bellum* – he who wants peace shall be prepared for war' had been 'the basic idea [*der Grundgedanke*] of the building of this warship'. Evoking Prussian military tradition, he continued: 'May the guns and machines of the *Yorck* be operated only by men with iron hearts and an iron will, men who know no other order than to put their lives at risk when the might, the greatness and the honour of the German people are being fought for'.[185] The *Breslauer General-Anzeiger*, reporting from the launch of the *Helgoland*, employed the same idea. The public ritual had been 'a serious warning for ourselves and those out there': Germany was prepared for war and was 'keeping its sword sharpened'.[186] The central maxim for the Imperial Navy, declared the *Tägliche Rundschau* in 1911, was '*Si vis pacem, para bellum*'.[187] So much did this phrase dominate speeches, articles and conversations that Eulenburg reflected: 'It is impossible that the fleet should simply follow the old cliché [*abgeleierten Grundsatze*]: *si vis pacem para bellum*'.[188] In the absence of any other guiding idea, he wrote, this cliché was presented as the fleet's only *raison d'être*. The navy's real purpose, however, Eulenburg considered, was to challenge Britain, an aim which he foresaw would ultimately mean war. 'That however is not wanted by the Kaiser or the government. So why?'[189]

Eulenburg's puzzlement illustrates the tension between rhetoric and reality that was at the heart of the naval theatre. For the leadership in the

---

[182] *Newcastle Daily Journal*, 21 March 1912.

[183] *Portsmouth Evening News*, 12 Feb 1906; PRO, ADM 1/8048:*Visit of the Fleet to the Thames. Report to the Court of Common Council from the Special Navy Entertainment Committee. Presented 7th October, 1909.*

[184] *Observer*, 5 May 1909. The speech was reported to Bethmann by Metternich: PA-AA, R 5590, 5 May 1909.

[185] BA-MA, RM 3/9958, Bl. 85: launch of SMS Yorck, 14 May 1904.

[186] *Breslauer General-Anzeiger*, 26 Sept 1909.   [187] *Tägliche Rundschau*, 16 Dec 1911.

[188] *Philipp Eulenburgs politische Korrespondenz*, vol. 3, doc. 1554, p. 2203.

[189] Ibid., p. 2205. For the Kaiser's endorsement of *si vis pacem para bellum* as a rationale for the navy see PA-AA, R 5585: Bericht des Marine-Attachés in London, Nr. 55, 3 Feb 1910.

two countries it was of central importance that they could tell the difference between sabre-rattling and serious preparation for war. However, even for those experienced in this international game, the messages conveyed in it were deeply ambiguous. As Admiral Hopman and Count von Hutten-Czapski observed, the Wilhelmine naval theatre projected a will for unbridled expansion and naval domination, while behind the scenes there was just as much nervousness and longing for peace. Unfortunately, the second aspect was lost on the public stage: 'The later developments have shown that the others [i.e. those outside Germany] saw in the military pomp of such displays only the expression of the German claim to power and the Kaiser's arrogance'.[190] Both the German and British naval leadership repeatedly mistook ostentatious muscle-flexing for war preparations. The most poignant example was the German review of 1911, which caused considerable alarm in London. Wilhelm Widenmann, German naval attaché in London, wrote to Tirpitz, the Kaiser and the *Auswärtiges Amt* two months after the event:

A most reliable source [*allerbester Quelle*] tells me about the following incident which took place in the house of an influential London banker at the end of August.

After dinner the invited ladies and gentlemen reconvened [in another room], but Mr. Churchill, who was one of the guests, abstained and read the evening news instead. A lady known for her quick-wittedness was evidently annoyed by this lack of politeness. She asked Mr. Churchill if he found politics even in the presence of ladies so interesting that he preferred the newspaper to a conversation with them. – Mr. Churchill answered very sharply that he had indeed no time for chit-chat with ladies at such a serious hour; and pointing to an article which dealt with the approaching naval review at Kiel, he continued: *Let them come, they can have war, if they want.*[191]

The Kaiser's response to Churchill's reaction is the most illuminating aspect of this episode. Reading Widenmann's report, Wilhelm II underlined Churchill's statement – '<u>Let them come, they can have war, if they want</u>' – and wrote next to it: 'We are saying exactly the same. [However, We] Did not have the intention [to go to war]'.[192] While not actually contemplating war, the Kaiser had still insisted on staging a display that signalled belligerence and could be read as the preparation for hostilities. As Magnus Hirschfeld wrote in 1916, what made the public display of weapons so

---

[190] Hutten-Czapski, *Sechzig Jahre*, vol. 1, p. 269. See also Hopman, *Logbuch*, p. 372.
[191] PA-AA, R 5793, Widenmann to Tirpitz, 18 Nov 1911.
[192] Ibid., marginalia by Wilhelm II. See also his marginalia to the article 'Germany's Place in the Sun' in *The Standard*, 22 Jan 1912, contained in PA-AA, R5796.

30. Playing war. Official programme, naval review, Spithead, July 1912.

potent was that the instruments of war in themselves did not indicate whether they were intended for defensive purposes or for an attack.[193] This ambivalence was heightened by the sense of entertainment and enactment that the naval theatre exuded. What these many spectacles, from the fleet reviews at Spithead to the mock fights in the pools of the *Marineschauspiele*, had in common was the ability to evoke violence and conflict in an entertaining way. Rivalry and antagonism could be performed in isolation from the complexities of international affairs and the secret diplomacy of cabinets and courts. This game was so fascinating precisely because it brought together play and war. It allowed audiences to approach violence and aggression, otherwise 'serious topics', as something playful and entertaining. At its heart was the continuous ambiguity between *Spiel* and *Ernst*.[194] It was the performative 'as if', the opportunity to experience conflict while not having to engage with its reality that made the naval game so appealing: in this theatre you could play war without having to want it.[195]

False victories

The naval theatre not only turned international conflict into a form of entertainment; it also raised expectations of victory that were increasingly removed from the strategic realities in which Britain and Germany found themselves. Historians have argued that the great failure of British statesmen after the two world wars was that they missed opportunities to bring public aspirations into alignment with political realities. Correlli Barnett's four-volume history of Britain in the twentieth century takes the gap between pretensions and realities as a key theme.[196] Both after 1919 and after 1945, he argues, British statesmen did not dare to shatter the myth of a united and powerful empire.[197] Brian Harrison makes a similar point:

---

[193] Magnus Hirschfeld, *Kriegspsychologisches* (Berlin, 1916), p. 9. For another example see the British reaction to the Kaiser's review of the Imperial Fleet in Norwegian waters in 1913 (PRO, ADM 1/8356, Secretary Admiralty to Under Secretary of State, Foreign Office, 19 Aug 1913).

[194] For a satirical play on this ambiguity see *Kladderadatsch*, Nr. 31, 4 Aug 1912: 'Der kleine John und das kleine Lieschen'.

[195] On the seriousness of play: Johan Huizinga, *Homo Ludens: A Study in the Play-Elements in Culture* (London, 1980), ch. 5; Victor Turner, *From Ritual to Theatre: The Human Seriousness of Play* (New York, 1982); Schechner, *Performance Theory*, pp. 98–103. See also the section on theatricality and war games in Chapter 2.

[196] Correlli Barnett, *The Collapse of British Power* (New York and London, 1972), pp. 71–4, 220–7. See also his *The Audit of War* (London, 1986); *The Lost Victory: British Dreams, British Realities* (London, 1985), pp. 7–9; *The Verdict of Peace: Britain Between Her Yesterday and Her Future* (London, 2001).

[197] Barnett, *Collapse of British Power*, pp. 71–4, 220–7.

British politicians up to the present have lingered too long over the precariously won successes of the Second World War, they have encouraged revivals of 'the Dunkirk spirit' [...]. They have misled the voters into expecting far more from politicians than they can possibly deliver.[198]

The task, Harrison and Barnett argue, was not about projecting 'hope and glory'. It was about publicly recognizing the realities of the decline from world power status and the adjustment to new limits of strategic influence. Their argument is persuasive, but its chronology needs to be extended backward: it was not after 1918 or after 1945 that the politics of self-deception began, but rather in the decade before the First World War.

A multitude of studies have analysed the relative decline faced by Britain and her empire in the two decades before the First World War. The South African War in particular exposed the imperial overstretching, and highlighted the fundamental problems confronting the British Empire on a strategic, economic and military level.[199] Politicians knew about this underlying weakness of the imperial structure. They acknowledged privately that the United Kingdom's over-committed position was unsustainable in the mid-term. Yet, they were reluctant to communicate this to the public. Thus Joseph Chamberlain predicted, despite all the evidence to the contrary that mounted during the South African War: 'We shall emerge from this war stronger than we have ever been before'.[200] This rhetoric of continued expansion was at the heart of the naval theatre, projecting an image of imperial strength that belied the strategic realities.

In Imperial Germany, too, politicians raised expectations that they knew could not be fulfilled. It was highly doubtful that the *Kaiserreich* could ever 'wield the trident'. From the very beginning there were fundamental contradictions in the 'Tirpitz-Plan'. Its failure became apparent after 1909. Even for the prosperous *Kaiserreich* it was impossible to sustain a naval race devouring unprecedented sums without neglecting the army, by far the more important safeguard for Germany. The idea of a *Weltpolitik* based on a strong navy that challenged the British fleet was exposed as an illusion.[201] Yet the Kaiser and many politicians continued to talk of overseas expansion and the 'national deeds' that the

---

[198] Harrison, *Transformation*, p. 404.   [199] Compare Chapter 4.
[200] *Annual Register 1900* (London, 1901), p. 114.
[201] Kennedy, 'Maritime Strategieprobleme'; Kennedy, *Rise of Anglo-German Antagonism*, ch. 20; Berghahn, *Tirpitz-Plan*, pp. 594–7; Volker R. Berghahn, *Germany and the Approach of War in 1914*, second edition (Houndmills, 1993), ch. 7; Salewski, *Tirpitz*, pp. 91–3.

navy would accomplish.[202] Bülow's famous phrase about the 'place in the sun' promised increasing prestige on the seas, despite the obvious limits to *Weltpolitik*. Ambassador Anton Graf Monts deplored the lack of political courage to tell the truth:

> There was one thing that had to be expected from the leaders of the people, from the Kaiser, the Chancellor and the Chief of Staff down to the party and newspaper big wigs, namely that they would break with Bülow's phrases and methods of glossing over things [*Beschönigungsmethoden*], that they would be open with the naive German *Michel*. [...] The primacy at land *and* at sea was beyond the resources of even such a great and diligent people as the Germans.[203]

Reinen Wein einschenken, as Monts called it, to be – in the face of public pressure – frank about the realistic strategic and economic possibilities: politicians in both countries skirted around this task. At best, they kept quiet when faced with exuberant demands and populist agitation. At worst, they actively contributed to the raising of false expectations. This, in turn, meant that politicians were limiting their room for manoeuvre: participating in or acquiescing to public self-deception meant the exclusion of viable alternatives. If politics is the art of the possible – and the art of communicating the possible to the public – leading British and German statesmen must be regarded as having failed at one of the key political agendas of this period.

As a result, the naval theatre continued to raise false expectations. There is a curious relationship between the rise of this public stage and the decline of strategic influence and power. The weaker one's own position seemed, the more intensive did the muscle-flexing, the projecting of empire and power, become. In Britain, Victoria's Diamond Jubilee naval review of 1897 marked the apogee or 'high water mark' of British sea power.[204] From this point until 1914, the naval theatre rose, as Chapter 1 has shown, to unprecedented heights. At the same time, the position of Britain as a world and naval power started to decline. The answer to challenges from within and without was to put the empire on stage and celebrate it, to demonstrate its unity and invincibility. The naval theatre thus encouraged and amplified dreams of empire and expansion, making a realistic debate about the limits to such dreams ever more difficult.

---

[202] For a good example see PA-AA, R 2284, Wilhelm II to Reichskanzler, 11 Nov 1911. This dynamic is examined in detail by Thomas Meyer, *'Endlich eine Tat, eine befreiende Tat...'. Alfred von Kiderlen-Wächters 'Panthersprung nach Agadir' unter dem Druck der öffentlichen Meinung* (Husum, 1996).

[203] *Erinnerungen und Gedanken des Botschafters Anton Graf Monts*, edited by Karl Friedrich Nowak and Friedrich Thimme (Berlin, 1932), pp. 288–9 (emphasis in original).

[204] Massie, *Dreadnought*, p. xxv; Marder, *Anatomy*, p. 282.

It was this fundamental contradiction between the rhetoric of the naval theatre and the reality of international affairs that critical observers focused on. In June 1909, commenting on the unprecedented display staged by the Royal Navy during its 'visit' to the Thames, the *Labour Leader* commented that such shows had the effect that 'the public both at home and abroad' was 'extensively deceived'. The majority of politicians and the popular press were painting a wholly unrealistic picture of what was necessary and what was possible, the *Leader* wrote. With its exaggerated staging of power, the naval theatre was a self-perpetuating force, a cult feeding on itself – at a time when détente and a realistic assessment of the economic and strategic possibilities were needed more than ever:

Forty miles of warships at a stretch – the 'Daily Mail' said fifty, but then, stretching is a favourite pastime with the 'Daily Mail'. Forty miles of warships at a stretch, ranging from the latest fashion in Dreadnoughts to the most occult thing in submarines. A fleet of one hundred and fifty war vessels, extending from Southend to Westminster, is a naval pageant truly, and calculated to give one pause, if only for the money that has been lavished on building it, a sum which is computed at somewhere about £100,000,000, to say nothing of the upkeep; and this stupendous aggregation of war vessels, mind you, is only one part of the British Fleet. And still the naval megalomaniacs clamour for more. [...] The appetite for armaments grows with what it feeds on. Gluttony, in fact, is insatiable, and a tempting display of viands is just the very method to tempt it to further excess.[205]

In Germany, the naval theatre reflected an aspiration to translate the *Kaiserreich*'s economic and military might into sea power. It advertised and anticipated naval victory and in particular, though not always explicitly, victory over Britain. Indeed, the speeches given at launches and, to an even greater degree, the press coverage of these events often created the impression that such a victory was only a matter of time. It seemed inevitable that the Imperial Navy would repeat on the sea what the Prussian army had achieved on land.[206] As Johannes Haller wrote after the war:

The idea and spirit of the naval battle in which the Germans would win over the British [*die Engländer*] lived in the armour plates and the guns of our Dreadnoughts. Had they won, this would now be the *Leitmotiv* of countless histories of the building of the battle fleet. Tirpitz would stand high just like Roon and Moltke, who had forged the sword for the Kaiser by which the German nation's rule over the oceans had been reached like once the rule over the Continent by the army reform of Wilhelm I.[207]

[205] *Labour Leader*, 11 June 1909. Similar: *Hamburger Echo*, 11 Sept 1904, Erstes Beiblatt; Otto Hammann, *Bilder aus der letzten Kaiserzeit* (Berlin, 1922), pp. 61–2.
[206] Compare the section on 'Military tradition and a violent future' in Chapter 4.
[207] *Philipp Eulenburgs politische Korrespondenz*, vol. 3, doc. 1602, p. 2318: Johannes Haller to Eulenburg, 13 June 1920.

Independent observers were astonished by how the naval spectacle seemed to pre-emptively celebrate victories. Count Robert Zedlitz-Trützschler, the Kaiser's Controller of the Household, was present at the launch of the *Deutschland* in November 1904. Alluding to the pouring rain which marked the ceremony, Wilhelm II announced that this was 'the weather of the Katzbach', Katzbach being where Blücher had won a decisive victory over the French army in a flood of rain on 26 August 1813. Zedlitz found the comparison of a ship launch with a past military victory worrying. Reflecting on the prolific celebrating of victories that had not yet been won, he wrote:

These many speeches, these spectacles, all this ceremony [...] really seem as if they made some people think we had won a big battle. I should like to know how we could devise any special way of celebrating a victory, should we ever win one, for our celebrations are, as it is, the last word in outward splendour.[208]

Bodo von dem Knesebeck, the Kaiser's vice master of ceremonies, similarly observed that Wilhelmine public rituals resembled triumphant victory parades. Commenting on the Kaiser's visit to Kiel in 1911, he noted that the festivities seemed to him 'as if this was after a war'.[209] However, since there had been neither a war nor a victory, it seemed that these parades were rehearsing a grand triumph that Germany was to have in future. The false victories that Zedlitz and Knesebeck spoke of were celebrated in a range of genres: fleet reviews, mock fights, ship launches, but also in the many games and entertainments that re-enacted these rituals. The expectation of victory rested on the assumption of an all-out grand battle, a Trafalgar in the North Sea, in which the nation's future would be decided. At a time when the limits to grand victories, posed by both foreign and domestic considerations, had become evident, this projected a wholly unrealistic message. All this came at a time when international relations required a sobering influence and a dispassionate assessment of the limits to national expectations.

1914 and the Anglo-German misunderstanding

For those who publicly encouraged better Anglo-German relations, there was little doubt that the naval theatre was at the heart of what they saw as the deep misunderstanding between Britain and Germany. A number of small but vociferous groups of 'Germanophiles' and 'Anglophiles'

---

[208] Zedlitz-Trützschler, *Twelve Years*, p. 104.
[209] *Tagebuch der Baronin Spitzemberg*, p. 529 (5 June 1911).

existed in both countries.[210] Amongst them were such diverse characters as Norman Angell and Sir Max Waechter, 'an old gentleman who propagates the mad idea of world peace', as Helmuth von Moltke put it.[211] Their petitions and publications were characterized by an increasingly desperate call for a better 'understanding', for a *Verstehen* and *Verständigen* between the two countries.[212] What seemed puzzling to them – and has since been for historians – was that the naval theatre continued to flourish after the naval race had been decided.[213] From 1909 onwards it became clear that the Tirpitz-Plan was failing. This was put beyond doubt in 1912 when the German budget favoured the army substantially over the navy.[214] The Royal Navy had reaffirmed its lead and there was little chance that the German navy would be able to mount a successful challenge. Yet the staging and celebrating of the navy continued. Indeed, it expanded further: the biggest displays took place between 1909 and 1914. The naval theatre reached its climax precisely at a time when the naval race had effectively been won by the British and a scaling down of public posturing would have been appropriate.

The navy's strategic role had thus been overtaken by its symbolic function. Strategic concerns may initially have been decisive in giving rise to antagonism; however, the estrangement of the two countries was imagined, experienced and interpreted in a cultural sense, as a rising opposition in ideas and assumptions. 'It is not a question of diplomatic moves and countermoves; it is a question of mental states, a question of ideas and ideals', wrote Charles Sarolea in *The Anglo-German Problem* in 1912.[215] The naval theatre provided a powerful stage for the projection of those ideas and ideals. It mobilized, as previous chapters have shown,

---

[210] See Roger Chickering, *Imperial Germany and a Word Without War: The Peace Movement and German Society, 1892–1914* (Princeton, 1975), pp. 305–17; Günter Hollenberg, *Englisches Interesse am Kaiserreich. Die Attraktivität Preußen-Deutschlands für konservative und liberale Kreise in Großbritannien 1860–1914* (Wiesbaden, 1974); Steven Wai-Meng Siak, 'Germanophilism in Britain: Non-Governmental Elites and the Limits to Anglo-German Antagonism, 1905–1914', Ph.D. thesis, University of London (1997).

[211] Moltke, *Erinnerungen, Briefe, Dokumente*, p. 354.

[212] See Anglo-German Friendship Society, *Report of a Meeting held at the Mansion House, Nov. 2nd, 1911* (London, 1911), p. 1, calling for 'the removal of all existing misunderstandings with Germany'. Its German equivalent focused similarly on the 'understanding' that was lacking between the two countries: *Deutsch-Englisches Verständigungs-Komitee* (Berlin, 1911); *Nachrichten des Deutsch-Englischen Verständigungs-Komitees* (Berlin, 1911).

[213] Zara Steiner, *Britain and the Origins of the First World War* (London, 1977), p. 50.

[214] Epkenhans, *Wilhelminische Flottenrüstung*, pp. 313–407; Förster, *Der doppelte Militarismus*, pp. 208–96; Stevenson, *Armaments and the Coming of War*, chs. 4, 5.

[215] Charles Sarolea, *The Anglo-German Problem* (London, 1912), p. 365.

a bundle of cultural themes and values on imperial, national, regional and local levels. This fostering of aspirations and illusions would not simply die away when inconvenient for politicians or diplomats. It was aggravated by a number of factors that have been examined throughout this book. Chief amongst them were the naval theatre's transformation through mass politics and popular culture; its peculiar position at the intersection between domestic and foreign as well as political and cultural contexts; its role as an arena in which the claim to the sea, rivalry and deterrence were acted out, and that was charged with ideas about nationhood and empire; and finally, its function as a theatre which made these particular ideas all the more potent since it projected them as an entertaining form of rhetorical violence that did not have to reckon with the realities of conflict.

It was not only pacifists and socialists who saw a threat to Anglo-German relations in the continued public staging of the navy. There were also, as this chapter has made clear, liberal and conservative observers who saw the triumphant staging of 'false victories' as dangerous for both domestic and foreign politics, making any realistic debate, let alone an Anglo-German détente, impossible. When the *Australia* was launched in October 1911, the *Sydney Morning Herald*'s correspondent, sent to Britain to cover the spectacle, lamented the 'tumult and the shouting', and 'the shoals of effervescent enthusiasm and congratulations'. The pomp and circumstance, he wrote, threatened to undermine any serious discussion about the navy's role.[216] Nor was the deeply adverse effect that the public posturing over the navy had on Anglo-German relations lost on politicians and diplomats. Yet, they did very little to rein it in. At times – perhaps conveniently – they portrayed themselves as powerless to do so. Sir Edward Goschen, the United Kingdom's Ambassador at Berlin, wrote in July 1910:

I wrote a long despatch about Naval Affairs [. . .], there is no more to be said – and violent articles quite unnecessary. They might have been necessary once – on *the German side* to rouse the enthusiasm necessary to make the German public put its hand into its pocket for a big fleet; on *our side* – to rouse our public opinion to a sense of danger which threatened our Naval supremacy. Now Press violence only embittered relations and rendered any moderating influence quite powerless.[217]

---

[216] *Sydney Morning Herald*, 28 Oct 1911.
[217] *The Diary of Edward Goschen 1900–1914*, edited by Christopher Howard (London, 1980), p. 214 (29 July 1910), emphases in original. The 'long despatch about naval affairs' can be found in *BD*, vol. 6, doc. 386.

Privately, diplomats and politicians in both countries acknowledged the need to scale down displays of deterrence and the rhetoric of rivalry. Publicly, however, they failed to translate such insight into action.[218]

This contrast between the public celebration of the fleet and the private regret at its effects is particularly well illustrated by the example of the Lord Provost of Glasgow. As the figurehead of the 'Second City of the Empire', the Lord Provost was at the centre of naval events such as the launch of the *New Zealand* in 1911, to which he invited scores of colonial politicians as well as military and naval leaders. He also hosted displays of Anglo-Japanese alliance, such as the visit of Admiral Togo, and he was a driving force behind the celebration of the *Comet* Centenary, designed to impress 'the citizens', as he put it to Lord Kitchener.[219] The Lord Provost specifically asked the Admiralty to send warships to the *Comet* Centenary to give it a more national character, and lobbied Churchill to be a key speaker.[220] While staging such displays of naval might, he expressed his support to pacifists such as Max Waechter and Norman Angell and his wish for better Anglo-German relations to the mayors of Berlin, Hamburg and Bremen.[221] The Lord Provost seemed to have found no contradiction in continuously advertising naval expansion for the sake of Glasgow's prosperity while privately writing to Asquith about his worries concerning the Anglo-German antagonism:

Dear Mr. Asquith, I was in the House yesterday afternoon intending to ask for a few minutes' conversation with you, but I saw you were closely following the debate. I am much distressed at the bad effect which is being produced in Germany by the acceleration proposals of Mr. Churchill. They are almost certain to be followed by a corresponding speeding-up in Germany, and all the good that has been done in the way of improving our relationships will be thrown away.[222]

This example illustrates how the naval theatre contributed crucially to the 'misunderstanding' between Britain and Germany. It served to extend the gap between public rhetoric and strategic necessity. Commanding wide participation and appealing strongly to popular culture, it acted as a

---

[218] See on this point also Kießling, *Gegen den großen Krieg*, pp. 274–6, who argues that it was one of the main failures of Anglo-German diplomacy not to engage the public in wider strategies for détente.

[219] Glasgow City Archives, G 1/1/15: Lord Provost to Field-Marshal Viscount Kitchener, 10 July 1911; ibid.: Lord Provost to Sir Joseph Ward, 16 and 23 June 1911.

[220] Glasgow City Archives, G 1/1/16: Lord Provost to Mrs Winston Churchill, 19 April 1912; ibid., G 1/1/17: Lord Provost to Secretary of the Admiralty, 1 Aug 1912.

[221] Glasgow City Archives, G 1/1/16: Lord Provost to Burgomaster of Berlin, 30 Jan 1912; ibid., G 1/1/19: Lord Provost to Burgomasters of Berlin, Bremen, Hamburg and Lübeck, 25 July 1913; ibid.: Lord Provost to Sir Max Waechter, 6 May 1913.

[222] Glasgow City Archives, G 1/1/19: Lord Provost to Asquith, 11 June 1913.

catalyst for antagonism, raising false expectations and fostering illusionary aims. It encouraged a culture in which a triumphant intransigence and the preparation for war in the name of peace were central features. Rather than communicate the fundamental limitations that confronted both nations and which they had to accept in order to resolve their 'misunderstanding', the two countries' leading actors either kept quiet or exploited the naval theatre for their own agendas. When they realized that the culture of confrontation that had seemed acceptable and indeed useful at the domestic level was in fact causing conflict and antagonism abroad, they appeared puzzled. August Graf zu Eulenburg wrote to Philipp Eulenburg that, despite the rhetoric of rivalry and the evocation of future victories, the *Kaiserreich*'s naval celebrations were 'well intended', they were really about peace and détente – 'but this is not understood abroad'.[223]

There can thus be little doubt that the naval theatre nurtured the Anglo-German antagonism. Was it, however, one of the factors that led to the outbreak of the First World War? Certainly not in a direct sense: by July 1914, the main source of tension had shifted from sea to land. It was the race unfolding between the armies of the Franco-Russian and German-Austrian alliances that dominated the 'arming of Europe' during the years before 1914 and that posed potentially the biggest challenge to peace.[224] Yet a number of factors can be seen at work in the naval theatre that are crucial for an understanding of the underlying causes of the First World War. Two main aspects should be stressed. First, while historians working on the origins of the First World War have emphasized either domestic or foreign factors, this book has directed attention to the interaction between the two: it was in the public collision of national and international contexts that the real source of conflict lay.[225] The naval theatre played to both domestic and foreign audiences – but these audiences made contradictory demands. For the first time, the display of naval might in one country could be seen and experienced by mass audiences in another. Displays that were 'understood' at home could be 'misunderstood' abroad and vice versa, yet the *Reichsmarineamt* found it impossible to limit the consumption of and participation in the naval

[223] *Philipp Eulenburgs politische Korrespondenz*, vol. 3, doc. 1352, p. 1879: August Graf zu Eulenburg to Philipp Eulenburg, 27 Dec 1897.

[224] David G. Herrmann, *The Arming of Europe* (Princeton, 1996); Stevenson, *Armaments and the Coming of War*.

[225] For a survey of the debate see Annika Mombauer, *The Origins of the First World War: Controversies and Consensus* (Harlow, 2002), pp. 149–54; Mark Hewitson, *Germany and the Causes of the First World War* (Oxford and New York, 2004), pp. 21ff., 171ff., and Klaus Hildebrand, *Deutsche Außenpolitik 1871–1918*, second edition (Munich, 1994), pp. 93–106.

theatre to the domestic market. It watched rather powerlessly while the media and popular culture appropriated the naval stage and turned it into an international theatre in which the rivalry between powers and their mutual performance of deterrence was a fascinating and entertaining game that was played by mass audiences. The realm of foreign policy and diplomacy collided with mass politics and popular culture, with effects that could not easily be controlled.

Second, studying this Anglo-German theatre demonstrates how closely bound up culture and politics were in European relations before 1914. The 'great game for mastery in the North Sea'[226] was as much a cultural phenomenon as it was a political one. Historians who until recently focused entirely on economic and strategic questions have begun to acknowledge this. David Stevenson writes about the great powers in the decades before the First World War: 'The ability to threaten and to use force was central to their identity'.[227] The importance of the intersection between cultural and political contexts has been a recurrent theme of this book. The naval theatre celebrated not only a strategic weapon, but also a cultural symbol. This symbol was central for ideas about 'the nation' and the past, for concepts of gender, masculinity and modernity, for notions of national health and survival. The strategic conflict between Britain and Germany was thus charged with a host of cultural themes.

It is the merging of cultural and political as well as domestic and foreign dynamics that explains why the naval theatre continued to present a powerful stage on which the wider confrontation between the European powers was played out, even at a time when naval rivalry had effectively been decided. In this theatre, 'the other' was not just a naval adversary, but the opposition to the values and aspirations represented by that *Kulturgerät*, the navy. More than in any other public arena, it was in the naval theatre, with its ostentatious displays of loyalty and unity, readiness and strength, that an image of two increasingly firm alliances facing each other in Europe was created. Long before the North Sea became a theatre of war in August 1914, it was a theatre of power and identity. It translated the increasing willingness to run the risk of war – while not necessarily intending to go to war – into a multi-faceted spectacle that was watched by domestic and foreign audiences alike. It nurtured a culture of conflict that limited the scope for diplomacy and détente. It contributed directly to the character of international relations in the decade before 1914, which has been described by diplomatic historians as 'ruthless' or 'reckless', and which they rightly see as essential for an understanding of

---

[226] Clarke, *Hope and Glory*, p. 56.
[227] Stevenson, *Armaments and the Coming of* War, p. 417.

the causes of the First World War.[228] Taken together, these factors indicate that if historians want to understand why war broke out in 1914, they can no longer study the strategic and diplomatic developments of this period in isolation from the important cultural transformations in which they were embedded.

[228] Paul W. Schroeder, 'International Politics, Peace and War, 1815–1914', in T. C. W. Blanning (ed.), *Short Oxford History of Europe: The Nineteenth Century* (Oxford, 2000), p. 208; David Stevenson, 'Militarization and Diplomacy in Europe before 1914', *International Security* 22 (1997), pp. 155–6.

Epilogue: no more parades

In July 1914, the public theatre that had celebrated the navy and the nation with such exuberance turned from spectacle to war. On 16 July, the Royal Navy had begun to assemble its squadrons at Spithead for what the Admiralty had declared to be a test mobilization.[1] There was not to be a formal royal review, but an 'inspection' at which the fleet would sail past the King. While the difference was lost on most of the press, the departure from the standard programme of Spithead spectacles created additional excitement. For the first time the show exercises would include a 'processional flight' of the navy's new aircraft before the King.[2] When the fleet was fully assembled it counted 205 vessels, 55 of them battleships, arranged in eleven long lines. On Saturday, 18 July, with a cold and strong easterly sweeping the Solent, the crowd had reached hundreds of thousands. Portsmouth police had asked for support from the Metropolitan Police and other forces in the South of England. The naval dockyard had teams of stretcher-bearers on stand-by, under the orders of a fleet surgeon. Vendors were busy selling guides and souvenirs, amongst them handkerchiefs showing the royal couple framed by the British colours.[3] At 5 pm a gunshot from HMS *Victory*, Nelson's old flagship, announced the arrival of the King. The fleet responded with the royal salute, enshrouding the Solent in wreaths of smoke. At the same time, a formation of planes flew over the navy, displaying a 'V' 2000 feet above the ships.

At 9 pm, when the sun had set, a single rocket shot up from the *Iron Duke*, the flagship of Admiral Sir George Callaghan. The battleships and cruisers responded by switching on their powerful searchlights, extending long beams into the night. According to a well-rehearsed choreography,

---

[1] The following account is based on the material contained in PRO, ADM 116/1372, including the Portsmouth Fleet Assembly Orders for July 1914.
[2] Twenty seaplanes and four airships took part, see PRO, ADM 116/1372: Assembly of Aircraft at Spithead, 18 to 22 July.
[3] RNM: Programme and Souvenir of the Royal Naval Inspection of the Home Fleets, Saturday, July, 18th, 1914.

251

the beams were then slowly lowered and trained onto the crowds watching at the beaches and on the vessels all around the fleet. One observer
claimed that on shore it was possible to read a newspaper without any
other light.[4] Finally, the beams swept horizontally and vertically, as if
directed by an invisible hand, revealing glimpses of the fleet, as well as the
spectators afloat and on land. Then, on orders of the King, the whole
programme was repeated: having watched from ashore, he now wanted to
see the spectacle of light and darkness from the sea. By 11pm, after two
hours, the strikingly modern display of technology and power was over. 'I
have seen many fleets illuminated', wrote the naval correspondent of *The
Times*, 'but no display exceeding this for beauty and brilliance'.[5]

On Monday, 20 July, the fleet weighed anchor at 9am, preparing to
proceed past the King. Half an hour later the royal yacht anchored close
to the Nab End buoy, off St Helens. From here George V inspected the
fleet sailing past him to sea. The First Fleet was led by four battlecruisers
in single line, headed by the *Lion*. Then the latest battleships came out in
two parallel columns, led by the *Iron Duke* and the *King George V*. Moving
at eleven knots, they were manned with Marine guards, and bands
paraded on the forecastles. As each ship reached the stern of the
Victoria and Albert, the seamen took off their hats, holding them out and
cheering, the bands played the national anthem and the Marines presented arms. Last in the procession were the cruisers and, following in
their wake, the fifty-six destroyers of the First Fleet, arranged in sections
of four.[6] After a short pause, another string of grey hulls followed. These
were the Second and Third Fleets, especially mobilized for the exercises
in the Channel. Again, battle squadrons were followed by cruisers,
destroyers and auxiliaries. In two long columns, led by the *Lord Nelson*
and the *Prince of Wales*, they passed the King, each ship saluting. In total,
the line of warships was twenty-two miles long. On the royal yacht,
George V noted: 'it was a very fine sight, they took just over two hours
to pass us and I remained on the bridge all the time and saluted each ship,
it made one feel very proud to see such a magnificent fleet'.[7] A 'grim, as
well as a grand, panorama', was what the correspondent of the *Naval and
Military Record* called it.[8] 'It constituted incomparably the greatest

---

[4] *Daily Telegraph*, 20 July 1914.
[5] *Times*, 20 July 1914.
[6] This excluded the fourth flotilla, which had been detached to the coast of Ireland out of
concern that Irish nationalists would exploit the opportunity to land arms. See PRO,
ADM 116/1313: Secretary of the Admiralty to Commander-in-Chief, Queenstown,
30 June 1914.
[7] RA King George V's diary, 20 July 1914.
[8] *Naval and Military Record*, 22 July 1914.

assemblage of naval power ever witnessed in the history of the world', wrote Winston Churchill nine years later.[9] The naval theatre had reached a new climax, upstaging all previous displays. It was not only power and might that were being celebrated in this arena, but also national identity. As *The Times* declared in its leading article, the unprecedented display posed a reminder of the nation's insularity, in a decidedly positive sense, and of what Britishness was all about. 'It is as islanders that Britons have built up that Fleet; it is as islanders that they look to maintain it'. Neither French-influenced plans to build a Channel Tunnel, nor the German Kaiser and his navy should ever be allowed to destroy this 'island status'.[10]

The King went back to Buckingham Palace on the next day while tourist steamers continued to hover around the warships at Spithead, filled with spectators keen to see the navy. Officers entertained their families and friends who had come to watch the spectacle. The papers printed the King's message to the Fleet ('I am proud of my Navy') and discussed the meaning of the inspection. Most commentators agreed that the main effect of the display had been to leave a visual and emotional impression of British sea power on domestic and foreign audiences. The aim had been to convey an 'effective picture of our strength', wrote the *Naval and Military Record.*[11] As at so many occasions before, there was a strong sense that the theatrical had outweighed the functional: demonstrating preparedness seemed more important than preparation itself.

On 23 July, more than three weeks after the assassination of Archduke Franz Ferdinand, the Austrian government presented its ultimatum to Serbia. Two days later, and strongly supported by the German government, it rejected the Serbian reply. On 26 July, Prince Battenberg, the First Sea Lord, ordered on his own initiative that the First Fleet and flotillas not return to their bases from the Spithead assembly. This was not quite the master-stroke it is often portrayed as.[12] Battenberg's order meant that the fleet did not disperse, as originally ordered, but instead stayed put, while Churchill, the First Lord, was on his way back from the countryside. Churchill arrived in London the same evening, so that

---

[9] Winston Churchill, *The World Crisis 1911–1918*, abridged and revised edition (London, 1931), p. 108. For a local account of the 1914 review see Portsmouth Record Office, 748A/1/1: Diary of Harry Joseph Atkins of Fareham, a retired teacher who witnessed all the major fleet displays between 1902 and 1914.

[10] *Times*, 21 July 1914, leading article.

[11] *Naval and Military Record*, 29 July 1914.

[12] Marder, *From the Dreadnought to Scapa Flow*, vol. i, p. 433 and Dan van der Vat, *Standard of Power: The Royal Navy in the Twentieth Century* (London, 2000), p. 73 both use this phrase.

Battenberg's initiative had saved not much more than a few hours. What in fact gave the Royal Navy a head start in the general mobilizing for war that was to follow was a remarkable coincidence: that the European crisis triggering the First World War should break out exactly at the moment when the Royal Navy had assembled at Spithead for what officers called 'show exercises', namely a test mobilization and royal inspection.[13]

On 28 July, Austria declared war on Serbia. In London, Sir Edward Grey, the foreign secretary, indicated to the German ambassador that the United Kingdom could not remain neutral in a war involving Germany and France. The Admiralty, in the meantime, had put the navy upon a 'preparatory and precautionary basis'. A day later Churchill gave orders for the Home Fleet to proceed to its war stations. It was here, in the evening of 29 July, that the grand Spithead show, the latest and most spectacular in a long series of public rituals, tilted towards war. On board HMS *Cumberland*, Lieutenant (later Admiral Sir) Louis Henry Hamilton captured the moment:

Wednesday, July 29th. At Cowes. Had a day-on. About 7 pm we got a telegram en code 'Prepare to Mobilize'. From then until midnight was one big succession of telegrams going and coming. Haddon and D-H arrived on board at 11.30 pm, having been dining at Osborne, their accounts of the panic reigning there was most amusing.[14]

What Hamilton witnessed was the shift from spectacle to war, from decorum to deployment (and, at least for some of the royal family at Osborne, from harmless summer entertainment to sheer panic). Five days later German troops invaded Belgium, triggering the British demand for a 'satisfactory explanation' by 11pm Greenwich Mean Time on 4 August. When this ultimatum expired, the British government announced a state of war with Germany.

Amongst the many diverse reactions to the outbreak of war in August 1914 was a remarkable scene in Trafalgar Square, that 'emblem of empire'.[15] Captured on a Pathé newsreel, men and boys pushed self-made warships, one of them a small rowing boat made to look like a destroyer, into the fountains of the Square. At the feet, as it were, of Nelson, they played 'ship launching', enacting one of the key public spectacles that had celebrated the navy and the nation during the decades before.[16] While such unofficial rituals continued, the official celebration

---

[13] NMM, HTN/202a: Admiral Sir Louis Henry Hamilton, private diary, 29 July 1914.
[14] Ibid.
[15] Rodney Mace, *Trafalgar Square: Emblem of Empire* (London, 1976).
[16] British Pathé News Library, reel ON 81 K. On the question of war enthusiasm in August 1914 and crowds in public spaces see Jeffrey Verhey, *The Spirit of 1914: Militarism, Myth,*

of the fleet ceased abruptly. Both in Britain and Germany the naval authorities declared launching ceremonies to be private affairs. The press and public were prohibited, and ceremonial was kept to a minimum. Only months earlier, warship launches had filled the newspapers with exclusive pictures, verbatim speeches and lengthy special reports. Now not more than a small paragraph notified the public of a new ship's successful launch.[17] Pompous ceremonies did not seem appropriate in time of war. They were not only difficult in a practical sense, but also morally problematic: how could celebrations at home be justified when soldiers were dying in the trenches and victory was far from certain?[18]

The war that unfolded between August 1914 and November 1918 turned out to be radically different from what it had been imagined as in the naval theatre. It became clear just how much the celebration of the navy had actively fostered public illusions about the nature of conflict. It had reflected the demands of stage directors and their audiences rather than an analysis of what war at sea would be like in the twentieth century. It had combined a strong sense of entertainment and play with romantic notions about heroism and masculinity. War at sea had been imagined and played as a serious game, in which honour and chivalry dominated. Officers and audiences alike had referred to it as a 'contest' or 'tournament'.[19] In the naval theatre, the past had been staged as a guide to the future. In Britain, Nelson had been cultivated as the guiding star for future conflicts. There had been very few speeches, programmes or guides disseminated at these rituals that did not evoke Nelson and Trafalgar. Even if internally the Admiralty was less obsessed with the past and more ready to develop new technologies and strategies than historians had thought until recently,[20] public ritual and ceremonial meant that the nation, if not most of the navy, had been 'hypnotized by its past'.[21]

and Mobilization in Germany (Cambridge, 2000), chs. 1–3 and Thomas Raithel, *Das 'Wunder' der inneren Einheit. Studien zur deutschen und französischen Öffentlichkeit bei Beginn des Ersten Weltkriegs* (Bonn, 1996).

[17] PRO, ADM 198/51, Secretary Admiralty to Ship Branch, 8 Sept 1914; BA-MA, RM3/9961, Bl. 33 ff.

[18] There was one notable exception. In Sydney, where the young Australian navy launched its first Australian-built cruiser, the *Brisbane*, in September 1915, national pride outweighed the moral objections to the staging of public spectacle in times of war. An audience of 10,000 reportedly watched the launch: NAA, A11804, 1915/315: *Launching of HMAS Brisbane; Report of Speeches at the Launching of the Cruiser "Brisbane" at the Commonwealth Naval Dockyard on the 30th September, 1915*, p. 1.

[19] Victoria Wemyss, *The Life and Letters of Lord Wester Wemyss* (London, 1935), p. 157; Ernst von Weizsäcker, *Erinnerungen*, edited by Richard von Weizsäcker (Munich, 1950), p. 17.

[20] Lambert, *John Fisher's Naval Revolution.*

[21] Marder, *From the Dreadnought to Scapa Flow*, vol. 5, p. 305.

In Germany, too, yesterday's wars and heroes had been paraded as a guide to the future. Prussian army tradition and the triumphant commemoration of wars against France had been core elements of the Wilhelmine cult of the navy, as if future victories at sea would repeat past victories on land.[22] The effect was the same in both countries: the raising of false expectations that imploded painfully during the war. When Commander Ernst von Weizsäcker, who was to become state secretary in the German Foreign Office in the late 1930s, rushed to Wilhelmshaven on 31 July 1914, he was anxious not to miss 'the sea battle' that he confidently expected to take place any day between Britain and Germany.[23] His growing disappointment about the lack of a 'quick decision' in the months and years that followed is palpable in his memoirs. In the end, he wrote, the fleet 'had lost its real purpose (*eigentlichen Zweck*)'.[24]

Neither in Germany nor in Britain was there to be a modern-day Nelson. Fred T. Jane, the naval author and publisher, observed in August 1914, only two weeks after the outbreak of war, that

people are disappointed that we have not had a Trafalgar or Tshushima. Events of that sort make very fine reading and also fine pieces for picture palaces, but they are not modern warfare.[25]

The war at sea, Jane predicted, would be long and with few spectacular events. He warned that the British would have to be prepared for a lengthy period during which attrition and the economics of war would be decisive. Jane's prediction proved largely right. There was no all-decisive sea battle, no heroic tournament, no Trafalgar in the North Sea. Instead, there was waiting. For four years, the North Sea witnessed a stalemate dominated by the Royal Navy. The Grand Fleet's control of the sea remained unimpaired throughout the war, but this control was not translated into a defeat of the German fleet. There were a number of battles, most prominently at Jutland, but none of them brought a decisive overall victory. It was the submarines rather than the traditional battle fleet that became the main focus. Hoping it might change the course of the war, the German leadership turned to the U-Boat, seen as 'un-chivalrous' and as the 'weapon of the weak' before 1914.[26] Yet what decided the war at sea was ultimately what happened on land.

---

[22] See the section 'Military tradition and a violent future' in Chapter 3.
[23] Weizsäcker, *Erinnerungen*, p. 30.   [24] Ibid., p. 40.
[25] *Hampshire Telegraph*, 14 Aug 1914. Similar: L. Persius, 'Geduld!', *Berliner Tageblatt*, 19 Sept 1914, title page.
[26] Rüger, 'U-Boot', pp. 263–4.

On 11 November 1918, the armistice came into effect. On 19 November, the German High Seas Fleet sailed into its internment at Scapa Flow, escorted by the Royal Navy. Seven months later it sank itself, an act that demonstrated once more just how much the thinking about the navy was governed by rhetoric and theatre. It was a rather desperate attempt at a heroic gesture and not much of an *Ersatz* for the aspirations invested in the Imperial Navy in the Wilhelmine era. Many in Germany understood it in the sense intended by Ludwig von Reuter, the commander of the interned fleet: as a tragic, but somehow honourable evasion of having to hand over the undefeated fleet. However, there were alternative readings: did not the scuttle symbolically send the pride and aspiration of Wilhelmine Germany to the bottom of the sea? Did it not represent the futility of two decades of naval building and national dreaming?[27] For the Imperial Navy, the sinking of the fleet presented a rhetorical escape similar to the *Dolchstoß* myth that the army's leadership cultivated (the idea that it had been civilians who had lost the war while the 'men in the field' had remained undefeated). Both the pseudo-heroic scuttle at Scapa Flow and the *Dolchstoß* myth were symbolic refusals to accept defeat and responsibility; and both were to play a key role for German political culture in the inter-war years.[28]

A lack of display

For many in Britain, the end of the High Seas Fleet at Scapa Flow symbolized their disappointment at the Royal Navy's failure to accomplish a decisive victory over the German navy. Even a self-ebullient character such as Admiral Beatty could not hide the fact that this was not quite the Nelson-like triumph at sea that the navy and the nation had grown to expect in the pre-war years. While publicly claiming that Germany's defeat was as much a triumph for the navy as it was for the army, he struck a more demure note when addressing the War Cabinet in the weeks before the armistice. Acknowledging that it was the army that had the lion's share in the victory over Germany, he declared that the Royal Navy's triumph was a 'passive' one. Yet, 'because our victory is a passive victory it is no reason why the Navy should not reap the fruits of that victory'.[29] Indeed, at the time of the armistice, there seems to have

---

[27] Andreas Krause, *Scapa Flow. Die Selbstversenkung der wilhelminischen Flotte* (Berlin, 1999).

[28] Ulrich Heinemann, *Die verdrängte Niederlage. Politische Öffentlichkeit und Kriegsschuldfrage in der Weimarer Republik* (Göttingen, 1983).

[29] *The Beatty Papers*, vol. 2, edited by B. McL. Ranft (Aldershot, 1993), p. 7, doc. 1: Notes on Armistice, 21 October 1918 (added emphasis).

been very little triumphant jubilation in the navy. Ian Sanderson, a midshipman aboard HMS *Malaya*, wrote to his father:

I'm afraid that the poor old Grand Fleet will never have the show of which we were so certain a short time ago. I suppose the GF will go down to history as the classic example of sea power which was so powerful that it was exercised without any fight worth mentioning. Which may be jolly good for historians but distinctly unsatisfactory for the ships' companies.[30]

More than a sense of glory and victory, there was, as the First Sea Lord, Wester Wemyss, put it, a feeling of 'incompleteness'. Three days after the armistice he wrote to Beatty:

There can be no naval officer who does not see the end of this war without a feeling of incompleteness, & with the knowledge that that incompleteness does not arise from any sense of failure. We all feel it – deeply – at the Admiralty & realise how much more this must be the case with you in the Grand Fleet. The Navy has won a victory even more complete in its effects than Trafalgar, but less spectacular, and, because of this *lack of display*, one feels that the unthinking do not fully realise what the nation – indeed what the whole world, owes to the British Navy. The way in which this fact is being ignored, (I will not say studiedly ignored), the way in which Foch and his part is being exalted by the Press and the politicians, is a matter not so much of resentment on our part, as of real national danger. It is impossible to protest – you & I are in the same boat in that way and any action on our part would only be attributed to personal motives.[31]

Wemyss's letter underlined the extent to which sea power had been thought of in terms of display and spectacle rather than merely strategy and administration. What the navy missed in the hour of their 'passive victory' was, in the words of their leading officer, a *display* of victory.

Such a public gesture was not to come for some time. There was a parade of the fleet on 21 November 1918 when the German High Seas Fleet, escorted by the Royal Navy, arrived in the Firth of Forth. Yet this assembly marking the 'Day of Surrender', as Beatty called it, was without royal and with only very low public attendance.[32] Far removed from the navy's traditional ceremonial arena in the Solent, this was the opposite of the Spithead spectacles that had seen hundreds of thousands, even millions, celebrate the fleet and the monarch before 1914. Nor was there much symbolic acknowledgement of the navy's role during the peace celebrations in July 1919. In fact, the navy's part in the ceremonies was conspicuously small. True, a large detachment of officers and sailors, led by Beatty, was amongst the long columns of soldiers that marched

---

[30] Ian Sanderson to his father, 10 Nov 1918, quoted in Marder, vol. 5, p. 188, n. 40.
[31] *Beatty Papers*, vol. 2, p. 12, doc. 3: Wemyss to Beatty, 12 or 13 Nov 1918 (emphasis added).
[32] Krause, *Scapa Flow*, pp. 187–92.

triumphantly through London on 19 July. But there was no royal inspection of the victorious armada, no triumphal Spithead review, no saluting
of the King in the amphitheatre that had seen so many celebrations of the
nation and the navy in the decades before the war. The ships and submarines assembled at Southend for the occasion constituted nothing
close to the displays which press and public had grown to expect from
the navy in the pre-war years. As *The Times* pointed out rather politely,
this was 'not a large fleet'.[33] Neither the King nor the Prime Minister
visited the ships under the command of Admiral Sir Charles Madden. It
was clearly the army that dominated the peace celebrations of July 1919.
The lack of a triumphal naval spectacle was a public reminder of the
junior part that the 'senior service' had played in winning the war.

It was not until five years later that the Royal Navy was given an
opportunity to 'reap the fruits of victory'. The occasion came in July
1924 when the Reserve Fleet was mobilized for manoeuvres for the first
time since the armistice. The Admiralty turned the exercise into a grand
spectacle, the first Spithead review since 1914, very much staged to
appear in the tradition of pre-war ritual. It assembled 193 warships in
the Solent. However, this fleet, inspected by the King on 26 July, was
radically different from that paraded at Spithead ten years before. Where
there had been fifty-five battleships, there were now only ten. And where
there had been fifty-nine battlecruisers and cruisers there were now,
again, only ten.[34] Some of these losses were due to the war, but a large
number of vessels had been scrapped voluntarily in 1919 and 1920 in
anticipation of the Washington Conference that was to reduce the number of capital ships further. The large gaps left by the war and the armament negotiations following it were filled by destroyers and minesweepers
and a number of older vessels that were propped up for the display.
Should there have been any doubts about the navy's role during the war
and, more to the point, about the foundations of its future, they were not
meant to show in its public celebration.[35] The significance of the review
lay in its re-opening of the naval theatre. Like much of the press, *The
Times* went along with the official emphasis on continuity. It recalled the
Spithead review of 1889, staged in honour of the German Kaiser, and the
assembly of July 1914, the greatest of such spectacles just before the
outbreak of war. German emperors came and went, *The Times* commented, but the British Empire and its bulwark, the navy, remained a
constant. Embodied by the fleet, empire and nation had 'come together'

---

[33] *Times*, 19 July 1919.   [34] *Times*, 25 July 1924.   [35] PRO, ADM 179/61.

at Spithead, 'the traditional parade-ground of the Fleet in peace and in war'.[36]

On the surface, such comments would seem to suggest that the revival of naval pageantry was uncontroversial. Yet there was very much an alternative, even if it did not appear in the main British newspapers: a choice between the uncritical return to pre-war pageantry and the attempt to rethink past rituals in the face of new realities. While the first attitude prevailed on the public stage, there were strong voices that suggested the necessity of the second. Indeed, the official re-mobilization of pre-war pageantry came at a time when past uses of such rituals were revisited critically for the first time. In the wake of war novels and trench poetry came a strong call for 'no more parades'. This was the title of a novel by Ford Madox Ford, a book that marked the intellectual discrediting of military ceremonial more than any other literary work. The novel, part of the tetralogy *Parade's End*, describes the brutal awakening of a generation in the trenches.[37] Ford achieves this to a large degree by offsetting the experience of war with the naïve and clean image of military ceremonies. It is the contrast between the harmless image of soldiers on parade and the brutal reality of trench warfare that carries much of the novel's tension.

Indeed, 'parade' has to be seen as the novel's *Leitmotiv*, its symbolic hinge. 'He had imagined himself making a good impression on parade, standing up, straight and tall', is noted about a Canadian officer who finds that dirt, deterioration and death compose the reality of war.[38] The novel's main characters experience the shattering of pre-war assumptions and illusions. And putting this experience into words, they reinterpret the meaning of ceremonies and parades. These are no longer honourable spectacles of military pride, but hollow, hypocritical rituals. In a key passage, the novel's (anti-)hero announces this farewell to parades:

'At the beginning of the war,' Tietjens said, 'I had to look in on the War Office, and in a room I found a fellow . . . What do you think he was doing . . . what the hell do you think he was doing? He was devising the ceremonial for the disbanding of a Kitchener battalion. You can't say we were not prepared in one matter at least. . . . Well, the end of the show was to be: the adjutant would stand the battalion at ease: the band would play *Land of Hope and Glory*, and then the adjutant would say:

---

[36] *Times*, 25 July 1924.
[37] On *Parade's End* and *No More Parades* see Arthur A. Meixner, *Ford Madox Ford's Novels: A Critical Study* (Minneapolis, Minnesota, 1962); Ambrose Gordon, *The Invisible Tent: The War Novels of Ford Madox Ford* (Austin, Texas, 1964), pp. 100–18 and Hynes, *A War Imagined*, pp. 430–33. On Ford see Alan Judd, *Ford Madox Ford* (London, 1990) and S. J. Strange (ed.), *The Presence of Ford Madox Ford* (Philadelphia, 1981).
[38] Ford Madox Ford, *No More Parades* (London, 1925), p. 14.

There will be no more parades. .... Don't you see how symbolical it was: the band playing *Land of Hope and Glory*, and then the adjutant saying *There will be no more parades?* ... For there won't. There won't, there damn well won't. No more Hope, no more Glory, no more parades for you and me any more. Nor for the country ... Nor for the world, I dare say ... None ... Gone ... No more ... parades!'[39]

Could there have been a more powerful indictment of pre-war pomp and pageantry? In Ford's novel, the parading of soldiers was morally corrupt. In the face of four years of mass warfare on an unprecedented scale, this 'anti-monument' displayed little tolerance for public ceremonial.[40]

And yet, while for critical observers such as Ford a return to pre-war pageantry seemed impossible, the naval theatre had re-opened with the Spithead review of 1924. Already in February 1920 the Admiralty had restored launches of warships as public spectacles, announcing that it would revert to 'the practice as to the admission of the public which was in vogue prior to the outbreak of war'.[41] The 1920s were thus characterized by a tension between the resuscitation of pre-war ceremonial, emphasizing continuity and the return to 'normality' on the one hand; and the critical, at times bitter voices such as Ford Madox Ford's, that called for an end to public parades, on the other.

Weimar and the Nazi cult of the navy

In Germany, neither launches of warships nor naval reviews were to be staged in the pre-war fashion until well into the 1930s. There was little to parade: the main fleet had sunk itself at Scapa Flow and the Versailles Treaty allowed for little more than a small coastal defence force. What was more, the new republic suffered from a fundamental discrediting of state-sponsored ceremonial, which made it difficult to find a new, shared symbolic language that could be employed in public ritual. This discrediting came both from the right and the left. For many liberal and socialist critics of the *Kaiserreich*, the war had revealed the hollow character of past public celebrations. When novelist Alfred Döblin assessed the legacy of the *Kaiserreich* in 1920, he asked his readers to remember in particular 'the byzantine emptiness and falsity of the spectacle and of the theatricality of the parades'.[42]

While critics such as Döblin called, not unlike Ford Madox Ford in Britain, for an end to parades, the radical parties and a range of

---

[39] Ibid., pp. 34–5.
[40] The term 'anti-monument' is taken from Samuel Hynes, *A War Imagined: The First World War and English Culture* (London, 1990), p. 283.
[41] PRO, ADM 198/51: Ship Branch, 13 Feb 1920.
[42] Alfred Döblin, 'Republik', *Neue Rundschau* 1 (1920), p. 78.

paramilitary organizations questioned the legitimacy of state-sponsored military ceremonial from a dramatically different point of view. Since it had, in their eyes, deserted the soldiers who had allegedly remained 'undefeated on the battlefield', the new republic was not entitled to speak for them at public rituals. Consequently, many of the veterans' leagues and paramilitary associations refused to participate in state-sponsored ceremonies and staged their own instead. This was an important departure from the political culture of the *Kaiserreich*. Before 1914, the 'radical right' had often enough publicly criticized the government, but it had never openly questioned the legitimacy of state and monarchical ceremonial. Now, after 1919, as part of the radicalization and fragmentation of political culture in the Weimar Republic, a range of leagues and paramilitary organizations developed their own ceremonies and parades. Such 'counter rituals' were employed both by the radical right and left.[43] They were designed to advertise opposition to the new republic, to mobilize support and intimidate opponents. This 'street theatre' brutally expressed the lack of acceptance for a unifying set of state-sponsored ceremonies and the absence of a 'legitimizing founding myth' on which a republican tradition of public ritual could have been built.[44]

When the naval theatre re-opened in Germany after the Nazi assumption of power in January 1933, it did so on an unprecedented scale. The rapid re-armament under Hitler was paralleled by a new rise in ceremonies and celebrations. Naval reviews and launches of warships became prime sites of Nazi ritual. They lent themselves to the symbolic representation of unity between people, Führer and armed forces that was a main theme of Nazi propaganda, while combining this with the traditional appeal and fascination of these spectacles. As one propaganda publication put it:

Ship launch! For everyone who has ever been present, this conjures up inextinguishable memories. Such days are made perfect when the Führer appears. The dockyard and the surrounding shore cannot contain the people who jubilate

---

[43] Sven Reichardt, *Faschistische Kampfbünde. Gewalt und Gemeinschaft im italienischen Squadrismus und in der deutschen SA* (Cologne, 2002), ch. 5; Richard Bessel, *Political Violence and the Rise of Nazism: The Storm Troopers in Eastern Germany, 1925–1934* (New Haven and London, 1984); Bernd Weisbrod, 'Gewalt in der Politik. Zur politischen Kultur in Deutschland zwischen den beiden Weltkriegen', *Geschichte in Wissenschaft und Unterricht* 43 (1992), pp. 391–404.

[44] Peukert, *Weimarer Republik*, p. 15. See also Peter Fritzsche, *Rehearsals for Fascism: Populism and Political Mobilization in Weimar Germany* (Oxford, 1990); Richard Bessel, *Germany after the First World War* (Oxford, 1993), ch. 9; Hans Mommsen, 'Nationalismus in der Weimarer Republik', in Otto Dann (ed.), *Die deutsche Nation. Geschichte, Probleme, Perspektiven* (Vierow, 1994), pp. 83–95 and Wolfgang Schivelbusch, *Die Kultur der Niederlage* (Darmstadt, 2001), ch. 3.

towards the Führer in gratitude. [...] At the christening [of the ship] tens of thousands of workers are assembled around the first worker of the nation.[45]

As before the First World War, these rituals simultaneously addressed foreign and domestic audiences. They were designed to project the confidence and unity of the nation, as well as its demand for a new role in international relations. Clearly, the Nazi stage directors borrowed extensively from their Wilhelmine predecessors. While they discarded what they saw as anachronistic or sentimental elements, they adopted the core procedures as Wilhelm II had established them. And they employed a number of additional features that had become standard practice under the Kaiser, notably the searchlight displays first pioneered by the Royal Navy. These *Scheinwerferspiele* appealed to the Nazi obsession with light and darkness. They facilitated the image of one unified mass, expressing the will of *Führer* and people; and they constructed a symbolic link between this mass and the power expressed by the weaponry and technology of the navy.[46]

Beyond such elements, however, there was little direct continuity between the Wilhelmine and Nazi cult of the navy. Contemporaries such as Count Zedlitz who had witnessed the rise of public rituals in the *Kaiserreich* had thought that these constituted the 'last word' in production and stagecraft.[47] Yet not even the Kaiser could have dreamt of the extremes to which 'his' rituals would be re-invented by the Nazis. A wholly new arsenal of technology was brought to bear on the staging of the navy. Microphones, loudspeakers and the radio were employed for the first time. They were used not just as a means of amplification and dissemination, but also as tools of choreography that moulded 'the masses' in an entirely new way. Nazi stagecraft translated the participation of audiences into a seemingly homogenous experience. For the launch of the cruiser *Prinz Eugen* in 1938, as at most of these events, loudspeakers were set up in the Kiel dockyard. They transmitted the radio coverage, creating a sense of suspense before the arrival of Hitler; and they amplified the 'storm of excitement' and 'hurricane-like jubilation' that the newspapers wrote about.[48] Indeed, commentators

---

[45] *Der Hamburger Hafen. Ein Bildwerk der Landesbildstelle Hansa Hamburg*, with a preface by Gauleiter and Reichsstatthalter Karl Kaufmann (Hamburg, n.d.), p. iii. See also StA Hamburg, 331–1I, Nr. 869: Stapellauf des schweren Kreuzers 'Admiral Hipper', 6 Feb 1937; Stapellauf eines KdF-Schiffes ('Wilhelm Gustloff') in Anwesenheit des Führers, 5 May 1937; Stapellauf eines zweiten KdF-Schiffes ('Robert Ley') in Anwesenheit des Führers, 12 March 1938.
[46] See Siegfried Bayer, *Flottenparaden und Repräsentationen der Marine 1925–1940* (Wölfersheim-Berstadt, 1997), p. 29 for an example.
[47] Zedlitz-Trützschler, *Twelve Years*, p. 104.
[48] *Hamburger Fremdenblatt*, 30 March 1938 (Rundschau im Bilde).

suggested that the new technology allowed for a feeling of simultaneity between the audience present at the launch and the general public listening to it on the radio.[49]

The discontinuity with the *Kaiserreich*'s rituals went beyond the use of new technologies and new styles of stage-management. The Wilhelmine ritual had insisted on reserving the inner core of ceremonies for military representation, and to demarcate a clear line between this military and predominantly male space on the one hand and the unstructured 'general audience' on the other. Under the Nazi dictatorship there was no such division between military and civilian spheres. Much of the Nazi techno-pageantry was designed to overcome the heterogeneous impression of 'the crowd' that had characterized Wilhelmine spectacles. It did so by marshalling and parading audiences like soldiers. Audiences were instructed to do the Hitler greeting towards *Führer* and ship simultaneously with the uniformed rows and blocks of detachments sent by the army, navy, SS and SA.[50] In addition, the *Blockeinteilung*, which was a standard feature of most public Nazi rituals, structured the masses of spectators into clearly defined, orderly segments, preferably squares, resembling party and army formations.[51] This *Blocken* of the audience signalled that, in the Nazi cult of the navy, the civil society of the *Kaiserreich* had ceased to exist.[52]

In rhetoric, too, the naval spectacle of the Nazi period signalled discontinuity with Wilhelmine Germany. Hitler was eager to stress the rupture with the Hohenzollern past at these occasions. At the launch of the battleship *Bismarck* in February 1939, he gave a speech that Goebbels called 'short, but classically beautiful and clear'.[53] As Goebbels noted, its main message was 'sharp criticism of Imperial Germany'.[54] Hitler evoked

[49] *Deutsche Allgemeine Zeitung*, 22 Aug 1938 (Montag Abend), title page; *Völkischer Beobachter*, 24 Aug 1938: 'Deutschland zeigt seine Wehr zur See'. On the role of amplification and the radio at Nazi rituals see also Fritzsche, *Germans into Nazis*, pp. 145–6 and Sabine Behrenbeck, *Der Kult um die toten Helden. Nationalsozialistische Mythen, Riten und Symbole 1923 bis 1945* (Vierow, 1996), p. 365.

[50] For an example see *Der Hamburger Hafen*, p. 10: 'Stapellauf des Schlachtschiffes "Bismarck" in Anwesenheit des Führers am 14.2.1939'.

[51] For an example of this effect as captured in propaganda photographs see *Völkischer Beobachter*, South German edition, 3 April 1939: 'Festlicher Tag in Wilhelmshaven'. For the orchestration of the 'blocks' of spectators see StA Hamburg, 331-1I, 869: Stapellauf eines zweiten KdF-Schiffes ("Robert Ley") in Anwesenheit des Führers am 12. März 1938: Plan der Blockeinteilung. See also Behrenbeck, *Kult um die toten Helden*, pp. 343–436.

[52] See also Manfred Messerschmidt, 'Das neue Gesicht des Militarismus in der Zeit des Nationalsozialismus', in Wolfram Wette (ed.), *Militarismus in Deutschland 1871 bis 1945, Zeitgenössische Analysen und Kritik* (Münster, 1999), p. 87.

[53] *Die Tagebücher von Joseph Goebbels*, part 1, vol. 6 (Munich, 1998), p. 258 (15 Feb 1939).

[54] Ibid.

Bismarck as a symbol against the Hohenzollern monarchy: while Bismarck had given the nation new power and new respect, the monarchy had dismissed the 'iron chancellor' in an act of a 'shameful ungratefulness':[55]

Princes and dynasties, politicizing priests of the *Zentrum* and Socialdemocracy, Liberalism, regional parliaments and parties in the Reichstag, they all exist no longer. They who hindered the historical struggle of this man, they only survived his death for a few decades. National Socialism, however, has created in its movement and in the German *Volksgemeinschaft* the [...] elements that are suited to annihilate the *Reich's* enemies from now on and for ever.[56]

The dominant impression conveyed by the speech was that what Bismarck had achieved in the foreign arena had been ruined by opposition 'from within'. Under the Nazis, in contrast, both internal and external enemies would be dealt with ruthlessly.[57]

It was this idea of the German nation being confronted by foreign and domestic enemies that presented the unifying theme of most speeches given in the naval theatre between Hitler's assumption of power and the outbreak of the Second World War. In essence, the Nazi cult of the navy recreated the situation of 1914, or rather what Hitler and Goebbels propagated as that situation: the encirclement of Germany by external enemies, leading to a war that was lost because of the 'betrayal' through internal enemies, in particular Socialists and Jews. In this re-enactment of 1914, Nazi rhetoric emphasized Britain as the major rival: first only indirectly, by stressing how 'the English' were reacting to the new rise of the German navy;[58] then, when Hitler had decided to abandon the naval agreement of 1935, directly, by naming Britain as the instigator of the encirclement that had supposedly led to war in 1914.

After the launch of the battleship *Tirpitz* in Wilhelmshaven in April 1939, Hitler gave a speech that encapsulated this violent uniting of Germany against internal and external enemies. 'We know now from

---

[55] *Völkischer Beobachter*, South German edition, 15 Feb 1939. An edited version of the speech can be found in Werner Johe (ed.), *Hitler in Hamburg. Dokumente zu einem besonderen Verhältnis* (Hamburg, 1996), p. 206: Taufrede Adolf Hitlers für das Schlachtschiff "Bismarck", 4 Feb 1939.

[56] *Völkischer Beobachter*, South German edition, 15 Feb 1939.

[57] On the uses of the 'Bismarck myth' in Nazi propaganda see Robert Gerwarth, *The Bismarck Myth: Weimar Germany and the Legacy of the Iron Chancellor* (Oxford, 2005), ch. 8.

[58] *Deutsche Allgemeine Zeitung*, 23 Aug 1938: 'Der Eindruck der Flottenschau in England'; *Völkischer Beobachter*, South German edition, 24 Aug 1938, both reporting on the reaction in Britain to the biggest naval spectacle of the Nazi period staged on 22 August 1938 when Hitler and the Hungarian leader Horthy attended the launch of the *Prinz Eugen* and then reviewed the fleet assembled off Kiel.

the historical files that the policy of encirclement had been instigated systematically by England', he claimed. Wilhelmine Germany had seen the danger in the years before 1914, but had not acted against it: 'Its greatest mistake was to watch the encirclement without defending itself in time'.

The result was the World War! In that war the German people – although it was in no way the best armed – has fought heroically. No nation can credit itself with having brought us to our knees. [...] Germany remained unbeaten and undefeated on land, at sea and in the air. And still we lost the war. We know the power that defeated Germany. It was the power of the lie [...]. I took my position then as an unknown soldier of the World War. It was a short and simple programme: the removal of the inner enemies of the nation, an end to the fragmentation of Germany, the bringing together of all the national power of our people in a new community and the breaking of the peace treaty in one way or another![59]

Hitler concluded his speech by claiming that the sacrifices of the war had not been in vain: Germany had risen again and was not to be intimidated. Such rhetoric offered the illusion of being able to 'right' the supposed wrong of the past. Hitler invited his audiences to re-fight the First World War in this theatre, without parliaments and princes, without the 'betrayal' through 'internal enemies' and without humiliation for Germany.[60]

Margaret Anderson has written that the *Kaiserreich*'s 'worst legacy to the next generation was not its political culture, but its war'.[61] The way in which the naval theatre unfolded under the Nazis underlines her assertion. Certainly, the Wilhelmine masters of ceremony had attempted to influence and manipulate their audiences. They had seen the navy as a powerful cultural instrument that could be used to create a sense of national unity at home and project prestige abroad. Yet they had never been the sole actors in this theatre, which was shaped just as much by independent media and market forces. Nor had they questioned the legitimacy of these forces. It was the war that radicalized and fragmentized the political culture in which the Nazis subsequently rose. And it was the trauma of the war, the currency it gave to ideas about encirclement, betrayal and inner enemies, which gave the Nazi staging of the navy and the nation its rhetorical power.

[59] *Völkischer Beobachter*, South German edition, 3 April 1939.
[60] For the way in which Nazi spectacle and rhetoric re-staged the 'August Days' of 1914 during Hitler's assumption of power in January 1933 see Fritzsche, *Germans into Nazis*, pp. 141–2.
[61] Anderson, *Practicing Democracy*, p. 436.

Losing the ocean throne

Against the backdrop of the rise of Nazi Germany and its public pageantry, the naval theatre reached a new climax in Britain in the 1930s. The dual challenges of a rising rival on the Continent and a chronically overstretched empire abroad motivated a wave of renewed rituals which were designed to project confidence and continuity. In the 1930s, statesmen in Australia, South Africa and Canada realized that it was doubtful whether the United Kingdom would be in a position to send forces to their assistance if the need arose. Yet no such doubts about the viability of the empire were to show on the naval stage. The royal navy was, as Prime Minister Stanley Baldwin declared in the House of Commons in May 1936, 'the repository of the spirit and the tradition of our nation'.[62] Whatever the 'spirit and tradition' of the British constituted exactly, it was to be displayed confidently on the naval stage to domestic and foreign audiences alike.

Unity and tradition were key themes. Like so many fleet assemblies before, the Spithead pageant celebrating George V's jubilee in 1935 combined royal and national with imperial iconography. This was underlined by the ships and representatives sent from all over the empire. And if the number of vessels assembled by the Royal Navy was smaller than at pre-war occasions, it helped that the merchant navy had been assigned a more active role, filling in the gaps. After two days of displays and mock exercises in the Solent, the King sent a message to the First Lord of the Admiralty that went simultaneously to all newspaper offices:

> I shall not easily forget the impressive spectacle of the review in which I am pleased to think the Merchant Navy have, for the first time, taken part, while the success with which the Fleet exercises have been carried out today bears witness to the traditional efficiency of the Royal Navy.[63]

There had been public voices arguing against the jubilee and its pageantry, but they showed little in the main newspapers, which emphasized consensus and continuity.[64] The festivities encapsulated 'Britain's story', wrote *The Times* in a leading article: 'As the King's yacht glided through the lines the nature and the very names of the ships seemed to recapture and interpret much of English history'. And 'running through the whole of it' was 'the building of an Empire'.[65] As at so many occasions before,

---

[62] Hansard, Fifth Series, House of Commons, vol. 311, cl. 1537. The occasion was the government's introduction of a motion to erect a memorial to Admiral of the Fleet Earl Beatty.
[63] *Daily Telegraph*, 18 July 1935.
[64] PRO, MEPO 38/144: Jubilee celebrations 1935: anti-Jubilee literature.
[65] *Times*, 17 July 1935, leading article: 'The King's Navy'.

the newspapers turned to Rudyard Kipling to underline the imperial message.[66] The Toronto *Globe* wrote that 'there may have been justification for the thought that the "Poet of Empire" was "written out"', but there were few other authors who seemed to offer a similarly powerful imperial rhetoric than Kipling.[67] Indeed, *The Times* even published a new poem that he had written especially to mark the jubilee. Called 'The King and the Sea', it brought together empire, monarchy and naval power in the heady and romantic language that had made Kipling famous before the war.[68]

A year later, after the accession of Edward VIII, the Admiralty suggested that the spectacle be repeated. The Treasury objected and Buckingham Palace was hesitant. As Alexander Hardinge, Edward VIII's private secretary, wrote to the War Office:

I do not think that The King is very keen about having any Reviews at all, because it is such a short time since the Jubilee Reviews, and also His Majesty likes to see the Services at work informally.[69]

The Admiralty, however, *was* very keen on having another Spithead show, and with persistent lobbying it overcame the King's objections.[70] The abdication crisis and the accession of George VI changed plans somewhat, so that a fully-fledged 'coronation fleet review' was held in 1937. There was some wrangling behind the scenes to ensure as complete an imperial representation as possible for the occasion, but the Admiralty and the Foreign Office managed to keep up appearances – with one notable exception. Canberra flatly refused to send its flagship yet again. As the Australian Prime Minister told the Secretary of State for Dominion Affairs, it was 'not considered desirable for a ship to leave the station at this juncture, and it is therefore regretted that His Majesty's Government in the Commonwealth of Australia will not be represented at the Review'.[71] The internal correspondence preceding the decision shows

---

[66] *Daily Mail*, 17 July 1935; *Daily Telegraph*, 17 July 1935.

[67] *The Globe* (Toronto), 18 July 1935.

[68] *Times*, 17 July 1935: 'The King and the Sea'. George V was so pleased with the poem that he had a note sent to Kipling indicating 'how delighted he was' (RA PS/GV/PS 55208/17/15/MAIN: Hardinge to Kipling, 18 July 1935). Kipling replied that 'His Majesty's message about my verses makes me the proudest subject in His Empire' (ibid., 20 July 1935).

[69] RA PS/GVI/PS 01000/060/004: Hardinge to Adjutant-General to the Forces, War Office, 28 Sep 1936, private.

[70] RA PS/GVI/PS 01000/060/003: R. U. E. Knox, Treasury, to Hardinge, 25 Sep 1936; RA PS/GVI/PS 01000/060/007: Hardinge to Knox, 7 Oct 1936; RA PS/GVI/C 020/1: Memorandum by Hardinge on 'Naval Matters'.

[71] NAA, CP4/2, 5: Prime Minister, Canberra, to Secretary of State for Dominion Affairs, London, 30 Jan 1937.

that Canberra believed that the Australian navy had more important things to do than to sail around the globe again to partake in what its leadership saw as a meaningless ritual.[72] The naval theatre of the 1930s was designed to affirm the unity of empire at a time when this unity was being challenged more than ever before. The press published 'loyal greetings from the empire'.[73] In recalling past ceremonies and printing lists of previous pageants, journalists and commentators stressed the sense of tradition and continuity that the spectacle was intended to convey. Articles entitled 'The King and His Navy: Former Reviews Recalled' and 'Sea Pageants of the Past'[74] suggested that this latest spectacle brought a long and uninterrupted story forward. The Victoria and Albert Museum contributed to this impression during the festivities by organizing an exhibition of 'Old Fêtes and Pageants', celebrating past coronation processions, triumphal entries and public displays.[75] It emphasized a context in which public ritual was understood to signify continuity and tradition rather than an expression of change.

The Spithead ceremonies of the inter-war years themselves reinforced this idea. Elements of innovation were only accepted at the margins. Thus the royal review of 1937 was the first outdoor event to be broadcast 'live' on the radio, with mixed success.[76] While such innovation took place at the fringes, the choreography of these events remained unchanged, notably so the procession through the lines of warships. At its head, preceding the royal yacht, was the Trinity yacht, as it had been throughout the nineteenth century. Already in 1911 the *Encyclopaedia Britannica* had explained to its readers that the services of this maritime harbinger were no longer needed, but that the privilege of the Trinity Brethren preceding the royal yacht at Spithead reviews was upheld for ceremonial reasons.[77]

---

[72] As the Australian Naval Board wrote to the Australian Prime Minister, it was paramount 'to proceed with intensive training in order to restore the Squadron to a state of efficiency' rather than to send any ships to participate in another British spectacle: NAA, CP4/2, 5, Commonwealth Naval Board to Secretary, Prime Minister's Department, 20 Jan 1937.
[73] *Times*, 17 May 1937.   [74] *Times*, 16 July 1935.
[75] Victoria and Albert Museum, *Kings and Queens of England, 1500–1900: The Catalogue of an Exhibition Arranged in Honour of the Coronation of King George VI and Queen Elizabeth* (London, 1937). See also *Times*, 24 May 1937.
[76] This was the occasion when Lieutenant-Commander Woodrooffe, the BBC's man aboard HMS *Nelson*, famously reported the fleet illuminations on 20 May 1937 in a fashion that the Admiralty found less than dignified: 'At the present moment, the whole fleet's lit up. When I say 'lit up', I mean lit up by fairy lamps'. The BBC interrupted the commentary and issued a statement regretting 'that the commentary was unsatisfactory and for that reason it was curtailed' (PRO, ADM 178/140). On the episode see also Asa Briggs, *History of Broadcasting in the UK*, vol. 2 (1965), p. 98.
[77] *Encyclopaedia Britannica*, vol. 27 (Cambridge, 1911), p. 286.

It was more superfluous than ever to engage a pilot to chart the waters of the Solent at these occasions, but to abandon 'ancient prescription' and 'ancient privilege' was unthinkable.[78] Dress regulations also remained unchanged, despite the fact that many participants thought modernization was long overdue. George VI's private secretary wrote to the First Lord of the Admiralty in the days before the review: 'The King will be in uniform, and the proper dress for you, I am afraid, will be top hat. This may be rather inconvenient to you and I shall be a fellow sufferer, but I can think of no alternative to suggest to the King!'[79]

The 'splendid anachronism' of Britain's public pageantry in the 1930s stood in stark contrast to Nazi public ritual, which stressed the functional and modern.[80] Indeed, the opposition between an 'old' and sentimental, pageantry-laden kingdom in the British Isles and a 'young', ruthlessly efficient and modernizing nation in Germany became a central theme in Nazi depictions of Britain.[81] The war itself, however, was characterized by a short, but dramatic suspension of royal and naval pageantry. The only event that came close to a fleet review was George VI's inspection of the Allied forces assembled for the invasion in May 1944. But this was a strictly private visit, kept 'top secret'. It was on board an ordinary motor launch and with careful avoidance of any traditional ritual that the monarch 'inspected' the fleet that was to lead the landing in Normandy.[82]

When Britain's empire unravelled after the end of the Second World War, the language describing this process was permeated by naval and maritime metaphors. Churchill famously called it a 'scuttle' when the Attlee government granted independence to Burma in 1948.[83] As if to counter any impression of decline, Elizabeth II's coronation was

---

[78] RA, PS 01000/060/071: Captain Arthur Morrell, Deputy Master of Trinity House, to Rt. Hon. Lord Wigham, Buckingham Palace, 18 Jan 1937.

[79] RA, PS 01000/060/066: Hardinge to Sir Samuel Hoare, First Lord of the Admiralty, 13 May 1937.

[80] Cannadine, 'Context, Performance and Meaning of Ritual', pp. 145–9. 'Splendid anachronism' is taken from Cannadine, *Ornamentalism*, p. 130.

[81] Gerwin Strobl, *The Germanic Isle: Nazi Perceptions of Britain* (Cambridge, 2000).

[82] RA PS/GVI/PS 04408/12/01/WARNAVY: Rear-Admiral Sir Philip Vian, Naval Commander, Eastern Task Force, to Alan Lascelles, H. M. Private Secretary, 13 April 1944, top secret; George VI's diary entry in RA GVI/PRIV/DIARY, 24 May 1944; RA PS/GVI/PS 04408/12/03/WARNAVY: Vian to Lascelles, 2 May 1944, top secret. The programme of the inspection, which was planned under the code name 'Aerolite', is contained in RA PS/GVI/PS 04408/12/05/WARNAVY: Visit of His Majesty the King to the Eastern Task Force, top secret.

[83] Wm. Roger Louis, 'The Dissolution of Empire', in Judith M. Brown and W. Roger Louis (eds.), *The Oxford History of the British Empire*, vol. 4: *The Twentieth Century* (Oxford, 1999), p. 337. On the cultural impact of 'decolonization' on Britain see Stuart Ward (ed.), *British Culture and the End of Empire* (Manchester, 2001) and Cannadine, *Ornamentalism*, ch. 11.

celebrated with a grand fleet review in June 1953. While dramatic changes in Britain's international role had taken place, the pageantry at Spithead remained the same. The navy assembled in the Solent and saluted the new monarch, who sailed through the lines on board the royal yacht according to the ritual established in the nineteenth century. The same image of continuity in the face of profound change was still on display in 1977 when Elizabeth II celebrated her jubilee in the naval theatre in the same fashion as Victoria and George V had done.[84]

It was only towards the end of the twentieth century that public spectacle came more into alignment with political realities. In 1997 the new Labour government announced that the royal yacht would not be replaced after its decommissioning at the end of that year. This meant not only that an important instrument of monarchical representation ceased to exist, but also that the tradition of the naval theatre at Spithead was thrown into doubt. The ritual calendar of the navy and the monarchy foresaw a fleet review as part of the Queen's jubilee in 2002. Yet no review was held. The absence of a royal yacht played a strong role in this decision, as did the lack of government funds. The jubilee was, as the official website declared, an occasion 'to look at all the changes that have occurred in Britain in the last fifty years'.[85] One of the most visible expressions of change was the absence of a naval review. From 1887 to 1977, the coronations and jubilees of British monarchs had been celebrated without fail with a grand fleet review at Spithead. In 2002, however, there was no royal yacht and no assembly of the fleet in the Solent. A decidedly nineteenth-century imperial and monarchical tradition had come to an end.

What did this mean for British self-images and attitudes to the monarchy? In December 2001, during a parliamentary debate on the jubilee festivities, the Secretary of Defence, Adam Ingram, explained that the 'size and scope of any previous Jubilee celebrations have no bearing on the Golden Jubilee'.[86] This was a remarkable departure. During the long nineteenth century, in the inter-war years and after 1945, the aim had been to sustain the impression that royal and naval ceremonial was unchangeable. However, by 2001, as the Labour government made clear, the ritualized repetition of past ceremonial was no longer binding. It was now possible for monarchical traditions to come to an end and for public spectacle to reflect change.

---

[84] PRO, ADM DEFE 69/182.
[85] Her Majesty The Queen's Golden Jubilee Official Site, www.goldenjubilee.gov.uk/content/serve.pcgi/en/std/gj/About_the_Golden_Jubilee, accessed on 20 Mar 2002.
[86] Hansard, House of Commons, 13 Dec 2001, col. 969w.

The commemoration of Trafalgar three years later provided a case in point. The fleet assembled in the Solent for the occasion was less British than international. Of the 167 assembled vessels, only 65 belonged to the Royal Navy and the Royal Fleet Auxiliary. The largest warship on display, the aircraft-carrier *Charles de Gaulle*, was French. Official terminology reinforced the fact that the event was consciously designed as a departure from the long tradition of Spithead pageants. This was an 'international fleet review' that was meant to be more 'maritime' than 'naval', as its organizers stressed, and 'less formal than previous maritime reviews'.[87] The vessel on board which the Queen sailed through the colourful combination of tall ships, yachts, merchant vessels and warships on 28 June 2005 was a less than elegant ice-breaker. It resembled the local Gosport ferry more than a royal yacht. None of the newspapers referred to this as a royal procession.[88] As the *Guardian* put it, 'Nelson could never have conceived of a monarch reviewing the fleet from the deck of an ice-breaker'.[89]

In June 2005, it appeared as if the naval theatre was close to coming to an end. The Spithead spectacle had been changed beyond recognition. There was no royal yacht and no 'ocean throne' any more. The changed nature of monarchical and national ceremonial indicated that the gap between display and substance had narrowed. In retrospect, the jubilee review of 1977 appears now as a last grand attempt to mobilize the 'pseudo-empire'.[90] Since then, public display has come more into alignment with strategic and political realities. The fact that Britannia no longer rules the waves is not only clear to most contemporaries, it seems also no longer necessary for admirals, politicians and monarchs to pretend otherwise.

---

[87] Letter by Mrs R. Briggs, Trafalgar 200 Project, HM Naval Base, Portsmouth, to author, 30 Nov 2002.
[88] *Daily Telegraph*, 29 June 2005; *Times*, 29 June 2005; *Guardian*, 29 June 2005; *Independent*, 29 June 2005.
[89] *Guardian*, 29 June 2005, title page.
[90] Simon Schama, *A History of Britain*, vol. 3, *The Fate of Empire 1776–2000* (London, 2002), pp. 413–4.

Bibliography

PRIMARY SOURCES

ARCHIVAL SOURCES

Britain

The National Archives (formerly the Public Record Office), Kew
ADM 1 (Admiralty and Secretariat Papers)
ADM 7 (Naval Instructions, Standing Orders, Admiralty and other Circulars)
ADM 12 (Admiralty Indexes and Compilations, Series iii)
ADM 116 (Admiralty Secretary's Casebooks)
ADM 167/30–48 (Board Minutes and Memoranda)
ADM 179 (Portsmouth Station, Records and Correspondence)
ADM 182/1–5 (Admiralty Weekly Orders)
ADM 198 (Precedent Books)
CAB 41 (Cabinet Letters to the Monarch)
LC 2 (Lord Chamberlain's Department, Records of Special Events)
MEPO 2 (Commissioner of the Metropolitan Police, Correspondence and Papers)
FO 371 (Germany)
FO 634 (Embassy and Consular Archives Germany)
MT 9 (Ministry of Transport, Marine Department)

Royal Archives, Windsor
Victorian Archive
Victorian Additional Archive
Queen Victoria's Journal
King George V Archive
King George V's Diaries
King George VI Archive
Queen Elizabeth II Archive
Press Cuttings

National Maritime Museum, Greenwich
Edward Fraser Papers
HTN (Admiral Sir Louis Henry Hamilton)
GBK/1 (Dockyard Notes Lord Charles Beresford)
RIC1 (Admiral Sir Herbert William Richmond)
JOD (Journals and Diaries)

Armstrong Co Ltd., Launch Books
Guides, Programmes, Souvenirs of Naval Reviews
Photographs Collection

Imperial War Museum, London
Midshipmen's Journals
Private Diaries
Naval Films
Naval Photographs (Q Series)

Cambridge University Library, Vickers Archive
Vickers-Armstrong Ltd.
Palmers Shipbuilding Co. Ltd.

Churchill Archives, Churchill College, Cambridge
FISR (Admiral of the Fleet John Arbuthnot Fisher)
BGGF (Sir Bryan Godfrey-Faussett)
HURD (Sir Archibald Hurd)
MCKN (Reginald McKenna)

Corporation of London Record Office, London Metropolitan Archives
Common Council Minutes and Reports
Visit of the Men of the Fleet to the Guildhall

Portsmouth City Records Office
SB/DF/P (Portsea District Police)
CCM 1 (Portsmouth Council Records, Watch Committee)
Diaries and Journals
Postcard Collection

Portsmouth Central Library
Prescott Frost Collection of Dockyard Photographs
Naval & Lily Lambert McCarthy Collections

Royal Naval Museum, Portsmouth
Midshipmen's Journals
Private Diaries
Collection of Souvenirs, Guides and Programmes
Letters of Admiral of the Fleet John Fisher, Baron Fisher of Kilverstone

Glasgow City Archives
C 1 (Corporation of Glasgow, Minutes)
E 1/6 A (Corporation of Glasgow, Police Department, Minutes)
G 1/1 (Corporation of Glasgow, Lord Provost's Letter Books)
G 2/1 (Corporation of Glasgow, Official Visits)
MP (Miscellaneous Prints)
UCS (Fairfield Shipbuilding and Engineering)

Glasgow University Archives, Business Records Centre
UGD 100 (William Beardmore & Co.)
GD 319 (Scotts Shipbuilding and Engineering Ltd.)
UCS 1 (John Brown & Co.)
Photograph Albums

Cumbria Record Office, Barrow-in-Furness
Ba/BP/1 (Barrow Corporation, Chief Constable, Letter Book)
BDB 16/L (Vickers Library Collection)
Ba/C (Newscuttings Books)
Barrow Council Minutes
Launch Programmes and Invitations

Tyne and Wear Archives Service, Newcastle
Armstrong Whitworth and Co. Ltd.
Palmers Shipbuilding and Iron Co. Ltd.
Newcastle Upon Tyne Borough Police, Chief Constable's Committee Minutes
Newcastle Upon Tyne Borough Police, General Orders
Newcastle Upon Tyne City Council Minutes

British Film Institute, National Film Archives, London
Hepworth & Co.
Barker Motion Photography
Gaumont Company
Warwick Trading Company
Charles Urban Trading Company
Jury's Imperial Pictures
British and Colonial Kinematography Company

British Pathé Film Archives, London
Early Pathé Newsreels
Pathé Animated Gazette

Germany

Bundesarchiv-Militärarchiv, Freiburg
RM 1 (Kaiserliche Admiralität)
RM 2 (Kaiserliches Marinekabinett)
RM 3 (Reichsmarineamt)
RM 4 (Kaiserliches Oberkommando der Marine)
RM 5 (Admiralstab der Marine)
RM 20 (Marinekommandoamt)
RM 31 (Marinestation der Ostsee)
RM 47 (Kommando der Hochseestreitkräfte)
N 253 (Nachlass Tirpitz)
Militärgeschichtliche Sammlung

Bundesarchiv, Berlin
R43 (Reichskanzlei)
R901 (Auswärtiges Amt)
R1501 (Reichsministerium des Innern)
R8034II (Reichslandbund, Pressearchiv)

Bundesarchiv-Filmarchiv, Berlin
Newsreels and Films (SP and SL Series)

Geheimes Staatsarchiv Preussischer Kulturbesitz, Berlin
I. HA, Rep. 89 (Geheimes Zivilkabinett)
I. HA, Rep. 77 (Ministerium des Innern)
I. HA, Rep. 90, Rep 90a (Staatsministerium)
BPH, Rep. 113 (Oberhofmarschallamt)

Politisches Archiv des Auswärtigen Amtes, Berlin
R 2224–2274 (Deutschland 138: Die kaiserliche Marine)
R 2278–2284 (Deutschland 138 secr.: Die kaiserliche Marine)
R 2296–2298 (Deutschland 138, Nr. 5: Der deutsche Flottenverein)
R 2417–2420 (Deutschland 148 secr.: Verhandlungen mit England)
R 5835–5853 (England 78, Nr. 3 secr.: Frage einer Verständigung Deutschlands
     mit England über Flottenbau)
R 5663–5766 (England 78: Die polit. Beziehungen Englands zu Deutschland)
R 5767–5798 (England 78 secr.: Beziehungen zu Deutschland)
R 5512–5595 (England 71b: Die Marine)
R 5596 (England 71b secr.: Die Marine)
R 5612–5643 (England 73: Die englische Presse)
R 5644 (England 73 secr.: Die englische Presse)
R 5647 (England 73, Nr. 2: Varia – Zeitungsartikel)
R 5855 (England 78, Nr. 3 adh. 1 secr.: Pressestimmen)
R 19710–19737 (Büroakten Nr. 4: Programme für die Reisen Seiner Majestät des
     Kaisers und Königs)
R 3576 (Correspondenz Seiner Majestät des Kaisers und Koenigs mit dem Prinz-
     Regenten von Bayern)
R 3585 (Correspondenz Seiner Majestät des Kaisers und Koenigs mit den
     Senaten der Hansestaedte)

Staatsarchiv der Freien Hansestadt Bremen
2-M.6 (Senat, Stapelläufe)
3-S.2.a (Senat, Schiffahrtssachen, Stapelläufe und Probefahrten)
3-P.1 (Senat, Polizeisachen)
3-B.16 (Senat, Besuche und Empfänge)
3-M.2.q (Senat, Militärsachen, Kaiserliche Marine, Stapelläufe)
4,14/1 (Polizeidirektion, Allgemeine Registratur, Politische Polizei)
4,19 (Bremisches Amt Vegesack, politische Überwachung und Hafen)
4,20 (Bremisches Amt Bremerhaven, öffentliche Feiern)
4,70 (Hanseatische Gesandtschaft Berlin)

Staatsarchiv der Freien und Hansestadt Hamburg
132–1I (Senatskommission für die Reichs- und auswärtigen Angelegenheiten)
132–5/2 (Hanseatischen Gesandtschaft in Berlin, Neuere Registratur)
331–1 I (Polizeibehörde)
331–3 (Politische Polizei)
614–2/1 (Deutscher Flottenverein)
622–1 (Blohm)
622–1 (Burchard)
622–1 (Mönckeberg)
622–1 (Predöhl)
Archiv Blohm & Voss

Landesarchiv Schleswig-Holstein, Schleswig
Abt. 301 (Oberpräsident der Provinz Schleswig-Holstein).
Abt. 309 (Regierung zu Schleswig)

Stadtarchiv Kiel
I.3 (Höchste und allerhöchste Personen)
VII.a (Hafenverwaltung)
IX (Polizeiverwaltung)
Naval Photographs

Historisches Archiv Krupp, Essen
FAH 3 B 181, FAH 4 C 55 (Germaniawerft: Stapellauf verschiedener Schiffe)
FAH 4 C 198 (Privatbüro Krupp von Bohlen und Halbach, Korrespondenz mit
    Hermann und Rudolf Blohm)
FAH 4 C 200 (Privatbüro Krupp von Bohlen und Halbach, Korrespondenz mit
    Albert Ballin, 1913–1918)
FAH 4 E 782, FAH 4 E 810 (Privatbüro Krupp von Bohlen und Halbach,
    Korrespondenz mit Wilhelm II.)
FAH 4 E 1141 (Privatbüro Krupp von Bohlen und Halbach, Korrespondenz mit
    Admiral von Tirpitz)
WA 16 (Werksalben)
Kruppsche Mitteilungen

Bibliothek für Zeitgeschichte, Württembergische Landesbibliothek, Stuttgart
Marinearchiv
Fotoarchiv

Wissenschaftliches Institut für Schiffahrts- und Marinegeschichte Peter Tamm
Collection of Postcards and Ephemera

Australia

National Archives of Australia, Canberra
Prime Minister's Department
Department of Defence

Screen Sound Archives, Canberra, Australia
Movietone News

PRINTED SOURCES

Newspapers and Periodicals

Abhandlungen zur Verkehrs- und Seegeschichte
Annual Register
Army and Navy Gazette
Barrow News
Berliner Lokal-Anzeiger
Berliner Morgenpost
Berliner Tageblatt
Bioscope
Brassey's Naval Annual
Bremer Nachrichten
Breslauer General-Anzeiger
British Journal of Photography
Daily Express
Daily Mail
Daily News
Daily Record and Mail (Glasgow)
Daily Telegraph
Danziger Neueste Nachrichten
Deutsche Allgemeine Zeitung
Deutsche Marinezeitung
Deutsche Rundschau
Deutsche Tages-Zeitung
Die Flotte
Frankfurter Zeitung
Gartenlaube
Glasgow Herald
Glasgow News
Hamburger Echo
Hamburger Fremdenblatt
Hamburger Hausfrau
Hamburger Nachrichten
Hamburgischer Correspondent
Hampshire Telegraph
Hansische Geschichtsblätter
Illustrated Chronicle (Newcastle)
Illustrated London News
Illustrierter Deutscher Flottenkalender
Jarrow Guardian
Kieler Neueste Nachrichten
Kieler Zeitung
Kinematograph Yearbook

Kladderadatsch
Kölnische Volkszeikung
Kölnische Zeitung
Labour Leader
Leipziger Illustrierte Zeitung
Mariner's Mirror
Marine-Rundschau
Marineverordnungsblatt
Morning Post
Münchener Neueste Nachrichten
Nauticus. Jahrbuch für Deutschlands Seeinteressen
Naval and Military Record
Naval Warrant Officer's Journal
Navy League Journal (continued as *The Navy*)
Neue Hamburger Zeitung
Neue Stettiner Zeitung
Newcastle Daily Journal
Newcastle Illustrated Chronicle
Norddeutsche Allgemeine Zeitung
North-Western Daily Mail
Observer
Portsmouth Evening News
Punch
Schulthess' Europäischer Geschichtskalender
Scotsman
Simplicissimus
Sphere
Sydney Morning Herald
Tägliche Rundschau
The Age (Melbourne)
The Times
Travel
Überall. Zeitschrift des Deutschen Flottenvereins
Ulk
Völkischer Beobachter
Vorwärts
Vossische Zeitung
Weser-Zeitung
Western Morning News
Die Zukunft

Edited Documents, Official Publications

British Documents on Foreign Affairs: Reports and Papers from the Foreign Office Confidential Print edited by Kenneth Bourne and D. C. Watt, part 1, *From the Mid-Nineteenth Century to the First World War*, Series F, *Europe 1848–1914*, vols. 18 to 21, *Germany 1848–1914*, edited by John F. V. Keiger and David Stevenson (Frederick, 1990).

British Documents on the Origins of the War, 1898–1914, edited by G. P. Gooch and Harold W. V. Temperley, 11 vols. (London, 1926–38).

British Naval Documents 1204–1960, edited by J. B. Hattendorf, R. J. B. Knight, A. W. H. Pearsall, N. A. M. Rodger, G. Till, A. B. Sainsbury (Aldershot, 1993).

Bülow, Bernhard Fürst von, *Deutsche Politik*, edited and introduced by Peter Winzen (Bonn, 1992).

Collection of Admiralty Office Memoranda (London, 1907).

Despatches from His Majesty's Ambassador at Berlin Respecting an Official German Organisation for Influencing the Press of Other Countries. Presented to both Houses of Parliament, September 1914, Cd.7595 (London, 1914).

Die Große Politik der Europäischen Kabinette 1871–1914. Sammlung der Diplomatischen Akten des Auswärtigen Amtes, edited by Johannes Lepsius, Albrecht Mendelssohn Bartholdy and Friedrich Thimme (Berlin, 1922–27).

English Historical Documents, vol. XII (1), 1833–1874, edited by G. M. Young (London, 1956); vol. XII(2), 1874–1914, edited by William D. Handcock (London, 1977).

Graf Bülows Reden nebst urkundlichen Beiträgen zu seiner Politik, collected and edited by Johannes Penzler, 3 vols. (Berlin, 1907–9).

Großherzog Friedrich I. von Baden und die Reichspolitik 1871–1907, edited by Walther Peter Fuchs, 4 vols. (Stuttgart, 1968–1980).

Hansard Parliamentary Debates, House of Commons, House of Lords; Third, Fourth and Fifth Series.

Das Kaiserreich am Abgrund. Die Daily-Telegraph-Affäre und das Hale-Interview von 1908. Darstellung und Dokumentation, edited by Peter Winzen (Stuttgart, 2002).

Klaußmann, A. O. (ed.), *Kaiserreden. Reden und Erlasse, Briefe und Telegramme Kaiser Wilhelms des Zweiten* (Leipzig, 1902).

Kohl, Horst (ed.), *Die politischen Reden des Fürsten Bismarck*, vol. 2 (Stuttgart, 1892).

Minutes of the Corporation of Glasgow (Glasgow, 1900–1914).

Proceedings of the Tyne Improvement Commissioners 1911–1912 (Newcastle, 1912).

Quellen zu den Beziehungen Deutschlands zu seinen Nachbarn im 19. und 20. Jahrhundert, vol. 3, *Quellen zu den deutsch-britischen Beziehungen 1815–1914*, edited by Reiner Pommerin and Michael Fröhlich (Darmstadt, 1997).

Quellen zum politischen Denken der Deutschen im 19. und 20. Jahrhundert, vol. 7, *Unter Wilhelm II., 1890–1918*, edited by Hans Fenske (Darmstadt, 1982).

Reden des Kaisers. Ansprachen, Predigten und Triksprüche Wilhelms II., edited by Ernst Johann (Munich, 1966).

Die Reden Kaiser Wilhelms II., edited by Johannes Penzler, 4 vols. (Leipzig, 1897–1913).

Report of Speeches at the Launching of the Cruiser "Brisbane" at the Commonwealth Naval Dockyard on the 30th September, 1915 (Sydney, 1915).

Rüstung im Zeichen der wilhelminischen Weltpolitik. Grundlegende Dokumente 1890–1914, edited by Volker R. Berghahn and Wilhelm Deist (Düsseldorf, 1988).

Stenographische Berichte über die Verhandlungen des Reichstages (Berlin, 1897–1914).

Untertan in Uniform. Militär und Militarismus im Kaiserreich 1871–1914, Quellen und Dokumente, edited by Bernd Ulrich, Jakob Vogel and Benjamin Ziemann (Frankfurt, 2001).
Verfassung der freien Hansestadt Bremen (Bremen, 1854).
Verhandlungen der Bürgerschaft (Bremen, 1909).
Verhandlungen zwischen dem Senate und der Bürgerschaft (Bremen, 1909).

Contemporary Publications

Alten, Georg von (ed.), *Handbuch für Heer und Flotte* (Berlin, 1913).
Altenloh, Emelie, *Zur Soziologie des Kinos* (Jena, 1914).
Anglo-German Friendship Society, *Report of a Meeting Held at the Mansion House, Nov. 2nd, 1911* (London, 1911).
Bagehot, Walter, *The English Constitution* (London, 1867).
Barker, Ellis, *Modern Germany* (London, 1905).
Bernstein, Eduard, *Die englische Gefahr und das deutsche Volk* (Berlin, 1911).
Bestimmungen für den Dienst an Bord (Berlin, 1894).
Blatchford, Robert, *Germany and England* (London, 1909).
Bleibtreu, Karl, *Deutschland und England* (Berlin, 1909).
Blüher, Hans, *Die Rolle der Erotik in der männlichen Gesellschaft. Eine Theorie der menschlichen Staatsbildung nach Wesen und Wert*, vol. 2, *Familie und Männerbund* (Jena, 1919).
Bodley, John E. C., *The Coronation of Edward the Seventh: A Chapter of European and Imperial History* (London, 1903).
Bonheur, Theo, *The Dreadnought: Descriptive Fantasia* (London, 1906).
Brand, W. F., *Allerlei aus Albion* (Leipzig, 1891).
England von heute (Dresden, 1907).
Bridge, Cyprian A. G., *Sea-Power and Other Studies* (London, 1910).
Britannia: Naval War Game (London, 1894).
Brommy, Admiral R., *Die Marine. Eine gemeinfassliche Darstellung des gesammten Seewesens* (Vienna, 1878).
Brunner, Karl, *Der Kinematograph von heute – eine Volksgefahr* (Berlin, 1913).
Bullen, Frank T., *Our Heritage the Sea* (London, 1906).
Bülow, Bernhard von, *Imperial Germany* (London, 1914).
Castner, Julius (ed.), *Militär-Lexikon* (Leipzig, 1882).
Celebration of Centenary of Launch of Steamer Comet, Built for Henry Bell: Official Programme, 29th, 30th, and 31st August, 1912 (Glasgow, 1912).
Childers, Erskine, *The Riddle of the Sands* (London, 1903).
Clarke, George Sydenham, *Russia's Sea-Power: Past and Present of the Russian Navy* (London, 1898).
Clowes, Sir William, *The Royal Navy: A History from the Earliest Times to the Death of Queen Victoria*, 7 vols. (London, 1897–1901).
Collier, Price, *Germany and the Germans* (London, 1913).
Coronation of H. M. King George V: Programme of Facilities for Witnessing the Royal Naval Review at Spithead on June 24th and the Coronation Processions in London on June 22nd and 23rd 1911 (London, 1911).
Cramb, John A., *Germany and England* (London, 1914).

Daenell, Ernst Robert, *Geschichte der deutschen Hanse in der zweiten Hälfte des 14. Jh.* (Leipzig, 1897).

Die Blütezeit der deutschen Hanse, 2 vols. (Berlin, 1905).

Delbrück, Hans, *Deutschland als Weltmacht* (Berlin, 1911).

Deutschland zur See (Leipzig, 1914).

Denicke, Harry, *Von der deutschen Hansa. Eine historische Skizze* (1884).

Der Hamburger Hafen. Ein Bildwerk der Landesbildstelle Hansa Hamburg. Vorwort: Gauleiter und Reichsstatthalter Karl Kaufmann (Hamburg, n.d.).

Deutschlands Flotte im Kampf. Eine Phantasie (Minden, 1908).

Dilke, Charles and Henry Spenser Wilkinson, *Imperial Defence* (London, 1892).

Döblin, Alfred, 'Republik', *Neue Rundschau* 1 (1920).

Dumas, F. G. (ed.), *The Franco-British Exhibition Illustrated Review 1908* (London, 1908).

Ein Weck- und Mahnruf unseres Kaisers. Ansprache S. M. des deutschen Kaisers an die Fähnriche der Marine bei Einweihung der Marineschule in Mürwik, 21. November 1910 (Leipzig, 1910).

Die Einweihung der Kruzifixgruppe vor der Marine-Garnisonkirche in Kiel (Berlin, 1900).

Eisenhart, Hans, *Ein deutsches Flottenbuch* (Stuttgart, 1905).

Encyclopaedia Britannica, eleventh edition (Cambridge, 1911).

Esenbeck, Hans Nees von, 'Die Feier der Eröffnung des Kaiser-Wilhelm-Kanals', *Marine-Rundschau* 6 (1895), pp. 393–417.

Exerzier-Reglement für die Infanterie (Berlin, 1889).

Flaggen-, Salut- und Besuchsordnung (Berlin, 1904).

Fletcher, C. R. L. and Rudyard Kipling, *A School History of England* (Oxford, 1911).

Ford, Ford Madox, *No More Parades* (London, 1925).

Fox, Frank, *Ramparts of Empire* (London, 1910).

Franco-British Exhibition, London, 1908: Official Catalogue (Derby and London, 1908).

Franco-British Exhibition, London, 1908: Official Guide (Derby and London, 1908).

Fraser, Edward, *Bellerophon* (London, 1909).

The Romance of the King's Navy (London, 1908).

Freemantle, E. R., *The Navy As I Have Known It, 1848–99* (London, 1904).

Friedag, B., *Führer durch Heer und Flotte* (Berlin, 1913).

Frobenius, H. (ed.), *Militär-Lexikon. Handwörterbuch der Militärwissenschaften* (Berlin, 1901).

Militär-Lexikon. Ergänzungshefte, 3 vols. (Berlin, 1902–1906).

Gildemeister, A., *Deutschland und England. Randbemerkungen eines Hanseaten* (Berlin, 1906).

Goedel, G., *Ethymologisches Wörterbuch der deutschen Seemannssprache* (Kiel and Leipzig, 1902).

Halle, Ernst von, *Die Seemacht in der deutschen Geschichte* (Leipzig, 1907).

Hannay, David, *The Navy and Sea Power* (London, 1913).

Harnack, Adolf, 'Protestantismus und Katholizismus in Deutschland', *Preußische Jahrbücher* 127 (1907), pp. 294–311.

Henrici, B., *Deutsches Flottenbüchlein* (Hamm, 1907).

Hirschfeld, Magnus, *Kriegspsychologisches* (Berlin, 1916).

Hirst, Francis W., *The Six Panics and Other Essays* (London, 1913).

Hislam, Percival A., *The Admiralty of the Atlantic: An Enquiry Into the Development of German Sea Power, Past, Present and Prospective* (London, 1908).

The North Sea Problem (London, 1913).

Hobson, J. A., *Imperialism* (London, 1902).

Psychology of Jingoism (London, 1901).

Horn, Paul, *Deutsche Soldatensprache* (Giessen, 1899).

Imme, Theodor, *Die deutsche Soldatensprache* (Dortmund, 1917).

Jane, Frederick T., *Heresies of Sea Power* (London, 1906).

Hints on Playing the Jane Naval War Game (London, 1903).

How to Play the "Naval War Game": With a Complete Set of the Latest Rules, Full Instructions, and Some Examples of "Wars" That Have Actually Been Played: Official Rules, 1912, Cancelling all Others (London, 1912).

Rules for the Jane Naval War Game (London, 1898).

Kaiser Wilhelm II. als Soldat und Seemann. Zugleich Geschichte des Reichsheeres und der Flotte seit 1871. Ein Jubiläumsbuch für das deutsche Volk, edited by Joseph Kürschner (Berlin, 1902).

Kipling, Rudyard, *A Fleet in Being: Notes of Two Trips with the Channel Squadron* (London, 1898).

Klöpper, Clemens, *Englisches Reallexikon*, 2 vols. (Leipzig, 1897–9).

Kluge, F., *Seemannssprache* (Halle, 1911).

Koch, Paul, *Geschichte der deutschen Marine* (Berlin, 1902).

Lacy, Charles J. de, 'The Cost of Placing a Battleship in the Water', *Boy's Own Paper*, 15 Feb 1908, pp. 311–14.

Le Bon, Gustave, *The Crowd: A Study of the Popular Mind* (London, 1896).

Le Queux, William, *Spies of the Kaiser: Plotting the Downfall of England* (London, 1909).

The Invasion of 1910 (London, 1906).

Lecky, H. St, *The King's Ships Together With the Important Historical Episodes Connected with the Successive Ships of the Same Name from Remote Times, and a List of Names and Services of Some Ancient War Vessels*, 6 vols. (London, 1913).

Lenschau, Thomas (ed.), *England in deutscher Beleuchtung* (Halle, 1906).

Leyland, John, 'The Navy and the Coronation', *Mariner's Mirror* 1 (1911), pp. 165–7.

Liesegang, Paul, *Das lebende Lichtbild. Entwicklung, Wesen und Bedeutung des Kinematographen* (Düsseldorf, 1910).

Lindenberg, Paul (ed.), *Pracht-Album photographischer Aufnahmen der Berliner Gewerbe-Ausstellung 1896 und der Sehenswürdigkeiten Berlins und des Treptower Parks* (Berlin, 1896).

Lindner, Theodor, *Die deutsche Hanse. Ihre Geschichte und Bedeutung dargestellt für das deutsche Volk* (Leipzig, 1899).

List, Georg Friedrich, 'Die deutsche Flagge', *Das Zollvereinsblatt*, no. 2, 8 Jan 1843.

Lookout (pseud.), *Englands Weltherrschaft und die deutsche 'Luxusflotte'* (Berlin, 1912).

Mahan, Alfred Thayer, *The Life of Nelson: The Embodiment of the Sea Power of Great Britain*, 2 vols. (London, 1897).
The Influence of Sea Power Upon History, 1660–1783 (London, 1890).
The Influence of Sea Power Upon the French Revolution and Empire, 1793–1812 (London, 1892).
Malchin, W., *Deutschland zur See* (Leipzig, 1913).
Mantels, Wilhelm, 'Der Hansische Geschichtsverein', *Hansische Geschichtsblätter* 1 (1874), pp. 3–8.
Martin, Rudolf Emil, *Deutschland und England. Ein offenes Wort an den Kaiser* (Hannover, 1909).
Martyn, Arthur, *Souvenir Song: The Naval Pageant* (London, 1909).
Meredith, George, *Celt and Saxon* (London, 1911).
Meyers Konversationslexikon, fourth edition (Leipzig, 1888).
Fifth edition (Leipzig, 1897).
Sixth edition (Leipzig and Vienna, 1908).
Müller, Conrad, *Altgermanische Meeresherrschaft* (Gotha, 1914).
Nachrichten des Deutsch-Englischen Verständigungs-Komitees (Berlin, 1911).
Naubert, Carl, *Land und Leute in England, neu bearbeitet von Dr. Eugen Oswald*, third edition (Berlin, 1906).
Naval Encyclopaedia (Philadelphia, 1881).
The Navy League Guide to the Naval Review: Plan of the Fleet and Index to Ships (London, 1897).
The Navy League Guide to the Coronation Review, June 28th, 1902, edited by H. W. Wilson (London, 1902).
The Navy League Guide to the Thames Review, 17th to 24th July 1909: Many Illustrations and Diagrams and Plans of the Fleet, edited by Benedict W. Ginsburg (London, 1909).
Neudeck, Georg and Heinrich Schröder, *Das kleine Buch von der Marine. Ein Handbuch alles Wissenswerten über die deutsche Flotte nebst vergleichenden Darstellungen der Seestreitkräfte des Auslands* (Kiel and Leipzig, 1899).
Newbolt, Henry, *Admirals All* (London, 1897).
The Island Race (London, 1898).
Official Programme of the Great Naval Review Westminster to Southend, July 17 to 24, 1909, Containing Plan of the Fleet and the Story of the Navy (London, 1909).
Official Programme of the Coronation Review, Spithead, June 24th, 1911: All About the Ships: All About the Guns and Men (London, 1911).
Official Programme of the Great Naval Review Spithead July 1912 (London, 1912).
Our German Cousins (London, 1909).
Pasley, L. M. Sabine, *Service to be Used at the Launching of Ships of His Majesty's Navy* (London, 1902).
Peez, Alexander von, *England und der Kontinent*, third edition (Vienna and Leipzig, 1909).
Perris, George, *Germany and the German Emperor* (London, 1912).
Petherick, Rosa, *Toy Boats* (London, 1910).
Poten, Bernhard von (ed.), *Handwörterbuch der gesamten Militärwissenschaften*, 9 vols. (Bielefeld and Leipzig, 1877–80).
Presse-Stimmen zur Flotten-Parade (Berlin, 1911).

Programm für die Informationsreise der Bundesratsmitglieder und Reichstagsabgeordneten nach Kiel vom 3. bis 8. Juni (Berlin, 1907).

Programme and Souvenir of the Royal Naval Inspection of the Home Fleets, Saturday, July, 18th, 1914 (London, 1914).

Quidde, Ludwig, *Caligula. Eine Studie über Cäsarenwahnsinn* (Leipzig, 1894).

Ran an den Feind! (Leipzig, 1913).

Rassow, Wilhelm, *Deutschlands Seemacht*, 25th edition (Elberfeld, 1910).

Ratzel, Friedrich, 'Der Lebensraum. Eine biogeographische Studie', in K. Bücher et al. (eds.), *Festgaben für Albert Schäffle zur siebzigsten Wiederkehr seines Geburtstages am 24. Februar 1901* (Tübingen, 1901), pp. 101–89.

Das Meer als Quelle der Völkergrösse. Eine politisch-geographische Studie (Munich and Leipzig, 1900).

Rawnsley, H. D., *The Child and the Cinematograph Show and the Picture Post-Card Evil* (London, 1913).

Reventlow, Graf Ernst, *Deutschland in der Welt voran?* (Berlin, 1905).

Die deutsche Flotte (Zweibrücken, 1901).

Die englische Seemacht (Halle, 1906).

Kaiser Wilhelm II. und die Byzantiner, second edition (Munich, 1906).

Richter, A. and O. Szczesny, *Ratgeber für den Dienstbetrieb in der kaiserlichen Marine* (Berlin, 1913).

Robinson, William, *The British Tar in Fact and Fiction* (1909).

Rollerton, Charles J., *The Age of Folly* (London, 1911).

Rudyard Kipling's Verse: Inclusive Edition, 1885–1918 (Edinburgh, 1922).

Sarolea, Charles, *The Anglo-German Problem* (London, 1912).

Schäfer, Dietrich, *Aufsätze, Vorträge und Reden*, 2 vols. (Jena, 1913).

Die deutsche Hanse. Mit 99 Abbildungen (Bielefeld und Leipzig, 1903).

Scheel, Willy, *Deutschlands Seegeltung* (Halle, 1905).

Scheibert, Justus (ed.), *Illustriertes deutsches Militär-Lexikon* (Berlin, 1897).

Schultzky, Otto, *England und Deutschland* (Mainz, 1909).

Schulz, Friedrich, *Die Hanse und England* (Berlin, 1910).

Schulze-Gaevernitz, G. von, *England und Deutschland*, second edition (Berlin, 1908).

Schurtz, Heinrich, *Altersklassen und Männerbünde* (Berlin, 1902).

Service to be Used at the Launching of Ships of His Majesty's Navy (London, 1902).

Sewill, Henry, *A German Invasion and the Real German Peril* (London, 1912).

The Ships of the Royal Navy with the Meanings and Pronunciations of Their Names (London, 1898).

Silburn, Percy, *The Evolution of Sea-Power* (London, 1912).

The Silver Jubilee Book (London, 1935).

Skrine, John Huntley, *The Ocean Throne: Verse for the Celebration of the Fiftieth Year of the Reign of Victoria* (Uppingham, 1887).

Smith, Logan Pearsall, 'English Sea-Terms', *English Review*, Nov 1912, pp. 541–59.

Souvenir of the Diamond Jubilee Naval Review at Spithead, June 28th, 1897 (London, 1897).

Special-Catalog No. 32 über Projections- und Aufnahmeapparate für lebende Photographie, Films, Graphophons, Nebelbilder-Apparate etc. der Fabrik für optisch-mechanische Präcisions-Instrumente von Ed. Messter (Berlin, 1898).

Spies, Heinrich, *Das moderne England. Einführung in das Studium seiner Kultur. Mit besonderem Hinblick auf einen Aufenthalt im Lande* (Straßburg, 1911).

Steer, Valentia, *The Romance of the Cinema: A Short Record of the Development of the Most Popular Form of Amusement of the Day* (London, 1913).

Stein, Walther, *Beiträge zur Geschichte der deutschen Hanse bis um die Mitte des 15. Jahrhunderts* (Giessen, 1900).

Zur Entstehung und Bedeutung der Deutschen Hanse (Lübeck, 1911).

Stenzel, Alfred, *Helgoland und die deutsche Flotte* (Berlin, 1891).

Deutsches seemännisches Wörterbuch (1904).

Stephen, Adrian, *The 'Dreadnought' Hoax* (London, 1936).

Stevenson, Robert Louis, *Virginibus Puerisque* (London, 1881).

Stöwer, Willy, *Deutschlands Kriegsflotte* (Berlin, 1898).

Deutsche Flottenmanöver (Braunschweig, 1900).

(ed.), *Kaiser Wilhelm II. und die Marine* (Berlin, 1912).

Strachey, Mary 'Amabel' Nassau, *The Sea-Power of England: A Play for a Village Audience* (London, 1913).

Teutsch-Lerchenfeld, Bernhard, *Deutschland zur See in Wort und Bild dargestellt*, fourth edition (Leipzig, 1909).

Urban, Charles, *The Cinematograph in Science, Education and Matters of State* (London, 1907).

Valois, Vice-Admiral, *Deutschland als Seemacht, sowie Betrachtungen marine-politischen Inhalts* (Leipzig, 1908).

Seemacht, Seegeltung, Seeherrschaft (Berlin, 1899).

Victoria and Albert Museum, *Kings and Queens of England, 1500–1900: The Catalogue of an Exhibition Arranged in Honour of the Coronation of King George VI and Queen Elizabeth* (London, 1937).

Visit of the French Fleet 1905: Illustrated Guide with Special Chart (Portsmouth, 1905).

Vogel, Walther, *Kurze Geschichte der Hanse* (Munich and Leipzig, 1915).

Ward, Thomas Humphry (ed.), *The Reign of Queen Victoria* (London, 1887).

The Web of Empire: Diary of the Indian Tour of T.R.H. the Duke and Duchess of York (London, 1901).

Weber, Max, *Gesammelte politische Schriften*, edited by J. Winckelmann, third edition (Tübingen, 1971).

Wendt, G., *England. Seine Geschichte, Verfassung und staatliche Einrichtungen*, third edition (Leipzig, 1907).

West, Alfred, *Our Navy: A Synopsis of the Life-Work of Alfred West, FRGS, Depicting Scenes of Life in Our Navy and Our Army, Our Mercantlile Marine: An Illustrated and Descriptive Catalogue* (London, 1912).

Westerman, Percy F., *The Sea Monarch* (London, 1912).

The Dreadnought of the Air (London, 1914).

Whitman, Sidney, *German Memories* (London, 1912).

Wilkinson, Henry Spenser, *The Command of the Sea* (London, 1894).

The Great Alternative (London, 1894).

Wislicenus, Georg, *Deutschlands Seemacht sonst und jetzt. Nebst einem Überblick über die Geschichte der Seefahrt aller Völker*, third edition (Leipzig, 1909).

Wolf, Arthur, *Denkschrift betreffend die Kinematographentheater* (Berlin, 1913).
Wyatt, Harold F. and L. G. H. Horton-Smith (eds.), *The Passing of the Great Fleet* (London, 1909).
God's Test by War (London, 1912).
Zimmermann, Alfred, 'Der deutsch-englische Gegensatz', *Zeitschrift für Politik* 2 (1909), pp. 236–51.
Zur feierlichen Einweihung des Nord-Ostsee-Kanals im Juni 1895. Amtliche Zusammenstellung der für die Festlichkeiten getroffenen Einrichtungen und Veranstaltungen (Kiel and Leipzig, 1895).
Zur Flottenfrage. Darlegungen der Norddeutschen Allgemeinen Zeitung (Berlin, 1899).

Memoirs, Diaries, Letters

The Beatty Papers, edited by B. McL. Ranft, 2 vols. (Aldershot, 1989–93).
Bethmann Hollweg, Theobald, *Betrachtungen zum Weltkriege*, 2 vols. (Berlin 1919–21).
Bülow, Bernhard von, *Denkwürdigkeiten*, edited by Franz von Stockhammern, 4 vols. (Berlin, 1930–1).
Chair, Dudley de, *The Sea is Strong* (London, 1961).
Denkwürdigkeiten des General-Feldmarschall Alfred von Waldersee, edited by Heinrich Otto Meisner, 3 vols. (Stuttgart and Berlin, 1922).
The Diaries of Colonel the Honourable Robert Fulke Greville, Equerry to His Majesty the King George III, edited by Frank McKno Bladon (London, 1930).
The diary of Edward Goschen 1900–1914, edited by Christopher Howard (London, 1980).
Eckardstein, Baron Hermann von, *Lebenserinnerungen und politische Denkwürdigkeiten*, 3 vols. (Lepizig, 1919–21).
Erinnerungen und Gedanken des Botschafters Anton Graf Monts, edited by Karl Friedrich Nowak and Friedrich Thimme (Berlin, 1932).
Fear God and Dreadnought: The correspondence of Admiral of the Fleet Lord Fisher of Kilverstone, edited by Arthur J. Marder, vol. 1 (London, 1952).
Groener, Wilhelm, *Lebenserinnerungen*, edited by Hiller von Gaertringen (Göttingen, 1957).
Hammann, Otto, *Bilder aus der letzten Kaiserzeit* (Berlin, 1922).
Hase, Georg von, *Die zwei weissen Völker! Deutsch-englische Erinnerungen eines deutschen Seeoffiziers* (Lepizig, 1923).
Hohenlohe-Ingelfingen, Prinz Kraft zu, *Aus meinem Leben*, 4 vols. (Berlin, 1897–1907).
Hohenlohe-Schillingsfürst, Fürst Chlodwig zu, *Denkwürdigkeiten*, edited by Friedrich Curtius, 2 vols. (Stuttgart, 1907).
Hopman, Albert, *Das Logbuch eines deutschen Seeoffiziers* (Berlin, 1924).
Hutten-Czapski, Bogdan Graf von, *Sechzig Jahre Politik und Gesellschaft*, 2 vols. (Berlin, 1936).
Inside Asquith's Cabinet: From the Diaries of Charles Hobhouse, edited by Edward David (London, 1977).

The Jellicoe Papers: Selections from the Private and Official Correspondence of Admiral of the Fleet Earl Jellicoe of Scapa, edited by A. Temple Patterson, 2 vols (Aldershot, 1966–68).

Der Kaiser ... Aufzeichnungen des Chefs des Marinekabinetts Admiral Georg Alexander v. Müller über die Ära Wilhelms II., edited by Walter Görlitz (Göttingen, 1965).

Kerr, Alfred, *Wo liegt Berlin? Briefe aus der Reichshauptstadt 1895–1900*, edited by Günther Rühle (Berlin, 1998).

Kessler, Harry Graf, *Das Tagebuch 1880–1937*, vols. 2–4 (Stuttgart, 2004–5).

King-Hall, Stephen, *A North Sea Diary 1914–1918* (London, 1936).

Kipling, Rudyard, *Something of Myself and Other Autobiographical Writings*, edited by Thomas Pinney (Cambridge, 2000).

Lantern Slides: The Diaries and Letters of Violet Bonham Carter, edited by Mark Bonham Carter and Mark Pottle (London, 1996).

The Letters of Charles Lamb, edited by Russell Davis Gillman (London, 1907).

Letters and Papers of Professor Sir John Knox Laughton, 1830–1915, edited by Andrew Lambert (Aldershot, 2002).

Moltke, Helmuth von, *Erinnerungen, Briefe, Dokumente, 1877–1916*, edited by Eliza von Moltke (Stuttgart, 1922).

The Life and Letters of David, Earl Beatty, Admiral of the Fleet, edited by W. S. Chalmers (London, 1951).

The Navy and Defence: The Autobiography of Admiral of the Fleet Lord Chatfield (London, 1942).

The Papers of Admiral Sir John Fisher, edited by P. K. Kemp, 2 vols. (Aldershot, 1960–4).

Paul von Hintze. Marineoffizier, Diplomat, Staatssekretär. Dokumente einer Karriere zwischen Militär und Politik, 1903–1918, edited by Johannes Hürter (Munich, 1998).

Philipp Eulenburgs politische Korrespondenz, edited by John C. G. Röhl, vol. 3, *Krisen, Krieg und Katastrophen, 1895–1921* (Boppard, 1983).

Pound, R. and G. Harmsworth, *Northcliffe* (London, 1960).

Raeder, Erich, *Mein Leben*, vol. 1 (Tübingen, 1956).

Regierte der Kaiser? Kriegstagebücher, Aufzeichnungen und Briefe des Chefs des Marine-Kabinetts Admiral Georg Alexander von Müller 1914–1918, edited by Walter Görlitz (Göttingen, 1959).

Stumpf, Richard, *Tagebuch des Matrosen Richard Stumpf* (Berlin, 1928).

Das Tagebuch der Baronin Spitzemberg. Aufzeichnungen aus der Hofgesellschaft des Hohenzollernreiches, edited by Rudolf Vierhaus (Göttingen, 1960).

Tirpitz, Alfred von, *Erinnerungen* (Leipzig, 1919).

Politische Dokumente. Der Aufbau der deutschen Weltmacht (Stuttgart, 1924).

Valentini, Rudolf von, *Kaiser und Kabinettschef* (Oldenburg, 1931).

Widenmann, Wilhelm, *Marine-Attaché an der kaiserlich-deutschen Botschaft in London 1907–1912* (Göttingen, 1952).

Wilhelm II, *Ereignisse und Gestalten aus den Jahren 1878–1918* (Leipzig and Berlin, 1922).

Aus meinem Leben, 1859–1888 (Lepizig, 1927).

Zedlitz-Trützschler, Count Robert, *Twelve Years at the Imperial German Court* (London, 1924).

SECONDARY LITERATURE

Abrams, Lynn, 'From Control to Commercialization: The Triumph of Mass Entertainment in Germany, 1900–1925', *German History* 8 (1990), pp. 278–93.

Workers' Culture in Imperial Germany: Leisure and Recreation in the Rhineland and Westphalia (New York, 1992).

Abrams, Lynn and Elizabeth Harvey (eds.), *Gender Relations in German History: Power, Agency and Experience from the Sixteenth Century* (Durham, NC, 1996).

Adas, Michael, *Machines as the Measure of Men: Science, Technology, and Ideologies of Western Dominance* (Ithaca and London, 1989).

Afflerbach, Holger, *Das entfesselte Meer. Die Geschichte des Atlantik* (Munich, 2001).

Agulhon, Maurice, 'La fabrication de la France. Problèmes et controverses', in M. Segalen (ed.), *L'autre et le semblable* (Paris, 1989), pp. 109–20.

Marianne au combat. L'imagerie et la symbolique républicaines de 1789 à 1880 (Paris, 1979).

Marianne au pouvoir. L'imagerie et la symbolique républicaines de 1880 à 1914 (Paris, 1989).

Alewyn, Richard, *Das große Welttheater. Die Epoche der höfischen Feste*, reprint of the second edition (Munich, 1989).

Alter, Peter, *Nationalismus* (Frankfurt, 1985).

Altick, Richard D., *The Shows of London* (Cambridge, MA, 1978).

Anderson, B., *Imagined Communities: Reflections on the Origins and Spread of Nationalism* (London, 1983).

Anderson, Margaret, *Practicing Democracy: Elections and Political Culture in Imperial Germany* (Princeton, 2000).

Anderson, Pauline R., *The Background of Anti-English Feeling in Germany, 1890–1903* (Washington, 1939).

Andrew, Christopher, *Théophile Delcassé and the Making of the Entente Cordiale: A Reappraisal of French Foreign Policy, 1898–1905* (London, 1968).

Secret Service (London, 1985).

Applegate, Celia, *A Nation of Provincials: The German Idea of Heimat* (Berkeley, 1990).

'Localism and the German Bourgeoisie: The "Heimat" Movement in the Rhenish Palatinate before 1914', in David Blackbourn and Richard J. Evans (eds.), *The German Bourgeoisie* (London, 1991), pp. 224–54.

Armitage, David, 'Greater Britain: A Useful Category of Historical Analysis?', *American Historical Review* 104 (1999), pp. 427–45.

The Ideological Origins of the British Empire (Cambridge, 2000).

Arnstein, Walter, 'Queen Victoria Opens Parliament: The Disinvention of Tradition', *Historical Research*, 63 (1990).

Queen Victoria (Houndmills, 2003).

Assmann, Jan, *Das kulturelle Gedächtnis* (Munich, 1992).

Assmann, Jan and Tonio Hölscher (eds.), *Kultur und Gedächtnis* (Frankfurt, 1988).

Attridge, Steve, *Nationalism, Imperialism, and Identity in Late Victorian Culture: Civil and Military Worlds* (Basingstoke, 2003).

August, Thomas G., *The Selling of the Empire: British and French Imperialist Propaganda 1890–1940* (London, 1985).

Bakhtin, Mikhail, *Rabelais and His World*, translated by Hélène Iswolsky (Cambridge, MA, 1968).

Barczewski, Stephanie, *Myth and National Identity in Nineteenth-Century Britain: The Legends of King Arthur and Robin Hood* (Oxford, 2000).

Barnes, John, *The Rise of Cinema in Great Britain* (London, 1983).

The Beginnings of the Cinema in England, 1894–1901, 4 vols. (Exeter, 1998).

Barnett, Correlli, *The Collapse of British Power* (Gloucester, 1972).

The Lost Victory (London, 1985).

The Audit of War (London, 1986).

The Verdict of Peace (London, 2001).

Barraclough, Geoffrey, *From Agadir to Armageddon: Anatomy of a Crisis* (New York, 1982).

Bassett, Judith, ' "A Thousand Miles of Loyalty": The Royal Tour of 1901', *New Zealand Journal of History* 21 (1987), pp. 125–38.

Bassin, Mark, 'Imperialism and the Nation State in Friedrich Ratzel's Political Geography', *Progress in Human Geography* 11 (1987), pp. 473–95.

Bauer, Franz J., *Gehalt und Gestalt in der Monumentalsymbolik. Zur Ikonologie des Nationalstaates in Deutschland und Italien 1860–1914* (Munich, 1992).

Bauerkämper, Arnd, *Die "radikale Rechte" in Großbritannien. Nationalistische, antisemitische und faschiste Bewegungen vom späten 19. Jahrhundert bis 1945* (Göttingen, 1991).

Bayer, Siegfried, *Flottenparaden und Repräsentationen der Marine 1925–1940* (Wölfersheim-Berstadt, 1997).

Beckett, W. N. T., *A Few Naval Customs, Expressions, Traditions and Superstitions*, second edition (Portsmouth, 1932).

Beer, Gillian, 'The Island and the Aeroplane: The Case of Virginia Woolf', in H. K. Bhabha (ed.), *Nation and Narration* (London, 1990), pp. 265–90.

Behrenbeck, Sabine, *Der Kult um die toten Helden. Nationalsozialistische Mythen, Riten und Symbole 1923 bis 1945* (Vierow, 1996).

Behrenbeck, Sabine and Alexander Nützenadel (eds.), *Inszenierungen des Nationalstaats. Politische Feiern in Italien und Deutschland seit 1860/71* (Cologne, 2000).

Behrmann, Cynthia F., *Victorian Myths of the Sea* (Athens, OH, 1977).

Bell, Catherine, *Ritual Theory, Ritual Practice* (Oxford, 1992).

Ritual: Perspectives and Dimensions (Oxford, 1997).

Bell, Christopher M., *The Royal Navy, Seapower and Strategy between the Wars* (Stanford, 2000).

Bell, P. M. H., *France and Britain 1900–1940: Entente and Estrangement* (London and New York, 1996).

Bell, Quentin, *Virginia Woolf*, vol. 1 (London, 1972).

Bendikat, Elfi, 'Die Massenagitation der Parteien in Deutschland und Großbritannien', *Historische Mitteilungen* 5 (1992), pp. 53–77.

Berding, Helmut (ed.), *Nationales Bewußtsein und kollektive Identität: Studien zur Entwicklung des kollektiven Bewußtseins in der Neuzeit* (Frankfurt, 1994).

Berghahn, Volker R., 'Zu den Zielen des deutschen Flottenbaus unter Wilhelm II.', *Historische Zeischrift* 210 (1970), pp. 34–100.

Der Tirpitz-Plan. Genesis und Verfall einer innenpolitischen Krisenstrategie unter Wilhelm II. (Düsseldorf, 1971).

Rüstung und Machtpolitik. Zur Anatomie des "kalten Krieges" vor 1914 (Düsseldorf, 1973).

Militarism: The History of an International Debate 1861–1979 (Leamington Spa, 1981).

Germany and the Approach of War in 1914, second edition (London, 1993).

Imperial Germany, 1871–1914: Economy, Society, Culture and Politics, second edition (Providence and Oxford, 2005).

Bessel, Richard, *Germany after the First World War* (Oxford, 1993).

Political Violence and the Rise of Nazism: The Storm Troopers in Eastern Germany 1925–1934 (New Haven and London, 1984).

Bhabha, H. K. (ed.), *Nation and Narration* (London, 1990).

Biddis, Michael, *The Age of the Masses: Ideas and Society in Europe since 1870* (Harmondsworth, 1977).

Bidlingmaier, Gerhard, *Seegeltung in der deutschen Geschichte. Ein seekriegsgeschichtliches Handbuch* (Darmstadt, 1967).

Bird, Keith W., *German Naval History: A Guide to the Literature* (New York, 1985).

Birk, Gerhard, 'Der Tag von Sedan. Intentionen, Resonanz und Widerstand (1871–1895)', *Jahrbuch für Volkskunde und Kulturgeschichte* 25 (1982), pp. 95–110.

Birke, Adolf M. and Kurt Kluxen (eds.), *Deutscher und britischer Parlamentarismus* (Munich, 1985).

Blackbourn, David, *Populists and Patricians: Essays in Modern German History* (London, 1987).

Marpingen: Apparitions of the Virgin Mary in Nineteenth-Century Germany (Oxford, 1993).

' "Taking the Waters": Meeting Places of the Fashionable World', in Martin H. Geyer and Johannes Paulmann (eds.), *The Mechanics of Internationalism: Culture, Society, and Politics from the 1840s to the First World War* (Oxford, 2001), pp. 435–57.

History of Germany, 1780–1918: The Long Nineteenth Century (Oxford, 2002).

The Conquest of Nature: Water, Landscape and the Making of Modern Germany (London, 2006).

Blackbourn, David and Geoff Eley, *The Peculiarities of German History: Bourgeois Society and Politics in Nineteenth-Century Germany* (Oxford, 1984).

Blaicher, Günther, *Das Deutschlandbild in der englischen Literatur* (Darmstadt, 1992).

Blanning, T. C. W. (ed.), *Short Oxford History of Europe: The Nineteenth Century* (Oxford, 2000).

Blaschke, Olaf, 'Das 19. Jahrhundert: ein zweites konfessionelles Zeitalter?', *Geschichte und Gesellschaft* 26 (2000), pp. 38–75.

Katholozismus und Antisemitismus im Kaiserreich, second edition (Göttingen, 1999).

Blessing, Werner K., 'Der monarchische Kult, politische Loyalität und die Arbeiterbewegung im deutschen Kaiserreich', in Gerhard A. Ritter (ed.), *Arbeiterkultur* (Königstein, 1979), pp. 185–208.

'Fest und Vergnügen der "kleinen Leute"', in Richard van Dülmen and Norbert Schindler (eds.), *Volkskultur. Zur Wiederentdeckung des vergessenen Alltags (16.–20. Jahrhundert)* (Frankfurt, 1984), pp. 352–79.

Bloch, Marc, *Les rois thaumaturges. Essai sur le caractère surnaturel attribué à la puissance royale particulièrement en France et en Angleterre* (Paris, 1961).

Bloch, Maurice, *Ritual, History and Power: Selected Papers in Anthropology* (London, 1989).

Blom, Ida, Karen Hagemann and Catherine Hall (eds.), *Gendered Nations: Nationalisms and Gender Order in the Long Nineteenth Century* (Oxford, 2000).

Bölke, Stefan, *Die Marineschule Mürwik. Architekturmonographische Untersuchung eines Repräsentationsbaus der Kaiserlichen Marine* (Frankfurt, 1998).

Bösch, Frank, 'Volkstribune und Intellektuelle: W. T. Stead, Harden und die Transformation des politischen Journalismus in Großbritannien und Deutschland im 19. und 20. Jahrhundert', in Clemens Zimmermann (ed.), *Politischer Journalismus, Öffentlichkeiten, Medien im 19. und 20. Jahrhundert* (Ostfildern, 2006), pp. 99–120.

Bollinger, Ernst, *Die goldenen Jahre der Massenpresse*, second edition (Freiburg, 2002).

Bonner-Smith, D., 'Religious Ceremony at Launches', *Mariner's Mirror* 35 (1949), pp. 43–6.

Bourdieu, Pierre, *Language and Symbolic Power*, edited and introduced by John B. Thompson, translated by Gino Raymond and Matthew Adamson (Oxford, 1991).

Bourke, Joanna, *Dismembering the Male: Men's Bodies, Britain and the Great War* (London, 1996).

Working-Class Cultures in Britain 1890–1960: Gender, Class and Ethnicity (London, 1993).

Boyce, George (ed.), *Newspaper History from the Seventeenth Century to the Present Day* (London, 1978).

Brantlinger, Patrick, *Bread and Circuses: Theories of Mass Culture as Social Decay* (Ithaca, 1983).

Rule of Darkness: British Literature and Imperialism, 1830–1914 (Ithaca, 1988).

Braudel, Fernand, *The Mediterranean and the Mediterranean World in the Age of Philip II*, translated by Sian Reynolds, 2 vols. (Berkeley, 1995).

Braun, Rudolf and David Guggerli, *Macht des Tanzes – Tanz der Mächtigen. Hoffeste und Herrschaftszeremoniell 1550–1914* (Zurich, 1993).

Bremmer, Jan and Herman Roodenburg (eds.), *A Cultural History of Gesture: From Antiquity to the Present Day* (Cambridge, 1991).

Brendon, Piers, *Thomas Cook* (London, 1991).

Breuilly, John (ed.), *The State of Germany: The National Idea in the Making, Unmaking and Remaking of a Modern Nation State* (London, 1992).

Labour and Liberalism in 19th Century Europe: Essays in Comparative History (Manchester, 1992).

Breymayer, Ursula, Bernd Ulrich, and Karin Wieland (eds.), *Willensmenschen. Über deutsche Offiziere* (Frankfurt/Main, 1999).

Briggs, Asa, *History of Broadcasting in the UK*, vol. 2 (1965).

Brooks, Richard, *Fred T. Jane: An Eccentric Visionary* (Coulsdon, 1997).

Brook-Shepherd, Gordon, *Uncle of Europe: The Social and Political Life of Edward VII* (London, 1975).

Brophy, James M., 'Carnival and Citizenship: The Politics of Carnival Culture in the Prussian Rhineland, 1823–1848', *Journal of Social History* 30 (1997), pp. 873–904.

Brown, J. M., and W. R. Louis (eds.), *The Oxford History of the British Empire*, vol. 4, *The Twentieth Century* (Oxford, 1999).

Buckner, Phillip, 'The Royal Tour of 1901 and the Construction of an Imperial Identity in South Africa', *South African Historical Journal* 41 (2000), pp. 324–48.

Budick, Sanford and Wolfgang Iser (eds.), *The Translatability of Cultures: Figurations of the Space in Between* (Stanford, CA, 1996).

Buhr, Hermann de, 'Darstellung und Funktion der Hanse in den deutschen Schulbüchern der letzten hundert Jahre', *Geschichte in Wissenschaft und Unterricht* 29 (1978), pp. 693–701.

Burckhardt, Jacob, *Geschichte der Renaissance in Italien* (Stuttgart, 1878). *Die Kultur der Renaissance in Italien. Ein Versuch* (Lepizig, 1926).

Burke, Peter, *The Fabrication of Louis XIV* (New Haven and London, 1992). *Varieties of Cultural History* (Cambridge, 1997). *What is Cultural History?* (Cambridge, 2004). (ed.), *New Perspectives on Historical Writing* (Cambridge, 1991).

Burns, Elizabeth, *Theatricality* (London, 1972).

Burton, Anthony, *The Rise and Fall of British Shipbuilding* (London, 1994).

Buse, Dieter K., 'Urban and National Identity: Bremen, 1860–1920', *Journal of Social History* 26 (1993), pp. 521–37.

Cain, Peter and Tony Hopkins, *British Imperialism 1688–2000*, second edition (London, 2001).

Calhoun, Craig (ed.), *Habermas and the Public Sphere* (Cambridge, MA, 1992).

Campbell, M. and M. Rollins, (eds.), *Begetting Images: Studies in the Art and Science of Symbol Production* (New York, 1989).

Canetti, Elias, *Macht und Masse* (Hamburg, 1960).

Cannadine, David, 'War and Death, Grief and Mourning in Modern Britain', in Joachim Whaley (ed.), *Mirrors of Mortality: Studies in the Social History of Death* (London, 1981), pp. 187–242.
'The Transformation of Civic Ritual in Modern Britain: The Colchester Oyster Feast', *Past & Present* 94 (1982), pp. 107–30.
'The Context, Performance and Meaning of Ritual: The British Monarchy and the "Invention of Tradition", c. 1820–1977', in Eric Hobsbawm and Terrence Ranger (eds.), *The Invention of Tradition* (Cambridge, 1983), pp. 101–64.
The Decline and Fall of the British Aristocracy (London, 1990).
Class in Britain (London, 1998).
Ornamentalism: How the British Saw Their Empire (London, 2001).

Cannadine, David and Simon Price (eds.), *Rituals of Royalty: Power and Ceremonial in Traditional Societies* (Cambridge, 1987).

Carey, John, *The Intellectuals and the Masses: Pride and Prejudice amongst the Literary Intelligentsia, 1880–1939* (New York, 1992).

Carroll, Eber M., *Germany and the Great Powers 1866–1914: A Study in Public Opinion and Foreign Policy* (Hamden, CT, 1938).

Cattaruzza, Marina, *Arbeiter und Unternehmer auf den Werften des Kaiserreichs* (Stuttgart, 1988).

'Das Kaiserbild in der Arbeiterschaft am Beispiel der Werftarbeiter in Hamburg und Stettin', in John C. G. Röhl (ed.), *Der Ort Kaiser Wilhelms II. in der deutschen Geschichte* (Munich, 1991), pp. 131–44.

Cecil, Lamar, *Alfred Ballin* (Princeton, 1967).

Wilhelm II: Prince and Emperor, 1859–1900 (Chapel Hill and London, 1989).

Wilhelm II: Emperor and Exile, 1900–1941 (Chapel Hill and London, 1996).

Charney, Leo and Vanessa R. Schwartz (eds.), *Cinema and the Invention of Modern Life* (Berkeley, 1995).

Chartier, Roger, *Cultural History: Between Practices and Representations*, translated by Lydia G. Cochrane (Cambridge, 1988).

Chickering, Roger, *Imperial Germany and a World Without War: The Peace Movement and German Society, 1892–1914* (Princeton, 1975).

We Men Who Feel Most German: A Cultural Study of the Pan-German League, 1886–1914 (London, 1984).

(ed.), *Imperial Germany: A Historiographical Companion* (Westport and London, 1996).

Christian Fälschle, *Rivalität als Prinzip. Die englische Demokratie im Denken des Wilhelminischen Deutschland 1900–1914* (Frankfurt, 1991).

Churchill, Winston, *A History of the English-Speaking Peoples* (London, 1956–8).

Clark, Anna, 'Contested Space: The Public and Private Spheres in Nineteenth-Century Britain', *Journal of British Studies* 35 (1996), pp. 269–76.

Clark, Christopher, *Kaiser Wilhelm II* (Harlow, 2000).

Clark, Christopher and Wolfram Kaiser (eds.), *Culture Wars: Secular-Catholic Conflict in Nineteenth-Century Europe* (Cambridge, 2003).

Clark, J. C. D., 'English History's Forgotten Context: Scotland, Ireland, Wales', *Historical Journal* 32 (1989), pp. 211–28.

'Protestantism, Nationalism, and National Identity, 1660–1832', *Historical Journal* 43 (2000), pp. 249–79.

Clarke, I. F., *Voices Prophesying War: Future Wars 1763–3749*, second edition (Oxford, 1992).

Clarke, Peter, *Hope and Glory: Britain 1900–1990* (Harmondsworth, 1996).

Coetzee, Marilyn S., *The German Army League: Popular Nationalism in Wilhelmine Germany* (Oxford, 1990).

Cohen, Deborah and Maura O'Connor (eds.), *Comparison and History: Europe in Cross-National Perspective* (New York and London, 2004).

Coleman, K. M., 'Launching into History: Aquatic Displays in the Early Empire', *Journal of Roman Studies* 83 (1993), pp. 48–74.

Colley, Linda, 'Britishness and Otherness: An Argument', *Journal of British Studies* 31 (1992), pp. 309–29.

Britons: Forging the Nation 1707–1837 (London, 1994).

Colls, Robert, *The Identity of England* (Oxford, 2002).

Colls, Robert and P. Dodd, (eds.), *Englishness: Politics and Culture 1880–1920* (London, 1986).

Confino, Alon, *The Nation as a Local Metaphor: Württemberg, Imperial Germany, and National Memory, 1871–1918* (Chapel Hill and London, 1997).

Conrad, Sebastian and Jürgen Osterhammel, *Das Kaiserreich transnational* (Göttingen, 2004).

Conze, Werner and Michael Geyer, 'Militarismus', in Otto Brunner, Werner Konze, Reinhart Koselleck (eds.), *Geschichtliche Grundbegriffe*, vol. 4 (Stuttgart, 1978), pp. 1–47.

Coppet, Daniel de (ed.), *Understanding Rituals* (London, 1992).

Corbin, Alain, *The Lure of the Sea: The Discovery of the Seaside in the Western World 1750–1840* (London, 1995).

Crary, Jonathan, *Techniques of the Observer: On Vision and Modernity in the Nineteenth Century* (Cambridge, MA, 1992).

Cross, Gary S. *The Playful Crowd: Pleasure Places in the Twentieth Century* (New York, 2005).

Cubitt, Geoffrey and Allen Warren (eds.), *Heroic Reputations and Exemplary Lives* (Manchester University Press, 2000).

Cunningham, Hugh, 'The Language of Patriotism, 1750–1914', *History Workshop Journal* 12 (1981), pp. 8–33.

Czisnik, Marianne, *Horatio Nelson: A Controversial Hero* (London, 2005).

Daniel, Ute and Wolfram Siemann (eds.), *Propaganda. Meinungskampf, Verführung und politische Sinnstiftung 1789–1989* (Stuttgart, 1994).

Daniels, Stephen, *Fields of Vision: Landscape, Imagery and National Identity in England and the United States* (Cambridge, 1993).

Dann, Otto, *Nation und Nationalismus in Deutschland 1770–1990* (Munich, 1993).

(ed.), *Die deutsche Nation. Geschichte, Probleme, Perspektiven* (Vierow, 1994).

Darnton, Robert, 'The Symbolic Element in History', *Journal of Modern History* 58 (1986), pp. 218–34.

Daunton, Martin J. (ed.), *The Cambridge Urban History of Britain*, vol. 3, *1840–1950* (Cambridge, 2000).

Daunton, Martin J. and Bernhard Rieger (eds.), *Meanings of Modernity: Britain in the Age of Imperialism and World Wars* (Oxford, 2001).

David, Robert G., *The Arctic in the British Imagination 1818–1914* (Manchester, 2000).

Davidoff, Leonore, *The Best Circles: Society, Etiquette and the Season* (London, 1986).

Worlds Between: Historical Perspectives on Gender and Class (Cambridge, 1995).

Davies, Norman, *The Isles* (London, 1999).

Davis, Natalie Zemon, *Society and Culture in Early Modern France* (Stanford, 1975).

Dawson, Graham, *Soldier Heroes: British Adventure, Empire and the Imagining of Masculinities* (London, 1994).

Debord, Guy, *The Society of the Spectacle*, translated by Donald Nicholson-Smith (New York, 1992, first published in 1967).

Dehio, Ludwig, *Gleichgewicht oder Hegemonie. Betrachtungen über ein Grundproblem der neueren Geschichte* (Krefeld, 1948).

Deist, Wilhelm, *Flottenpolitik und Flottenpropaganda. Das Nachrichtenbureau des Reichsmarineamtes 1897–1914* (Stuttgart, 1976).

Militär, Staat und Gesellschaft. Studien zur preußisch-deutschen Militärgeschichte (Munich, 1991).

Delap, Lucy, '"Thus Does Man Prove His Fitness to Be the Master of Things": Shipwrecks, Chivalry and Masculinities in Nineteenth and Twentieth-Century Britain', *Cultural and Social History* 3 (2006), pp. 45–74.

Dening, Greg, *Mr Bligh's Bad Language: Passion, Power and Theatre on the Bounty* (Cambridge, 1992).

Dering, Florian, Margarete Gröner and Manfred Wegner, *Heute Hinrichtung. Jahrmarkts- und Varietéattraktionen der Schausteller-Dynastie Schichtl* (Munich, 1990).

Deutsche Militärgeschichte in sechs Bänden, edited by the Militärgeschichtliches Forschungsamt, vol. 5, *Marinegeschichte der Neuzeit* (Herrsching, 1983).

Diekmann, Irene, Peter Krüger and Julius H. Schoeps (eds.) *Geopolitik: Grenzgänge im Zeitgeist*, vol. 1 (Potsdam 2000).

Dockrill, Michael and Brian J. C. McKercher (eds.), *Diplomacy and World Power: Festschrift Zara Steiner* (Cambridge, 1996).

Doerry, Martin, *Übergangsmenschen. Die Mentalität der Wilhelminer und die Krise des Kaiserreichs* (Weinheim, 1986).

Döhring, R.: 'Nationalfeiertag und sozialistisches Geschichtsbewusstsein', *Beiträge zur Geschichte der Arbeiterbewegungen* 31 (1989), pp. 595–604.

Dörner, Andreas, *Politischer Mythos und symbolische Politik. Sinnstiftung durch symbolische Formen am Beispiel des Hermannsmythos* (Opladen, 1995).

Dotzauer, Winfried, 'Die Ankunft des Herrschers. Der fürstliche "Einzug" in die Stadt (bis zum Ende des alten Reiches)', *Archiv für Kulturgeschichte* 55 (1973), pp. 245–88.

Douglas, Mary, *Purity and Danger: An Analysis of the Concepts of Pollution and Taboo* (London, 1996).

Duchhardt, Heinz, 'Die Hanse und das europäische Mächtesystem des frühen 17. Jahrhunderts', in Antjekathrin Grassmann (ed.), *Niedergang oder Übergang? Zur Spätzeit der Hanse im 16. und 17. Jahrhundert* (Cologne, Weimar, Vienna, 1998), pp. 11–24.

Düding, Dieter, 'Deutsche Nationalfeste im 19. Jahrhundert. Erscheinungsbild und politische Funktion', *Archiv für Kulturgeschichte* 69 (1987), pp. 371–388.

Düding, Dieter, Peter Friedemann and Paul Münch (eds.), *Öffentliche Festkultur. Politische Feste in Deutschland von der Aufklärung bis zum Ersten Weltkrieg* (Reinbek, 1988).

Dudink, Stefan, Karen Hagemann and John Tosh (eds.), *Masculinities in Politics and War: Gendering Modern History* (Manchester, 2004).

Dülffer, Jost and Karl Holl (eds.), *Bereit zum Krieg. Kriegsmentalität im wilhelminischen Deutschland, 1890–1914* (Göttingen, 1986).

Dülmen, Richard van and Norbert Schindler (eds.), *Volkskultur. Zur Wiederentdeckung des vergessenen Alltags* (Frankfurt, 1987).

Duppler, Jörg, *Der Juniorpartner. England und die Entwicklung der Deutschen Marine 1848–1890* (Herford, 1985).
Germania auf dem Meere. Bilder und Dokumente zur Deutschen Marinegeschichte 1848–1998 (Hamburg, 1998).
Durkheim, Emile, *The Elementary Forms of Religious Life*, translated and with an introduction by Karen E. Fields (New York, 1995).
Eco, Umberto, *Travels in Hyperreality*, translated by William Weaver (San Diego, 1986).
Edelman, Murray, *The Symbolic Use of Politics* (Urbana, 1964).
Constructing the Political Spectacle (Chicago, 1988).
Eisenberg, Christiane, 'Pferderennen zwischen "Händler-" und "Heldenkultur". Verlauf und Dynamik einer englisch-deutschen Kulturbegegnung', in Hartmut Berghoff and Dieter Ziegler (eds.), *Pionier und Nachzügler? Vergleichende Studien zur Geschichte Englands und Deutschlands im Zeitalter der Industrialisierung* (Bochum, 1995), pp. 235–258.
"English sports" und deutsche Bürger. Eine Gesellschaftsgeschichte 1800–1939 (Paderborn, 1999).
Eley, Geoff, 'State Formation, Nationalism and Political Culture in Nineteenth-Century Germany', in Raphael Samuel and Gareth Stedman Jones (eds.), *Culture, Ideology and Politics: Essays for Eric Hobsbawm* (London, 1982), pp. 277–30.
'The View from the Throne: The Personal Rule of Kaiser Wilhelm II', *Historical Journal* 28 (1985), pp. 469–85.
From Unification to Nazism: Reinterpreting the German Past (London, 1986).
Reshaping the German Right: Radical Nationalism and Political Change after Bismarck, with new introduction (Ann Arbor, 1991).
(ed.), *Society, Culture and the State in Germany, 1870–1930* (Ann Arbor, 1996).
Eley, Geoff and James Retallack (eds.), *Wilhelminism and its Legacies: German Modernities, Imperialism, and the Meaning of Reform, 1890–1930: Essays for Hartmut Pogge von Strandmann* (Oxford, 2003).
Eley, Geoff and Ronald Grigor Suny (eds.), *Becoming National* (Oxford, 1996).
Elias, Norbert, *Die höfische Gesellschaft* (Darmstadt, 1969).
Ellis, John S., 'Reconciling the Celt: British National Identity, Empire, and the 1911 Investiture of the Prince of Wales', *Journal of British Studies* 37 (1998), pp. 391–418.
Elsaesser, Thomas, 'Wilhelminisches Kino: Stil und Industrie', *Kintop* 1 (1992), pp. 10–27.
(ed.), *A Second life: German Cinema's First Decades* (Amsterdam, 1996).
Filmgeschichte und frühes Kino. Archäologie eines Medienwandels (Munich, 2002).
Elsner, Tobias von, *Kaisertage. Die Hamburger und das Wilhelminische Deutschland im Spiegel öffentlicher Festkultur* (Frankfurt, 1991).
Elvert, Jürgen, Jürgen Jensen and Michael Salewski (eds.), *Kiel, die Deutschen und die See* (Stuttgart, 1992).
Epkenhans, Michael, *Die wilhelminische Flottenrüstung 1908–1914. Weltmachtstreben, industrieller Fortschritt, soziale Integration* (Munich, 1991).

'Aspekte des deutschen Englandbildes 1800–1914: Vorbild und Rivale', *Westfälische Forschungen* 44 (1994), pp. 329–42.

'Die kaiserliche Marine im Ersten Weltkrieg', in Wolfgang Michalka (ed.), *Der Erste Weltkrieg. Wirkung, Wahrnehmung, Analyse* (Munich, 1994), pp. 319–40.

'"Der Dreizack gehört in unsere Faust." Die Bedeutung von "Seemacht" im kaiserlichen Deutschland', in *Liberalismus, Parlamentarismus und Demokratie: Festschrift für Manfred Botzenhart zum 60. Geburtstag* (Göttingen, 1994), pp. 191–211.

'Alfred von Tirpitz (1849–1930)', in Michael Fröhlich (ed.), *Das Kaiserreich. Portrait einer Epoche in Biographien* (Darmstadt, 2001), pp. 228–39.

Espagne, Michel, 'Sur les limites du comparatisme en histoire culturelle', *Genèses* 17 (1994), pp. 112–21.

Les transferts culturels franco-allemands (Paris, 1999).

Espagne, Michel and Michaël Werner (eds.), *Transferts: les relations interculturell dans l'espace franco-allemand, XVIIIe et XIX siècle* (Paris, 1988).

Esser, Frank, *Die Kräfte hinter den Schlagzeilen. Englischer und deutscher Journalismus im Vergleich* (Freiburg, 1998).

Evans, Ellen L., *The Cross and the Ballot: Catholic Political Parties in Germany, Switzerland, Austria, Belgium and the Netherlands, 1785–1985* (Boston, 1999).

Evans, Eric, 'From English to Britons? Nationhood in the Nineteenth Century', in Claus Bjørn (ed.), *Social and Political Identities in Western History* (Copenhagen, 1994), pp. 193–213.

Evans, Richard J., *The Feminist Movement in Germany, 1894–1933* (London, 1976).

'"Red Wednesday" in Hamburg: Social Democrats, Police and *Lumpenproletariat* in the Suffrage Disturbances of 17 January 1906', *Social History* 4 (1979), pp. 1–31.

Death in Hamburg: Society and Politics in the Cholera Years, 1830–1910 (Oxford, 1987).

Rethinking German History: Nineteenth-Century Germany and the Origins of the Third Reich (London, 1987).

Kneipengespräche im Kaiserreich. Die Stimmungsberichte der Hamburger Politischen Polizei 1892–1914 (Reinbek/Hamburg, 1989).

Rituals of Retribution: Capital Punishment in Germany 1600–1987 (Oxford, 1996).

Rereading German History from Unification to Reunification, 1800–1996 (London, 1997).

In Defence of History (London, 1997).

Eyck, Erich, *Das persönliche Regiment Wilhelms II. Politische Geschichte des deutschen Kaiserreichs von 1890 bis 1914* (Zurich, 1948).

Featherstone, Donald F., *Naval War Games: Fighting Sea Battles with Model Ships* (London, 1965).

Fehrenbach, Elisabeth, *Wandlungen des deutschen Kaisergedankens 1871–1918* (Munich, 1969).

'Über die Bedeutung der politischen Symbole im Nationalstaat', *Historische Zeitschrift* 213 (1971), pp. 296–357.

Ferguson, Niall, *The Pity of War* (London, 1998).

Fesser, Gerd, *Der Traum vom Platz an der Sonne. Deutsche 'Weltpolitik' 1897–1914* (Bremen, 1996).

Reichskanzler Fürst von Bülow. Architekt der deutschen Weltpolitik (Leipzig, 2003).
Finamore, Daniel (ed.), *Maritime History as World History* (Gainsville, 2004).
Findling, John E. (ed.), *Historical Dictionary of World's Fairs and Expositions, 1851–1988* (New York, 1990).
Firchow, Peter E., *The Death of the German Cousin: Variations on a Literary Stereotype, 1890–1920* (Lewisburg, 1986).
Fischer, Fritz, *Griff nach der Weltmacht. Die Kriegszielpolitik des kaiserlichen Deutschland 1914/18* (Düsseldorf, 1961).
Krieg der Illusionen. Die deutsche Politik von 1911 bis 1914 (Düsseldorf, 1969).
Fischer, Jörg-Uwe, *Admiral des Kaisers. Georg Alexander von Müller als Chef des Marinekabinetts Wilhelms II.* (Frankfurt, 1992).
'Die Faszination des Technischen. Die parlamentarische Studienreise zur kaiserlichen Flotte vor 1914', *Zeitschrift für Geschichtswissenschaft* 40 (1992), pp. 1150–6.
Flacke, Monika (ed.), *Mythen der Nationen. Ein europäisches Panorama* (Berlin, 1998).
Föhles, Eleonore, *Kulturkampf und katholisches Milieu in den niederrheinischen Kreisen Kempen und Geldern und der Stadt Viersen* (Viersen, 1995).
Förster, Stig, *Der doppelte Militarismus. Die deutsche Heeresrüstungspolitik zwischen Status-quo-Sicherung und Aggression 1890–1913* (Stuttgart, 1985).
Foucault, Michel, *Discipline and Punish: The Birth of the Prison*, translated by Alan Sheridan (London, 1977).
'Of Other Spaces', *Diacritics* 16 (1986), pp. 22–7.
François, Etienne and Hagen Schulze (eds.), *Deutsche Erinnerungsorte*, 3 vols. (Munich, 2001).
François, Etienne, Hannes Siegrist and Jakob Vogel (eds.), *Nation und Emotion. Deutschland und Frankreich im Vergleich. 19. und 20. Jahrhundert* (Göttingen, 1995).
French, David, 'Spy Fever in Britain, 1900–1915', *Historical Journal* 21 (1978), pp. 355–70.
Frevert, Ute (ed.), *Bürgerinnen und Bürger. Geschlechterverhältnisse im 19. Jahrhundert* (Göttingen, 1988).
Militär und Gesellschaft im 19. und 20. Jahrhundert (Stuttgart, 1997).
Die kasernierte Nation. Militärdienst und Zivilgesellschaft in Deutschland (Munich, 2001).
Ehrenmänner. Das Duell in der bürgerlichen Gesellschaft (Munich, 1991).
'Soldaten, Staatsbürger. Überlegungen zur historischen Konstruktion von Männlichkeit', in T. Kühne (ed.), *Männergeschichte – Geschlechtergeschichte. Männlichkeit im Wandel der Moderne* (Frankfurt, 1996), pp. 65–91.
Friedberg, Aaron L., *The Weary Titan: Britain and the Experience of Relative Decline, 1895–1905* (Princeton, 1988).
Friedjung, Heinrich, *Das Zeitalter des Imperialismus 1884–1914*, 3 vols. (Berlin, 1919–22).
Friedrich, Karin (ed.), *Festive Culture in Germany and Europe from the Sixteenth to the Twentieth Century* (Lewiston, 2000).
Friedrichsmeyer, Sara, Sara Lennox and Susanne Zantop (eds.), *The Imperialist Imagination: German Colonialism and its Legacy* (Ann Arbor, 1998).

Fritzsche, Peter, *Rehearsals for Fascism: Populism and Political Mobilization in Weimar Germany* (Oxford, 1990).

A Nation of Fliers: German Aviation and the Popular Imagination (Cambridge, MA, 1992).

Reading Berlin 1900 (Cambridge, MA, 1996).

Germans into Nazis (Cambridge, MA, 1998).

Fröhlich, Michael, *Von Konfrontation zu Koexistenz. Die deutsch-englischen Kolonialbeziehungen in Afrika zwischen 1884 und 1914* (Bochum, 1990).

(ed.), *Das Kaiserreich. Portrait einer Epoche in Biographien* (Darmstadt, 2001).

Fuchs, Peter, 'Vaterland, Patriotismus und Moral. Zur Semantik gesellschaftlicher Einheit', *Zeitschrift für Soziologie* 20 (1991), pp. 89–103.

Fullerton, R. A., 'Toward a Commercial Popular Culture in Germany', *Journal of Social History* 12 (1978/79), pp. 489–511.

Gade, Christel, *Gleichgewichtspolitik oder Bündnispflege? Maximen britischer Außenpolitik, 1909–1914* (Göttingen and Zurich, 1997).

Garvin, James L. and Julian Amery, *The Life of Joseph Chamberlain*, 6 vols. (London, 1932–69).

Gavin, C. M., *Royal Yachts* (London, 1932).

Gay, Peter, *The Cultivation of Hatred: The Bourgeois Experience: Victoria to Freud* (London, 1993).

Gebhardt, Hardtwig, '"Der Kaiser kommt!". Das Verhältnis von Volk und Herrschaft in der massenmedialen Ikonographie um 1900', in Anette Graczyk (ed.), *Das Volk. Abbild, Konstruktion, Phantasma* (Berlin, 1996), pp. 63–82.

Geertz, Clifford, *The Interpretation of Cultures* (London, 1975).

'Centers, Kings and Charismas: Reflections on the Symbolics of Power', in J. Ben-David and T. N. Clark (eds.), *Culture and its Creators* (Chicago, 1977).

Negara: The Theatre-State in Nineteenth-Century Bali (Princeton, 1980).

Local Knowledge (New York, 1983).

Geisthövel, Alexa, 'Der Strand', in Alexa Geisthövel and Habbo Knoch (eds.), *Orte der Moderne: Erfahrungswelten des 19. und 20. Jahrhunderts* (Frankfurt, 2005), pp. 121–130.

Gennep, Arnold van, *The Rites of Passage* (Chicago, 1960).

Gerwarth, Robert, *The Bismarck Myth: Weimar Germany and the Legacy of the Iron Chancellor* (Oxford, 2005).

Giessler, Klaus-Volker, *Die Institution des Marineattachés im Kaiserreich* (Boppard, 1976).

Girouard, Mark, *The Return to Camelot: Chivalry and the English Gentleman* (New Haven, 1981).

Glaser, Hermann, *Die Kultur der wilhelminischen Zeit. Topographie einer Epoche* (Frankfurt, 1984).

Golby, J. M. and A. W. Purdue, *The Civilisation of the Crowd: Popular Culture in England 1750–1900* (London, 1984).

Gollin, Alfred M., 'England Is No Longer an Island: The Phantom Airship Scare of 1909', *Albion* 13 (1981), pp. 43–57.

No Longer an Island: Britain and the Wright Brothers, 1902–1909 (Stanford, 1984).

Goltermann, Svenja, *Körper der Nation. Habitusformierung und die Politik des Turnens 1860–1880* (Göttingen, 1998).

Gordon, Ambrose, *The Invisible Tent: The War Novels of Ford Madox Ford* (Austin, Texas, 1964).

Gough, Barry M., 'The Royal Navy and the British Empire', in Robin W. Winks (ed.), *The Oxford History of the British Empire*, vol. 5, *Historiography* (Oxford, 2000).

Grant, Alexander and Keith J. Stringer (eds.), *Uniting the Kingdom? The Making of British History* (London, 1996).

Grassmann, Antjekathrin (ed.), *Niedergang oder Übergang? Zur Spätzeit der Hanse im 16. und 17. Jahrhundert* (Cologne, Weimar, Vienna, 1998).

Grebing, Helga, *Der 'deutsche Sonderweg' in Europa 1806–1945. Eine Kritik* (Stuttgart, 1986).

Green, Abigail, *Fatherlands: State-Building and Nationhood in Nineteenth-Century Germany* (Cambridge, 2001).

Greenhalgh, Paul, 'Art, Politics, and Society at the Franco-British Exhibition of 1908', *Art History* 8 (1985), pp. 434–52.

Ephemeral Vistas: The Expositions Universelles, Great Exhibitions and World's Fairs, 1851–1939 (Manchester, 1988).

Gries, Rainer and Wolfgang Schmale (eds.), *Kultur der Propaganda* (Bochum, 2004).

Grießmer, Axel, *Massenverbände und Massenparteien im wilhelminischen Reich. Zum Wandel der Wahlkultur 1903–1912* (Düsseldorf, 2000).

Groh, Dieter, 'Cäsarismus, Bonapartismus, Führer, Chef, Imperialismus', in Otto Brunner, Werner Konze, Reinhart Koselleck (eds.), *Geschichtliche Grundbegriffe*, vol. 1 (Stuttgart, 1972), pp. 726–71.

Grüttner, Michael, *Arbeitswelt an der Wasserkante. Sozialgeschichte der Hamburger Hafenarbeiter 1886–1914* (Göttingen, 1984).

Gunzenhäuser, Max, 'Die Marine-Rundschau 1890–1914. Bericht und Bibliographie', *Jahresbibliographie der Bibliothek für Zeitgeschichte* 49 (1977), pp. 417–61.

Habermas, Jürgen, *Strukturwandel der Öffentlichkeit. Untersuchungen zu einer Kategorie der bürgerlichen Gesellschaft. Mit einem Vorwort zur Neuauflage 1990* (Frankfurt, 1995).

Hale, Oron J., *Publicity and Diplomacy: With Special Reference to England and Germany 1890–1914* (New York, 1940).

Hall, Catherine (ed.), *Cultures of Empire: Colonizers in Britain and the Empire in the Nineteenth and Twentieth Centuries* (Manchester, 2000).

Hamilton, C. I., 'Naval Hagiography and the Victorian Hero', *Historical Journal* 23 (1980), pp. 381–98.

Hamilton, W. Mark, *The Nation and the Navy: Methods and Organization of British Navalist Propaganda, 1889–1914* (New York and London, 1986).

Hammerton, Elizabeth and David Cannadine, 'Conflict and Consensus on a Ceremonial Occasion: The Diamond Jubilee in Cambridge in 1897', *Historical Journal* 24 (1981), pp. 111–46.

Handelman, Don, *Models and Mirrors: Towards an Anthropology of Public Events* (Cambridge, 1990).

Hansen, C. B., 'Schiffstaufen', in Volker Plagemann (ed.), *Übersee. Seefahrt und Seemacht im deutschen Kaiserreich* (Munich, 1988), pp. 140–2.

Hardtwig, Wolfgang, *Geschichtskultur und Wissenschaft* (Munich, 1990).

Hardtwig, Wolfgang and Hans-Ulrich Wehler (eds.), *Kulturgeschichte heute* (Göttingen, 1996).

Harley, Basil, *Toy Boats* (Haverfordwest, 1987).

Harrington, Ralph, '"The Mighty Hood": Navy, Empire, War at Sea and the British National Imagination, 1920–60', *Journal of Contemporary History* 38 (2003), pp. 171–85.

Harris, Jose, *Private Lives, Public Spirit: Britain 1870–1914* (Harmondsworth, 1993).

Harrison, Brian, *Peaceable Kingdom: Stability and Change in Modern Britain* (Oxford, 1982).

The Transformation of British Politics (Oxford, 1996).

Hartmann, Jürgen, *Staatszeremoniell* (Cologne, 1990).

Hartung, Fritz, 'Das persönliche Regiment Kaiser Wilhelms II.', *Sitzungsberichte der deutschen Akademie der Wissenschaften zu Berlin* 3 (1952), pp. 4–20.

Hastings, Adrian, *The Construction of Nationhood: Ethnicity, Religion and Nationalism* (Cambridge, 1997).

Hattendorf, John B. (ed.), *The Influence of History on Mahan: The Proceedings of a Conference Marking the Centenary of Alfred Thayer Mahan's 'The Influence of Sea Power Upon History, 1660–1783'* (Newport, RI, 1991).

Ubi sumus? The State of Naval and Maritime History (Newport, RI, 1994).

Haug, Walter and Rainer Warning (eds.), *Das Fest* (Munich, 1989).

Haupt, Heinz-Gerhard and Jürgen Kocka (eds.), *Geschichte und Vergleich* (Frankfurt, 1996).

'Comparative History: Methods, Aims, Problems', in Deborah Cohen and Maura O'Connor (eds.), *Comparison and History: Europe in Cross-National Perspective* (New York and London, 2004), pp. 23–39.

Hävernick, Walter, *Der Matrosenanzug der Hamburger Jungen 1890–1939* (Hamburg, 1962).

Hawkins, *Social Darwinism in European and American Thought 1860–1945: Nature as Model and Nature as Threat* (Cambridge, 1997).

Headrick, Daniel R., *The Invisible Weapon: Telecommunications and International Politics, 1851–1945* (New York, 1991).

The Tools of Empire: Technology and European Imperialism in the Nineteenth Century (Oxford, 1991).

Heinemann, Ulrich, *Die verdrängte Niederlage. Politische Öffentlichkeit und Kriegsschuldfrage in der Weimarer Republik* (Göttingen, 1983).

Hennock, E. P., *Fit and Proper Persons: Ideal and Reality in Nineteenth-Century Urban Government* (London, 1973).

Herrmann, David G., *The Arming of Europe* (Princeton, 1996).

Herwig, Holger, *Das Elitekorps des Kaisers. Die Marineoffiziere im Wilhelminischen Deutschland* (Hamburg, 1977).

'Luxury' Fleet: The Imperial German Navy 1888–1918 (London, 1980).

'The Failure of German Sea Power, 1914–1915: Mahan, Tirpitz, and Raeder Reconsidered', *International History Review* 10 (1988), pp. 68–105.

'The German Reaction to the Dreadnought Revolution', *International History Review* 13 (1991), pp. 273–83.

Hettling, Manfred and Paul Nolte (eds.), *Bürgerliche Feste. Symbolische Formen politischen Handelns im 19. Jahrhundert* (Göttingen, 1993).

Hewitson, Mark, 'The Kaiserreich in Question: Constitutional Crisis in Germany Before the First World War', *Journal of Modern History* 73 (2001), pp. 725–80.

Germany and the Causes of the First World War (Oxford and New York, 2004).

Higson, Andrew (ed.), *Young and Innocent? The Cinema in Britain, 1896–1930* (Exeter, 2002).

Hildebrand, Klaus, '"British Interests" und "Pax Britannica". Grundfragen englischer Außenpolitik im 19. und 20. Jahrhundert', *Historische Zeitschrift* 221 (1975), pp. 623–39.

'Zwischen Allianz und Antagonismus. Das Problem bilateraler Normalität in den britisch-deutschen Beziehungen des 19. Jahrhunderts (1870–1914)', in *Weltpolitik. Europagedanke. Regionalismus. Festschrift Gollwitzer* (Münster, 1982), pp. 305–31.

Deutsche Außenpolitik 1871–1918, second edition (Munich, 1994).

Das vergangene Reich. Deutsche Außenpolitik von Bismarck bis Hitler 1871–1945 (Stuttgart, 1995).

(ed.), *Das Deutsche Reich im Urteil der Großen Mächte und europäischen Nachbarn, 1871–1945* (Munich, 1995).

Hiley, Nicholas, 'The Failure of British Counter-Espionage against Germany, 1907–1914', *Historical Journal* 28 (1985), pp. 835–62.

Hillmann, Jörg and Reinhard Scheiblich, '*Das rote Schloß am Meer'. Die Marineschule Mürwik seit ihrer Gründung* (Hamburg, 2002).

Hinsley, Francis H. (ed.), *British Foreign Policy under Sir Edward Grey* (Cambridge, 1977).

Hobsbawm, Eric, *The Age of Empire 1875–1914* (London, 1987).

Nations and Nationalism Since 1780: Programme, Myth, Reality, second edition (Cambridge, 1994).

Hobsbawm, Eric and Terrence Ranger (eds.), *The Invention of Tradition* (Cambridge, 1983).

Hobson, Rolf, *Imperialism at Sea: Naval Strategic Thought, the Ideology of Sea Power and the Tirpitz Plan, 1875–1914* (Boston and Leiden, 2002).

Holl, Karl, Hans Kloft and Gerd Fesser (eds.), *Caligula – Wilhelm II. und der Cäsarenwahnsinn. Antikenrezeption und wilhelminische Politik am Beispiel des 'Caligula' von Ludwig Quidde* (Bremen, 2001).

Hollenberg, Günter, *Englisches Interesse am Kaiserreich. Die Attraktivität Preußen-Deutschlands für konservative und liberale Kreise in Großbritannien 1860–1914* (Wiesbaden, 1974).

Homans, Margaret and Adrienne Munich (eds.), *Remaking Queen Victoria* (Cambridge, 1997).

Honold, Alexander and Klaus R. Scherpe (eds.), *Mit Deutschland um die Welt. Eine Kulturgeschichte des Fremden in der Kolonialzeit* (Stuttgart, 2004).

Hopkins, A. G., 'Back to the Future: From National History to Imperial History', *Past & Present* 164 (1999), pp. 218–36.

Hopkins, Keith, *Death and Renewal: Sociological Studies in Roman History* (Cambridge, 1983).

Horden, Peregrine and Nicholas Purcell, *The Corrupting Sea: A Study of Mediterranean History* (Oxford, 2000).

'The Mediterranean and "the New Thalassology"', *American Historical Review* 111 (2006), pp. 722–40.

Hormann, Jörg-Michael, *Willy Stöwer. Marinemaler der Kaiserzeit. Leben und Werk* (Hamburg, 2001).

Howard, Michael, *Studies in War and Peace* (London, 1970).

The Continental Commitment: The Dilemma of British Defence Policy in the Era of the Two World Wars, second edition (London, 1989).

Hubatsch, Walther, *Die Ära Tirpitz. Studien zur deutschen Marinepolitik 1890–1918* (Göttingen, 1955).

Der Admiralstab und die obersten Marinebehörden in Deutschland 1848–1945 (Frankfurt, 1958).

(ed.), *Navalismus. Wechselwirkung von Seeinteressen, Politik und Technik im 19. und 20. Jahrhundert* (Koblenz, 1983).

Huber, Ernst Rudolf, *Deutsche Verfassungsgeschichte seit 1789*, vol. 4, *Struktur und Krisen des Kaiserreichs* (Stuttgart, 1969).

'Das persönliche Regiment Kaiser Wilhelms II.', in Ernst-Wolfgang Böckenförde (ed.), *Moderne deutsche Verfassungsgeschichte (1815–1918)* (Cologne, 1972), pp. 282–303.

Huizinga, Johan, *Homo Ludens: A Study in the Play-Elements in Culture* (London, 1980, first published in 1938).

Hull, Isabel V., *The Entourage of Kaiser Wilhelm II, 1888–1918* (Cambridge, 1982).

Absolute Destruction: Military Culture and the Practices of War in Imperial Germany (Ithaca, 2005).

Hunt, Lynn (ed.), *The New Cultural History* (Berkeley, 1989).

Hynes, Samuel, *The Edwardian Turn of Mind* (Princeton, 1968).

A War Imagined: The First World War and English Culture (London, 1990).

Jaacks, Gisela, 'Hermann, Barbarossa, Germania und Hammonia. Nationalsymbole in Hamburger Festzügen des Kaiserreichs', *Beiträge zur deutschen Volks- und Altertumskunde* 18 (1979).

Jeismann, Michael, *Das Vaterland der Feinde. Studien zum nationalen Feindbegriff und Selbstverständnis in Deutschland und Frankreich 1792–1918* (Stuttgart, 1992).

Jenkins, Jennifer, *Provincial Modernity: Local Culture and Liberal Politics in Fin-de-Siècle Hamburg* (Ithaca, 2003).

Jensen, Jürgen and Peter Wulf (eds.), *Geschichte der Stadt Kiel* (Neumünster, 1991).

Johe, Werner (ed.), *Hitler in Hamburg. Dokumente zu einem besonderen Verhältnis* (Hamburg, 1996).

Joll, James, *1914. The Unspoken Assumptions: An Inaugural Lecture* (London, 1968).

The Origins of the First World War, second edition (London, 1992).

Jones, Larry Eugene and James Retallack (eds.), *Elections, Mass Politics, and Social Change in Modern Germany* (Washington, DC, 1992).

Jones, Max, *The Last Great Quest: Captain Scott's Antarctic Sacrifice* (Oxford, 2003).

Joyce, Patrick, *Visions of the People: Industrial England and the Question of Class, 1848–1914* (Cambridge, 1991).

Judd, Alan, *Ford Madox Ford* (London, 1990).

Judd, Denis, *Empire: The British Imperial Experience from 1765 to the Present* (London, 1996).

Kaelble, Hartmut, *Der historische Vergleich. Eine Einführung zum 19. und 20. Jahrhundert* (Frankfurt, 1999).

Kaelble, Hartmut and Jürgen Schriewer (ed.), *Vergleich und Transfer. Komparatistik in den Sozial-, Geschichts- und Kulturwissenschaften* (Frankfurt and New York, 2003).

Kamberger, Klaus, *Flottenpropaganda unter Tirpitz. Öffentliche Meinung und Schlachtflottenbau, 1897–1900* (Vienna, 1966).

Kantorowicz, Ernest, *Laudes Regiae: A Study in Liturgical Acclamations and Medieval Ruler Worship* (Berkeley, 1946).

The King's Two Bodies: A Study in Medieval Political Theology (Princeton, 1957).

Selected Studies (New York, 1965).

Kaschuba, Wolfgang, 'Ritual und Fest. Das Volk auf der Straße. Figurationen und Funktionen populärer Öffentlichkeit zwischen Frühneuzeit und Moderne', in R. Van Dülmen (ed.), *Dynamik der Tradition* (Frankfurt, 1992), pp. 240–67.

Kearny, Hugh, *The British Isles: A History of Four Nations* (Cambridge, 1989).

Kehr, Eckart, *Schlachtflottenbau und Parteipolitik 1894–1901. Versuch eines Querschnitts durch die innenpolitischen, sozialen und ideologischen Voraussetzungen des deutschen Imperialismus* (Berlin, 1930).

Der Primat der Innenpolitik. Gesammelte Aufsätze zur preußisch-deutschen Sozialgeschichte im 19. und 20. Jahrhundert, edited by Hans-Ulrich Wehler, second edition (Berlin, 1970).

Kemp, Peter (ed.), *The Oxford Companion to Ships and the Sea* (Oxford, 1988).

Kenefick, William, *'Rebellious and Contrary': The Glasgow Dockers, 1853 to 1932* (East Linton, 2000).

Kennedy, Paul M., 'Idealists and Realists: British Views of Germany, 1864–1939', *Transactions of the Royal Historical Society*, 5th Series, 24 (1975), pp. 137–56.

(ed.), *The War Plans of the Great Powers 1880–1914* (Boston, 1979).

The Rise of the Anglo-German Antagonism 1860–1914 (London, 1980).

The Rise and Fall of the Great Powers: Economic Change and Military Conflict from 1500 to 2000 (New York, 1987).

The Rise and Fall of British Naval Mastery, third edition (London, 1991).

Kennedy, Paul and Anthony Nicholls (eds.), *Nationalist and Racialist Movements in Britain and Germany before 1914* (London, 1981).

Kern, Stephen, *The Culture of Space and Time, 1880–1918* (Cambridge, MA, 2003).

Kertzer, David I., *Ritual, Politics, and Power* (New Haven and London, 1988).

Kieler Stadt- und Marinebilder. 150 Jahre Foto-Atelier Renard (Neumünster, 1993).

Kießling, Friedrich, *Gegen den großen Krieg? Entspannung in den internationalen Beziehungen, 1911–1914* (Munich, 2002).

Killingray, David and David Omissi (eds.), *Guardians of Empire: The Armed Forces of the Colonial Powers c. 1700–1964* (Manchester, 2000).

Kirsch, Martin, *Monarch und Parlament im 19. Jahrhundert. Der monarchische Konstitutionalismus als europäischer Verfassungstyp – Frankreich im Vergleich* (Göttingen, 1999).

Klein, Bernhard and Gesa Mackenthun (eds.), *Sea Changes: Historicizing the Ocean* (New York, 2004).

Klenke, Dietmar, 'Zwischen nationalkriegerischem Gemeinschaftsideal und bürgerlich-ziviler Modernität. Zum Vereinsnationalismus der Sänger, Schützen und Turner im Kaiserreich', *Geschichte in Wissenschaft und Unterricht* 45 (1994), pp. 207–23.

Kloosterhuis, Jürgen, *"Friedliche Imperialisten". Deutsche Auslandsvereine und auswärtige Kulturpolitik 1906–1918*, 2 vols. (Frankfurt, 1994).

Kludas, Arnold, 'Der Wettkampf der Ozeanriesen: Deutsche Schiffe als Auslöser und Höhepunkt des großen friedlichen Wettrüstens vor 1914', *Jahrbuch der Schiffbautechnischen Gesellschaft* 79 (1985), pp. 67–76.

Die Geschichte der deutschen Passagierschiffahrt, 5 vols. (Hamburg, 1986–90).

Kluxen, Kurt, *Geschichte und Problematik des Parlamentarismus* (Frankfurt, 1983).

Kocka, Jürgen, 'Asymmetrical Historical Comparison: The Case of the German *Sonderweg*', *History and Theory* 38 (1999), pp. 40–50.

Kohlrausch, Martin, *Der Monarch im Skandal. Die Logik der Massenmedien und die Transformation der wilhelminischen Monarchie* (Berlin, 2005).

Kohut, Thomas, *Wilhelm II and the Germans: A Study in Leadership* (Oxford, 1991).

Koop, Gerhard, Kurt Galle and Fritz Klein, *Von der Kaiserlichen Werft zum Marinearsenal. Wilhelmshaven als Zentrum der Marinetechnik seit 1870* (Munich, 1982).

Koselleck, Reinhart, 'Volk, Nation, Nationalismus, Masse', in Otto Brunner, Werner Konze, Reinhart Koselleck (eds.), *Geschichtliche Grundbegriffe*, vol. 7 (Stuttgart, 1992), pp. 141–431.

Vergangene Zukunft. Zur Semantik geschichtlicher Zeiten, third edition (Frankfurt, 1995).

Kritik und Krise. Eine Studie zur Pathogenese der bürgerlichen Welt, eighth edition (Frankfurt, 1997).

Koselleck, Reinhart and Michael Jeismann (eds.), *Der politische Totenkult. Kriegerdenkmäler in der Moderne* (Munich, 1994).

Koshar, Rudy, *Germany's Transient Pasts: Preservation and National Memory in Twentieth Century Germany* (Chapel Hill, 1998).

From Monuments to Traces: German Artifacts of Memory, 1870–1990 (Berkeley, 2000).

Koss, Stephen, *The Rise and Fall of the Political Press in Britain*, 2 vols. (London, 1984).

Krause, Andreas, *Scapa Flow. Die Selbstversenkung der wilhelminischen Flotte* (Berlin, 1999).

Krebs, Paula M., *Gender, Race, and the Writing of Empire: Public Discourse and the Boer War* (Cambridge, 1999).

Kuckuk, Peter, 'Schiffstaufen, ein maritimes Ritual', *Deutsches Schiffahrtsarchiv* 15 (1992), pp. 389–410.

Kühne, Thomas, *Dreiklassenwahlrecht und Wahlkultur in Preußen 1867–1914. Landtagswahlen zwischen korporativer Tradition und politischem Massenmarkt* (Düsseldorf, 1994).

Kuhn, Robert and Bernd Kreutz, *Der Matrosenanzug. Kulturgeschichte eines Kleidungsstückes* (Dortmund, 1989).

Kuhn, William M., *Democratic Royalism: The Transformation of the British Monarchy, 1861–1914* (London, 1996).

Kundrus, Birthe (ed.), *Phantasiereiche. Zur Kulturgeschichte des deutschen Kolonialismus* (Frankfurt, 2003).

Kunz, Georg, *Verortete Geschichte. Regionales Geschichtsbewußtsein in den deutschen Historischen Vereinen des 19. Jahrhunderts* (Göttingen, 2000).

Lambert, Andrew, 'The Royal Navy 1856–1914: Deterrence and The Strategy of World Power', in Keith Neilson and Elizabeth Jane Errington (eds.), *Navies and Global Defense: Theories and Strategy* (London, 1995).

The Foundations of Naval History: Sir John Laughton, the Royal Navy and the Historical Profession (London, 1998).

Lambert, Nicholas A., *Sir John Fisher's Naval Revolution* (Columbia SC, 1999).

Lambi, Ivo Nikolai, *The Navy and German Power Politics, 1862–1914* (Boston, 1984).

Lange-Fuchs, Hauke, *Der Kaiser, der Kanal und die Kinematographie* (Schleswig, 1995).

Langer, William L., *Diplomacy of Imperialism 1890–1902*, second edition (New York, 1951).

Langewiesche, Dieter, 'Nation, Nationalismus, Nationalstaat: Forschungsstand und Forschungsperspektiven', *Neue politische Literatur* 40 (1995), pp. 190–236.

Lant, Jeffrey L., 'The Spithead Naval Review of 1887', *Mariner's Mirror* 62 (1976), pp. 67–79.

Insubstantial Pageant: Ceremony and Confusion at Queen Victoria's Court (New York, 1979).

Lawrence, Jon, *Speaking for the People: Party, Language and Popular Politics in England, 1867–1914* (Cambridge, 1998).

'The Transformation of British Public Politics after the First World War', *Past & Present* 190 (2006), pp. 188–94.

Ledger, Sally, 'The New Woman and the Crisis of Victorianism', in Sally Ledger and Scott McCracken (eds.), *Cultural Politics at the Fin de Siècle* (Cambridge, 1995), pp. 22–44.

Lee, Alan J., *The Origins of the Popular Press in England 1855–1914* (London, 1976).

Lees-Milne, James, *The Enigmatic Edwardian: The Life of Reginald, 2nd Viscount Esher* (London, 1986).

Lekan, Thomas M., *Imagining the Nation in Nature: Landscape Preservation and German Identity 1885–1945* (Cambridge, MA, 2004).

Lepenies, Wolf, *The Seduction of Culture in German History* (Princeton, 2006).

Lepsius, M. Rainer, *Interessen, Ideen und Institutionen* (Opladen, 1990).

'Militärwesen und zivile Gesellschaft', in Ute Frevert (ed.) *Militär und Gesellschaft im 19. und 20. Jahrhundert* (Stuttgart, 1997), pp. 359–70.

Lerman, Katharine A., *The Chancellor as Courtier: Bernhard von Bülow and the Governance of Germany 1900–1909* (Cambridge, 1990).

'Bismarck's Heir: Chancellor Bernhard von Bülow and the National Idea, 1890–1918', in John Breuilly (ed.), *The State of Germany: The National Idea in the Making, Unmaking and Remaking of a Modern Nation State* (London, 1992), pp. 103–27.

Lewis, Michael, *Spithead: An Informal History* (London, 1972).

Lincoln, Margarette, 'Naval Ship Launches as Public Spectacle 1773–1854', *Mariner's Mirror* 83 (1997), pp. 466–72.

Representing the Royal Navy: British Sea Power, 1750–1815 (Aldershot, 2002).

Linden, Marcel van der and Gottfried Mergner (eds.), *Kriegsbegeisterung und mentale Kriegsvorbereitung. Interdisziplinäre Studien* (Berlin, 1991).

Link, Jürgen and Wulf Wülfing (eds), *Nationale Mythen und Symbole in der zweiten Hälfte des 19. Jahrhunderts* (Stuttgart, 1991).

Loiperdinger, Martin, 'Wie der Film nach Deutschland kam', *KINTop* 1 (1992), pp. 114–8.

'Kaiser Wilhelm II. Der erste deutsche Filmstar', in Thomas Koebner (ed.), *Idole des deutschen Films* (Munich, 1997), pp. 41–53.

Lorenz, Chris, 'Comparative Historiography: Problems and Perspectives', *History and Theory* 38 (1999), pp. 25–39.

Loth, Wilfried, *Das Kaiserreich. Obrigkeitsstaat und politische Mobilisierung*, second edition (Munich, 1997).

Louis, Wm. Roger, 'The Dissolution of Empire', in Judith M. Brown and W. Roger Louis (eds.), *The Oxford History of the British Empire*, vol. 4: *The Twentieth Century* (Oxford, 1999), pp. 329–56.

Low, Rachael, *The History of the British Film, 1906–1914* (London, 1948).

Low, Rachael and Roger Manvell, *The History of the British Film, 1896–1906* (London, 1948).

Lowry, Donal (ed.), *The South African War Reappraised* (Manchester, 2000).

Lowry, R. G., *The Origin of Some Naval Terms and Customs* (London, 1930).

Loxley, Diana, *Problematic Shores: The Literature of Islands* (Houndmills, 1990).

Lüdtke, Alf, 'Organisational Order or Eigensinn? Workers' Privacy and Workers' Politics in Imperial Germany', in Sean Wilentz (ed.), *Rites of Power: Symbolism, Ritual and Politics Since the Middle Ages* (Philadelphia, 1985), pp. 303–33.

'Cash, Coffee-Breaks, Horseplay: *Eigensinn* and Politics Among Factory Workers in Germany circa 1900', in Michael Hanagan and Charles Stephenson (eds.), *Confrontation, Class Consciousness and the Labor Process: Studies in Proletarian Class Formation* (New York, 1986), pp. 65–95.

Eigen-Sinn. Fabrikalltag, Arbeitererfahrung und Politik vom Kaiserreich bis in den Faschismus (Hamburg, 1993).

Lühr, Dora, 'Matrosenanzug und Matrosenkleid. Entwicklungsgeschichte einer Kindermode von 1770 bis 1920', *Beiträge zur deutschen Volks- und Altertumskunde* 5 (1960/61), pp. 19–42.

Lunn, K. and R. Thomas, 'Naval Imperialism in Portsmouth, 1905–1914', *Southern History* 10 (1988), pp. 142–59.

Maase, Kaspar, *Grenzenloses Vergnügen. Der Aufstieg der Massenkultur, 1850–1970* (Frankfurt, 1997).

Maase, Kaspar and Wolfgang Kaschuba (eds.), *Schund und Schönheit. Populäre Kultur um 1900* (Cologne, 2001).

MacAloon, John, (ed.), *Rite, Drama, Festival, Spectacle: Rehearsals toward a Theory of Cultural Performance* (Philadelphia, 1984).

MacDonald, Robert H., *The Language of Empire: Myths and Metaphors of Popular Imperialism, 1880–1918* (Manchester, 1994).

Mace, Rodney, *Trafalgar Square: Emblem of Empire* (London, 1976).

Mack, W. P. and W. Connell, *Naval Ceremonies, Customs and Traditions* (Annapolis, 1980).

Mackay, R. F., *Fisher of Kilverstone* (Oxford, 1973).

MacKenzie, John M., *Propaganda and Empire: The Manipulation of British Public Opinion, 1880–1960* (Manchester, 1984).

(ed.), *Imperialism and Popular Culture* (Manchester, 1986).

(ed.), *Imperialism and the Natural World* (Manchester, 1990).

Popular Imperialism and the Military 1850–1950 (Manchester, 1992).

'Empire and Metropolitan Cultures', in Andrew Porter (ed.), *The Oxford History of the British Empire*, vol. 3 (Oxford, 1999), pp. 290–2.

'Nelson Goes Global: The Nelson Myth in Britain and Beyond', in David Cannadine (ed.), *Admiral Lord Nelson: Context and Legacy* (Basingstoke, 2005), pp. 144–65.

Mandler, Peter, 'Against "Englishness": English Culture and the Limits to Rural Nostalgia', *Transactions of the Royal Historical Society*, 6th series, 7 (1997), pp. 155–75.

'The Problem with Cultural History', *Cultural and Social History* 1 (2004), pp. 5–28.

Mangan, James A. (ed.), *Making Imperial Mentalities: Socialisation and British Imperialism* (Manchester, 1990).

'Duty unto Death: English Masculinity and Militarism in the Age of the New Imperialism', *International Journal of the History of Sport* 12 (1995), pp. 10–38.

Manning, T. D. and C. F. Walker, *British Warship Names* (London, 1959).

Marchand, Suzanne and David Lindenfeld (eds.), *Germany at the Fin de Siècle: Culture, Politics and Ideas* (Baton Rouge, 2004).

Marder, Arthur J., *From the Dreadnought to Scapa Flow: The Royal Navy in the Fisher Era, 1904–1919*, 5 vols. (Oxford, 1961–78).

The Anatomy of British Sea Power: A History of British Naval Policy in the Pre-Dreadnought Era, 1880–1905, second edition (London, 1964).

Marienfeld, Wolfgang, *Wissenschaft und Schlachtflottenbau in Deutschland 1897–1906* (Frankfurt, 1957).

Marschall, Brigitte, *Reisen und Regieren. Die Nordlandfahrten Kaiser Wilhelms II.* (Hamburg, 1991).

Marvin, Carolyn, *When Old Technologies Were New: Thinking about Electric Communication in the Late Nineteenth Century* (New York and Oxford, 1988).

Massie, Robert K., *Dreadnought: Britain, Germany and the Coming of the Great War* (London, 1991).

Castles of Steel: Britain, Germany, and the Winning of the Great War at Sea (New York and London, 2003).

Matthew, Colin, 'Public Life and Politics', in Colin Matthew (ed.), *Short Oxford History of the British Isles: The Nineteenth Century* (Oxford, 2000), pp. 85–133.

(ed.), *Short Oxford History of the British Isles: The Nineteenth Century* (Oxford, 2000).

Maurer, John H., 'The Anglo-German Naval Rivalry and Informal Arms Control, 1912–1914', *Journal of Conflict Resolution* 36 (1992), pp. 284–308.

Maurer, Michael, 'Feste und Feiern als historischer Forschungsgegenstand', *Historische Zeitschrift* 253 (1991), pp. 101–30.

McClintock, Anne, *Imperial Leather: Race, Gender and Sexuality in the Colonial Contest* (New York, 1995).

McCord, Norman, *British History 1815–1906* (Oxford, 1991).

McLaren, Angus, *The Trials of Masculinity: Policing Sexual Boundaries 1870–1930* (Chicago, 1997).

McLean, Roderick R., *Royalty and Diplomacy in Europe 1890–1914* (Cambridge, 2001).

Meixner, Arthur A., *Ford Madox Ford's Novels: A Critical Study* (Minneapolis, Minnesota, 1962).

Melman, Billie, 'Claiming the Nation's Past: The Invention of the Anglo-Saxon Tradition', *Journal of Contemporary History* 26 (1991), pp. 575–95.

Mergel, Thomas, 'Überlegungen zu einer Kulturgeschichte der Politik', *Geschichte und Gesellschaft* 28 (2002), pp. 574–606.

Meyer, Juerg, *Die Propaganda der deutschen Flottenbewegung 1897–1900* (Bern, 1967).

Meyer, Thomas, *'Endlich eine Tat, eine befreiende Tat ...' Alfred von Kiderlen-Wächters 'Panthersprung nach Agadir' unter dem Druck der öffentlichen Meinung* (Husum, 1996).

Middell, Matthias (ed.), *Kulturtransfer und Vergleich* (Leipzig, 2000).

Miller, Jacques and Robert Forbes, *Toy Boats 1870–1955: A Pictorial History* (Cambridge, 1979).

Mock, Wolfgang, 'Entstehung und Herausbildung einer "radikalen Rechten" in Großbritannien 1900–1914', *Historische Zeitschrift*, Beiheft 8 (Munich, 1983), pp. 5–45.

Mollat, Michel du Jourdin, *Europe and the Sea* (Oxford, 1993).

Mollin, Gerhard T., '"Schlachtflottenbau" vor 1914: Überlegungen zum Wesen des deutsch-britischen Antagonismus', in *Pionier und Nachzügler? Vergleichende Studien zur Geschichte Großbritanniens und Deutschlands im Zeitalter des Imperialismus. Festschrift für Sidney Pollard zum 70. Geburtstag* (Bochum, 1995).

Mombauer, Annika, *Helmuth von Moltke and the Origins of the First World War* (Cambridge, 2001).

The Origins of the First World War: Controversies and Consensus (Harlow, 2002).

Mombauer, Annika and Wilhelm Deist (eds.), *The Kaiser: New Research on Wilhelm II's Role in Imperial Germany* (Cambridge, 2003).

Mommsen, Hans, 'Nationalismus in der Weimarer Republik', in Otto Dann (ed.), *Die deutsche Nation: Geschichte, Probleme, Perspektiven* (Vierow, 1994), pp. 83–95.

Mommsen, Wolfgang J., *Das Zeitalter des Imperialismus* (Frankfurt, 1969).

(ed.), *Der moderne Imperialismus* (Stuttgart, 1971).

'Zur Entwicklung des Englandbildes der Deutschen seit dem Ende des 18. Jahrhunderts', in *Studien zur Geschichte Englands und der deutsch-britischen Beziehungen. Festschrift für Paul Kluke* (Munich, 1981).

'The Topos of Inevitable War in Germany in the Decade before 1914', in Volker R. Berghahn and Martin Kitchen (eds.), *Germany in the Age of Total War* (London, 1981).

Two Centuries of Anglo-German Relations: A Reappraisal (London, 1984).

Der autoritäre Nationalstaat. Verfassung, Gesellschaft und Kultur des deutschen Kaiserreiches (Frankfurt, 1990).

'Die Kultur der Moderne im Kaiserreich', in Wolfgang Hardtwig and Harm-Hinrich Brandt (eds.), *Deutschlands Weg in die Moderne: Politik, Gesellschaft und Kultur im 19. Jahrhundert* (Munich, 1993), pp. 254–74.

Bürgerstolz und Weltmachtstreben. Deutschland unter Wilhelm II. 1890 bis 1918 (Berlin, 1995).

War der Kaiser an allem schuld?. Wilhelm II. und die preußisch-deutschen Machteliten (Berlin, 2002).

Monger, George W., *The End of Isolation: British Foreign Policy 1900–1907* (London, 1963).

Morat, Daniel, 'Das Kino', in Habbo Knoch and Alexa Geisthövel (eds.), *Orte der Moderne* (Frankfurt, 2005).

Morris, A. J. A., *Radicalism against War, 1906–1914: The Advocacy of Peace and Retrenchment* (London, 1972).

The Scaremongers: The Advocacy of War and Retrenchment 1896–1914 (London, 1984).

Morris, Jan, *Farewell the Trumpets: An Imperial Retreat* (London, 1978).

The Spectacle of Empire (London, 1982).

Mosse, George L., 'Caesarism, Circuses and Monuments', *Journal of Contemporary History* 6 (1971), pp. 167–82.

The Nationalisation of the Masses: Political Symbolism and Mass Movements in Germany from the Napoleonic Wars Through the Third Reich (New York, 1975).

'Nationalism and Respectability', *Journal of Contemporary History* 17 (1982), 221–46.

The Image of Man: The Creation of Modern Masculinity (New York and Oxford, 1996).

Muhs, Rudolf, Johannes Paulmann and Willibald Steinmetz (eds.), *Aneignung und Abwehr. Interkultureller Transfer zwischen Deutschland und Großbritannien im 19. Jahrhundert* (Bodenheim, 1998).

Muir, Edward, *Civic Ritual in Renaissance Venice* (Princeton, 1981).

Ritual in Early Modern Europe (Cambridge, 1997).

Müller, Gerhard H., *Friedrich Ratzel (1844–1904). Naturwissenschaftler, Geograph, Gelehrter: neue Studien zu Leben und Werk und sein Konzept der "Allgemeinen Biogeographie"* (Stuttgart, 1996).

Myerly, Scott Hughes, '"The Eye Must Entrap the Mind": Army Spectacle and Paradigm in Nineteenth-Century Britain', *Journal of Social History* 26 (1992), pp. 105–31.

British Military Spectacle: From the Napoleonic Wars through the Crimea (Cambridge, MA, 1996).

Nathans, Eli, *The Politics of Citizenship in Germany: Ethnicity, Utility and Nationalism* (Oxford and New York, 2004).

'Naumachie', *Paulys Realencyclopaedie der classischen Altertumswissenschaften, neue Bearbeitung, begonnen von Georg Wissowa*, vol. 32 (Stuttgart, 1935), cl. 1970–74.

Nicholson, John, 'Popular Imperialism and the Provincial Press: Manchester Evening and Weekly Papers, 1895–1902', *Victorian Periodicals Review* 13 (1980), pp. 85–96.

Nipperdey, Thomas, 'Nationalidee und Nationaldenkmal in Deutschland im 19. Jahrhundert', *Historische Zeitschrift* 206 (1968), pp. 529–85.

'Wehlers Kaiserreich. Eine kritische Auseinandersetzung', in Thomas Nipperdey, *Gesellschaft, Kultur Theorie. Gesammelte Aufsätze zur neueren Geschichte* (Göttingen, 1976), pp. 360–89.

Nachdenken über die deutsche Geschichte (Munich, 1990).

Deutsche Geschichte 1866–1918, 2 vols. (Munich, 1990–2).

Nora, Pirerre (ed.), *Les lieux de mémoire*, 3 vols. (Paris, 1984–92).

Omissi, David and Andrew S. Thompson (eds.), *The Impact of the South African War* (Basingstoke, 2002).

Osterhammel, Jürgen, *Geschichtswissenschaft jenseits des Nationalstaats. Studien zu Beziehungsgeschichte und Zivilisationsvergleich* (Göttingen, 2001).

Otte, Thomas G., '"An Altogether Unfortunate Affair": Great Britain and the Daily Telegraph Affair', *Diplomacy & Statecraft* 5 (1994), pp. 196–233.

Overlack, Peter, 'An Instrument of "Culture": The Imperial Navy, the Academics and Germany's World Mission', in Andrew Bonnell, Gregory Munro and Martin Travers (eds.), *Power, Conscience and Opposition: Essays in German History in Honour of John A. Moses* (New York, 1996), pp. 3–24.

Ozouf, Mona, *Festivals and the French Revolution*, translated by Alan Sheridan (Cambridge, MA, 1988).

Padfield, Peter, *Rule Britannia: The Victorian and Edwardian Navy* (London, 1981).

The Great Naval Race: Anglo-German Naval Rivalry 1900–1914 (London, 1974).

Palmowski, Jan, 'Liberalism and Local Government in Late Nineteenth-Century Germany and England', *Historical Journal* 45 (2002), pp. 381–409.

Paris, Michael, *Warrior Nation: Images of War in British Popular Culture, 1850–2000* (London, 2000).

Paulmann, Johannes, 'Internationaler Vergleich und interkultureller Transfer. Zwei Forschungsansätze zur europäischen Geschichte des 18. bis 20. Jahrhunderts', *Historische Zeitschrift* 267 (1998), pp. 649–85.

Pomp und Politik. Monarchenbegegnungen in Europa zwischen Ancien Régime und Erstem Weltkrieg (Paderborn, 2000).

Peckham, Robert Shannan, 'The Uncertainty of Islands: National Identity and the Discourse of Islands in Nineteenth-Century Britain and Greece', *Journal of Historical Geography* 29 (2003), pp. 499–515.

Pelling, Henry M., *Popular Politics and Society in Late Victorian Britain* (London, 1968).

Penny, H. Glenn, *Objects of Culture: Ethnology and Ethnographic Museums in Imperial Germany* (Chapel Hill, 2003).

Peters, Michael, *Der Alldeutsche Verband am Vorabend des Ersten Weltkrieges* (Frankfurt, 1992).

Peukert, Detlev, *Die Weimarer Republik. Krisenjahre der Klassischen Moderne* (Frankfurt, 1997).

Pick, Daniel, *War Machine: The Rationalisation of Slaughter in the Modern Age* (New Haven, 1993).

Pieper, Josef, *Zustimmung zur Welt. Eine Theorie des Festes* (Munich, 1963).

Plagemann, Volker (ed.), *Industriekultur in Hamburg. Des Deutschen Reiches Tor zur Welt* (Munich, 1984).

(ed.), *Übersee. Seefahrt und Seemacht im deutschen Kaiserreich* (Munich, 1988).

Plunkett, John, *Victoria: First Media Monarch* (Oxford, 2003).

Pocock, J. G. A., 'British History: A Plea for a New Subject', *Journal of Modern History* 47 (1975), pp. 601–21.

'The Limits and Divisions of British History: In Search of the Unknown Subject', *American Historical Review* 87 (1982), pp. 311–36.

Pollard, Sidney, '"Made in Germany" – die Angst vor der deutschen Konkurrenz im spätviktorianischen England', *Technikgeschichte* 53 (1987), 183–95.

Pollard, Sidney and Paul Robertson, *The British Shipbuilding Industry, 1870–1914* (Cambridge, MA, 1979).

Porter, Andrew (ed.), *Oxford History of the British Empire*, vol. 3, *The Nineteenth Century* (Oxford, 1999).

Potter, Elmar B. and Chester W. Nimitz (eds.), *Sea Power: A Naval History* (New Jersey, 1960).

Prager, Hans-Georg, *Blohm + Voss* (Herford, 1977).

Price, Richard, *An Imperial War and the British Working Class: Working-Class Attitudes and Reactions to the Boer War 1899–1902* (London, 1972).

Radkau, Joachim, *Technik in Deutschland. Vom 18. Jahrhundert bis zur Gegenwart* (Frankfurt, 1989).

'Die Wilhelminische Ära als nervöses Zeitalter, oder: Die Nerven als Netz zwischen Tempo- und Körpergeschichte', *Geschichte und Gesellschaft* 20 (1994), pp. 211–41.

Das Zeitalter der Nervosität. Deutschland zwischen Bismarck und Hitler (Munich, 1998).

Raithel, Thomas, *Das 'Wunder' der inneren Einheit. Studien zur deutschen und französischen Öffentlichkeit bei Beginn des Ersten Weltkriegs* (Bonn, 1996).

Rappaport, Erika, *Shopping for Pleasure: Women in the Making of London's West End* (Princeton, 2000).

Readman, Paul, 'The Place of the Past in English Culture c.1890–1914', *Past & Present* 186 (2005), pp. 147–99.

'Landscape Preservation, "Advertising Disfigurement", and English National Identity, c. 1890–1914', *Rural History* 12 (2001), pp. 61–83.

'The Conservative Party, Patriotism, and British Politics: The Case of the General Election of 1900', *Journal of British Studies* 40 (2001), pp. 107–45.

Rebentisch, Jost, *Die vielen Gesichter des Kaisers. Wilhelm II. in der deutschen und britischen Karikatur* (Berlin, 2000).

Reckner, James R., *Teddy Roosevelt's Great White Fleet* (Annapolis, 1988).

Reichardt, Sven, *Faschistische Kampfbünde. Gewalt und Gemeinschaft im italienischen Squadrismus und in der deutschen SA* (Cologne, 2002).

Reinermann, Lothar, *Der Kaiser in England. Wilhelm II. und sein Bild in der britischen Öffentlichkeit* (Paderborn, 2001).

Reinhard, Wolfgang (ed.), *Imperialistische Kontinuität und nationale Ungeduld im 19. Jahrhundert* (Frankfurt, 1991).

Rembold, Elfie, *Die festliche Nation. Geschichtsinszenierungen und regionaler Nationalismus in Großbritannien vor dem Ersten Weltkrieg* (Berlin, 2000).

Repp, Kevin, *Reformers, Critics, and the Paths of German Modernity: Anti-Politics and the Search for Alternatives, 1890–1914* (Cambridge, MA, 2000).

Requate, Jörg, 'Öffentlichkeit und Medien als Gegenstände historischer Analyse', *Geschichte und Gesellschaft* 25 (1999), pp. 5–32.

Retallack, James, *Notables of the Right: The Conservative Party and Political Mobilisation in Germany 1876–1918* (Boston, 1988).

'From Pariah to Professional? The Journalist in German Society and Politics, from the late Enlightenment to the Rise of Hitler', *German Studies Review* 16 (1993), pp. 175–223.

Germany in the Age of Kaiser Wilhelm II (Basingstoke, 1996).

'"Why Can't a Saxon Be More Like a Prussian?" Regional Identities and the Birth of Modern Political Culture in Germany, 1866–7', *Canadian Journal of History* 32 (1997), pp. 26–55.

'Demagogentum, Populismus, Volkstümlichkeit. Überlegungen zur "Popularitätshascherei" auf dem politischen Massenmarkt des Kaiserreichs', *Zeitschrift für Geschichtswissenschaft* 48 (2000), pp. 309–325.

'Saxon Signposts: Cultural Battles, Identity Politics, and German Authoritarianism in Transition', *German History* 17 (2000), pp. 455–69.

Reulecke, Jürgen, 'Das Jahr 1902 und die Ursprünge der Männerbund-Ideologie in Deutschland', in Gisela Völger and Karin von Welck (eds.), *Männerbande – Männerbünde: zur Rolle des Mannes im Kulturvergleich*, vol. 1 (Cologne, 1990), pp. 3–10.

Reynolds, David, *Britannia Overruled: British Policy and World Power in the Twentieth Century*, second edition (London, 2000).

Richards, Thomas, *The Commodity Culture of Victorian England: Advertising and Spectacle, 1851–1914* (Stanford, 1990).

Rieger, Bernhard, '"Modern Wonders": Technological Innovation and Public Ambivalence in Britain and Germany, 1890s to 1933', *History Workshop Journal* 55 (2003), pp. 152–76.

Technology and the Culture of Modernity in Britain and Germany, 1890–1945 (Cambridge, 2005).

Ritchie, L. A. (ed.), *The Shipbuilding Industry: A Guide to Historical Records* (Manchester, 1992).

Ritter, Gerhard, *Staatskunst und Kriegshandwerk. Das Problem des "Militarismus" in Deutschland*, 4 vols. (Munich, 1954–68).

Ritter, Gerhard A. (ed.), *Arbeiterkultur* (Königstein, 1979).

Ritter, Gerhard A. and Klaus Tenfelde, *Arbeiter im Deutschen Kaiserreich, 1871 bis 1914* (Bonn, 1992).

Ritter, Gerhard A. and Peter Wende (eds.), *Rivalität und Partnerschaft. Studien zu den deutsch-britischen Beziehungen im 19. und 20. Jahrhundert. Festschrift für Anthony J. Nicholls* (Paderborn, 1999).

Robbins, Keith, *Nineteenth-Century Britain: Integration and Diversity* (Oxford, 1988).

'National Identity and History', *History* 75 (1990), pp. 369–87.

History, Religion and Identity in Modern Britain (London, 1993).

Great Britain: Identities, Institutions and the Idea of Britishness (London, 1998).

Rodger, N. A. M., *The Safeguard of the Sea: A Naval History of Britain, 660–1649* (London, 1997).

The Command of the Ocean: A Naval History of Britain, 1649–1815 (London, 2004).

'Queen Elizabeth and the Myth of Seapower in English Politics, 1568–1815', *Transactions of the Royal Historical Society*, 6th series, vol. 14 (2004), pp. 155–76.

Roedel, Christian, *Krieger, Denker, Amateure. Alfred von Tirpitz und das Seekriegsbild vor dem Ersten Weltkrieg* (Stuttgart, 2003).

Röhl, John C. G., 'Kaiser Wilhelm II., Grossherzog Friedrich I. und der "Königsmechanismus" im Kaiserreich', *Historische Zeitschrift* 263 (1983), pp. 539–77.

Kaiser, Hof und Staat. Wilhelm II. in der deutschen Geschichte (Munich, 1987).

(ed.), *Der Ort Kaiser Wilhelms II. in der deutschen Geschichte* (Munich, 1991).

Wilhelm II. Die Jugend des Kaisers, 1859–1888 (Munich, 1993).

The Kaiser and His Court: Wilhelm II and the Government of Germany (Cambridge, 1994).

Wilhelm II. Der Aufbau der persönlichen Monarchie (Munich, 2001).

Röhl, John C. G. and Nicolaus Sombart (eds.), *Kaiser Wilhelm II: New Interpretations* (Cambridge, 1982).

Röhr, Albert, *Handbuch der Marinegeschichte* (Oldenburg, 1963).

Rohkrämer, Thomas, *Der Militarismus der 'kleinen Leute'. Die Kriegervereine im Deutschen Kaiserreich. 1871–1914* (Munich, 1990).

'Das Militär als Männerbund? Kult der soldatischen Männlichkeit im Deutschen Kaiserreich', *Westfälische Forschungen* 45 (1995), pp. 169–87.

Eine andere Moderne? Zivilisationskritik, Natur und Technik in Deutschland, 1880–1933 (Paderborn, 1999).

Rolo, P. J. V., *Entente Cordiale: The Origins and Negotiations of the Anglo-French Agreements of 8 April 1904* (London, 1969).

Roper, Michael and John Tosh (eds.), *Manful Assertions: Masculinities in Britain since 1800* (London, 1991).

Rosenbach, Harald, *Das Deutsche Reich, Großbritannien und der Transvaal, 1896–1902. Anfänge deutsch-britischer Entfremdung* (Göttingen, 1993).

Ross, Ronald J., *The Failure of Bismarck's Kulturkampf: Catholicism and State Power in Imperial Germany, 1871–1887* (Washington D.C., 1998).

Rubinstein, W. D., *Capitalism, Culture and Decline in Britain, 1750–1990* (London, 1993).

Rüger, Jan, 'Nation, Empire and Navy: Identity Politics in the United Kingdom 1887–1914', *Past & Present* 185 (2004), pp. 159–87.

'Das U-Boot', in Alexa Geisthövel and Habbo Knoch (eds.), *Orte der Moderne* (Frankfurt, 2005), pp. 259–69.

'"The Last Word in Outward Splendour": The Cult of the Navy and the Imperial Age', in David Stevens (ed.), *The Navy and the Nation* (Crows Nest, 2005), pp. 48–65.

Russell, Mark, 'The Building of Hamburg's Bismarck Memorial, 1898–1906', *Historical Journal* 43 (2000), pp. 133–156.

Sahlins, Marshall, *Historical Metaphors and Mythical Realities* (Ann Arbor, 1981).

Islands of History (Chicago, 1985).

Sahlins, Peter, *Boundaries: The Making of France and Spain in the Pyrenees* (Berkeley, 1989).

'Natural Frontiers Revisited: France's Boundaries Since the Seventeenth Century', *American Historical Review* 95 (1990), pp. 1435–43.

Said, Edward W., *Culture and Imperialism* (London, 1994).

Salewski, Michael, *Tirpitz. Aufstieg, Macht, Scheitern* (Göttingen, 1979).

'Über historische Symbole', in Julius H. Schoeps (ed.), *Religion und Zeitgeist im 19. Jahrhundert* (Stuttgart and Bonn, 1982), pp. 157–83.

'Kiel und die Marine', in Jürgen Jensen and Peter Wulf (eds.), *Geschichte der Stadt Kiel* (Neumünster, 1991), pp. 272–94.

Die Deutschen und die See (Stuttgart, 1998).

Samuel, Raphael (ed.), *Patriotism: The Making and Unmaking of British National Identity*, 3 vols. (London, 1989).

Island Stories: Unravelling Britain (London, 1998).

Saunders, David, *Britain's Maritime Memorials and Mementoes* (Sparkford, 1996).

Schama, Simon, *A History of Britain*, vol. 3, *The Fate of Empire 1776–2000* (London, 2002).

Schechner, Richard, *Between Theatre and Anthropology* (Philadelphia, 1985).

Performance Theory (New York and London, 1988).

Schellack, Fritz, *Nationalfeiertage in Deutschland von 1871 bis 1945* (Frankfurt, 1990).

Schencking, J. Charles, 'The Imperial Japanese Navy and the Constructed Consciousness of a South Seas Destiny', *Modern Asian Studies* 33 (1999), pp. 767–96.

Making Waves: Politics, Propaganda, and the Emergence of the Imperial Japanese Navy, 1868–1922 (Stanford, 2005).

Schenk, Willy, *Die deutsch-englische Rivalität vor dem Ersten Weltkrieg in der Sicht deutscher Historiker. Mißverstehen oder Machtstreben?* (Aarau, 1967).

Schieder, Theodor, *Nationalismus und Nationalstaat. Studien zum nationalen Problem im modernen Europa*, edited by Otto Dann and Hans-Ulrich Wehler (Göttingen, 1991).

Das deutsche Kaiserreich von 1871 als Nationalstaat, second edition (Göttingen, 1992).

Schivelbusch, Wolfgang, *Die Kultur der Niederlage* (Darmstadt, 2001).

Schmoll, Friedemann, *Verewigte Nation. Studien zur Erinnerungskultur von Reich und Einzelstaat im württembergischen Denkmalskult des 19. Jahrhunderts* (Tübingen and Stuttgart, 1995).

Schneer, Jonathan, *London 1900: The Imperial Metropolis* (New Haven and London, 1999).

Schneider, Ute, 'Einheit ohne Einigkeit: der Sedantag im Kaiserreich', in Sabine Behrenbeck and Alexander Nützenadel (eds.), *Inszenierungen des*

Nationalstaats. Politische Feiern in Italien und Deutschland seit 1860/71 (Cologne, 2000), pp. 27–44.

Schniewind, P., 'Seezeremoniell', *Marine Rundschau* 35 (1930), pp. 558–62.

Schöllgen, Gregor, '"Germanophobia". Deutschland, England und die orientalische Frage im Spiegel der britischen Presse 1900–1903', *Francia* 8 (1980), pp. 407–26.

'Die Großmacht als Weltmacht. Idee, Wirklichkeit und Perzeption deutscher "Weltpolitik" im Zeitalter des Imperialismus', *Historische Zeitschrift* 248 (1989), pp. 79–100.

Das Zeitalter des Imperialismus, third edition (Munich, 1994).

Imperialismus und Gleichgewicht. Deutschland, England und die orientalische Frage 1871–1914, third edition (Munich, 2000).

Schoenbaum, David, *Zabern 1913: Consensus Politics in Imperial Germany* (London, 1982).

Schopf, Roland (ed.), *England und die Engländer in Schulbüchern des Kaiserreichs und der Weimarer Republik. Texte mit Kommentar* (Frankfurt, 1990).

Schottelius, Herbert and Wilhelm Deist (eds.), *Marine und Marinepolitik im kaiserlichen Deutschland 1871–1914* (Düsseldorf, 1972).

Schöttler, Peter, 'The Rhine as an Object of Historical Controversy in the Interwar-Years: Towards a History of Frontier Mentalities', *History Workshop Journal* 39 (1995), pp. 1–21.

Schramm, Percy Ernst, *Herrschaftszeichen und Staatssymbolik*, 3 vols. (Stuttgart, 1954–6).

Schröder, Karsten, *Parlament und Außenpolitik in England 1911–1914, dargestellt an der englischen Deutschlandpolitik von der Agadirkrise bis zum Beginn des Ersten Weltkrieges* (Göttingen, 1974).

Schroeder, Paul W., 'International Politics, Peace and War, 1815–1914', in T. C. W. Blanning (ed.), *Short Oxford History of Europe: The Nineteenth Century* (Oxford, 2000), pp. 158–209.

Schümer, Dirk, 'Die Hanse', in Etienne François and Hagen Schulze (eds.), *Deutsche Erinnerungsorte*, vol. 2 (Munich, 2001), pp. 369–86.

Schultz, Uwe (ed.), *Das Fest. Eine Kulturgeschichte von der Antike bis zur Gegenwart* (Munich, 1988).

Schulz, Andreas, 'Der Aufstieg der "vierten Gewalt". Medien, Politik und Öffentlichkeit im Zeitalter der Massenkommunikation', *Historische Zeitschrift* 270 (2000), pp. 65–97.

Schulze, Hagen, *Staat und Nation in der europäischen Geschichte*, second editon (Munich, 1995).

(ed.), *Nation-Building in Central Europe* (Leamington Spa, 1987).

Schwarz, Bill (ed.), *The Expansion of England: Race, Ethnicity and Cultural History* (London and New York, 1996).

Schweinitz, Jörg, *Prolog vor dem Film. Nachdenken über ein neues Medium 1909–1914* (1992).

Scott, Joan W., *Gender and the Politics of History* (New York, 1988).

See, Klaus von, 'Politische Männerbund-Ideologie von der wilhelminischen Zeit bis zum Nationalsozialismus', in Gisela Völger and Karin von Welck (eds.),

Männerbande – Männerbünde. Zur Rolle des Mannes im Kulturvergleich, vol. 1 (Cologne, 1990), pp. 93–102.

Sellin, Volker, 'Nationalbewußtsein und Partikularismus in Deutschland im 19. Jahrhundert', in Jan Assmann and Tonio Hölscher (eds.), *Kultur und Gedächtnis* (Frankfurt, 1988), pp. 241–64.

Sheehan, James J., 'What is German History? Reflections on the Role of the Nation in German History and Historiography', *Journal of Modern History* 53 (1981), pp. 1–23.

'Nation und Staat. Deutschland als "imaginierte Gemeinschaft"', in Manfred Hettling and Paul Nolte (eds.), *Nation und Gesellschaft in Deutschland. Historische Essays* (Munich, 1996), pp. 33–45.

'Nineteenth-Century Culture', in T. C. W. Blanning (ed.), *Short Oxford History of Europe: The Nineteenth Century* (Oxford, 2000), pp. 126–57.

Shields, Rob, *Places on the Margin: Alternative Geographies of Modernity* (London, 1991).

Shimazu, Naoko, 'The Making of a Heroic War Myth in the Russo-Japanese War', *Waseda Journal of Asian Studies* 25 (2004), pp. 83–96.

Sievers, Kai Detlev, 'Öffentliche Festveranstaltungen in Kiel während der wilhelminischen Zeit', *Zeitschrift für Volkskunde* 75 (1979), pp. 1–22.

'Die "Kieler Woche" im wilhelminischen Deutschland. Ihre nationale und soziale Bedeutung', *Mitteilungen der Gesellschaft für Kieler Stadtgeschichte* 67 (1980), pp. 213–28.

Sievert, Hedwig, 'Die Kieler Woche', in Volker Plagemann (ed.), *Übersee. Seefahrt und Seemacht im deutschen Kaiserreich* (Munich, 1988), pp. 49–52.

Smellie, Kingsley, *A History of Local Government* (London, 1946).

Smith, A. D., *National Identity* (Harmondsworth, 1992).

Smith, Helmut Walser, *German Nationalism and Religious Conflict: Culture, Ideology, Politics, 1870–1914* (Princeton, 1995).

Smith, Tori, '"Almost Pathetic ... But Also Very Glorious": The Consumer Spectacle of the Diamond Jubilee', *Histoire Sociale* 29 (1996).

Sösemann, Bernd, 'Die sog. Hunnenrede Wilhelms II. Textkritische und interpretatorische Bemerkungen zur Ansprache des Kaisers vom 27. Juli 1900 in Bremerhaven', *Historische Zeitschrift* 222 (1976), pp. 342–58.

Sombart, Nicolaus, 'Männerbund und politische Kultur in Deutschland', in J. H. Knoll and J. H. Schoeps (eds.), *Typisch deutsch. Die deutsche Jugendbewegung* (Opladen, 1988), pp. 155–76.

'The Kaiser in his Epoch: Some Reflexions on Wilhelmine Society, Sexuality and Culture', in John C. G. Röhl and Nicolaus Sombart (eds.), *Kaiser Wilhelm II: New Interpretations* (Cambridge, 1982), pp. 287–311.

Sondhaus, Lawrence, *Preparing for Weltpolitik: German Sea Power Before the Tirpitz Era* (Annapolis, 1997).

Sontag, Raymond J., *Germany and England: Background of Conflict, 1848–1894*, second edition (New York, 1969).

Später, Jörg, *Vansittart. Britische Debatten über Deutsche und Nazis, 1902–1945* (Göttingen, 2003).

Sperber, Jonathan, *The Kaiser's Voters: Electors and Elections in Imperial Germany* (Cambridge, 1997).

Stansky, Peter, *On Or About December 1910: Early Bloomsbury and Its Intimate World* (Cambridge, MA, 1996).
Stargardt, Nicholas, *The German Idea of Militarism: Radical and Socialist Critics, 1866–1914* (Cambridge, 1994).
Stark, Gary D. and Bede Karl Lackner (eds.), *Essays on Culture and Society in Modern Germany* (Arlington, Texas, 1982).
Stedman Jones, Gareth, *Languages of Class: Studies in English Working-Class History 1832–1933* (Cambridge, 1983).
Stein, Hans-Peter, *Symbole und Zeremoniell in deutschen Streitkräften vom 18. bis zum 20. Jahrhundert*, second edition (Herford and Bonn, 1986).
Steinberg, Jonathan, 'The Copenhagen Complex', *Journal of Contemporary History* 1 (1988), pp. 23–46.
'The *Novelle* of 1908: Necessities and Choices in the Anglo-German Naval Arms Race', *Transactions of the Royal Historical Society*, 5th Series, 21 (1971), pp. 25–43.
Yesterday's Deterrent: Tirpitz and the Birth of the German Battle Fleet (London, 1965).
'The Kaiser's Navy and German Society', *Past & Present* 28 (1964), pp. 102–10.
Steiner, Zara, *The Foreign Office and Foreign Policy, 1898–1914* (Cambridge, 1969).
Britain and the Origins of the First World War (London, 1977).
Steinmetz, Willibald, 'Anbetung und Dämonisierung des Sachzwangs. Zur Archäologie einer deutschen Redeform', in Michael Jeismann (ed.), *Obsessionen: Beherrschende Gedanken im wissenschaftlichen Zeitalter* (Frankfurt, 1995), pp. 293–333.
Stern, Fritz, *The Politics of Cultural Despair: A Study in the Rise of Germanic Ideology* (Berkeley, 1961).
Sternberger, Dolf, *Panorama oder Ansichten vom 19. Jahrhundert* (Hamburg, 1946).
Stevenson, David, *The First World War and International Politics* (Oxford, 1991).
Armaments and the Coming of War: Europe, 1904–1914 (Oxford, 1996).
'Militarization and Diplomacy in Europe before 1914', *International Security* 22 (1997) pp. 125–61.
Stibbe, Matthew, *German Anglophobia and the Great War, 1914–1918* (Cambridge, 2001).
Stöber, Gunda, *Pressepolitik als Notwendigkeit. Zum Verhältnis von Staat und Öffentlichkeit im Wilhelminischen Deutschland 1890–1914* (Stuttgart, 2000).
Stöber, Rudolf, 'Der Prototyp der deutschen Massenpresse. Der "Berliner Lokal-Anzeiger" und sein Blattmacher Hugo von Kupffer', *Publizistik* 39 (1994), pp. 314–30.
Storch, Robert D. (ed.), *Popular Culture and Custom in Nineteenth-Century England* (London, 1982).
Strachan, Hew, *The First World War*, vol. 1, *To Arms* (Oxford, 2002).
Strange, S. J. (ed.), *The Presence of Ford Madox Ford* (Philadelphia, 1981).
Strobl, Gerwin, *The Germanic Isle: Nazi Perceptions of Britain* (Cambridge, 2000).
Strong, Roy, *Art and Power: Renaissance Festivals 1450–1650* (Woodbridge, 1984).
The Cult of Elizabeth (London, 1977).
Stürmer, Michael (ed.), *Das kaiserliche Deutschland* (Kronberg, 1977).
Das ruhelose Reich. Deutschland, 1866–1918 (Berlin, 1983).

Süssmuth, Hans (ed.), *Deutschlandbilder in Dänemark und England, in Frankreich und den Niederlanden* (Baden-Baden, 1996).

Sumida, Jon Tetsuro, 'The Royal Navy and Technological Change', in R. Haycock and K. Neilson (eds.), *Men, Machines and War* (Ontario, 1988), pp. 75–91.

In Defence of Naval Supremacy: Finance, Technology and British Naval Policy, 1889–1914 (Boston, 1989).

'British Naval Administration and Policy in the Age of Fisher', *Journal of Modern History* 54 (1990), pp. 1–26.

'Sir John Fisher and the *Dreadnought*: The Sources of Naval Mythology', *Journal of Military History* 59 (1995), pp. 619–37.

Inventing Grand Strategy and Teaching Command: The Classic Works of Alfred Thayer Mahan Reconsidered (Washington, 1997).

Summers, Anne, 'Militarism in Britain before the Great War', *History Workshop Journal* 2 (1976), pp. 104–23.

'The Character of Edwardian Nationalism: Three Popular Leagues', in Paul Kennedy and Anthony Nicholls (eds.), *Nationalist and Racialist Movements in Britain and Germany Before 1914* (London, 1981), pp. 68–87.

Suval, Stanley, *Electoral Politics in Wilhelmine Germany* (Chapel Hill, 1985).

Syon, Guillaume de, *Zeppelin! Germany and the Airship, 1900–1939* (Baltimore, 2002).

Tacke, Charlotte, *Denkmal im sozialen Raum. Nationale Symbole in Deutschland und Frankreich im 19. Jahrhundert* (Göttingen, 1995).

Taylor, A. J. P., *The Struggle for Mastery in Europe 1848–1918* (Oxford, 1954).

The Trouble Makers: Dissent Over Foreign Policy 1792–1939, with a new introduction by Paul Addison (London, 1993).

Taylor, Antony, '*Reynolds's Newspaper*, Opposition to Monarchy and the Radical Anti-Jubilee', *Historical Research* 68 (1995), pp. 318–37.

'*Down with the Crown': British Anti-Monarchism and Debates About Royalty Since 1790* (London, 1999).

Taylor, Miles, 'John Bull and the Iconography of Public Opinion in England, c. 1712–1929', *Past & Present* 134 (1992), pp. 93–128.

Tenfelde, Klaus, 'Adventus. Zur historischen Ikonologie des Festzugs', *Historische Zeitschrift* 235 (1982), pp. 45–84.

Thomas, Roger, 'Empire, Naval Pageantry and Public Spectacle: The Launch of HMS Iron Duke in Portsmouth Dockyard, October 12th 1912', *Mariner's Mirror*, 88 (2002), pp. 202–13.

Thompson, Andrew, 'The Language of Imperialism and the Meaning of Empire: Imperial Discourse in British Politics, 1895–1914', *Journal of British Studies* 36 (1997), pp. 147–77.

Thornton, A. P., *The Imperial Idea and its Enemies: A Study in British Power* (London, 1959).

Toeplitz, Jerzy, *Geschichte des Films*, vol. 1, *1895–1928* (Munich, 1975).

Transfeldt, Walter, *Wort und Brauch in Heer und Flotte*, ninth edition, edited by Hans-Peter Stein (Stuttgart, 1986).

Trebilcock, Clive, *The Vickers Brothers: Armaments and Enterprise* (London, 1977).

Trentmann, Frank (ed.), *The Making of the Consumer: Knowledge, Power and Identity in the Modern World* (Oxford and New York, 2006).

Turner, Victor, *Dramas, Fields and Metaphors* (Ithaca, 1974).

The Ritual Process: Structure and Anti-Structure (Harmondsworth, 1974).

From Ritual to Theatre: The Human Seriousness of Play (New York, 1982).

The Anthropology of Performance (New York, 1989).

Ullmann, Hans-Peter, *Das Deutsche Kaiserreich 1871–1918* (Frankfurt, 1995).

Ullrich, Volker, *Die nervöse Großmacht. Aufstieg und Untergang des deutschen Kaiserreichs, 1871–1918* (Frankfurt, 1997).

Umbach, Maiken, 'Made in Germany', in Etienne François and Hagen Schulze (eds.), *Deutsche Erinnerungsorte*, vol. 2 (Munich, 2001), pp. 405–18.

'A Tale of Second Cities: Autonomy, Culture and the Law in Hamburg and Barcelona in the Long Nineteenth Century', *American Historical Review* 110 (2005), pp. 659–92.

Unsworth, Barry, *Losing Nelson* (London, 1999).

Van Gennep, Arnold, *The Rites of Passage*, translated by M. B. Vizedom and G. L. Caffee (Chicago, 1960).

Verhey, Jeffrey, *The Spirit of 1914: Militarism, Myth, and Mobilization in Germany* (Cambridge, 2000).

Veyne, Paul, *Le pain et le cirque* (Paris, 1976).

Vickery, Amanda, 'Golden Age to Separate Spheres? A Review of the Categories and Chronology of English Women's History', *Historical Journal* 36 (1993), pp. 383–414.

Völger, Gisela and Karin von Welck (eds.), *Männerbande – Männerbünde. Zur Rolle des Mannes im Kulturvergleich*, 2 vols. (Cologne, 1990).

Vogel, Jakob, *Nationen im Gleichschritt. Der Kult der 'Nation in Waffen' in Deutschland und Frankreich, 1871–1914* (Göttingen, 1997).

'"En revenant de la revue": Militärfolklore und Folkloremilitarismus in Deutschland und Frankreich 1871–1914', *Österreichische Zeitschrift für Geschichtswissenschaften* 9 (1998), pp. 9–30.

'Military, Folklore, Eigensinn: Folkloric Militarism in Germany and France, 1871–1914', *Central European History* 33 (2000), pp. 487–504.

Waller, P. J., *Town, City and Nation: England 1850–1914* (Oxford, 1983).

Walton, John K., *The English Seaside Resort: A Social History, 1750–1914* (Leicester, 1983).

Walvin, James, *Beside the Seaside: A Social History of the Popular Seaside Holiday* (London, 1978).

Ward, Stuart (ed.), *British Culture and the End of Empire* (Manchester, 2001).

Warneken, Bernd Jürgen (ed.), *Massenmedium Straße. Zur Kulturgeschichte der Demonstration* (Frankfurt, 1991).

Weber-Kellermann, Ingeborg, *Der Kinder neue Kleider. 200 Jahre deutscher Kindermoden in ihrer sozialen Zeichensetzung* (Frankfurt, 1985).

Wehler, Hans-Ulrich, *Krisenherde des Kaiserreichs 1871–1918. Studien zur deutschen Sozial- und Verfassungsgeschichte* (Göttingen, 1970).

Das Deutsche Kaiserreich 1871–1918, seventh edition (Göttingen, 1994).

Deutsche Gesellschaftsgeschichte, vol. 3, *Von der 'Deutschen Doppelrevolution' bis zum Beginn des Ersten Weltkrieges 1849–1914* (Munich, 1995).

'Nationalismus und Nation in der deutschen Geschichte', in Helmut Berding (ed.), *Nationales Bewußtsein und kollektive Identität* (Frankfurt, 1996), pp. 163–75.

(ed.), *Ludwig Quidde, Caligula. Schriften über Militarismus und Pazifismus* (Frankfurt, 1977).

Weisbrod, Bernd, 'Gewalt in der Politik. Zur politischen Kultur in Deutschland zwischen den beiden Weltkriegen', *Geschichte in Wissenschaft und Unterricht* 43 (1992), pp. 391–404.

Welch, David, 'Cinema and Society in Imperial Germany, 1905–1918', *German History* 8 (1990), pp. 28–45.

Wells, Gerard, *Naval Customs and Traditions* (London, 1930).

Wendt, Bernd-Jürgen (ed.), *Das britische Deutschlandbild im Wandel des 19. und 20. Jahrhunderts* (Bochum, 1984).

Wernecke, Klaus, *Der Wille zur Weltgeltung. Außenpolitik und Öffentlichkeit im Kaiserreich am Vorabend des Ersten Weltkrieges*, second edition (Düsseldorf, 1970).

Werner, Michaël and Bénédicte Zimmermann, 'Penser l'historie croisée. Entre empirie et réflexivité', *Annales* 58 (2003), pp. 7–36.

West, Shearer (ed.), *The Victorians and Race* (Aldershot, 1996).

Wette, Wolfram (ed.), *Militarismus in Deutschland 1871 bis 1945. Zeitgenössische Analysen und Kritik* (Münster, 1999).

Wiedemann, Thomas, *Emperors and Gladiators* (London, 1992).

Wiener, Joel H. (ed.), *Papers for the Millions: The New Journalism in Britain 1850 to 1914* (New York and London, 1988).

Wiener, M. J., *English Culture and the Decline of the Industrial Spirit, 1850–1980* (Cambridge, 1981).

Wigen, Kären, 'Oceans of History', *American Historical Review* 111 (2006), pp. 717–21.

Wilderotter, Hans and Klaus-Dieter Pohl (eds.), *Der letzte Kaiser* (Gütersloh, 1991).

Wilentz, Sean (ed.), *Rites of Power: Symbolism, Ritual and Politics Since the Middle Ages* (Philadelphia, 1985).

Wilkinson, Glenn R., '"The Blessings of War": The Depiction of Military Force in Edwardian Newspapers', *Journal of Contemporary History* 33 (1998), pp. 97–115.

Willems, Emilio, *A Way of Life and Death: Three Centuries of Prussian-German Militarism: An Anthropological Approach* (Nashville, 1986).

Williams, Rhodri, *Defending the Empire: The Conservative Party and British Defence Policy 1899–1915* (New Haven and London, 1991).

Williams, Richard, *The Contentious Crown: Public Discussion of the British Monarchy in the Reign of Queen Victoria* (Aldershot, 1997).

Wilson, Angus, *The Strange Ride of Rudyard Kipling: His Life and Works* (London and New York, 1977).

Wilson, Kathleen, *The Island Race: Englishness, Empire, and Gender in the Eighteenth Century* (London, 2003).

Wilson, Keith M., *The Policy of the Entente: Essays on the Determinants of British Foreign Policy 1904–1914* (Cambridge, 1985).

Empire and Continent: Studies in British Foreign Policy from the 1880s to the First World War (London and New York, 1987).

'Sir Eyre Crowe on the Origin of the Crowe Memorandum of 1 January 1907', in *Bulletin of the Institute of Historical Research* 56 (1983), pp. 238–41.

Channel Tunnel Visions 1850–1945: Dreams and Nightmares (London, 1994).

Winkler, Heinrich August, *Nationalismus* (Königstein, 1978).

Streitfragen der deutschen Geschichte: Essays zum 19. und 20. Jahrhundert (Munich, 1997).

Der lange Weg nach Westen, vol. 1, *Deutsche Geschichte 1806–1933* (Munich, 2000).

(ed.), *Griff nach der Deutungsmacht. Zur Geschichte der Geschichtspolitik in Deutschland* (Göttingen, 2004).

Winks, Robin W. (ed.), *The Oxford History of the British Empire*, vol. 5, *Historiography* (Oxford, 2000).

Winter, Jay, *Sites of Memory, Sites of Mourning: The Great War in European Cultural History* (Cambridge, 1995).

'Propaganda and the Mobilization of Consent', in *The Oxford Illustrated History of the First World War* (Oxford, 1998), pp. 216–26.

Winter, Jay and Blaine Bagget, *The Great War and the Shaping of the 20th Century* (London, 1996).

Winzen, Peter, *Bülows Weltmachtkonzept. Untersuchungen zur Frühphase seiner Außenpolitik 1897–1901* (Boppard, 1977).

Withey, Lynne, *Grand Tours and Cook's Tours: A History of Leisure Travel, 1750–1915* (London, 1997).

Wittek, Thomas, *Auf ewig Feind? Das Deutschlandbild in den britischen Massenmedien nach dem Ersten Weltkrieg* (Munich, 2005).

Wohl, Robert, *A Passion for Wings: Aviation and the Western Imagination, 1908–1918* (New Haven and London, 1994).

Woodward, E. L., *Great Britain and the German Navy* (Oxford, 1935).

Wulle, Arnim, *Der Stettiner Vulcan* (Herford, 1989).

Yuval-Davis, Nira, *Gender and Nation* (London, 1997).

Zischler, Hanns, *Kafka geht ins Kino* (Reinbek, 1998).

Dissertations

Birmele, Jutta, 'The Mass-Circulating Press and the Crisis of Legitimation in Wilhelmine Germany, 1908–1918', Ph.D. thesis, Claremont Graduate School (1991).

Deckart, Gerald, 'Deutsch-englische Verständigung. Eine Darstellung der nicht-offiziellen Bemühungen um eine Wiederannäherung der beiden Länder zwischen 1905 und 1914', Dr. phil. thesis, University of Munich (1967).

Ehlers, Hans, 'Farbige Wörter im England der Kriegszeit. Ein Beitrag zur Entwicklungsgeschichte von Schlagwörtern, Modewörtern, geflügelten Wörtern und ähnlichen', Dr. phil. thesis, University of Leipzig (1922).

Gregory, B., 'The Spectacle Plays and Exhibitions of Imre Kiralfy, 1887–1914', Ph.D. thesis, Manchester University (1988).

Hilbert, Lothar Wilfried, 'The Role of Military and Naval Attachés in the British and German Services with Particular References to those in Berlin and London and their Effect on Anglo-German Relations, 1871–1914', Ph.D. thesis, University of Cambridge (1954).

Jahrl, Harald, 'Deutschlands Urteil über England im Spiegel deutscher Publizistik 1890 bis 1901', Dr. phil. thesis, Heidelberg University (1950).

O'Brien, Phillips Payson, 'The Cabinet, Admiralty and the Perceptions Governing the Formation of British Naval Policy: 1909, 1921–1922, 1927–1936', Ph.D. thesis, University of Cambridge (1992).

Rieger, Bernhard, 'Public Readings of Technology: Film, Aviation and Passenger Shipping, 1890s–1930s', Ph.D. thesis, University of London (1999).

Rodgers, Silvia, 'The Symbolism of Ship Launching in the Royal Navy', D.phil. thesis, University of Oxford (1983).

Schepper, Regi, 'Nationenbilder in Wandel. Zur Entwicklung von Deutschlandbildern in Großbritannien', Dr. phil. thesis, University of Duisburg (1990).

Schütz, Rüdiger, 'Die deutsch-englische Entfremdung im Spiegel der britischen Presse von 1897–1903', Dr. phil. thesis, University of Aachen (1969).

Siak, Steven Wai-Meng, 'Germanophilism in Britain: Non-Governmental Elites and the Limits to Anglo-German Antagonism, 1905–1914', Ph.D. thesis, University of London (1997).

Tilley, Heather, '"Oh Might our Marges Meet Again": Arnold, the Self, and Mid-Nineteenth-Century Representations of the Sea', M.A. thesis, Birkbeck College, University of London (2004).

Index

Italic page numbers indicate illustrations.

Lightning Source UK Ltd.
Milton Keynes UK
09 September 2010

159693UK00001B/52/P

9 780521 114615